# Transition to Democracy in Latin America: The Role of the Judiciary

# Transition to Democracy in Latin America: The Role of the Judiciary

EDITED BY

## Irwin P. Stotzky

**Westview Press**

BOULDER • SAN FRANCISCO • OXFORD

Copyright © 1993 by Westview Press, Inc.

Published in 1993 in the United States of America by Westview Press, Inc., 5500 Central Avenue, Boulder, Colorado 80301-2877, and in the United Kingdom by Westview Press, 36 Lonsdale Road, Summertown, Oxford OX2 7EW

Library of Congress Cataloging-in Publication Data
Transition to democracy in Latin America : the role of the judiciary /
edited by Irwin P. Stotzky.
   p.  cm.
  Includes bibliographical references.
  ISBN 0-8133-8456-7
  1. Judicial process—Latin America.  2. Political questions and
judicial power—Latin America.  3. Human rights—Latin America.
I. Stotzky, Irwin P.
KG495.T7  1993
342.8'066—dc20
[348.0266]                                        93-13943
                                                          CIP

Printed and bound in the United States of America

The paper used in this publication meets the requirements of the American National Standard for Permanence of Paper for Printed Library Materials Z39.48-1984.

10    9    8    7    6    5    4    3    2    1

*To Aaron
(Dr. Dunk)*

# Contents

# PART SIX
## Judicial Review and Remedies

# PART SEVEN
## Conclusion

# Acknowledgments

The idea for this book first occurred to me in 1990 after discussions with Carlos S. Nino and Owen M. Fiss. Subsequently, I spent part of 1991 and 1992 as a Fulbright Scholar in Argentina, where I worked at the Center for Institutional Studies (Centro de Estudios Institucionales). There, I had the opportunity to speak with many courageous and experienced people who have played and continue to play important roles in the transition process in several different Latin American nations. These meetings included discussions with academics, political activists, common citizens, and current and former government officials. I also gave lectures in several cities in Argentina and Chile and taught a course in constitutional theory at the center. The people I met during my trips across Argentina and Chile and the participants in the course convinced me of the importance of exploring the role of the judiciary in a transition process.

After intense analysis of the issues, Carlos Nino and I decided to facilitate discussion and scholarship among Latin and North Americans on the institutional importance of the judiciary in the transition to democracy and its consolidation. To achieve this goal, we met with a variety of very talented people with broad experience in this area. This created an intriguing dynamic. Indeed, the level of debate and interaction among these people was truly extraordinary. On the basis of these experiences, I decided to solicit articles for this book.

There are so many persons to whom I am indebted and grateful that it would be difficult to acknowledge adequately all those who have helped. Nevertheless, I shall attempt to acknowledge those persons who have been the most helpful.

I am especially grateful to Owen Fiss for first introducing me to the ideas involved in the transition to democracy in Latin America and for all of his encouragement and support over the years as a teacher and friend. I am also deeply grateful to Carlos Nino for all of his support, friendship, and interest in this project. His involvement was crucial for the success of the project. Jaime Malamud-Goti played an indispensable role in helping to make sense out of some of the ideas and essays and in his very helpful editing suggestions. His experience and friendship were invaluable. Nora Whitlock played an equally important role in the entire scheme of things.

She helped organize the meetings and worked extremely hard and with great skill on editing the essays and finding footnotes for the articles. Melanie Trexler's first-rate help in finding footnotes, editing, cite checking, and proofreading proved invaluable. She never wavered, even in the face of impossible deadlines and unreasonable demands. She deserves special praise. Joanne Harvest Koren's work on Roberto Gargarella's article was outstanding. Vivien Toomey Montz did an equally good job on Carlos Nino's chapter. Martha Seijas did a wonderful job of helping to translate and edit the chapter of Raúl R. Alfonsín. Sarah Clasby also did an excellent job on the editing of Alfonsín's chapter. Audrey R. Goldman's editing suggestions on my article and her support of this project were indispensable. David B. Feingold's support was also extremely important.

The University of Miami Library staff was always helpful. In particular, I am indebted to Ruth Parlin, whose research was indispensable. Edgardo Rotman also provided important research help. I am deeply grateful to all of the library's staff.

In addition, there were many students whose energy and talent eased my research and proofreading burdens as the work progressed: Laurie Adams, Suzanne R. Amster, Lisa R. Askowitz, Mary Elizabeth Borja, Floyd Chapman, Cheryl Cooper, James G. Dodrill II, John B. Duer, Rosemary Ernst, Dianne O. Fischer, Anthony Lauriello, Wendy Miller, Gary Murphree, and Reed Slogoff.

I wish also to thank the secretaries who helped in typing various parts of the manuscript: Jennifer Alexander, Lidia Grumberg, Haydee Gonzalez-Pola, and Phyllis Taggett. Evelyn Medina did an excellent job of helping to put the book into camera-ready form. Barbara Wingard deserves special mention. She combined intelligence with competence and hard work and almost single-handedly typed several drafts of the book. Trenesia Green-Smith also deserves special praise for her competence, intelligence, and dedication to the project. She not only did an excellent job of putting the book into camera-ready form but also made helpful suggestions concerning format, style, and substance. Her work was truly first-rate.

I am also indebted to Barbara Ellington, senior editor, Westview Press. Her editorial suggestions and patience were crucial to the timely completion of the book.

Finally, I am grateful to the University of Miami Law School, the University of Miami North-South Center, and the Fulbright Commission for financial support for this project.

*Irwin P. Stotzky*

# PART ONE

## Introduction

# 1

# The Difficulties of the Transition Process

*Irwin P. Stotzky and*
*Carlos S. Nino*

In the past decade, many Latin American nations have been involved in a remarkable political experiment. The historically ubiquitous authoritarian regimes, usually in the form of military juntas and dictators, have gradually been replaced by constitutional democracies.[1] This process -- usually referred to as the transition from authoritarianism to democracy -- is, however, far from complete.

Economic, political, and social stability has not yet been secured. Corporatist political and social structures have not yet been transformed to allow for a more equitable distribution of goods and services so that the neediest members of society gain access to the basic necessities required for a life of dignity. Institutional structures must be developed and stabilized. The rule of law has to be consolidated and become a basic, accepted requirement of government practice and daily life.

These issues are more complicated than they first appear. Although these issues may be theoretically severable, they are also inextricably intertwined. The rule of law, for example, must be consolidated not only to protect human rights, but also to help secure a satisfactory level of economic, political, and social development. Moreover, virtually no Latin American nation remains free from these problems. Indeed, even in the nations that claim to have been the most successful in making this transition, problems abound.

One of the best examples of the promises and pitfalls of such an undertaking in Latin America is Argentina. The 1983 election of Raúl Alfonsín, the leader of the Radical Party, came after one of the bleakest periods in Argentine history. From 1976 until 1983, a series of military juntas ruled Argentina.[2] They conducted a "dirty war" against leftist terrorism resulting in the disappearances of anywhere between 7,000 and 30,000 mostly innocent people,[3] started and lost a war with Great Britain over the Falkland/

Malvinas Islands,[4] and left the country almost bankrupt with a staggering 45 billion dollar debt.[5]

The political, social, and economic developments in Argentina and other developing Latin American democracies, such as Chile, have been widely discussed.[6] The question of the role of the judicial power in strengthening a democratic system of government has not, however, been as openly debated. Indeed, the Alfonsín and Menem Administrations present a unique opportunity to study the transition process from a military government to two successive civilian governments, something that has not happened in Argentina in more than sixty years. Moreover, what this peaceful transfer of power represents both in terms of the consolidation of human rights values and more generally in the consolidation of democracy, and what role the judiciary has played and could conceivably play in this process, has yet to be analyzed. Further, Argentina under Alfonsín and Menem is a valuable case study of the relationship between economic instability and the ability of a society to guarantee protection for human rights. Analysis of the developments in Argentina and other Latin American nations should, therefore, prove helpful in understanding the role of the judiciary in the development of democracies worldwide.

The role of the judiciary in the transition process is, of course, extremely complicated. One major complication is the fact that the institutional structures necessary for a viable democracy remain in varying stages of development. The transition to democracy in Latin America is usually represented in one of two distinct stages. In one stage of development, a country is attempting to adjust norms or institutions towards the strictures of the democratic rule of law. Stated otherwise, the institutional structures associated with a democratic government, such as an independent judiciary or competition between different political parties, must be developed. In the other stage of development, the democratic institutional structures exist in a developed form, but their stability is not completely secured. Social tensions and conflicts sometimes coercively interfere with the institutional structures. Indeed, this transition from dictatorship to democracy is a fragile and uncertain process, and it has met with varying degrees of success. There are many extremely difficult choices to be made in a society that desires to be free and none of them are easy.[7] The wrong choices can often prove fatal to the democracy and thus lead to serious deprivations of human rights.

One of the most difficult choices facing these budding democracies is whether military and police officials should be prosecuted for human rights abuses they committed during the years of dictatorship or whether a blanket amnesty should be declared. Putting human rights violators on trial is, of course, extremely important to the development of institutional structures

-- such as an independent judiciary -- which the people respect and whose opinions they accept as valid. Nevertheless, serious problems arise no matter which choice is made about such prosecutions. In Argentina, for example, the decision to prosecute these government sponsored criminals led to several military mutinies during the last years of President Raúl Alfonsín's term (1987-1989)[8] and during the early years of President Carlos Menem's term (1989-1990).[9] Brazil, which chose to forget these atrocities, has kept its enlisted soldiers out of the streets and in the barracks, but the top military officials continue to control many of the major governmental decisions.[10] More recently, the military coup leaders in Haiti continue to bar the first democratically elected Haitian President in 200 years, Jean-Bertrand Aristide, from returning to Haiti unless he agrees to a general amnesty for these murderous military officials. But even that act may not be sufficient to guarantee his return.[11]

Even with these problems, however, Latin America continues to move steadily away from dictatorship to democracy. In 1989, voters in Paraguay elected a new president, only three months after the overthrow of one of the most infamous dictators, General Alfredo Stroessner.[12] In December, 1989, Chileans selected a new president to replace General Augusto Pinochet.[13] Other Latin American nations have embarked on a path of economic and social stabilization. Nevertheless, the military shadow always remains in the background. Civilian rulers continue to be disturbingly weak when confronted by democracy's inherently difficult choices.[14] To put it another way, there is a fine line separating democracy and oppression.

If civilian democratic government is less than effective in Latin America, who should be blamed? Much of the fault lies with unprincipled military officials who quietly left office instead of facing up to the economic, political, and social disasters they created. Moreover, they stepped aside without any intention of surrendering real power or living within the demands of a constitutional government. Many, but not all of these military officials, stubbornly refuse to adhere to the rule of law while insidiously working for the collapse of civilian rule so that they may return to power.

The new civilian leaders must also accept some of the blame. They either made no real attempt to restrain their armed forces and educate them to become responsible members of their nations, or were simply ineffective in attempting to do so. In Brazil, for example, the government simply made no serious attempt to control the military. By contrast, in Argentina, the government first made a strong effort to prosecute the military, but finally had to come to terms with the reality that full prosecution of commanders and torturers was not possible without causing a military uprising which might conceivably overthrow the democratically elected government.

The newly re-enfranchised citizens of Latin America are also at fault. They have too quickly grown impatient with their democratically elected leaders. For example, many citizens unjustly blame their leaders for economic crises inherited from the dictators. They expect quick and painless solutions to almost insoluble problems.

The more developed Western nations cannot escape a great deal of the responsibility for the precarious state of these fledgling democracies. Western nations, while claiming to be models for these democracies, hold the major portion of Latin America's multi-billion dollar foreign debt. They often push these new democracies into economic chaos by refusing to extend loans or by demanding interest payments during critical moments in the history of these societies. These actions, of course, leave the democracies exposed to the distinct possibility of a return to military dictatorships.

Moreover, Western banks must also accept much of the blame for the precariousness of these democracies. While many of these nations are trying to lure the flight capital back to their countries, some of the world's leading financial institutions are aggressively working to hang on to the money. Citibank, for example, which in 1989 had 7.7 billion dollars outstanding in Latin American loans, also held approximately 20 billion dollars of private Latin American deposits.[15] Thus, it appears that some of the major banks are attempting to cover possible losses on their third world loans by soliciting private Latin American wealth. By helping to remove the private capital from these countries, however, the banks make it extremely difficult for Latin American nations to build up their economies, a prerequisite to the repayment of the debts.

The problem runs even deeper. It is clear that many Latin Americans have not internalized the significance and legitimacy of a constitutional system based on the rule of law. Moreover, the Latin American culture appears to be strongly resistant to the internalization of universal standards of achievement and competition necessary to an equitably functioning democracy. Rather, Latin Americans appear to have internalized a belief in the overpowering importance of status and connections, thus crippling the transition to a constitutional democracy. It is a sobering thought that the problems associated with any transition to democracy may be intractable. Is it possible to instill the belief in people -- struggling for their very existence -- that the moral bases of a democracy must be adhered to for their, and their children's, lives to improve?

The democratization process needs further elucidation if we are to begin to answer this question. The issue is further complicated by the fact that the concept of transition to democracy has unclear and shifting boundaries. Indeed, the very question of whether certain Latin American and European nations remain in the transition towards democracy or have already completed the journey is one which requires both empirical corroboration and conceptual clarification.

One possibility is to declare the transition complete when democracy seems to be sufficiently consolidated. Setting aside the complex question of which democracy has been consolidated, which we believe depends implicitly upon justificatory conceptions of democracy, the concept of consolidation presents difficult problems of its own. The idea of consolidation is intimately connected with the stability of a given political system, and it is plausible to argue that the latter is itself an arrangement -- a dispositional property -- which in turn depends upon certain predictions.

Yet predictions about any political process, and particularly those in Latin America, are problematic at best. We thus do not intend to make such predictions. We do, however, wish to discuss briefly some of the most prominent features of the present consolidation process taking place in the Southern part of Latin America. These features are useful in formulating those predictions on which the claim that the transition to democracy has or has not been completed depends.

The first significant feature of the consolidation is the fact that the process of democratization has taken place in most of those countries -- with perhaps the exception of Chile -- during one of the worst economic and social crises in the history of these nations. In general, this crisis manifested itself in enormous external debts, hyperinflation, the collapse of systems of social welfare, huge rates of unemployment, increases in infant mortality, epidemics, and a variety of other social catastrophes.[16] Furthermore, there is great controversy in the region about whether this crisis is leading to a change in the economic and social structures of the countries necessary to allow for a new oligopolization of the economy. Stated otherwise, it is not clear whether a new oligopolization will develop which will greatly restrict the avenues of access for the powerless sectors of society to the goods necessary for leading a life of dignity, or whether on the contrary, the crisis is leading to a more efficient scheme of production which will ultimately benefit all sectors of society.

A second prominent feature of the consolidation, and integrally connected to this first significant feature, is the clear fact that the corporatist political and social structure that characterized the region is in a process of transformation.[17] This corporatism has been described as bi-frontal. On the one hand, it served the state by allowing it to control different sectors of civil society, and, on the other, it involved the establishment of cleavages of privilege and domination on the part of different social groups within the very structure of the state. The groups which formed the constellation of corporative power varied from country to country: in Argentina, for example, it included the armed forces, the Catholic Church, the trade unions, and different economic groups. Presently, the armed forces have lost power and influence in some countries of the region and have generally been more accepting of democratic practices and institutions. In several nations, the Church is reluctantly ceding its claim that the state enforce its vision of private, personal life.[18] In many of the nations of the region, the trade unions have been enormously affected by unemployment and by the reduction -- sometimes adversely affecting parties normally allied with governments -- of the welfare state. The great enigma, which is related to the controversy surrounding the assessment of the first feature -- the economic and social crisis -- is whether the previous dominant economic groups remain all-powerful, or even increase their power, by having changed their positions as privileged contractors of the state to positions as owners and thus monopolistic providers of the recently privatized public services.

Strongly interconnected in several ways with the two above described features of the process of democratic consolidation is a final one, which is extremely relevant to the transition process and to the themes of this book -- the deficiency in the fulfillment of the requirements of the rule of law. This deficiency pervades the region. Indeed, the consequences of this failure to recognize the primacy of the rule of law have made international headlines in extreme cases. For example, in Peru, President Alberto Fujimori unconstitutionally closed down Congress and removed the Supreme Court.[19] He based his actions on the pretext that these bodies were infected by corruption and thus harmed his policies of economic recovery and combating terrorism. In Brazil, President Fernando Collor resigned after having been impeached by Congress, and only minutes after the Brazilian Senate had begun an impeachment trial, for serious acts of corruption.[20]

In Argentina, attacks on the rule of law are perhaps slightly more subtle, but nevertheless pervasive. Deeds of corruption by governmental officials are reported almost daily. Yet judicial procedures have not been helpful in investigating them. Indeed, despite persistent rumors of corruption by the highest officials in the Menem government, few, if any, serious judicial investigations have taken place against these officials. These acts of corruption generally undermine the credibility of democratic institutions.

Even more debilitating to a democracy than these acts of corruption, however, are the attempts by the Menem Administration to dominate the other state powers. For example, in 1990, Menem packed the Supreme Court with those loyal to his government.[21] He took advantage of the majority which he enjoys in both Houses of Congress to pass a law expanding the number of Supreme Court Justices and requiring that the confirmation of candidates to fill the new positions be handed down swiftly by the Senate.[22] Moreover, many of the officials whose offices are charged with the duty of observing and enforcing the rule of law, and many of the officials of the bodies which control the financial dealings of the government -- the Attorney General (historically part of the Supreme Court and appointed with Senatorial confirmation until the present administration), most of the members of the Tribunal of Accounts, the Attorney for Administrative Investigations, and so forth -- have been removed.[23] The Menem Administration has also enacted decrees of so-called "urgency and need," thus circumventing Congress in the adoption of significant reforms, economic and otherwise. Congress has even delegated many of its responsibilities to the Menem Administration.[24] Moreover, the Menem Administration clearly abused its power of vetoing Congressional bills, even resorting to the device of enacting part of the bill vetoed, which is a way of creating a new statute more agreeable to its policies. Several provinces have been placed in "receivership;" that is, their elected officials and their Supreme Court Justices have been removed by executive decree. This is a contravention of Article 6 of the Argentine Constitution, which in its standard construction ascribes that power to the Federal Congress in cases of internal upheavals.[25] Finally, a new assault on the judicial power is presently occurring on the occasion of the adoption of a new code of federal criminal procedure. Since adoption of the code will require a doubling of the number of judges, the government is appointing political and personal friends to fill these openings.[26]

The violation of legal norms, however, is not restricted to the Menem Administration, though it has certainly been exacerbated by it. In point of fact, it is a distinguishing mark of Argentine political and social life evident throughout its history.[27] This rule-oblivious mentality has been permanently depicted and even celebrated in Argentine literature, and manifests itself in both social practices and in the actions of governmental bodies.

These acts reflect a general disregard for the rule of law. This tendency of unlawfulness does not, however, only infect public officials, it infects the general society. To put it another way, this unlawfulness mentality correlates with a general trend towards anomie in society as a whole. It manifests itself in such things as an enormous black market, tax evasion, corruption in private economic activities, non-observance of efficient economic norms, and non-compliance with the most basic rules of society, such as elementary traffic and urban regulations. This general tendency towards illegality in public and social life normally appears in one of two ways. People in Argentina may adopt a "finalist attitude," where they agree with the goals of a rule but do not follow the commands of the rule. Conversely, they may adopt a "formalist attitude," where they blindly comply with the commands of the rule but ignore its goals. Both of these attitudes are incompatible with and thus contribute to the continuing difficulty of securing adherence to the rule of law.

The problem runs deeper. The tendency towards unlawfulness in Argentine public and social life is often the product and the cause of collective action problems, such as those which have structures that game theory labels "prisoners' dilemma," "assurance game," "chicken game," and so forth. Frequently, the combination of expectations, interests, possibilities of actions, and their respective pay-offs are such that the rational course of action for each individual participant in the process of political or social interaction advises her not to comply with a certain norm, despite the fact that general compliance with it would have been for the benefit of everybody, or almost everybody. This kind of anomie may be called "dumb anomie," since it refers to situations in which the compliance of a certain norm would have led the social actors to a more efficient result -- in Pareto's terms -- than what they obtain in the actual situation of not observing norms.[28]

It is clear that this "dumb anomie" is connected with the reversal, which occurred after the 1930s, of Argentina's economic and social development. (It has not, however, been perceived as such in the usual attempts to explain that reversal.) First, there is a direct conceptual connection between that kind of anomie and failures in economic productivity. Indeed, "dumb anomie" is identified by the inefficient results of processes of interaction, including economic ones, which do not observe certain norms. Second, it is clear that anomie affects the process of capital accumulation. For example, when the behavior of people intervening in the process of production -- even that of judges and governmental officials -- is not sufficiently predictable, productive investments decline or claim disproportionate profits.

Therefore, it is crucial for Argentina and other countries in the process of transition to democracy to consolidate the rule of law. This is important not only to secure respect for fundamental rights and for the observance of the democratic process, but also to achieve satisfactory degrees of economic and social development. Moreover, it is obvious that the consolidation of the rule of law, with the consequent overcoming of "dumb anomie," requires strengthening the independence, reliability, and efficiency of the judicial process.

To do this, nations must satisfy the guarantees which derive from the idea of due process of law. These guarantees are concerned with the way in which an act of State coercion -- which because of its very nature infringes upon an individual right and thus must be specially justified -- may be exerted against a particular individual. The general principle in a liberal democracy is that when a government act coercively deprives an individual of a vital good, as many independent powers of the state as possible should intervene to ensure that such an act is truly necessary for the good of society. The legislative branch of government necessarily intervenes in regulating constitutional rights. It draws a balance between constitutional rights and determines the conditions under which some of them may be limited for the sake of others. While the necessary generality of this legislation guarantees some degree of impartiality, it is clear that the power may be arbitrarily applied. Thus, the power of the state to exert an act of coercion against an individual must necessarily be mediated by an independent judicial power. Indeed, the ideal of a liberal democracy is that a judge should always intervene between an individual and an act of state coercion.

As many commentators argue,[29] there are two main justifications for interposing a measure of due process between the coercive deprivation of a good and the individual who is the victim of it: the first is an intrinsic value resulting from the fact that the individual in question is not merely an object to be manipulated, but rather is part of a dialogue in which the prosecution tries to convince him of the rightness of the coercion, as part of a cooperative search for truth. The second justification ascribes to due process an instrumental value; it is viewed as a mechanism for the impartial application of laws. Both justifications, of course, complement each other. To have a dialogue in which the person affected is an active part of the power process is the best way of achieving impartial applications of the law.

The general guarantee of due process of law implies a series of other guarantees; for example, those due process guarantees associated with access to the jurisdiction of courts. Thus, there must be guarantees related to the conditions for standing, the availability of appropriate remedies, such as *habeas corpus* and injunctions, which protect basic rights, the guarantee against being tried *in absentia*, the possibility of appeals, the availability of legal assistance, the proximity of courts, the openness of the judicial procedure, the efficiency and expedience of that procedure.

Also implied are those due process guarantees related to the characteristics that the judicial process must satisfy, which include: (a) the observance of the democratically enacted laws; (b) the unrestricted search for the truth about the facts; and (c) the impartiality of the judge between the parties involved in the process. Additional implied guarantees include those due process guarantees associated with the conditions that state coercion must fulfill, such as not imposing cruel or inhumane punishment, being rational in enforcing the purpose of social protection that the law was passed to meet, allowing the individual the possibility of avoiding prosecution and punishment if he complies with the legal requirement (an idea which rejects retroactive and vague legislation), and not punishing an individual for the commission of involuntary acts.

In Argentina and other Latin American nations, the ideal of due process of law has not been actively enforced. Indeed, respect for the guarantees of due process has suffered from considerable oscillations and from a combination of progressive constitutional and legislative acts and judicial decisions that intentionally disregard those guarantees. This has occurred despite the fact that such guarantees are recognized in most of their constitutions.

Moreover, although it is clear that the guarantees in the constitutions of these nations do not explicitly include remedial devices, such as *habeas corpus* and injunctions, which allow access to the administration of justice, it is obvious that without proper remedial devices the rights become meaningless. To put it another way, the existence of efficacious remedies inheres in the very rights guaranteed in a liberal democracy. In spite of this recognition, many Latin American nations do not have remedies sufficient to protect guaranteed rights.[30]

Legal assistance is another guarantee that is sorely lacking in Latin American nations. Such assistance in Argentina, as in many nations, is quite costly, in part as a result of the length of the judicial proceedings. Although there are some mechanisms for free legal assistance -- such as lawyers for poor and incompetent people -- the procedures for appointing lawyers to cases is extremely inefficient. In addition, these lawyers defend relatively few cases, mostly those involving minors or the mentally incompetent. There are also mechanisms for legal assistance organized by municipalities or lawyers associations, but these are equally inefficient and insufficient. It is also true that courts are not generally accessible to large segments of the population, both because of geographical location and because their procedures are too cumbersome, expensive, and slow for dealing with the kinds of controversies common to the large majority of the population.

The judicial process itself raises grave concerns. In Argentina, for example, there has historically been institutional instability because of the large degree of dependence by the courts, particularly by the Supreme Court, on the political process. The Argentine Supreme Court is unstable because it frequently reverses its own opinions and because its Justices are frequently replaced. Indeed, almost every new government has had a judiciary of their own choice. For example, during the military regimes, one of the first acts was to assault the judicial power. The military leaders selected judges who would legitimize the military's seizure of power. With the return of civilian government, the opportunity to shape the judiciary came directly after the previous military assault on it. Nevertheless, in some of the civilian governments, particularly President Alfonsín's government, the judiciary maintained its independence.[31]

The Argentine judiciary is also dependent on the political arena because of another factor: the proliferation of administrative courts. This has occurred despite the prohibition that article 95 of the Argentine Constitution imposes on the President with regard to exerting judicial functions and imposing penalties.[32]

The due process guarantees which should be granted in the course of the judicial process are further impaired in Argentina because of the extreme slowness of the proceedings, the secretness[33] and exaggerated ritualism in which they are conducted, the delegation of many judicial functions to clerical employees, the ex-parte communications many judges engage in, and so forth. All of these factors destroy the impartiality and expediency of the administration of justice.[34]

However depressing these factors appear to be, and however debilitating to the strengthening of the rule of law and the consolidation of democracy, all is not lost. There are signs of hope. For example, major progress in the procedural conditions for the protection of human rights has been effected by the 1984 ratification of several international agreements, such as the American Convention on Human Rights,[35] (approved by bill 23,054), and the United Nations Covenant on Civil and Political Rights,[36] with the optional protocol, and, in 1986, the International Covenant on Economic, Social, and Cultural Rights[37] (approved by bill 23,313).[38]

With respect to the conditions that the exercise of State coercion should satisfy, there are also several causes of dissatisfaction in the Argentine context. A major problem is the doctrine of *de facto* laws, which grants the same validity to the laws enacted by military regimes as that of democratic ones. The Alfonsín government attacked this concept in 1983. The amnesty law enacted by the military to protect them against prosecutions for massive human rights violations was declared null and void on the basis that *de facto* laws do not possess *a priori* validity as democratic laws do, and their content should thus be evaluated by *de jure* authorities in order to possess binding authority. This action was proposed by the President, approved by Congress and upheld by the Supreme Court. Unfortunately, the expanded Supreme Court, appointed by President Menem, abolished this new doctrine in 1990.[39]

There are also problems in complying with the requirement of legality under which coercion may be exerted by the State.[40] The major problems about the conditions that acts of coercion must satisfy have to do with the ways in which government detains people and treats them from arrest through imprisonment. The problem runs deeper. Large numbers of acts of torture and maltreatment on the part of the police are still reported, though they have certainly diminished since the re-establishment of democracy in 1983.[41]   Prisons are crowded, unhealthy and non-rehabilitative places.  There have been several inmate uprisings.  Perhaps the most grievous situation is that of people held in detention during the entire length of their trial, without any possibility of parole.  They are in almost the same conditions as convicts, and often the trial lasts so long that they serve the entire sentence for a crime for which they may later be found not guilty.  Moreover, they are not allowed any compensation for this preventive detention.  Further, many judges tend to convict a detainee after he has been in prison for such a long time.  In their minds, a retroactive conviction legitimates the detainee's imprisonment.

As the essays in this book show, there is still a long and perilous road to travel in Latin America before the guarantees of due process and the rule of law are sufficiently consolidated to overcome political and social anomie and to complete the transition to a valuable form of democracy.  Despite the recent setbacks, however, remarkable progress has been made.  Perhaps even more important, discussions about the present ailments in the administration of justice and ways of overcoming them are in the forefront of the public debate, and in the minds of concerned scholars.

This book is an example of that debate.  It analyzes the multiple factors necessary for a viable judiciary and its role in the transition to democracy.  In so doing, the essays in this book illustrate differing conceptions about the consolidation of democracy.  These differences, in turn, highlight the complexity and tension inherent in the process of transition itself.

The essays in this book are both specific and general: some of the essays analyze particular issues related to the judiciary and its role in the transition process in a particular nation.[42]   But these same essays also refer to the more general features of such a transition.  They are instructive for any nation making the transition to democracy.  Further, many of the other essays are more general in nature.  They do not necessarily refer to any particular nation, but speak instead to the role of the judiciary in any liberal democratic nation.[43]

Part Two analyzes the various roles that a judiciary serves in the transition to democracy.  Former President Alfonsín discusses his vision of the role of the judiciary and the role of law during his administration.  He describes the difficulties of democratizing the judicial process and he criticizes the present trend of the courts under the Menem Administration.  President Aristide has a rather different set of circumstances with which he must come to terms.  Unlike Argentina, Haiti does not have a mature set of institutions.  The most elementary concepts of democracy remain far distant from the current Haitian situation.  President Aristide thus speaks about the role the judiciary may serve in the transition process.  Finally, Marvin Frankel, a former United States District Judge and an international human rights advocate, speaks about these issues from a peculiarly American and international perspective. He foresees a time when juridical principles to protect democracy may be implemented in a civilized fashion.

In Part Three, the authors discuss rather complicated and diverse notions of independence. One notion of independence requires the judiciary to be independent from other institutions of government. A second notion of independence requires the judge to be independent from the parties to the litigation. Another type of independence concerns itself with the power of one judge over another. There is also a form of independence which assumes ideological independence. Owen Fiss discusses each of these forms of independence and argues that in the context of transition to democracy in Argentina and Chile, certain types of political interferences with the judiciary may be necessary to foster democracy. Paul Kahn offers a somewhat different vision of the concept of independence. Indeed, he believes that responsibility is as important a judicial norm as is independence, and it may therefore suggest a limit to the notion of independence. Jorge Correa Sutil looks at independence from the particular perspective of Chile. He also argues that too much judicial independence can be harmful to democracy. Finally, Roberto Gargarella looks at several models of impartiality and analyzes the impact of these models on the judiciary in a nation making the transition to democracy.

Part Four looks at the judicial process, with special emphasis on the differences between inquisitorial and common law systems in the criminal context. George Fletcher compares the common law system with the civil law jurisdictions to see if it is correct to argue that the former offers defendants greater procedural protections than the latter. He also examines the proposition that the civilian system offers defendants greater substantive protection than the common law system. Ruti Teitel argues that there is a strong relationship between the human rights violations of the military and the inquisitorial system of criminal process in Latin America. She claims, moreover, that the inquisitorial criminal justice system is itself a paradigm of the state's expression of the authoritarian exercise of power. Jonathan Miller takes a different position. He argues that the democratic transition process is profoundly influenced by and dependent upon the actions of the United States in the process of protecting human rights. Marcela Rodriguez attacks what she refers to as the mask of judicial neutrality, claiming that this idea merely allows the status quo power structure to dominate the judicial process. More specifically, she argues for the democratization of the administration of justice so that powerless voices, particularly women's voices, are incorporated into its processes. Finally, Stephen Schnably analyzes and criticizes the positions of the previous authors in this section. He argues that efforts to reform the judicial process are not helpful unless they are done with a clear understanding of the concrete social contexts in which that process operates. By understanding the particular social context, it is possible that more rather than less government intervention is sometimes necessary to protect democracy and human rights.

In Part Five, the authors discuss the role of the prosecution in the structure of a democratic government. Andrés D'Alessio writes about his experiences as a federal judge and the Attorney General of Argentina. He argues that prosecutors must have institutional independence and intra-institutional independence to prosecute successfully cases of human rights abuses. Philip Heymann explores the role of the prosecutor in dealing with human rights abuses. He begins by categorizing the types of governmental abuses, and analyzes their sources and the motivations for the abuses. He then examines the attitudes of high level government officials toward those abuses. He also discusses the power of these officials in relation to one another. Professor Heymann next looks at the relevance of independence and its ambiguities for the effectiveness of prosecutions and applies this analysis to abuses by security forces in the name of security. Jaime Malamud-Goti, former State Secretary and adviser on human rights to President Alfonsín, discusses the human rights trials in Argentina in the context of the general public distrust of the impartiality of the courts in trying these cases. He analyzes the ways in which the human rights trials may have contributed to the democratization of Argentine society by looking at the traditional utilitarian and retributive theories of punishment and concluding that they are inappropriate justifications for punishing human rights abuses. Diane Orentlicher addresses the challenges that a prosecutor confronts when investigating human rights abuses by security forces during the period of transition to democracy from the perspective of international law and policy. Finally, Elizabeth Iglesias examines the difficult issues related to an independent prosecutor's office and to the creation of the prosecutorial structure from an institutional perspective.

Part Six speaks to a variety of issues related to the question of judicial review and the tradition and practice of constitutional adjudication. Robert Burt argues that the notion of judicial supremacy in a democracy is a flawed one. Instead, he claims that the judiciary must respect and facilitate the democratic principle of mutual respect. Joseph Goldstein takes an unusual approach. He creates a fictitious Supreme Court Justice in Argentina, and writes a fictitious opinion which reflects on the communications function of judicial opinions in a democracy. Carlos Nino, adviser to former President Alfonsín, presents a theory that justifies judicial review on the basis that judges are guardians of democracy, personal autonomy, and the rule of law. He then analyzes the way in which judicial review has been performed in Argentina in light of this theory. Eduardo Rabossi, former Under Secretary of human rights under President Alfonsín, discusses the role of the judiciary during the 1983 human rights trials in Argentina. His approach is to examine both the philosophical underpinnings of the trials and their practical effects on democracy in Argentina. Irwin P. Stotzky examines the methods and results of the tradition of constitutional adjudication in the United States in the context of the Fourth Amendment's protection against unreasonable searches and seizures. He then proposes that this tradition can aid the development of democracy by creating a moral consciousness in the citizenry through the process of rational discourse. In his essay, Cass Sunstein discusses the relationship between property, democracy, and economic growth. He argues that property should be seen as a political right that helps to reduce dependence on the state and creates a kind of security which creates the basis for a genuine democracy. He then speculates on the contents of a constitution that is meant to create a market economy and thus promote the institutions of civil society. Finally, William Twining completes the collection of essays by looking at the transition to democracy from a peculiarly British perspective. He suggests that different conceptions of democracy -- from relatively weak to relatively strong -- lead to different conceptions of constitutional design. He then applies his analysis to the United Kingdom.

All of the chapters reflect on the difficulties of consolidating a democracy. Thus, there is a general convergence of ideas and themes. At the same time, however, a warning is in order. Context is paramount. To put it another way, each nation has its own peculiar cultural, social, political, economic, and legal history. The ideas presented in this book, while possessing cross-cultural significance, are, therefore, also limited by those differences. With this as the backdrop, we begin our journey.

## Notes

[1]We do not, of course, mean to say that the replacement of dictatorships by constitutional rule is necessarily equivalent to the transition to democracy. *See generally*, Adam Przeworski, *Democracy as a Contingent Outcome of Conflicts, in* CONSTITUTIONALISM AND DEMOCRACY 59 (Jon Elster & Rune Slagstad eds. 1988).

[2]*See* Paula K. Speck, *The Trial of the Argentine Junta: Responsibilities and Realities,* 18 INTER-AM. L. REV. 491 (1987).

[3]The official estimate is 8,960. *See* COMISIÓN NACIONAL SOBRE LA DESPARICIÓN DE PERSONAS, NUNCA MAS: INFORME DE LA COMISIÓN NACIONAL SOBRE LA DESPARICIÓN DE PERSONAS [NEVER AGAIN: REPORT OF THE ARGENTINE NATIONAL COMMISSION ON THE DISAPPEARED] 16 (9th ed. 1985); *Human Rights in the World: Argentina,* 31 REV. INT'L COMMISSION OF JURISTS 1 (1983) (claiming

the number of disappeared to be 15,000 due to underreporting); JUAN E. CORRADI, THE FITFUL REPUBLIC: ECONOMY, SOCIETY AND POLITICS IN ARGENTINA 120 (1985) (estimating the number of disappeared to be as high as 30,000).

[4]*See* CORRADI, *supra* note 3, at 136-45.

[5]Peter Passell, *The Long Road to Argentina's Financial Disaster*, N.Y. TIMES, June 18, 1989, at A16.

[6]*See, e.g.*, CORRADI, *supra* note 3, at 136-45.

[7]These choices include resolutions of extremely difficult economic, political, and social issues.

[8]*See* Eduardo Viola & Scott Mainwaring, *Transition to Democracy: Brazil and Argentina in the 1980's*, 38 J. INT'L AFF. 193 (1985).

[9]*See* Julia Michaels, *Argentina Reassesses Military Role*, CHRISTIAN SCI. MONITOR, July 16, 1991, at 6.

[10]RONALDO MONCK, LATIN AMERICA: THE TRANSITION TO DEMOCRACY 129-48 (1989).

[11]Steven A. Holmes, *U.S. Is Seeking to Prevent Vengeance Attacks if Haitian is Restored*, N.Y. TIMES, Jan. 28, 1993, at A4.

[12]James Brooke, *Paraguay General Wins Conclusively*, N.Y. TIMES, May 3, 1989, at A5. More recently, in addition to establishing a new constitution and holding free elections, the citizens of Paraguay are putting on trial four army generals accused of smuggling and corruption. This was made possible by Paraguay's new constitution, which authorizes civilian trials of military officers, and a brave whistle blower inside the military, Colonel Gonzalez Rojas. *The Heroes of Paraguay*, THE MIAMI HERALD, January 12, 1983, at 8A (Editorial).

[13]*See* Mark Falcoff, MODERN CHILE 1970-1989: A CRITICAL HISTORY 311-12 (1989).

[14]Moreover, some of the democratically elected presidents have themselves violated democratic norms. *Fujimori Says Peruvians Support His Crackdown*, THE HOUSTON CHRON., April 9, 1992, §A, at 20. *See also* Lee Hockstader, *Peruvian President Takes Case to OAS; Vow Expected on Faster Pace to Democracy*, THE WASH. POST, May 18, 1992, §1, at A12; James Brooke, *Venezuelan Chief Rules Out Resigning*, N.Y. TIMES, Nov. 30, 1992, §A, at 6; Pamela Constable, *Coup and Corruption; Venezuelan Leader Beats Rebels*, THE BOSTON GLOBE, Nov. 30, 1992, at 2.

[15]Matt Moffett, *Crippling Export: Mexico's Capital Flight Still Wrecks Economy Despite the Brady Plan*, WALL ST. J., Sept. 25, 1989, at A1.

[16]It is a common saying in Latin America that, in the past, crises of this magnitude would have unavoidably led to the destruction of the democratic system, and that it is a demonstration of the strength of that system that in all of these countries the democratically elected officials remained in office.

[17]The concept of corporatism refers to two distinct situations. In the traditional sense, corporatism refers to the control exercised by the state over organizations and interest groups. The more technical meaning, usually used in the political arena, refers to the contrary phenomena: where these same organizations and interest groups acquire considerable influence and exert persistent pressure against state

decisionmakers. *See generally* AUTHORITARIANISM AND CORPORATISM IN LATIN AMERICA (J. Malloy ed. 1977).

[18]The Church has played different roles in different nations. In Argentina, the Church has strongly supported the dictatorship. *See* EMILIO E. MIGNONE, WITNESS TO THE TRUTH: THE COMPLICITY OF CHURCH AND DICTATORSHIP IN ARGENTINA (1986); JOSE-MARIA GHIO, THE LATIN AMERICAN CHURCH IN WOJTYLAS' ERA: NEW EVANGELIZATION OR "NEO INTEGRATION" (Working Paper No. 159, May 1991). In other nations, such as Brazil and Chile, the Church has been very supportive of democracy. Indeed, the largest human rights organization in Chile during the 1970s and 1980s, the Vicaria de la Solidaridad, was run by the Church.

[19]*See e.g.*, Hockstader, *supra* note 14.

[20]Nathaniel C. Nash, *Brazilian Leader Quits as his Trial Starts in Senate*, N.Y. TIMES, Dec. 30, 1992, at A1.

[21]Former President Alfonsín forcefully denounced this practice in his essay. Raúl Alfonsín, *The Function of Judicial Power During the Transition*, in TRANSITION TO DEMOCRACY IN LATIN AMERICA: THE ROLE OF THE JUDICIARY 41 (Irwin P. Stotzky ed., 1993) [hereinafter TRANSITION].

[22]Horatio Verbitsky, *Argentina Retreats from Democracy*, N.Y. TIMES, Oct. 3, 1992, §1, at 23.

[23]This is so even though these officials were assumed, even by the military governments, to have tenure.

[24]The bill of "reform of the state" is but one example.

[25]CONST. ARG. art. 6.

[26]It is noteworthy that this branch of the judiciary will deal with, among other things, cases of governmental corruption.

[27]During the colonial era, for example, smuggling was one of the most important economic activities in Argentina.

[28]This is a different sort of anomie than that which may be due to social marginalization or to ideological conflicts, of which Argentina is presently largely exempt.

[29]*See generally*, Irwin P. Stotzky & Alan C. Swan, *Due Process Methodology and Prisoner Exchange Treaties: Confronting an Uncertain Calculus*, 62 MINN. L. REV. 733 (1978); LAURENCE H. TRIBE, AMERICAN CONSTITUTIONAL LAW 666-67 (2d ed. 1988).

[30]Argentina is a prime example. Between 1976 and 1983, during the reign of the military regimes, lawyers filed thousands of *habeas corpus* petitions in the name of each disappeared person. Several petitions were filed for each disappeared person. Except for one or two cases, the courts denied every petition. *See* NUNCA MAS, *supra* note 3.

[31]President Alfonsín felt compelled to have an independent judiciary because of his own convictions and because his party did not control the Senate.

[32]CONST. ARG. art. 95.

[33]Until the recent reforms, the entire trial was by written document and in the future will remain so for the preliminary investigation.

[34]The Supreme Court has issued some guidelines to deal with some of these issues. *See, e.g., Estevez,* 289 Fallos 183 (1974) (delay in judicial proceedings threatens the guarantee of due process); *Gordilla,* 312-2 Fallos 1934 (1989) (defendant must receive substantial and real legal assistance).

[35]O.A.S. OFF. REC. OEA/Ser. L/V/11.23, doc. 21 rev. 6 (1979), *entered into force* July 18, 1978.

[36]G.A. Res. 2200, 21st Sess. U.N. GAOR, Supp. No. 16, at 52, 54, U.N. Doc. A/6316 (1967).

[37]G.A. Res. 2200, 21st Sess., U.N. GAOR, Supp. No. 16, at 49, U.N. Doc. A/6316 (1966).

[38]The ratification of the Pact of San Jose, with the recognition of the obligatory jurisdiction of the Inter-American Court, has created an enormous improvement in the protection of basic rights. There have been many occasions on which the government had to retreat in some course of action because of the threat of resorting to the mechanisms provided by that court.

[39]In *Godoy,* [1991-C] L.L. 390 (1991), the Supreme Court held that de facto laws should be granted the same validity as democratic ones, regardless of the "affective or ideological value" we assign to democracy.

[40]For example, the Administration abused its power by enacting decrees of necessity and urgency to replace legislation.

[41]*See e.g.,* CLARIN (Buenos Aires, Arg., newspaper) Aug. 31, 1990, at 27.

[42]Argentina and Chile are the primary models. *See, e.g.,* Andrés J. D'Alessio, *The Function of the Prosecution in the Transition to Democracy in Latin America,* in TRANSITION, *supra* note 21, at 187; Jaime Malamud-Goti, *Human Rights Abuses in Fledgling Democracies: The Role of Discretion,* in TRANSITION, *supra* note 21, at 225; and Jorge Correa Sutil, *The Judiciary and the Political System in Chile: The Dilemmas of Judicial Independence During the Transition to Democracy,* in TRANSITION, *supra* note 21, at 89.

[43]*See, e.g.,* Owen Fiss, *The Right Degree of Independence,* in TRANSITION, *supra* note 21, at 55; Philip B. Heymann, *Should Prosecutors Be Independent of the Executive in Prosecuting Government Abuses?,* in TRANSITION, *supra* note 21, at 203; Irwin P. Stotzky, *The Tradition of Constitutional Adjudication,* in TRANSITION, *supra* note 21, at 347.

# PART TWO

# Various Roles of the Judiciary in the Transition to a Democratic Society

# 2

---

# Concerning the Role the Judiciary May Serve in the Proper Functioning of a Democracy

## *Marvin E. Frankel*

The subject of this chapter is one that is quite impossible to embrace in a comprehensive fashion. Thus I shall not attempt a thorough discussion but will instead give a more general and idiosyncratic "overview" of the area.

To begin, I offer a mildly disruptive observation when I mention the ambiguity of some of the key words that comprise rubrics for the theme of this book. When speaking of "the judiciary," the people of western democratic nations have a vision, I think, of men and women removed from the daily battle, pursuing "justice" with single minds, and enjoying essential independence in that pursuit. These are sacred conceptions for us.

It is relevant, however, to have in view that these conceptions, and the realities to which they relate, are by no means the same for other people in other places. For many people -- in the ghettos of this and other nations and in whole countries we can name -- the idea of The Law and the image of Justice are far from the positive ideals we cherish.

In too many places, the "law" is embodied in a uniformed thug who is the enemy -- the tool of the oppressors. "Justice" is a fake that The Man parades without fooling anyone. The judge's black robe is another hated uniform of another establishment tool. The idea of "equal justice under law" is a joke -- exploding every day in the contrasts between black and white, rich and poor, male and female, gay and straight, and so forth.

These gaps between the ideal and the reality exist in many places that are entitled to be called democracies, let alone nations that hope to be in transition to democracies from some less happy arrangements. The gaps have existed at various times and places in the United States, and still exist today. I mention this as what I trust is probably an unnecessary reminder that none of us is entitled to feel smug or perfectly confident about the practical meaning of the great concepts on which we proceed.

Our idea of the independence of the judiciary also generates complexities and ambiguities. It may be an automatic impulse to think of judicial independence in terms of the judge's freedom from unwanted external restraints -- usually from the executive branch of the government. But that idea is limited as well as useful. There are interesting questions about what we want our judges to be free from and how they propose to use their independence if they have it.

The premise is and should be that the judge is a proper judge and wants to be free to be fair, rigorous, and impartial. The ideal unravels, though, when the judge himself or herself does not desire or try to exercise independence. Judges in Nazi Germany, under a so-called law,[1] could be fired by Hitler at will. The judges in that regime did not have and did not aspire to independence. For most of our history, on the other hand, federal judges in the United States have enjoyed a wholesome measure of independence in the standard sense of the term. When people in the 1960s burned crosses on the lawns of southern judges who pursued racial equality, that was a familiar kind of threat to their independence. Some of our judges responded as heroes -- though it is a threat to the role of the judiciary in a tripartite government when a judge is called upon to be a hero to do his job. But when another species of federal judge -- in Mississippi -- referred to African-American litigants in his courtroom as "chimpanzees," the notion of independence went up in smoke.[2]

That judge was not independent in any sense that we care about. He was chained to a conception of his role that made the meaning and purpose of independence irrelevant. When the United Nations in 1985 promulgated the Basic Principles on the Independence of the Judiciary, it declared in Principle No. 6: "The principle of the independence of the judiciary *entitles and requires* the judiciary to ensure that judicial proceedings are conducted fairly and that the rights of the parties are respected."[3] The words "entitles and requires" are certainly well and carefully spoken ones. The judge who flouts the requirement of fairness and respect for the rights of the parties trashes the principle of independence -- and, of course, does not deserve to be called a judge at all.

This is elementary, but I think extraordinarily important to keep in mind in the efforts to use the judiciary as an institution to protect democratic processes. It refers to an unfortunately common and pervasive phenomenon -- in our time and at all times. It reminds us that we will have the kind of judiciary -- no better and no worse -- that the people who exercise the ultimate power of the state fight for and demand. It should also remind us that while we are fortunate in many ways in the United States, we still have many judges all over the land who are not worthy to preside over courtrooms in a democracy.

My next submission is that judges do not make or unmake revolutions. They do not even launch major social transitions. They may crystallize and advance ideas that start elsewhere in the processes of government. They may get out in front a little or try to hold back the political tides. But they do not initiate the great changes. In order to function, they need a mandate, a starting-place and pointed directions of the road or roads they may follow.[4] And even within those limits, there are varying possibilities and diverse factors -- not excluding the accidents of judicial personality.

Having broached a huge topic, I can only offer a couple of thoughts that I hope may be suggestive. For this purpose, I take as book-ends two momentous decisions of our Supreme Court a century apart: *Dred Scott v. Sandford*,[5] and *Brown v. Board of Education*.[6] For people like me, those cases mark the low point and the high point so far in American judicial history.

In both cases the Court found itself in the bright glare of publicity and inevitably in a political mine field. The *New York Herald* said that the case officially involved only "the freedom of a nigger of the name of Dred Scott,"[7] but that it was being realized that the Supreme Court was on trial before the people and the Constitution. Chief Justice Taney read three newspapers a day unlike his successor Holmes, who read none. Taney and his brethren could not be unaware of the spotlight and they should have been aware of the stakes -- though perhaps they were not.

Chief Justice Taney sank beneath the challenge to write the most infamous words in the Supreme Court reports. Unnecessarily, he found himself impelled to write that people of color, having been slaves, could not be citizens. He looked at what he found to be the "original intent" of the framers of the Constitution and found a vision of inhumanity and repression. African-Americans, he said, were "a subordinate and inferior class of beings."[8] He apparently could not bring himself to write "people." And he held that under the Constitution they "had no rights or privileges but such as those who held the power and the government might choose to grant them . . . no rights which the white man was bound to respect."[9]

The decision was a national disaster, a significant cause of the Civil War and what later Chief Justice Hughes called a "self-inflicted wound" for the Supreme Court as an institution.[10] It was an instance in which the Court had leeway and chose to decide in terms that can only be called grossly anti-democratic, even discounting for the nature of hindsight and the inevitably anachronistic quality of our perspective at this distance in time.

Did the Court lead us into the Civil War?[11] To say it led to or caused the war is probably too much, but it surely added a sharp push down the tragic road. And it shoved aside any opportunity to find the humane ideals of freedom and equality that were discoverable in a Constitution drawn hardly more than a decade after the Declaration of Independence.

A century after *Dred Scott*, in *Brown*, the Court was once again in the eye of a divided public and a political storm. The Justices in their marble palace were vividly aware of the risks and the tension -- perhaps more sensibly aware than Chief Justice Taney and some of his colleagues had been. They sensed keenly that a decision outlawing school segregation would touch the most sensitive of nerves, would threaten the foundations of the Court's own protected status, and could well lead to violence among its dangerous consequences.

The unanimous bench, in an opinion by another Chief Justice, Earl Warren, concluded that it could not take refuge in some supposed "original intent . . . [could not] turn the clock back to 1868 when the Fourteenth Amendment was adopted, . . . [but had to] consider public education in the light of its full development and its present place in American life . . . ."[12] The Court ruled for the descendants of the former slaves that "to separate them from others of similar age and qualification solely because of their race generates a feeling of inferiority as to their status in the community that may affect their hearts and minds in a way unlikely ever to be undone."[13]

The Court in *Brown*, undoubtedly at risk, took a long step on the road to democracy beyond what the executive and the legislature had been prepared to attempt -- and very possibly beyond what the majority of Americans were prepared to endorse. Despite the troubled history of this subject in the forty years since *Brown*, the decision remains an inspiration. And it contains, especially along with *Dred Scott*, important lessons about judges and democracy that could usefully inform us in any quest about the role of the judiciary in the transition to democracy.

I will not try to anticipate all of those lessons beyond reiterating and enlarging a thought I proposed earlier. Though it was dramatic and splendid, *Brown* does not contradict my thesis that judges cannot and do not launch historic transitions by the force of their own role and authority. Between *Dred Scott* and *Brown* -- and in some measure because of *Dred Scott* -- came the Fourteenth Amendment.[14] That was of course the mandate on which the Court proceeded in *Brown*.

Without that authority, the Court would have had no way to make its advance, however breathtaking. With that authority, the Court could declare in all good faith that it was simply doing its judicial duty, within the lines others had marked for the performance. Even then there were limits of prudence and professional responsibility to which the Justices were and had to be sensitive. But those limits are within the judicial competence, not outside of it.

I could, of course, say a great deal more about *Brown* as it reflects the power and the glory and the limits of the judiciary in relation to the struggle for liberty and equality. I wish only, however, to make a few points about this topic. The fragility of the Court's power and its need for support from the political branches were evident with respect to *Brown* through the 1950s and 1960s. President Eisenhower, in one of his dark moments, helped saboteurs by suggesting that the Court had done a questionable act.[15]

Perhaps encouraged by that among other things, Governor Faubus of Arkansas assured his bad name in history by proclaiming defiance of the Court's decree. Then Eisenhower took the vital and redemptive step of sending troops to Little Rock, Arkansas, to make federal supremacy a physical fact of life.[16] In both of his acts in that drama, President Eisenhower gave vivid reminders of the limits upon the powers of the judges. The miracle with us is how wonderfully these powers have worked -- from President Truman's yielding up the steel mills in 1954[17] to President Nixon's giving up the tapes in 1974.[18]

But miracles are not scientific laws. The American experience tells us how lucky we are, how prayerful and vigilant we have to be, and how chancy life is. The principal lesson of a general nature is that judges cannot lead in the political process unless those with the troops are prepared, somehow or other, to move in the same direction.

I mentioned earlier the Fourteenth Amendment to the American Constitution,[19] and that brings to mind another matter of consequence affecting the judicial role in furthering democracy. The Fourteenth Amendment became in this century a central bulwark in the American Bill of Rights. It stands as an example for the world of how valuable a bill of rights can be in enlisting the judiciary in the service of democracy. It is no guaranty, obviously; there are many countries where bills of rights lie uselessly on paper while human rights are routinely crushed.[20] There are countries, on the other hand, where there is no formal bill of rights but human rights are solidly respected.[21]

With these lawyer's qualifications, I cast a strong vote for a bill of rights as a powerful means for the judicial advancement of democracy. I stick with Jefferson's position that "[a] bill of rights is what the people are entitled to against every government on earth."[22]

Jefferson meant, of course, a genuine bill of rights, intended for use and not for show. We are all familiar with the roster of totalitarian countries where bills of wonderful-sounding rights have been a waste of the paper on which they were written. We all know of the derogation clauses that have been the subject of scholarly debate but are quite simply an anathema to my provincial American way of thinking. And we have all watched in anguish as one dictator after another simply announces that the bill of rights is suspended and that is that.

This is just one facet of my general proposition that the nations will have a judiciary that advances democracy if they first of all genuinely want and fight for democracy and then demand such a judiciary. As we observe the countries to the south of the United States, we are compelled to know that this kind of resolve has been in very short supply. Democracy, with the freedoms that are in the central definition of democracy, has been conspicuously absent for most of the history of most of the countries of Latin America.

In a society that is not free, and not committed to democratic principles, there will be no way that the judiciary can advance the cause of, or even the transition to, democracy. I know that other lawyers and scholars may well disagree with what I have just said, but I simply am not convinced by their counterarguments. For the time being, I am unable to rid myself of the belief that judges cannot fashion democracy but can only take up the baton when it is entrusted to them by those who have the physical power to prescribe and enforce the fundamental principles on which the nation is constituted.

Believing that, I believe that our friends in Latin America have a long, hard struggle to build the road to democracy and then to launch on that road the judges who can help with the journey. One clue to how tough the struggle will be emerges from a primitive aspect of the judicial office right now. Indeed, one cannot fail to have in mind how many of our most respected colleagues in the Latin American judiciary in recent years have been terrorized or killed in the line of duty, in Guatemala, in Colombia, in Peru, in Chile, in El Salvador and elsewhere.[23]

That is an appalling circumstance. What does it mean when in so many places judges are being murdered or threatened with death or the deaths of their families for having the gall to undertake to enforce the rule of law? It means, of course, that there is no semblance of an independent judiciary and not enough will or force in the nation to have one.

The terror means that the people who have power in the country do not want an effective, independent judiciary essential to the rule of law. And that means there is not a free, democratic society. It is a fundamental principle that an independent judiciary is necessary to a free, democratic society and that there can be no truly independent judiciary where the fundamental principles of limited, responsible government are not in force.

This again is elementary, but it is not so elementary that it can go without saying. So I mention here an omission on this subject that seems to me to be regrettable. Earlier in this chapter, I cited with appreciation the 1985 United Nations Basic Principles on the Independence of the Judiciary.[24] Those twenty principles are sound and admirable as far as they go. I note, however, that there is no principle enjoining a duty on the executive to see that judges are not harassed, threatened, beaten, or murdered for the earnest performance of their judicial duties.

By contrast, a set of draft principles adopted in Syracuse, Italy, in the spring of 1981, expressly covered this subject in an article numbered 27, which said: "It is the responsibility of the executive authorities to ensure the security and physical protection of members of the judiciary and their families, especially in the event of threats being made against them."[25] That is a model worth following.

To put it another way, the bedrock needs of an independent judiciary in a free society include not only secure tenure, decent compensation, self-regulation and other similar factors. They also include working conditions that make the lives of judges no less insurable than those of others in the sedentary professions.

I turn now to another subject that has been, one way or another, a matter of agonizing difficulty in the century that is now ending along with the millennium. What can the judges do -- what can or should *anyone* do -- if the people grow weary of the burdens of freedom and want to vote an end to the democratic experiment? The question has arisen in a variety of forms during this century, and it may be that I will be blurring some lines of distinction when I talk about supposed varieties of a single question. In any event, I mean to mention concerns that are obviously interrelated and obviously critical when they arise.

I think we would all agree with Justice Holmes when he indicated that the people in the United States democracy should not be hindered (at least not by the judges) if they choose to vote down free capitalist enterprise and replace it with some form of socialism.[26] But what would he have said if the people decided to scrap democracy altogether -- repeal the Bill of Rights -- and install a dictator? And what could he have said or done in his role as a judge?

The question can arise in a variety of forms -- and may even be viewed as a variety of questions. When Hitler came to power as Chancellor, I think it is correct to say he was installed in accordance with the rules and forms of the Weimar Republic. It is to be doubted that the judges could have done anything about that. They could have refused, of course -- those who were not sacked -- to enforce the racist laws of the Nazi regime. It does not appear that a great many did that. But no matter. The judges were largely irrelevant -- as judges -- to the transition away from democracy and to a barbarism that cannot be dignified as a mere retreat to the past.

In the United States, we had what many found it agreeable to see as an analogous threat of totalitarianism. Congress in the 1950s reacted to the "Communist Menace," as it was called, by making large inroads on the rights of free association and free expression. The judges might have done something about that. But a majority of the Supreme Court agreed with Justice Jackson's dissenting view in *Terminiello v. Chicago*[27] that the United States Constitution was not a "suicide pact"[28] and agreed with his comments in *Dennis v. United States*[29] that those who joined in propagating Communist doctrine could be jailed as criminal conspirators.[30]

After the 1950s it came to be generally agreed that the judges had gone too far in sanctioning the repression of revolutionary advocacy. Would it be different today? It is not easy to know with certainty. While I leave that and other questions hanging, let me turn finally in this speedy excursion to recent events in Algeria, which I choose to see as at least approximately related.

You will recall that in early 1992 the Islamic Salvation Front was on the verge of a huge victory in a seemingly free election in that country. The Islamic Salvation Front preaches Islamic fundamentalist doctrine and proposed to install the law of Islam -- *shari'a* -- as the law of the secular state. The full implications of that promise were vague. How women would fare, how non-Muslims would be treated, what kinds of retrograde criminal law and process might come to be installed -- a host of questions like these awaited the answers of a parlous future.

But the Algerian military and its political cohorts in what was still at best a shaky, incipient democracy did not wait passively for what answers might come to be given. They intervened, blocked the decisive round of elections, and nullified the whole process. Indeed, a substantial array of civil rights -- in general what we think of as the essentials of the democratic process -- were suspended in Algeria.

The rest of the world has responded quite gingerly in reacting to that Algerian situation. There was, as there should have been, a sharp denunciation of the military when it overturned the election result in Haiti. Similar outcries were heard against armed obstruction of democracy in Zaire. But the prospect of possible Islamic repression versus actual military repression now seemed to give many people pause. One can understand that. My personal view, for what it is worth, is that the Algerian military probably deserved to be condemned. At best, they appear to have moved too soon, on evidence that was insufficient for such drastic action. But the matter is far from perfectly simple. It is not necessarily the case that an election is the last word. Majority rule, as we all know, is not always consistent with the ultimate values of genuinely free societies.

What remains unclear is any rationale for justifying the obstruction of the will of democratic majorities in the interests of human rights. This is a problem suited for jurists -- for judges -- as I would suggest, and eminently suited for handling in the setting of international human rights. As one worries about what the judges may be doing in the transition to democracy, one may also worry about the perennial danger of detours along the way and reversals in a world that has learned that endless progress is not inevitable after all.

Without pretending to have any solid answers, I will suggest a few axioms for considering when and how a democratic majority may be thwarted:

First, free elections are basic human rights, but they are not absolutes -- as the Bills of Rights protecting minorities remind us every day.

Second, electoral majorities are not empowered to close down the process and bar either their own replacement or the democratic freedoms that make meaningful elections possible.

Third, and most controversially, an elected group or party may be denied office when it has made plain either by an explicit and unequivocal statement and/or by evidence convincing beyond rational doubt that it intends to use the power of government either (1) to foreclose free elections in the future or (2) to suppress such basic rights as those of religion, speech and freedom from discrimination on grounds of race, religion, gender, ethnic origin, or political belief.

In the past, and even today, a formula like this might be no more or less than a suggested justification for violent revolution or the kind of military intervention -- scary as it is -- that we witnessed in Algeria. There is something new now under the sun, however -- the primitive beginnings of an international order for the enforcement of human rights. Whatever Mr. Bush really had in mind in Iraq, given the variety of things he said in justifying that war, that may have been an early step on a good journey.

So there may come a time in a foreseeable future when juridical principles to prevent democracy from self-destructing will have a civilized means for their implementation. I have offered a first draft of the principles. I hope that this draft will, in the near future, be debated and perfected and that the international jurists will be able to apply them.

## Notes

[1]*See, e.g.,* DENNIS L. ANDERSON, THE ACADEMY FOR GERMAN LAW, 1933-1944, at 489-492 (1987) (citing 2 HITLER, REDEN UND PROKLAMATIONEN, 1932-1945, at 1865 (Max Domarus ed., 1963) (Hitler's April 26, 1942 speech calling for an end to a formally independent judiciary and insisting upon his right to rearrange institutions of justice without regard to existing laws or traditions)).

[2]*See U.S. Judge Voids a Major Charge in Rights Deaths*, N.Y. TIMES, Feb. 26, 1965, at 1, 14.

[3]Seventh United Nations Congress on the Prevention of Crime and the Treatment of Offenders, U.N. GAOR, 40th Sess., U.N. Doc. A/CONF. 121/22/Rev. 1 (1986) (emphasis added).

[4]The movement for racial equality in the United States amply demonstrates this point. The rigidly mandated dual school system, for example, could not have been dismantled without the use of federal troops, the Civil Rights Act of 1964, 42 U.S.C. §§ 1971, 1975a-1975d, 2000a-2000h-6 (1988), the lawsuits of the NAACP, the intervention of federal agencies, such as the Department of Justice, or the brave black citizens, fully cognizant that their lives were on the line, who became plaintiffs or marched and demonstrated to break the Jim Crow system and to obtain their rights. This is not to say, however, that the Warren Court did not act as a catalyst for further advancements in the area of civil rights.

[5]60 U.S. (19 How.) 393 (1857).

[6]347 U.S. 483 (1954).

[7]*New York Herald*, Dec. 25, 1856, *quoted in* 5 CARL B. SWISBER, HISTORY OF THE SUPREME COURT OF THE UNITED STATES - THE TANEY PERIOD 614 (1974).

[8]60 U.S. (19 How.) at 404.

[9]*Id.* at 404-405, 407.

[10]CHARLES E. HUGHES, THE SUPREME COURT OF THE UNITED STATES 50 (1928).

[11]For a discussion of the negative effects on the legal system when a judge, in his judicial capacity, is required to enforce a law which, as a private person, he regards as profoundly immoral, see ROBERT M. COVER, JUSTICE ACCUSED: ANTISLAVERY AND THE JUDICIAL PROCESS (1975).

[12]347 U.S. 483 at 492.

[13]*Id.* at 494. We may give thanks that the question of "original intent" came up before the Warren Court and not the Rehnquist Court.

[14]The Fourteenth Amendment provides, in pertinent part:
No State shall make or enforce any law which shall abridge the privileges and immunities of citizens of the United States; nor shall any State deprive any person of life, liberty, or property without due process of law; nor deny any person within its jurisdiction the equal protection of the laws.
U.S. CONST. amend. XIV, § 1.

[15]*See* 2 STEPHEN E. AMBROSE, EISENHOWER 337 (1984).

[16]*See* Ronald Smothers, *At Little Rock, 30 Years Later: Starting Over*, N.Y. TIMES, Sept. 27, 1987, at 10.

[17]*See* Youngstown Sheet & Tube Co. v. Sawyer, 343 U.S. 575 (1952).

[18]*See* United States v. Nixon, 418 U.S. 683 (1974).

[19]*See supra* note 14.

[20]For example, the former Soviet Union.

[21]The United Kingdom, with failings like every other nation, is a prime example.

[22]4 BUREAU OF ROLLS AND LIBRARY, U.S. DEP'T OF STATE, DOCUMENTARY HISTORY OF THE CONSTITUTION OF THE UNITED STATES OF AMERICA 1786-1870, at 412 (1901) (letter from Thomas Jefferson to James Madison, Dec. 20, 1787).

[23]*See, e.g., Colombian Judge Killed*, B.B.C. SUMMARY OF WORLD BROADCASTS, Sept. 21, 1992, at ME 1491 iii; *Nine Police and a Judge Die in Terrorist Attacks*, NOTIMEX MEXICAN NEWS SERVICE (Peru), July 13, 1992; *World Jurist Body Says 67 Lawyers, Judges Killed in 12 Months*, REUTERS LIBRARY REPORT, Aug. 21, 1990.

[24]*See supra* note 3.

[25]*Report of the Special Rapporteur, UN Sub-Commission on Discrimination and Minorities*, 34th Sess., U.N. Doc. E/CONF. 4/Sub. 2/481 Add. 1 (1981).

[26]Lochner v. New York, 198 U.S. 45, 74-76 (1905) (Holmes, J., dissenting).

[27]337 U.S. 1 (1949).

[28]*Id.* at 37 (Jackson, J. dissenting).

[29]341 U.S. 494 (1951).

[30]*Id.* at 561-79 (Jackson, J., concurring).

# 3

# The Role of the Judiciary in the Transition to Democracy

*President Jean-Bertrand Aristide*

When I assumed the Presidency of my country in February 1991, I did so based on a commitment and platform that provided explicitly for the maintenance of an independent judicial system free from corruption and influence. For the Haitian people, a functioning independent judiciary is necessary for several reasons. Most important, it is necessary for the prosecution of those who have committed crimes against the Haitian people. These crimes have taken many forms during the Duvalier era and what I will call the "Era of the Generals." They include the plundering of the public treasury and the taking of international funds for personal use. While the Haitian people suffered from the lowest per capita income and literacy rates and the highest infant mortality and unemployment rates in the Western Hemisphere, and while Haiti was being deprived of the necessary infrastructure to build the nation, the Duvaliers and the generals used the public's money to buy multi-million dollar homes and yachts, apartments at Trump Towers and other such places in the United States and France, held multi-million dollar parties, and obtained a level of decadence and corruption unimaginable. Before General Avril ended the commission investigating public corruption, that commission documented over $550 million dollars that were stolen from the Haitian people by Duvalier and his associates alone in less than a ten-year period. The manner in which the funds were stolen included taking checks directly out of the national security accounts and even stealing funds needed for the construction of a children's hospital. Under the rule of the generals, including Namphy, Regal, Avril and now Cedras, nothing has changed. The greed and corruption remain.

In order to perpetuate an environment that facilitates greed and corruption, those in power maintain an atmosphere of repression so thorough and so complete that the system functions much more like a totalitarian state than the authoritarian state suggested by some commentators. As a result, over the past thirty-five years, tens of thousands of Haitians have been summarily executed, tortured, and subjected to forced disappearances and unlawful incarceration for prolonged periods of time. Since the coup d'état against my government, most reliable international and domestic organizations have reported that between 1,500 and 2,500 of my countrymen have been murdered by the military. In addition, the old forces of repression have returned. Section chiefs under the Duvaliers and the generals have returned with a vengeance. The United States media has reported that they have burned villages to the ground, murdered supporters of democracy, and even attempted to kill a reporter for National Public Radio.

The need for a judicial system that will bring such persons to justice is the major concern, the major desire, and the major issue for most Haitians. We need to see that justice is done and that those who have committed such heinous crimes -- crimes against humanity -- will be brought to justice. This pledge, like that of the Holocaust survivors and the State of Israel, is a fundamental part of our national consciousness. This thirst for justice transcends even momentary economic hardship. It is for this reason that the poor of Haiti who suffer under the embargo support it the most. They support the embargo at great personal sacrifice because they know that this is the only way that justice will become a reality in our country.

When I assumed the office of President, I began the process of obtaining justice within a constitutional framework. We understood, like the survivors of the Holocaust, that bringing to justice those who had committed crimes against humanity would require time and commitment. We recognized that it would require painstaking documentation, thorough investigation, and a fair prosecution and trial within the constitutional framework.

We recognized further that to establish justice it is necessary to ensure that we provide for the administration of justice. Prior to the initiation of democracy in Haiti, there was no functioning system for administering justice. This maladministration of justice served precisely the needs of the non-democratic government. If persons are ignorant of their rights, and if the system designed to administer justice has no chance of succeeding, then raw power reigns supreme.

When I was elected President, we recognized that the existing justice system was not functional to serve the needs of a democratic society and state. We recognized that in order to have a judicial system consistent with the goals of democracy, it must be a system that functions at all levels. First, we must train the police, who must not only be well-equipped but must be educated and motivated. They must understand the basic, rudimentary procedures of conducting an investigation and must learn the basic scientific techniques of criminal justice, whether it be in the methods of securing evidence, cataloging criminal suspects, or identifying witnesses. They must also be knowledgeable about crime prevention as well as crime detection. This requires some knowledge of the law, the ability to inform the citizenry of their rights, and the ability to organize the citizenry to establish safe neighborhoods and cities.

Training in our criminal juice system must also include training concerning the treatment of those who are incarcerated. We must develop a system that does not allow people to languish in prison without a fair and expeditious trial. Persons who are incarcerated, either before trial or after, must be treated with the respect and dignity consistent with how democracy treats all human beings. The prisons must be modernized and prison guards educated as to the treatment of those incarcerated. Programs designed to rehabilitate and to give medical and psychological assistance to detained persons must be established in all prisons and jails throughout the nation.

A judiciary consistent with democratic values must also establish a functioning court system. Court clerks and court reporters must be well-trained and paid sufficient salaries so that they are not subject to intimidation or corruption. The courts must develop systems that provide for retrieval of information, regular and consistent court sessions, standardized rules of procedure, and education of citizens as to their legal rights.

Similarly, the legal profession itself must be elevated. Judges must be better trained, not only in the law, but in the administration of justice. The courts in Haiti have so few sessions that a person may remain in jail for months at a time without ever having the benefit of a hearing or trial. We need to establish fundamental rules involving the release of persons from custody awaiting trial, the establishment of a truly adversarial system, and the ability to have the fair and efficient administration of justice. A system of public prosecutors and public defenders must be established and at salary levels and substantial recognition so that they are not tempted to cast aside their oaths of office.

Finally, and perhaps most important, a judicial system can only work in a democratic society when the public knows what their rights are and when citizens have access to the system. Civic and legal education must be a fundamental part of the curriculum for all students throughout the nation. Adults must become aware through public forums and public meetings of the kinds of rights they have as citizens and the ways in which the judiciary is open to them.

A judicial system must exist, therefore, not only in theory, but in practice. Once there is a meaningful judicial system in place, such system furthers the democratic process by demonstrating to its citizens that all persons can have access to the legal system and can obtain a fair and expeditious hearing. A system such as the one envisioned would also allow the government to bring to justice persons who have committed past wrongs.

The recognition that such people could be brought to justice under a fair system furthers the democratic process by demonstrating that a democratically elected government can redress the wrongs of the past. In Haiti, our judicial system must and can do better. Although we have had a temporary setback, the Haitian people will not return to the past. They will no longer accept a judicial system in a democratic society that is not open to the public, that is not impartial, and that is not well-trained and well-organized.

In addition to establishing a domestic system of justice, a democratic society demands the internationalization of the fight against criminal conduct. For Haiti, the importance of the use of international forums and domestic forums of other countries to prevent injustice and to punish those for past injustices is critical. In addition to our own judiciary, we believe that international fora must be available to prosecute criminally and civilly crimes that have been committed against the Haitian people. In this vein, we have pursued claims against the Duvaliers and others in the courts of the United States and France. In a world where criminals and their capital are highly mobile, we must track down and bring to justice criminal conduct wherever such criminals and the rewards of their crimes are found. In addition, we believe that international courts must remain open for individual criminal and civil prosecutions to redress crimes committed against the Haitian people, including summary executions, torture, and forced disappearances.

The prosecution of such persons domestically and internationally profoundly reinforces democratic values. It demonstrates that those who have been traditionally powerless in society may still have their rights vindicated. It provides an important step toward empowerment and integration into the political life of the country. It serves as the foremost symbol that the government can function to right past injustice and can protect its citizens against future harm. It places Pharaohs, both old and new, on notice that their days are numbered and that they can no longer expect acceptance and passivity in the people's march to freedom. Upon the re-establishment of my government, we intend to utilize fully our courts to redress the crimes that have been committed against the Haitian people.

An independent judiciary also enforces and reinforces the rule of law. In a society so long subjected to abuses of power and corruption as Haiti, the rule of law must be the centerpiece for democratic rule. No official, no matter how high or petty, and no person, no matter how rich or poor or how educated or uneducated, can be beyond or above the law. The rule of law levels the playing field and allows all to participate in the benefits of democratic society. It also enhances the ability of the government to serve its people and to operate in the interest of its people. It means that public or private corruption will not be tolerated; that governmental laws as basic as collecting taxes and preventing crimes will not be subject to humor but humility; that the corrupting influence of drugs and drug proceeds will not infect Haitian society; and that those anti-democratic elements in society will be held accountable for their wrongdoing.

For those who were for so long disenfranchised in Haiti, the rule of law offers hope of equal treatment under law. For the children of Cite Soleil, Lasaline, Foncet, Belai, Rabotoa and Lasavan, and for all children in urban and rural areas, the rule of law holds out the promise that they will have an equal chance to survive, an equal share in society, and the equal right to succeed.

Finally, the judiciary plays the important role of establishing a forum for the resolution of disputes in society. The Haitian Constitution has a number of unique features in this respect. In addition to our court system, our Constitution provides for a separate independent court to address disputes against the State, government officials, public services, and even citizens involving financial and administrative disputes arising out of government expenditures or administrative abuse.

In addition, our Constitution contains a provision for the establishment of a Conciliation Commission which is responsible for settling disputes between the Executive Branch and the two Houses of the Legislature. Moreover, we have established the Office of Citizen Protection, which is designed to intervene on behalf of any complainant, without charge, in any court that has jurisdiction to hear the matter. We hope in this manner to provide support to those who may feel powerless or lost in the judicial system. The Protector of Citizens will work for and represent the interests of those who would be shut out of the judicial process because of the lack of funds or education.

The purpose of these provisions is to enhance lawful procedures as a means for resolving disputes. The political history of our country is, unfortunately, a history of extremes, of ultimatums, and of force as the only mechanisms for resolving disputes. The use of these dispute-resolution methods, including the courts, enhances the democratic process by demonstrating that there are alternatives to force as a way of resolving problems between citizens, between the government and its citizens, and within the government itself.

What I have discussed to this point is the form of judicial process that we have sought to develop in Haiti. Of course, the form of the judicial system is quite different than its substance. Until we establish both the form and substance of the rule of law in our society, we cannot begin to approach a just society. In our pursuit of justice we must not be naive about the institutions of government. The institutions, as we have painfully learned, are extraordinarily fragile. Justice can only survive in Haitian society when it is accepted and furthered at all levels of society. Like the Sophists during the time of Socrates, there are those in our society who believe that justice is determined solely by those who are most powerful. As long as such people remain in positions to assert unrestricted force, Haiti will remain an unequal, unjust, and impoverished society financially, morally, and spiritually. At the same time, justice cannot exist for the masses in Haiti without giving them the tools they demand and need to establish the rule of law in society. Haitians must be physically healthy, not malnourished. They must be literate, and with literacy understand the legal methods necessary to assert their rights. Persons who are ill-fed, ill-clothed, ill-housed and illiterate are easily brushed aside by those with money or guns, or both. The institutions that mete out justice in Haitian society are only as effective as the support they receive from those who demand justice. Those who have sought to rob democracy from the people of Haiti through their military coup have used force to stop the support of democratic institutions that were beginning to flourish in Haiti. Although successful in the very short run, it cannot and will not destroy the aspirations of the Haitian people. As the Haitian people become literate, and they will, as the Haitian people become healthy and strong, and they will, and as they become more vocal in their support of the rule of law and of equal justice under law, the generals and their supporters will be forced to give way to democracy. The promise of our society, the promise of the Haitian people, will be fulfilled.

# 4

# The Function of Judicial Power During the Transition

*Raúl Ricardo Alfonsín*

## I.
### The Initial Question: The Concept of "Democracy" in Argentina's Transition

Before undertaking an analysis of Argentina's transition to democracy, the meanings and ideas embodied by the term "democracy" must be set forth. The very powerful emotive significance of the term makes evident that democracy is an instrument that makes human self-actualization possible. As such, the term lends itself to use by the broadest array of political systems, not only diverse ones but also systems inherently opposed to one another.

This preliminary definition is needed to illuminate my perspective as the Argentinian president to whom the people entrusted the mandate of setting in motion Argentina's transition to a stable democracy. It is not intended to prevail over all others nor to set universal requisites for the term.

The mandate of the Argentine people was the establishment of a government capable of going beyond implementation of participatory democracy governed by laws, and a departure from autocratic heteronomous rule. For the Argentinian populace, the term "democracy" connotes more than representative and participatory government. It encompasses a rule of law bound by the central requisites of liberalism -- a set of traditional civil and political rights that serve to deter state action as well as permit economic, social, and cultural choices -- commonly referred to as "human rights," and which complements free popular elections. This conception of democracy is not compatible with an economic liberalism so exaggerated and impervious to economic forces that it prevents the State from stimulating modern production activity or extending protections to underprivileged segments of the community.

The term "democracy" must also include the components of a republican system of government: equality, accountability of elected officials to the electorate, separation of powers, and the existence of political opposition to those in control.

Our definition of democracy is complete when the concept of the inherent sanctity of rights is added. This sanctity of rights necessitates universal, public, and clearly stated laws and requires congruence between official state action and the content of the laws. Corruption, prejudice, and the human tendency to personalize power undermine this congruence. A political system wherein elected officials utilize power to enrich themselves and not to serve the people, where corruption and embezzlement reign, and where personal and not institutional interests are followed does not qualify as a democracy. Thus, the term "democracy" should include the concept of *democratic* rule of law, that is, popularly elected government.

These are the legitimate requirements for the legitimate use of the term "democracy." They are necessary if a democratic regime is to survive. In Argentina's experience, "transition to democracy" has been equivalent to the establishment of a regime that will neither self-destruct nor incite or invite its own destruction through a *coup d'état* by revealing deficiencies that render it vulnerable.

In sum, a democracy meets the following requirements: (1) its officials have acquired power, directly or indirectly, as a result of free popular elections; (2) it is bound by the central requisites of both political liberalism and social constitutionalism (human rights); (3) it observes and enforces rules that promote economic transformation and provides protection for the less privileged; (4) it incorporates the republican form of government (equality, accountability to the people, the presence of political opposition, and separation of powers); and (5) it promulgates rules universally, publicly, and in clear fashion, thus precluding corruption in their application.

## II.
## Human Rights

On December 10, 1983, I became President of the Republic of Argentina after more than seven years of military dictatorship. During this long period the absence of the rule of law, violence, and systematic violation of human rights plagued the country. The national constitution was suspended, constitutional rights and guarantees were disregarded, separation of powers of the branches of government and federalism were suppressed, and the power of the judiciary was threatened. Political and labor union activity was forbidden, the universities were occupied, and the press was censored.

Thousands of citizens were detained without due process of law; many of them were tortured and later assassinated in numerous detention centers. More than 10,000 people disappeared.

Throughout my presidential campaign, I continually emphasized the need to restore universal ethical values and the rule of law. The violence, cruelty, and absence of the rule of law characteristic of the military "juntas" and terrorist groups had to be eradicated from our country forever.

Our convictions were guided by five basic principles. The first is that all human beings have inherent human and moral rights, whether or not the government recognizes such rights, and regardless of race, gender, religion, or nationality. Second, the function of human rights is to prevent the use of human beings as instruments for the benefit of collective objectives or ideological positions. Third, human rights may be violated by both affirmative acts and omissions. The fourth principle is that the use of physical and moral force by the state is justified only if necessary to promote human rights. Finally, defense of human rights is the concern not only of governments but of society as a whole, and transcends national boundaries. It should be a responsibility assumed by the international community.

We began with the conviction that only through institutionalization of democratic procedures, dialogue, and participation would it be possible to lay the groundwork to establish the sovereignty of law. The task of reinstating the rule of law in Argentina demanded a profound transformation. We repeatedly emphasized that Argentina's transition to democracy should not be regarded as a restorative process, but rather as a process of creation -- of new institutions, new procedures, new habits, and new ways to cohabit peacefully. We were faced not with reconstructing an already functioning system, temporarily displaced by authoritarianism, but with the need to establish new foundations so that an authentic democratic system could emerge.

Our first objective was to implement effective judicial protection of human rights. Discriminatory penal laws which imposed excessive punitive measures for political crimes were modified, greater individual freedoms during the judicial process were guaranteed, the possibility of conditional penalties was increased, and penalties for recidivism were decreased. Excessive and cruel sentences characteristic of the dictatorship decreased, and those found guilty by military courts were given recourse to nullify sentences through *habeas corpus*.

My government initiated the passage of laws that rendered torture equivalent to homicide, made unlawful the failure to report torture in military or police quarters, and eliminated motion picture censorship. New legislation also made the rights of all children equal, whether born in or out of wedlock. The law allowing citizenship revocation was repealed. Legislation prohibiting discrimination and recognizing conscientious objector rights was also passed.

The International Agreement on Economic, Social and Cultural Rights was ratified as well as the Inter-American Covenant on Human Rights. Provisions of the Military Code of Justice that allocated judicial authority to preside over criminal trials of military officers were altered.

## III.
## The Role of Judges in a Democracy

The requisite components of a viable democracy outlined above presuppose an impartial, respected judiciary and the judiciary's working interrelationship with the other governmental branches.

In contrast, the judiciary in a typical authoritarian regime purports to be a separate branch of government, when in reality it is devoid of power. Judges are limited by blind obedience to the absolute will of those in power -- a fact they generally try to hide -- and pretend to function independently, when in reality they have no independence. We of course acknowledge that there are many intermediary situations.

A republican form of government assigns to the judiciary the role of effecting the notion of equality of all men, controlling the exercise of power by the executive and legislative branches, and complementing the creation of law, without interference from the other branches. Judicial power, like many forms of power, comprehends defining goals and objectives: when a tribunal enters a judgment it resolves more than a single dispute, it sets forth and gives notice to the community of the criteria that will govern subsequent disputes.

The judiciary is also charged with ensuring that elections be free of fraud; guaranteeing the existence, plurality and internal democratic functioning of political parties (the parties' adequate functioning is required to maintain the equilibrium necessary to a democracy), and presiding over disputes between the branches of government and between the states.

Another function of the judiciary is to test the constitutionality of laws created by the other branches, whether through diffuse control processes -- similar to the United States' -- or through abstract control methods. On occasion, the judiciary is called upon to validate the form or content of a constitutional reform. Finally, the judiciary is responsible for acting swiftly to protect constitutional rights and freedoms -- human rights -- through specific and summary procedures, including *habeas corpus* protection and injunction, without which civil liberties would not be duly protected, particularly from state action.

The main objective of a transition to democracy is to ensure that each branch of government does not exceed its constitutionally designated authority. This responsibility falls squarely on the judiciary. A system where constitutional guarantees are weak or absent will easily bring about a climate of fear and insecurity which, in turn, tends to undermine the democratic order.

The judiciary, and particularly the Supreme Court, must ensure that the Constitution and the laws are upheld. If they succeed, they will win the respect and following of the citizenry. If they fail, they will lose their prestige and power; moreover, this failure will open the doors to anarchy or oppression.

With these responsibilities comes judicial power. Judicial impartiality is a pre-requisite for the adequate exercise of this power. Where judicial independence does not exist, as in authoritarian or semi-authoritarian regimes, the protection of the citizens is not exclusively derived from laws, but is influenced by external factors, such as national or international politics, which render that protection uncertain.

A sense of security in the law can only result from a democratic system. Furthermore, the degree to which that protection exists is directly related to the degree to which the judges are able to exercise impartially their power.

## IV.
## Judicial Independence During
## the Democratic Transition in Argentina

Citizens in democratic systems know their judges are impartial. Lifetime tenure guarantees their independence and objectivity. The republican form of government mandates periodic elections of executive and legislative officials. In contrast, during a transition period the judicial branch suffers from the same lack of legitimacy that affects an authoritarian government's executive branch.

Argentina's *coup d'état* abolished, from 1955 onward, the existing power structure and mandated that all public officials, including the judges, follow the military's code. The only exception was the interregnum of 1962-1963 during which a legitimate judicial branch survived despite the dismantling of the other two branches of government.

Thus, democratically elected officials are responsible for the most difficult of transition tasks: total restoration of the judicial framework; yielding a judiciary profoundly committed to the values of the system; and offering guarantees that judicial action will be both independent from other governmental branches and beyond suspicion of being influenced by government officials.

We have no doubt that the first government of Argentina's democratic transition fully achieved its objective. It not only appointed judges whose prestige and reputation were beyond reproach, but it also appointed a large number of lower court judges who changed the general legal framework and restored democratic institutions, fully performing their obligation to be zealous protectors of the law and the Constitution. The transition government's judicial integration was neither dependent, submissive or even compliant to the executive branch.

During the transition period's first administration, the Judiciary was the branch most successful in revitalizing social confidence in the state's capacity to be an effective force of transformation. One of the reasons was that the Executive was authorized to appoint objective and independent judges. This was possible because a senate majority did not exist. Pursuant to the Constitution, had there been a senate majority, that body would approve the nominations.

The Judiciary was the branch that took decisive steps to extirpate the image, deeply rooted in Argentinian society, that the citizens had no protection against the state, and that important public officials were above the law. The work of the judiciary generated the citizens' sincere admiration, as judges made clear in many instances that long-lasting progress is made only by ethically unobjectionable actions. A good example is the diligence, efficiency, and integrity that were evident throughout the process universally known as the "trial of the military juntas," which constituted a culminating point in the history of the rule of law not only in a single country but perhaps in the entire world.

## V.
## Dysfunction in the Exercise of Judicial Power and the
## Transition to Democracy: The Democratization of the Process

The appointment of impartial, diligent, and effective judges only begins the long transition from authoritarianism to democracy. The successful consolidation of the judiciary as a legitimate representative of the state's power and, more important, the creation of a solid social awareness that the judicial branch is as powerful as the other governmental branches and that it effectuates necessary criteria for the resolution of disputes depends on how solutions to a number of social needs are presented. These include the need for clear and publicly known laws governing judges' activities; the effectiveness of those laws in guaranteeing individual freedoms throughout the judicial process, as well as more general freedoms that depend on the proper function of the criminal system; the availability of needed physical and human resources and the balanced use of these resources in the legal system and quest for justice; and the need for reasonably speedy trials, which comport with society's need for finality and security.

Meeting these needs becomes extremely complex in Argentina's case because of our long tradition of authoritarian government. This is evident in the following examples.

Before 1983, the penal process, which governs the concrete and maximum application of power by the State and represents the unit of measure by which to gauge the strength of individual rights, failed to translate into everyday activity the clear, constitutional declaration of the republican system of government. Argentina's penal process kept the basic institutions of an absolutist Spain, adding to the inquisitional character of the investigation -- where the judge combines the contradictory functions of protecting both the prosecutor and the accused -- formal written allegations. As the written allegations are brought before the courts without public disclosure or debate on the evidence, the public has no opportunity to participate in the process or control it.

The tension between a system designed to achieve bureaucratic justice and defend the interests of an absolute ruler, and a political regime where individual guarantees are essential and difficult to ignore -- especially after the prohibition of coercion to obtain confessions was implemented at the outset of the transition period -- brought to light the inefficiencies of coerced confessions. That technique is now defunct.

Misdemeanors were resolved by administrative authorities, for example, police judges, and appeals limited to appearing before an independent judge. Archaic and broad repressive rules governed these crimes; there were no small claims courts; and the disappearance of an authoritarian government which suppressed conflict led to a vertical growth in the demand for justice, particularly between employers and employees, including the State and its service agencies, and between the State and private citizens. The high volume of litigation against the State is due in great part to the carelessness and excesses of authoritarianism.

Moreover, the last authoritarian government plunged Argentina's society into poverty and debt, conditions that made it difficult to modernize rapidly and expand the judiciary. The complete absence of planning criteria to organize activity requiring permanent and prioritized follow-up made necessary an enormous effort to attend to unsatisfied needs.

The first government of the democratic transition met these needs by establishing priorities. Our principal goal was to modify completely the criminal justice system, in order to project a sense of democracy in everyday activities. The effort was also directed at establishing a judicial system that would ensure efficiency in the investigative process by delegating the indicting function exclusively to the attorney general's department, and the responsibility for guaranteeing rights to an independent judge who would conduct a public trial where all the evidence would be exposed and the citizens would participate in the judgment.

This task included establishment of a new trial system, and a corresponding organic law, as well as a detailed organization of the resources necessary to set the new regime in motion. These efforts were partially frustrated when the officials who gained power through constitutional succession -- after a two-year delay -- showed a preference for a judicial process which, while providing for a public trial, did not improve much on the traditional investigative methods originally inherited from the Spanish and which, contrary to constitutional law, prohibited the use of a jury.

In addition to completely modifying the penal system, the first government of the democratic transition also undertook the following tasks. First, it began an integral reform of indictment rules governing minor offenses, as well as a reform of the substantive laws governing such cases, and organization of the physical and human resources needed to implement such reforms. After a two-year delay the successor government showed interest in continuing the work we began.

Second, it undertook the establishment of small claims courts. After the initial delay, official action is being taken in an analogous direction. Third, efforts were made to increase the decisional output of the Supreme Court. The number of judges was increased from five to seven in an effort to make clear that a complacent majority would not rule the Court. The judges were appointed by a new government and a senate where the majority of the members came from the opposition party. An additional set of laws was established to expedite the appeal process. These objectives were not achieved, and later those particular projects were replaced by the new administration with a plan which aimed at restricting the independence of the judiciary.

Fourth, the scope of responsibility of courts presiding over non-commercial conflicts such as inheritance disputes was redefined, and courts to deal with family issues were established. Next, the duties of judges responsible for resolving labor disputes were broadened by doubling their number and by the creation and introduction of massive computerized investigative procedures to modernize and aid in the administration of justice. Finally, plans to improve technologically the federal and state system of investigative justice were implemented. The succeeding administration did not continue this effort.

## VI.
## The Supreme Court of Justice

A democratic consolidation requires serious and continuous effort over a long period. It does not result from a single grand gesture, nor is it the task of a single administration. It is a particularly lengthy process given the difficult conditions under which Latin American democracies operate -- harassed by the foreign debt crisis, the negative economic growth during the 1980s, the rising expectations of increasingly dissatisfied societies, the backwardness of their production systems, the necessary painful structural adjustments, and the internal and external limitations which affect their domestic productive capacity as well as their access to global markets.

After strong movement toward progress, Argentina's democratic transition suffered a serious setback. The present government, opting for immediate gains rather than long-term progress, saw fit to alter summarily the number of Supreme Court judges, and at the same time explicitly mandate that the Judiciary mirror its political goals. We denounced this intent to manipulate judicial decisions to affect favorably the government's political interests.

The new judicial appointments which followed confirmed our worst fears: far from respecting and preserving the pluralism necessary to a republican system of government, Argentina became the only western nation, in a mere few months, to fill two-thirds of its highest court's judicial seats with judges beholden to the government.

The Court's loss of independence had concrete repercussions. Its integrity was compromised by its bowing to government influence, and its subordination of social interests to the government's political interests became especially visible in rulings on serious criminal offenses. Moreover, the new government imposed a hierarchical structure analogous to the executive branch on the judiciary, ignoring the fact that judicial independence is the only protection judges have against undue influence from the executive branch or their colleagues.

Without judicial independence and security, guarantees of individual liberty, economic stability, investment and production growth cannot exist. Judicial security exists only within the framework of the rule of law, and an independent and impartial judiciary.

Since the present government's summary increase in the number of Supreme Court judges, it has consolidated an unwavering majority of the Court, influenced other judges, pressured magistrates to force their resignation, and removed officials, including those appointed with the Senate's consent. These steps have led to public distrust of the judiciary, which extends, perhaps unfairly, to judges of high integrity. Without maintaining even a façade of legality, the government made arbitrary judicial appointments and removals, and purposefully manipulated jurisdictional rulings.

During our democratic administration, the executive and the judiciary earned a high degree of respect and loyalty. Today, the converse is true; the judiciary is greatly distrusted. The number of citizens convinced that the judiciary is not fulfilling its obligation to guarantee their rights grows constantly.

Every transition process from authoritarianism to democracy requires a judicial branch independent from political influence and power. Since the 1930s, Argentina's judiciary has sanctioned decisions made by illegitimate governments as though they were constitutionally sound governments. For many decades Argentina's judiciary ignored basic constitutional laws. Electoral fraud, *coups*, human rights violations, abuse of presidential power, and declarations of states of emergency occurred regularly. There was also administrative corruption, and when constitutional reforms were introduced by the military the judiciary arbitrarily interpreted the law to legitimize the reforms. Perhaps the most ominous of jurisprudential tactics since the 1930s was the doctrine of *de facto* laws, used by Argentinian courts to assimilate the laws dictated during military rule into the laws established by democratic governments.

The first years of the democratic transition were unusually rich in that the judiciary participated in enforcing the rule of law and the protection of individual rights. Important decisions were made which, in contrast to the past, did not respond to the will or hegemony of a given sector, but rather were the result of ample public debate participated in by all pertinent parties.

Some of these issues reached the Supreme Court of Justice and new positions were adopted which reflected a profound jurisprudential shift in the Court's rulings on constitutional matters. These included the Court's abandonment of *de facto* laws, requiring that all such laws be either ratified or rejected explicitly or implicitly by constitutional governments.

Other important Court decisions delineated the extent of freedom of expression and the right to privacy, assured personal autonomy by keeping the State out of personal matters, and recognized conscientious objector status as to service in the armed forces. Importantly, the Court adopted the position that evidence illegally obtained in a criminal investigation is inadmissible.

Recently, however, the new Court's decisions are seriously affecting institutional mechanisms for participatory government and decentralization of power. Perhaps the most significant threat to the rule of law in recent years has been the unconstitutional delegation of powers to the President of the Republic. He has usurped legislative power by abolishing or replacing laws at will through presidential decrees.

The Supreme Court sanctioned this usurpation of legislative power, purportedly because of the Congress' inability to resolve problems efficiently during Argentina's state of emergency. In effect, the present government maintains that the nature of the problems and required solutions are inherently unresolvable by a large pluralistic body like the Congress. The Court rationalizes the Executive's usurpation by indicating that Congress' inefficiency stems from the delays in decision-making brought about by conflicting interests and pressures exerted by various interest groups.

The great contribution of Congress, in my view, is precisely that it serves as a forum to debate conflicting ideas and interests. These debates make possible the expression of interests of all relevant parties. Congress not only exercises control over decisions made by the Executive, but also generates consensus on fundamental national policies. In contrast, in a president-centered system, the legislature cannot guarantee the participation of opposing factions, a condition crucial to democracy.

In response to the argument that the Legislature is vulnerable to and inefficient because of pressure from lobbyists, it is obvious that corporations can much more easily influence one person, the President, than a group of lawmakers who represent different constituencies and must periodically account for their actions during elections.

Under the pretext that a state of emergency exists, the Executive controls the branches of government and the division of power, rendering moot the need for consensus to pass laws. Congressional inaction, rather than formal approval following a presidential decree, is considered sanctioning of the creation, alteration, or suppression of individual rights.

The present Court established constitutional doctrine wherein the President can, independent of the Legislature, remove government officials working in agencies responsible for the State's assets and administrative control. The government asked for the resignation of the Public Prosecutor in charge of administrative investigations as well as of four of the five members of the Accounting Board. The Attorney General was also asked to resign, without prior Senate approval, as prescribed by law and tradition.

Called upon to rule on one of the above-mentioned dismissals, the Court ruled that Congress could not have input into the criteria governing public official appointments and removals. The Court then declared unconstitutional certain laws promulgated by the Executive of the democratic government and dismantled the system by which the constitutionality of laws is enforced. Instead, another system was established which permitted suppression of laws limiting the government's power. These conditions produced a very serious consequence: the Court, contrary to legislative mandate, approved the removal of the official in charge of the Administrative agencies by a politically appointed department head. The current Court has made other retreats. It maintains, for example, that substantive laws dictated by *de facto* governments extend to *de jure* governments. Moreover, the current Court's limiting of the application of the exclusionary rule in criminal matters where evidence is illegally obtained may lead to the Court once again fully admitting illegally obtained evidence. Guarantees of personal autonomy and individual liberties have suffered a serious setback as a result of the current Court's rulings. Individual choice as to life style -- free of outside intervention, and particularly State intervention -- has been undermined by restrictions of the right of association, evidenced in a Court decision that denied legal recognition to an association which included a homosexual minority. This doctrine proclaims discrimination based on personal characteristics constitutionally valid, gutting the freedom of choice and self-determination of minorities. The Court's ruling validates intolerance and represents a corrosive authoritarian component within a democratic system.

## VII.
### Everyone's Responsibility

Democracy is more than the expression of the majority's will. It is a complex combination of will and reason, of preferences and principles. Democracy's development requires an atmosphere where freedom and criticism can exist, and where a single political will cannot be obeyed, even if backed by a majority. Democracy exists through discussion, and decisions may be called democratic when they result from public debate and free expression from which consensus is reached.

General awareness that judges -- particularly Supreme Court Justices -- do not fulfill their duties of guaranteeing rights or protecting the division of power among the branches is a grave symptom; a loss of confidence in institutions ultimately leads to social dissolution. Preserving the public trust is thus the most important duty of public officials.

Society's clamor for independent and impartial judges will be answered through proper conduct and changed attitudes. Indeed, although the transition to democracy is a long and arduous road, Argentina will, no doubt, succeed in reaching this goal.

# PART THREE

# The Independence of the Judiciary

# 5

# The Right Degree of Independence

*Owen M. Fiss*[1]

In the discussions concerning the transitions from dictatorship to democracy in Latin America, it is commonplace to make two assumptions. The first is that the judiciary will have an important role to play in the new democratic regimes and the second is that every effort must be made to assure its independence. I can readily embrace both assumptions, but hesitate because I believe that the concept of judicial independence is far more complex than first appears.

The term "independence" is generally used to characterize the relationship of the judiciary to other institutions or agencies.[2] An independent judge is one who is not under the influence or control of someone else. An element of ambiguity arises, however, because there are several different kinds of institutions or agencies from which the judge is to be independent. Judges are supposed to be independent, but from whom?

One notion of independence -- I will call it "party detachment" -- requires the judge to be independent from the parties in the litigation, not to be related to them or in any way under their control or influence. This aspect of independence is rooted in the idea of impartiality and is uncompromising in its demands -- the more detachment from the parties the better. The bribe is, of course, the extreme example of a violation of this demand. But a less blatant link to one of the parties, such as a cultural tie that could cause the judge to identify with one party more than the other, may also count as a transgression.

Another form of independence -- "individual autonomy" -- concerns collegial relationships or the power of one judge over another. In common law systems, judges feel the pressure of other judges through the doctrine of *stare decisis*. In both common and civil law countries, collegial control may also be exercised over lower court judges through the regular appellate procedures. These traditional forms of collegial control do not threaten the independence that rightly belongs to a judge. But another form of control, recently imported into the United States, may threaten a judge's independence, or more specifically the claim for autonomy from bureaucratic control. Here I am referring to arrangements such as those embodied in the 1980 Judicial Councils Reform Act[3] that allow one group of judges, acting through an organization rather than the normal appellate procedures, to review the work of an individual judge and discipline him or her. The 1980 Act gives the judicial councils of the circuit courts power to investigate complaints against trial judges and to impose a number of sanctions against them.

Such bureaucratic controls are commonplace in civil law countries, where the judiciary is professionalized, but their introduction in the United States has alarmed some who fear the potential inroads on the American tradition that promises to each judge a measure of individual autonomy.[4] This tradition is nourished by broad cultural norms and our individualistic ideology; it also stems from the practice, most prevalent in the federal courts, of recruiting judges laterally.

A third form of independence -- the most difficult to understand and the focus of this chapter -- concerns what I call "political insularity." The judiciary is a part of the state, exercising the state's coercive power and dedicated to fulfilling the state's purposes, yet we insist that the judiciary be independent of other governmental institutions. This form of independence overlaps with party detachment whenever one of the litigants before the court happens to be another branch of the state, say the executive, but it is more encompassing and is best understood as an additional requirement. Even when a case is wholly between private parties, the judge is expected to decide the case free of any influence or control from the other branches of government.

Political insularity enables the judiciary to act as a countervailing force within the larger governmental system. In the context of a dictatorship, conflict or the very possibility of conflict between the judiciary (if it is allowed to exist) and the ruling powers is all to the good -- the more political insularity the better. The situation is more complicated, however, when the judiciary is part of a democratic regime. Then, so I will argue, we must optimize rather than maximize independence. In contrast to impartiality, it simply is not true that the more insularity the better, for a judiciary that is insulated from the popularly controlled institutions of government -- the legislative and executive branches -- has the power to interfere with the actions or decisions of those institutions, and thus has the power to frustrate the will of the people. An independent judiciary can be a threat to democracy.

The tension between popular sovereignty and judicial independence is most pronounced where judges are appointed by the executive and have life tenure, as is true of the federal judiciary in the United States. However, this tension also exists where judges are elected or subject to popular recall, since the mechanisms by which the judiciary is held publicly accountable tend to be far cruder than those that hold the executive or legislative branches accountable. Judicial terms of office are longer, elections occur more irregularly, and information about the performance or qualifications of the judiciary is more difficult for the public to assess.

Admittedly, the power possessed by an independent judiciary may sometimes be used to further the power of the electorate. This occurs, for example, whenever the court protects the integrity of the electoral process or political freedoms. Even then, however, the tension between judicial independence and democracy is not altogether absent, since undemocratic means are being used to protect democratic ends. Granted, only an institution that is free of political control can serve as an effective watchdog of the political process. Yet there is no guarantee that the judicial power will be used to enhance rather than constrict the power or political freedom of the electorate. Judges enjoying a hefty measure of independence may be no more committed to the preservation of free and open debate than military officers who are similarly insulated from politics. Sometimes they are, and sometimes they are not.

An even more fundamental conflict between democracy and judicial independence arises when, as is often the case, the judiciary goes beyond protecting the electoral process or political freedoms and sets aside an executive or legislative act that could not possibly be said to interfere with or corrupt the representational process. Typically, those seeking to justify judicial independence and to lessen this conflict expand upon the notion of democracy and insist that it does not require a complete surrender to the demands of the present electorate.[5] Rather, democracy is presented as a nuanced theory of governance that requires the state to be responsive both to preferences and principles: the democratic state must respond to both the occurrent demands of the electorate and to certain transcendent values, such as the protection of human rights, or to core principles embodied in a constitution. Within this scheme, the judiciary appears as the privileged guardian of these core principles or transcendent values, not least because it is insulated from popular control and generally sequestered from politics. Independence allows the judiciary to take the long view.

Such interpretations of democracy, distinguishing it from an insistent populism and tying it to such notions as "constitutionalism" or the "rule of law," are commonplace today in both the United States and Latin America and account for much of the appeal of the ideal of political insularity. The fact remains, however, that the appeal is a qualified one. Democracy may be acknowledged to be a combination of principle and preference, but the proportion of each is never specified. Moreover, while political insularity may put the judiciary, as compared to the legislature or executive, in a privileged position to speak authoritatively on questions of principle, there is no guarantee that what it says will be correct. A politically neutral interpretation is not necessarily a correct one.[6]

We are thereby confronted with a dilemma. Independence is assumed to be one of the cardinal virtues of the judiciary, but in a democracy it must be acknowledged that too much independence may be a bad thing. We want to insulate the judiciary from the more popularly controlled institutions, but recognize at the same time that some elements of political control should remain. We are, in other words, ambivalent about independence. This attitude is reflected in the United States constitutional system, as I will describe in the first section of this essay. It is even more evident in the emerging democratic republics of Latin America. In these countries one sees in dramatic ways the truly limited and contingent nature of the ideal of an independent judiciary.

## I.

State and local courts are essential elements of the United States judicial system, but the federal courts are the more celebrated division of that system. They are treated as the fullest embodiment of the ideal of judicial independence and a model for all the world to emulate. We boast of the political insularity of the federal courts and point to Article III of the Constitution,[7] providing life tenure and protection against diminution of pay, as the essential guarantor of independence. In the same spirit, we explain how the work of the federal judiciary is protected against easy revision by the political branches. The Supreme Court's interpretations of the Constitution can be revised only by the cumbersome amendment process, which requires special majorities in each house of Congress and approval by three-fourths of the states.[8] As a consequence, in the two-hundred-year history of the nation, only three amendments -- the Eleventh,[9] Fourteenth[10] and Sixteenth[11] -- have reversed decisions of the Supreme Court.

This mythic picture of the federal judiciary is often buttressed with references to some of the more dramatic instances in which the Supreme Court defied the executive or legislature, as when the Court required President Nixon to surrender secret tapes of his conversations[12] or when it ordered Congress to accept Adam Clayton Powell as a member even though it had previously refused to seat him.[13] The truth, however, is more complex than this one-sided telling of victorious moments may convey. While the Constitution creates a measure of political insularity for the federal judiciary, a number of other factors -- some also rooted in the Constitution -- bring the judiciary to some extent under the sway of one or the other of the political branches. Independent to an important degree, the federal judiciary is nonetheless tied to the political branches in ways that sometimes constrict its independence and other times enhance it. The relationship among the branches is multifaceted and highly interdependent, and this is true whether the focus be the process by which judges are appointed, the guarantee of life tenure and protection against the diminution of pay, or the law-making function of the judiciary.

A natural starting point for this inquiry is, of course, the process by which judges are appointed. As an abstract matter, judges can be selected by other judges and thus truly insulated from popular pressure. In the United States, however, the power to appoint federal judges is vested by the Constitution in a political officer, specifically the President, and an element of political control over the judiciary is thereby introduced. Presumably, the President does not want someone to do his bidding, and recognizes that the judge's job is law, not politics. Nonetheless, he is likely to appoint someone whose concept of justice approximates his own and who is likely to further rather than impede the policies of his administration.

While the President's control over the appointment process provides the executive branch with a certain degree of influence over the judiciary, the President's control is not unconstrained. The bar and public expect a measure of professional and intellectual achievement for nominees to the federal bench. Moreover, the President's power over appointments is a shared one, since the Senate must confirm the President's nomination. The Senate is as much a political institution as is the presidency, but the very division of the appointment power limits the control of the President over appointments, and the interaction between the two institutions often creates a dynamic which is not wholly within the control of either one.

Time also works to lessen the influence of the President. The judge has life tenure while the President serves for four or possibly eight years. At the moment of selection, the judge is likely to be deeply grateful to those responsible for his or her appointment, above all the President, and may be inclined to transform that feeling of gratitude into a sense of loyalty, giving the President every benefit of doubt. As time passes, however, administrations change, and the judge confronts the policies of a President with whom he or she has had no relationship. As a result, the distance between the President and the judge grows. Indeed, at certain points in its history, the Supreme Court has been composed of justices who owe their appointments to an entire panoply of Presidents. In the mid-1960s, for example, the Court was constituted by justices appointed by Franklin Roosevelt, Harry

Truman, Dwight Eisenhower, and John Kennedy, each President strikingly different from the others and collectively representing almost all the political strands of the modern period.

The threat to independence posed by the President's power over appointments is further limited by certain understandings that have evolved about the process by which new judgeships are created. Every vacancy constitutes an opportunity for the President to enhance his control over the judiciary. The Constitution does not limit the number of federal judgeships, either on the Supreme Court or the lower federal courts. However, an informal understanding -- stemming from the court-packing incident of the late 1930s -- has partially filled that gap. Frustrated by a series of Supreme Court decisions invalidating various New Deal measures, President Roosevelt proposed creating new justiceships -- one for each justice over seventy -- because he was unwilling to await the normal creation of vacancies from deaths and retirements.[14] The effect of this proposal was the opposite of that intended. Not only did it engender great hostility in Congress and the bar, forcing its withdrawal, but it left us with the settled understanding that the number of judges cannot be increased solely to create the opportunity to make appointments.

Aside from the appointments process, a threat to independence may also arise from a judge's continued involvement with the President and his administration. In the past, such involvement was commonplace. Indeed, one of the most distinguished judges of the United States, Louis D. Brandeis, acted as an informal adviser to President Roosevelt.[15] Such involvement impairs the impartiality of the judge; he or she may one day be called on to adjudicate the legality of a government practice that he or she shaped. But even more, such involvement is likely to create informal ties and bonds of loyalty to the President and thus is likely to breach what I have called the political insularity of the judiciary. The threat posed by this kind of behavior has somewhat declined, however. In recent decades a general understanding has evolved requiring sitting justices to remove themselves from the councils of the President.[16] Justice Harlan took this new demand for political abstinence to extreme lengths by refusing even to vote.

Financial need may also increase the political vulnerability of the judiciary. The protection against diminution of salary is an important bulwark against political control. It is qualified, however, because it leaves judges subject to inflationary pressure: a decision by Congress or the President to hold judicial salaries constant in the face of spiraling inflation can act as a severe sanction.[17] Mindful of congressional and executive control over their salaries, judges trying to keep up with inflation may be motivated to tailor their actions in such a way as to win the good will of these branches. The judiciary's attachment to the incidental emoluments of office, such as secretaries, law clerks, and chauffeurs can have a like effect, for these too are within the control of Congress and the President.

Similarly, the provision for life tenure, another measure that is supposed to provide political insularity, is qualified by the fact that federal judges are subject to impeachment and removal for misconduct. The Constitution vests this power in Congress but does not specify the permissible grounds of impeachment. Article III speaks only in the most general terms, providing that judges "shall hold their Offices during good Behavior." Another provision provides for impeachment of all civil officers of the United States for "high Crimes and Misdemeanors."[18] In the early history of the nation, the power of impeachment was in fact used to express strong disagreement with judicial decisions.[19] No judge, however, has ever been removed for that reason, and with the exception of an attack on Justice Douglas in the late 1960s by then Representative Gerald Ford,[20] an understanding has evolved under which a judge can be impeached only for violation of the most elemental duties of office, for example, through drunkenness, corruption, or conviction of a crime.[21]

In addition to its impeachment power, Congress may also try to exercise power over the judiciary by reversing judicial decisions. While it is true that a constitutional decision cannot be altered by simple legislative enactment, Congress, with the concurrence of the President, can reverse a statutory interpretation by a simple majority. Moreover, there is considerable congressional power over the jurisdiction of the federal courts, especially the lower ones; in the past, particularly controversial decisions have led to proposals to withdraw jurisdiction of the federal courts over select subject matters as a way of curbing judicial power.[22] Few such measures have been enacted, but the threats of such action and concrete plans to actualize those threats remind the judiciary of the limits of its power.

Finally, the judiciary is likely to become dependent on the other branches of government -- and thus less insulated from politics than the more familiar account suggests -- when the moment of enforcement or implementation comes. Judges speak the law and hope that there will be voluntary compliance with all that they command, but realize that resistance may well be encountered. They know that requiring the release of a prisoner or the desegregation of the schools may provoke sharp and passionate reactions.[23] Judges may be sovereign in articulating rights, but they are not sovereign in enforcing them. The coercive machinery of the state -- the sword -- is in the immediate control of the executive, and the purse strings are in the hands of the legislature and executive.

It is thus apparent that even the mythic independence of the United States federal judiciary is substantially constrained. Whether it be through the appointments process, control over jurisdiction and financial matters, or the imperatives of the implementation process, the executive and legislative branches exercise significant influence over the courts.

## II.

The republics of Latin America subscribe to notions of judicial independence that are not radically different from those which govern the federal judiciary of the United States. In all these countries -- including Chile and Argentina, the special concerns of this volume -- political insularity is considered a virtue, although it is also understood that the separation between political institutions and the judiciary is and should always remain incomplete.

Sometimes the political insularity of the judiciary is greater in the Latin American republics than in the United States. In Chile, for example, where the judiciary is professionalized, Supreme Court justices play an important role in selecting lower court judges and choosing their own successors.[24] There, the justices create a short list of nominees for the Supreme Court and Court of Appeals from which the President makes his selection. In a similar vein, the provision in the Argentine Constitution protecting against the diminution of pay, though identical to that found in Article III of the United States Constitution, has been interpreted more broadly. This provision has been read to protect against diminution of pay through inflation, on the theory that it is concerned with real, not just nominal, income.[25]

In other ways, of course, the tie between political institutions and the judiciary has been considerably stronger in some Latin American countries than in the United States. While consultation between the President and the judiciary is exceptional in the United States, and today is frowned upon, it is commonplace in Argentina. President Alfonsín engaged in it, and so does President Menem. The norm against court-packing also seems distinctly less robust. In 1990, for example, President Menem proposed legislation increasing the number of justices from five to nine, and as soon as that legislation was enacted he proceeded to fill the newly created vacancies with candidates of his own choosing.[26] All this was done in a context where Menem's party controlled the Senate (which must confirm the appointments) and where party loyalty was essentially taken for granted. To make matters worse, President Menem was alleged to have earlier offered inducements in the form of ambassadorships to encourage his predecessor's appointees to resign.

A study of such controversies in Latin America may have an intrinsic interest, but the issues they present do not differ significantly from those we have explored with regard to the United States. In all these controversies, it is generally assumed that judicial independence is a virtue, but also that it should not be complete. As in the United States, it is taken as axiomatic that the judiciary's relationship to political institutions consists of a delicate balance of both separation and control. Sometimes the balance is struck in one direction, sometimes in another. As a practical matter, a great deal depends on how the balance is struck, but the understanding of independence is not essentially different from that prevailing in the United States.

An entirely new dimension, however, is added to our understanding of judicial independence when our focus shifts from these interstitial controversies to more elemental ones, such as those arising from the transitions from authoritarianism to democracy that countries such as Chile and Argentina underwent in the 1980s. These transitions suggest a new and important qualification to the ideal of judicial independence. Not only is independence an ideal that must be optimized rather than maximized, but it is also regime-relative. A look at the Latin American transitions to democracy suggests that the claim for independence or political insularity is sharply confined to the regime of which the judiciary is a part.

The regime-relative nature of independence can be illustrated by another reference to Argentina. In that country, a military dictatorship seized power in 1976 and governed until 1983, at which time the junta called for elections that resulted in the election of President Raúl Alfonsín, who then restored constitutional government and went so far as to prosecute the junta for human rights violations.[27] In the period from 1976 to 1983 the junta utilized pre-existing institutions, including the courts, to govern; but the junta did not use those institutions according to the norms established by the Constitution. For the most part, the junta left the lower courts alone, but appointed its own Supreme Court.[28]

When the transition occurred in Argentina in 1983, the Supreme Court justices appointed by the dictatorship tendered their resignations, as indeed was customary in Argentina in such circumstances.[29] I would argue that even if they had not been so accommodating, President Alfonsín could have demanded their resignations and tried to impeach them. As a practical matter, he may not have had the power to do so, but for our purposes what is important is that the norm of independence did not constrain him. Alfonsín should not have been required to respect the justices appointed by the previous regime.

Some might take a contrary position and suggest -- to continue this speculative exercise -- that if President Alfonsín had left the justices appointed by the dictatorship in place, the ideal of judicial independence would have been dramatically strengthened. Possibly such an action could have constrained others -- not just President Menem, who lawfully succeeded Alfonsín, but also some ruler who might one day unlawfully seize power. This seems implausible to me. The newly refurbished norm might possibly have deterred Menem from packing the court in 1990, but it is hard to believe that it could have much force on any dictator who might seize power unlawfully. Those who act by such means do not usually consider themselves bound by considerations of reciprocity ("I'll let your judges stay in office, because you let mine.").

Additionally, there is no philosophical basis for insisting that President Alfonsín should have respected the independence of the justices appointed by the junta. Those justices could have checked or constrained Alfonsín's exercise of power, thereby serving one of the ends of independence; but as the instruments of another regime, there is no reason to respect their effort to do so. We want exercises of power to be checked, but not by another government. Of course, if a democratic regime were overthrown by a dictatorship, we may well want the dictators to leave in office the justices appointed by the democratic government. But that desire derives from our commitment to the democratic nature of the old government and from the hope that the incumbent justices will use their power to further the values of the previous regime, not to any abstract notion of judicial independence.

The qualification I am proposing to the ideal of independence makes crucial the scope one assigns to the notion of a regime-shift. More than an ordinary change of administrations is required; there has to be a decisive break with the past, almost a constitutional change. By way of illustration one can point, as I have, to the events occurring in Argentina in 1983, since these can easily be characterized as a regime shift. In many other cases, however, it will be much harder to determine whether a change of this nature occurred. This is true of present-day Chile, where the presidency has been transferred -- through elections, as in the case of Argentina -- from General Pinochet to President Patricio Aylwin. Although there is all the difference in the world between the policies of Pinochet and Aylwin, it is harder to say that there had been a regime shift.

In 1973, General Pinochet seized power in violation of the 1925 Chilean Constitution.[30] From that time until 1980, Pinochet claimed that he ruled according to the Constitution, but that claim was a farce. He assumed the presidency through force, Congress was dissolved, generals were placed in control of civilian agencies and though the courts continued to function, the writ of *habeas corpus* was effectively suspended.[31] In 1980 Pinochet proposed a new Constitution, which was then adopted by a plebiscite conducted without free and open debate. The new Constitution radically revised and supplemented the 1925 Constitution, adding a new layer of authoritarianism.

The 1980 Constitution retained the presidential system, but restructured Congress and put off congressional elections until 1989. It further provided that Pinochet would retain the presidency until March 1989.[32] A plebiscite would be held prior to that date to determine whether the General would remain in office for another eight years. If he lost, elections would promptly be held to determine who would replace him as President. (Regardless of the outcome, Pinochet would remain Commander-in-Chief of the Army until 1997). Beginning in 1983, the reign of terror lessened and the political climate in Chile improved, but it was still something of a miracle when the opposition defeated Pinochet in the October 1988 plebiscite and then managed to have Aylwin rather than Pinochet's candidate chosen as President in the election of December 1989.[33] Aylwin is a Christian Democrat, but he was supported in that election by a coalition of some seventeen parties.

President Aylwin took office in March 1990. Since that time, President Aylwin has governed with a broad political base, but always within the terms of the 1980 Constitution -- even though that document was adopted during a reign of terror which deprives it of any moral claim upon him. The aging general has remained in control of the army and presumably is prepared to use that power to protect his Constitution. In July 1989, the newly elected Congress amended the Constitution to remove some of its more draconian provisions,[34] but further amendment is difficult. Crucial provisions can only be amended by a three-fifths vote of both houses,[35] and nine of the forty-seven Senators are appointed rather than elected. As the 1980 Constitution provided, two of the nine were directly appointed by Pinochet (acting as President), and the remaining seven were appointed by institutions controlled by Pinochet -- the National Security Council (which appointed four) and the Supreme Court (which appointed three).[36]

Not only is Aylwin encumbered by the 1980 Constitution, but he inherited a Supreme Court that was largely molded by Pinochet. When the General seized power in 1973, he dissolved Congress, but left the Supreme Court -- no friend of Allende -- in power.[37] The President of the Court, Enrique Urratia Manzano, placed the "presidential band" on the General and proudly declared, "I put the judiciary in your hands." Unlike the Argentina junta, Pinochet did not replace the individual justices when he came to power -- there was no need to -- and for the most part, the rulings of the Supreme Court supported or strengthened Pinochet's reign. The 1980 Constitution left the personnel and structure of the Supreme Court unchanged, only with one exception. While retirement at seventy-five became a constitutional requirement (previously it was an administrative regulation, but was breached during the Pinochet years), an exception was made for the incumbent justices.[38] They could serve for life.

In 1973, the Supreme Court consisted of twelve justices. Under Pinochet, the Court was expanded until in 1988 it had seventeen members. Between 1973 and 1988, five of the twelve original seats on the Court became vacant and were filled by Pinochet, which meant that at the time of the October 1988 plebiscite ousting Pinochet, ten of the seventeen justices were Pinochet appointees. Moreover, immediately after the plebiscite but before the December 1989 election, two pre-Pinochet justices left the Court (one died and one retired), and Pinochet offered the aging justices who remained generous pensions, so-called "golden parachutes."[39] Six accepted this offer -- two of whom were appointed before 1973 -- and Pinochet filled these vacancies too. This meant that by the time Aylwin took office in March 1990, he confronted a Supreme Court consisting of a total of four-teen Pinochet appointees, some newly appointed. The other three were not appointed by Pinochet -- one was appointed by Allende in 1971 and the two others were appointed in the mid-1960s by Eduardo Frei, a Christian Democrat -- but all served during the dictatorship. The new President therefore had to face the question -- only hypothetical in the case of Alfonsín in Argentina -- whether he had to respect the independence of those justices who were either appointed by the dictator or who had served him during his regime.

With Pinochet in control of the Army, it was not clear that Aylwin had the practical power to unseat any of the incumbent justices. Nor was it clear that those justices would actually use their power to frustrate the new President's policies or to interfere with his fragile and cautious steps toward democracy.[40] Today, the question of judicial independence grows less urgent as some of the Pinochet justices retire or die.[41] Still, in 1990 the prospect of judicial interference with the policies of the fledgling administration was considered real, and that brought to the fore the question of the proper scope of the ideal of judicial independence. What could Aylwin legitimately do to control the Court? One option, in particular, which drew both curiosity and fire was court-packing.[42]

In the hands of Presidents Roosevelt and Menem, court-packing was justly regarded as an improper assault on an independent judiciary. In neither the United States of the 1930s nor in 1990 Argentina had there been a transformation that one could characterize as a regime shift.[43] Both Roosevelt and Menem acquired power through the constitutionally pre-scribed mechanisms (although in the case of Menem there was one irregu-larity -- he took office six months early). Aylwin is, however, in a different and more complex situation. On the one hand, he derives his power from the 1980 Constitution, and thus is not altogether free from the constraints it lays down. On the other hand, given the non-democratic elements of the 1980 Constitution, the circumstances surrounding its adoption, and Aylwin's repudiation of Pinochet's dictatorial policies, Aylwin's administration represents a partial break with the predecessor regime -- a relation one might call a "partial regime shift."

Aylwin's Chile, in this regard, falls somewhere between Alfonsín's Argentina and the Argentina of Menem -- between a sharp regime shift and a simple change of administrations. In such an in-between situation, in-between remedies may be appropriate, and court-packing might be such a remedy. It is a classically intermediate solution to the problem of inheriting a hostile judiciary. Unlike impeachment, court-packing accepts the authority of the justices in office, but it dilutes their power by adding new ones. It weakens the stranglehold of the past, but does not break from it altogether.

Initially, court-packing might seem anathema to those who, like myself, envision an important role for the judiciary even in democratic regimes and count political insularity as essential to judicial legitimacy. The transitions in Argentina and Chile make clear, however, that American aversion to court-packing and other political interferences with the judiciary crucially depends on a judgment about the terms and conditions under which power has been acquired. Independence is not a transcendent ideal, but contingent upon certain assumptions about the structure of government. In the case of the United States, our understanding of the nature of judicial independence has been forged in the context of stability -- two hundred years of a shifting, but generally stable government structure. It would be a mistake of the highest order to apply mechanically and uncritically that understanding to countries that have had an entirely different history.

## Notes

[1] I am especially grateful to Irwin Stotzky, the organizing spirit and the editor of this volume. I also wish to thank Terence Anderson, Eric Beckman, Eric Bentley, Jr., Marcel Bryar, Rodrigo P. Correa Gonzáles, Steve Diamond, Kenneth Held, Elizabeth Iglesias, Stanley Katz, Jonathan Miller, Keith Rosenn, Pablo Ruiz-Tagle, and Kevin Russell for commenting on this chapter and giving me the benefit of their thoughts.

[2] Independence is an essential attribute of good judging, but it is not the only one, and nothing will be gained by letting it stand for all the judicial virtues. I therefore take exception to Professor Kahn's broadening of the notion of judicial independence to include "independence from ideology." Paul W. Kahn, *Independence and Responsibility in the Judicial Role, in* TRANSITION TO DEMOCRACY IN LATIN AMERICA: THE ROLE OF THE JUDICIARY 73 (Irwin P. Stotzky ed., 1993) [hereinafter TRANSITION]; *see also* Jorge Correa Sutil, *The Judiciary and the Political System in Chile: The Dilemmas of Judicial Independence During the Transition, in* TRANSITION, *supra* at 89. Judges can be independent, yet fail in discharging their most elemental duties because they do not understand the issues, lack courage, or are captured by an outworn and antiquated philosophy.

[3]The Judicial Councils Reform and Judicial Conduct and Disability Act of 1980, § 3, 28 U.S.C. § 372 (c)(6)(B) (1989).

[4]Owen M. Fiss, *The Bureaucratization of the Judiciary*, 92 YALE L.J. 1442, 1445 (1983).

[5]Owen M. Fiss, *The Forms of Justice*, 93 HARV. L. REV. 1 (1979); BRUCE ACKERMAN, WE THE PEOPLE (1991).

[6]Owen M. Fiss, *Objectivity and Interpretation*, 34 STAN. L. REV. 739, 744, 748-49 (1982).

[7]Article III provides in pertinent part: "The Judges, both of the supreme and inferior Courts, shall hold their Offices during good Behaviour, and shall, at stated Times, receive for their Services a Compensation, which shall not be diminished during their Continuance in Office." U.S. CONST. art. III §1.

[8]Article V provides in pertinent part:

The Congress, whenever two-thirds of both Houses shall deem it necessary, shall propose Amendments to this Constitution, or, on the Application of the Legislatures of two-thirds of the several States, shall call a Convention for proposing Amendments, which, in either Case, shall be valid to all Intents and Purposes, as part of this Constitution, when ratified by the Legislatures of three-fourths of the several States, or by Conventions in three-fourths thereof, as the one or the other Mode of Ratification may be proposed by the Congress.

U.S. CONST. art. V.

[9]The Eleventh Amendment provides: "The Judicial power of the United States shall not be construed to extend to any suit in law or equity, commenced or prosecuted against one of the United States by Citizens of another State, or by Citizens or Subjects of any Foreign State." U.S. CONST. amend. XI. The Eleventh Amendment was adopted in response to the Supreme Court's decision in Chisholm v. Georgia, 2 U.S. (2 Dall.) 419 (1793) (holding that a state could be sued by a citizen of another state and that the Supreme Court had original jurisdiction over such a suit).

[10]The Fourteenth Amendment confers citizenship on all persons born or naturalized in the United States and thus reversed the ruling of Scott v. Sandford, 60 U.S. (19 How.) 393 (1857), that denied persons of African ancestry the possibility of becoming citizens even when freed from slavery.

[11]The Sixteenth Amendment provides: "The Congress shall have power to lay and collect taxes on incomes, from whatever source derived, without apportionment among the several States, and without regard to any census or enumeration." U.S. CONST. amend. XVI. The Sixteenth Amendment was adopted in response to the Supreme Court's decision in Pollock v. Farmers' Loan & Trust Co., 157 U.S. 429 (1895); 158 U.S. 601 (1895) (holding that Congress' attempt to tax incomes without apportionment was unconstitutional).

[12]United States v. Nixon, 418 U.S. 683 (1974). Another instance of defiance is Youngstown Sheet and Tube Co. v. Sawyer, 343 U.S. 579 (1952) (holding that President Truman lacked the authority to seize the nation's steel mills during the Korean War).

[13]Powell v. McCormack, 395 U.S. 486 (1969).

[14]William E. Leuchtenberg, *The Origins of Franklin D. Roosevelt's "Court-Packing" Plan*, 1966 SUP. CT. REV. 347; WILLIAM H. REHNQUIST, THE SUPREME COURT: HOW IT WAS, HOW IT IS 219-34 (1987). Executive interference with the judiciary had an early start in American history. Under President Thomas Jefferson, Republican frustration towards the Federalist judiciary led to the initial refusal to issue commissions to certain judges President Adams had appointed, measures to repeal the Judiciary Act of 1801 (thereby abolishing the positions to which these new judges had been appointed), and legislation in 1802 which recessed the Supreme Court for fourteen months. In 1804, Jefferson engineered impeachment proceedings against one Supreme Court justice, and by 1808 he had expanded the Court from five members to seven, filling each new vacancy with a Republican. 2 GEORGE L. HASKINS & HERBERT A. JOHNSON, HISTORY OF THE SUPREME COURT OF THE UNITED STATES, FOUNDATIONS OF POWER: JOHN MARSHALL, 1801-1815, 136-245 (1981).

[15]BRUCE A. MURPHY, THE BRANDEIS-FRANKFURTER CONNECTION: THE SECRET POLITICAL ACTIVITIES OF TWO SUPREME COURT JUSTICES 98-185 (1982).

[16]Justice Fortas's continuing involvement as President Johnson's advisor was one factor that damaged his candidacy for the chief justiceship. LAURA KALMAN, ABE FORTAS: A BIOGRAPHY 293-357 (1990); BRUCE A. MURPHY, FORTAS: THE RISE AND RUIN OF A SUPREME COURT JUSTICE 234-68 (1988).

[17]*See* Atkins v. United States, 556 F.2d 1028 (Ct. Cl. 1977), *cert. denied*, 434 U.S. 1009 (1978) (holding that Congress had not violated the Article III Compensation Clause by failing to raise judicial salaries an amount equivalent to the rate of inflation). *But see* United States v. Will, 449 U.S. 200 (1980) (finding that Congress had violated Article III in passing legislation which repealed a salary increase already in effect and thus "diminished" the compensation of federal judges).

[18]Article II § 4 provides: "The President, Vice President and all civil Officers of the United States, shall be removed from Office on Impeachment for, and Conviction of, Treason, Bribery, or other high Crimes and Misdemeanors." U.S. CONST. art. II § 4.

[19]WILLIAM H. REHNQUIST, GRAND INQUESTS: THE HISTORIC IMPEACHMENTS OF JUSTICE SAMUEL CHASE AND PRESIDENT ANDREW JOHNSON 52-53, 58-60, 74-77, 90-93, 103-05 (1992); RAOUL BERGER, IMPEACHMENT: THE CONSTITUTIONAL PROBLEMS 224-51 (1973).

[20]EDWIN P. HOYT, WILLIAM O. DOUGLAS 149-51 (1979).

[21]In recent years, federal judges have been impeached for tax fraud, bribery and perjury. Mark A. Hutchinson, *Maintaining Public Confidence in the Integrity of the Judiciary: State Bar of Nevada v. Claiborne*, 1989 B.Y.U. L. REV. 283, 284; *see also* IMPEACHMENT TRIAL COMMITTEE ON THE ARTICLES AGAINST JUDGE ALCEE L. HASTINGS, PROCEEDINGS OF THE U.S. SENATE IN THE IMPEACHMENT TRIAL OF ALCEE L. HASTINGS, A JUDGE OF THE UNITED STATES DISTRICT COURT FOR THE SOUTHERN DISTRICT OF FLORIDA, S. Doc. No. 18, 101st Cong., 1st Sess. (1989); S. Rep. No. 164, 101st Cong., 1st Sess. 4 (1989) (on the impeachment of Judge Walter L. Nixon, Jr., of Mississippi). A failed challenge to Judge Nixon's

impeachment has been granted certiorari by the Supreme Court. Nixon v. United States, 938 F.2d 239 (D.C. Cir. 1991), *cert. granted*, 112 S. Ct. 1158 (1992). Judge Hastings's impeachment was recently declared invalid by the District of Columbia District Court. Hastings v. United States, 802 F. Supp. 490 (D.D.C. 1992).

[22]In the early 1980s, legislation was introduced to limit lower federal court jurisdiction over state anti-abortion laws. *See, e.g.*, S. 158, 97th Cong., 1st Sess., (1981); H.R. 3225, 97th Cong., 1st Sess. (1981); H.R. 900, 97th Cong., 1st Sess. (1981). Bills were also introduced to limit federal court powers to order school busing. *See, e.g.*, S. 1147, 97th Cong., 1st Sess. (1981); S. 1005, 97th Cong., 1st Sess. (1981); H.R. 3332, 97th Cong., 1st Sess. (1981); H.R. 1180, 97th Cong., 1st Sess. (1981). For a general discussion, *see* Lawrence G. Sager, *Constitutional Limitation on Congress' Authority to Regulate the Jurisdiction of the Federal Court*, 95 HARV. L. REV. 17-20 (1981).

[23]Fiss, *supra* note 5, at 2.

[24]CONSTITUTIÓN POLÍTICA DE LA REPÚBLICA DE CHILE art. 75 (1980) [hereinafter, CHILE CONST.]; Keith S. Rosenn, *The Protection of Judicial Independence in Latin America*, 22 BULLETIN OF THE CENTRE FOR THE PROTECTION OF JUDGES AND LAWYERS 13, 22 (1980).

[25]Bonorino Peró v. Estado Nacional, Supreme Court of Argentina, November 15, 1985, 116 E.D. 321 (1985) and decisions of December 4, 1985 and April 4, 1986 [1986-II] J.A. 376, 377; Rosenn, *supra* note 24, at 33. *But see id.* at 18 (noting the decreasing percentage of the Argentine national budget devoted to the federal judiciary).

[26]*Argentina: Controversy Surrounding the Judiciary*, 45 INT'L COMMISSION JURISTS REV. 1, 4 (1990).

[27]For a general discussion of Argentina's recent political history, see Irwin P. Stotzky, *The Fragile Bloom of Democracy*, 44 U. MIAMI L. REV. 105, 109-14 (1989); Carlos S. Nino, *The Duty to Punish Past Abuses of Human Rights Put Into Context: The Case of Argentina*, 100 YALE L.J. 2619, 2622-23 (1991).

[28]Alejandro M. Garro, *The Role of the Argentine Judiciary in Controlling Governmental Action Under a State of Siege*, 4 HUM. RTS. L.J. 311, 314-15 (1983).

[29]*Argentina: Controversy Surrounding the Judiciary*, supra note 26, at 2. *But see* Rosenn, *supra* note 24, at 30 (describing court changes prior to 1976 as dismissals); Garro, *supra* note 28, at 314-15 (describing these changes as purges).

[30]For a review of Chile's recent past, see JAY A. SIGLER ET AL., CONSTITUTIONS OF THE COUNTRIES OF THE WORLD: CHILE 15-36 (Albert P. Blaustein & Gisbert H. Flanz eds., 1991).

[31]Historical legal constraints were avoided by military trials which often involved summary proceedings and the violation of due process. Hugo Frühling, *Repressive Policies and Legal Dissent in Authoritarian Regimes: Chile 1973-81*, 12 INT'L J. SOC. L. 351, 354 (1984). The Supreme Court of Chile rejected writs of *habeas corpus* on the grounds that the Code of Military Justice did not allow the courts to intervene in martial law cases. *Id.* at 363-64, 370.

[32]CHILE CONST. transitory provision 14; SIGLER ET AL., *supra* note 30, at 28-29.

[33]MARK FALCOFF, MODERN CHILE 1970-1989: A CRITICAL HISTORY 311-12 (1989).

[34]For an analysis of one such provision, the notorious article 8, see Pablo Ruiz-Tagle, *Debate Publico Restringido en Chile (1980-1988)*, 16 REVISTA CHILENA DE DERECHO 111 (1989).

[35]CHILE CONST. art. 63.

[36]*Id.* art. 75 (as amended).

[37]One of the primary justifications for the military takeover was the restoration of constitutional order. Rosenn, *supra* note 24, at 34. The Allende government had refused to enforce Supreme Court decisions ordering the return of illegally occupied land and illegally seized factories. Eugenio Velasco, *The Allende Regime in Chile: An Historical and Legal Analysis (Part II)*, 9 LOY. L.A. L. REV. 711, 725-26 (1976).

[38]CHILE CONST. transitory provision 8.

[39]Letter from Rodrigo P. Correa Gonzáles to Owen M. Fiss (Oct. 19, 1992) (on file with Owen M. Fiss).

[40]The sensitivity of the Supreme Court to the limits of its power was revealed in its handling of a controversy involving Carlos Cerda, a court of appeals judge greatly admired by human rights groups in Chile. The controversy began in the mid-1980s, before Aylwin came to power, when Cerda undertook an investigation of the disappearance in 1976 of ten members of the Communist Party. The persons accused of this crime claimed that the investigation was barred by the 1978 amnesty law, and the Supreme Court agreed and ordered Cerda to desist from his investigation. When he refused, the Supreme Court suspended him for two months. That occurred in 1986. In 1990, after the plebiscite ousting Pinochet and after the election of Aylwin, Cerda resumed the investigation and the Supreme Court then responded by reaffirming its previous order requiring him to desist. Cerda stopped the proceedings but refused to dismiss the case altogether, and then the Supreme Court entered an order in effect requiring the President to remove Cerda from office. There was an immediate and enormous public uproar over this order, and following a formal request for reconsideration by Cerda, the Supreme Court backed down. During the summer of 1990, speculating on what action the Supreme Court might take in the Cerda matter, officials spoke informally of the possibility of impeachment and court-packing if the Court tried to remove Cerda from office. For Cerda's distinctive conception of judicial independence, what I have called "individual autonomy," see Pablo Ruiz-Tagle, *Analisis Comparado de la Función Judicial*, 39 REVISTA DE ESTUDIOS PUBLICO 131, 154-58 (1990).

[41]By 1992, Aylwin had the opportunity to fill three vacancies -- two of the three vacancies arose from the retirement of Frei appointees and one arose from the death of a justice appointed by Pinochet shortly before the election. In July 1992, a law was enacted creating as generous a retirement program as the one Pinochet established in 1989. It applied to those justices over seventy and who held office at the time the law was passed.

[42]Changes concerning the Chilean Constitutional Court (dissolved by Pinochet in 1973, but reinstated in the 1980 Constitution) were also considered at this time, but with less specificity and urgency, perhaps because the judges serve only for eight year terms. It is noteworthy that Germany and Italy established Constitutional Courts following World War II, as did Spain following the death of Franco. SUPRA-NATIONAL AND CONSTITUTIONAL COURTS IN EUROPE: FUNCTIONS AND SOURCES 6-11 (Igor I. Kavass ed., 1992). These courts might be seen as transitional devices -- as a way of constraining the influence of judges who were appointed by or served dictatorial regimes.

[43]Bruce Ackerman does not regard the New Deal as a regime shift, but describes it as a decisive moment in American history "at which deep changes in popular opinion gained authoritative constitutional recognition." BRUCE ACKERMAN, *supra* note 5, at 41, 47-50 (1991).

# 6

# Independence and Responsibility in the Judicial Role

## Paul W. Kahn

Judicial independence is a goal democracies strive to achieve. The judiciary should be independent from the parties to a conflict, independent from the political institutions of a government, and independent from contested political ideologies. An international bureaucratic corps of judges, well versed in state law and available to resolve domestic disputes, would certainly advance this concept of judicial independence. Most democratic states, however, would reject such a proposal because it ignores judicial responsibility. Responsibility, I will argue, is as important a judicial norm as is independence and it cuts against too much independence.

## I.
### A Wholly Independent Judiciary

It is not hard to propose a model for an independent court, even one that would survive radical variations in political regimes. If the judicial role requires independence, then why not internationalize the judiciary? One can imagine an international bureaucracy of judges who maintain an understanding of domestic legal systems and who are given jurisdiction to adjudicate at least major domestic controversies. These international, judicial, civil servants could be organized on a regional basis or, perhaps more appropriately, according to broad categories of legal systems. They could be appointed by a process that was wholly independent of national politics. For example, it could be a career bureaucracy that attorneys entered soon after the end of their formal education.

We can see some steps arguably moving in this direction. There are international associations that provide arbitrators when requested by the disputants.[1] There has been some movement toward international courts that consider not just disputes between states (for example, the International

Court of Justice) but also allegations of human rights abuses by particular regimes within their own jurisdictions.[2] But I am imagining something far more dramatic and intrusive in the ordinary judicial business of a country. Why would we expect massive rejection of such an effort to achieve judicial independence?

To understand this resistance requires an examination of the idea of judicial independence and of the closely related idea of judicial neutrality. Independence is the institutional or structural condition of neutrality in judicial decision-making. In some obvious sense, the proposed international judiciary would be both independent and neutral. Perhaps the problem is that we want less of these characteristics than we might at first suppose.

## II.
## Judicial Independence and the Legitimating Function of the Courts

We can distinguish three different kinds of judicial independence. First, there is the independence of judges from the parties that have an interest in a particular controversy before the court. The interested parties include both the formal parties to the case and those with a personal interest in the outcome of the case. Second, there is the independence of the judiciary from the political institutions of government. We expect a democratic political order to draw a distinction between politics and law and we expect to find that distinction reflected in institutional structure. Third, there is independence from particular political ideologies. To understand this aspect of independence requires an examination of the relationship between the ideology of law and the ideology of a democratic political order. I will discuss each of these in turn.

### A. *Judicial Independence with Respect to the Parties*
It is clearly not controversial to claim that a judge should be independent of the parties to the controversy before the court. In no system of law is it regarded as a matter of course that a party may try to bribe the judge or rely on a personal relationship to the judge that attaches outside of the terms of the controversy. This is not to say that such relationships are not regularly found in the practice of many countries. But in none are such practices seen as a legitimate aspect of the judicial role. We can, of course, make even this argument controversial by expanding the idea of an interested party to include more than those directly, whether formally or not, involved in the controversy. Nevertheless, I want to bracket such expansions and look at the paradigmatic case of adjudication of a private controversy.

We expect a court to be neutral as between the parties to the controversy for at least two reasons, which reflect two different roles that the judge serves. The judge is to settle a dispute between private parties and to do so by applying standards of public order. We can refer to these as the private and public functions of the judge.

One function the judge serves is that of an institutionalized arbitrator. If the parties to a controversy propose to resolve their dispute through arbitration, the success of that agreement depends upon their ability to agree upon an arbitrator who will treat them both "fairly." This means the arbitrator will treat each party as entitled to equal respect within the procedures of the arbitration -- equal entitlement to present a case, for example -- and treat neither party as having a greater right to success based on reasons that are independent of the grounds of their controversy. An arbitrator could not succeed in "settling" the dispute unless he or she met this criterion of fairness as impartiality. To violate this condition of impartiality is to enter the dispute. Instead of settling the controversy, the arbitrator would simply have expanded it to include additional parties.

Judicial resolution of private disputes requires no less of a judge. Partiality will not settle a dispute, but only expand it -- perhaps now into a dispute between a party and the state. While the judge must meet the conditions of private arbitration, the judge is not simply an institutionalized arbitrator. The judge differs from an arbitrator in the character of the rules of decision that the judge applies. In arbitration, the parties establish the terms, including the rules of decision. A judge, however, applies a rule of law that has its source outside of the particular parties, as well as outside of the personal beliefs and opinions of the judge.

Each time a controversy comes before a court, there is an implicit declaration that what had been a private dispute has become a matter of public concern. The courtroom transforms the private into the public. To enter the court's jurisdiction is to undergo a transformation in personal identity. The private person becomes the citizen, even if not formally recognized as such. To be a citizen is to recognize a reciprocal relationship of obligation and responsibility between the citizen and a set of political institutions. The parties recognize an obligation to comply with the judgment of the court; the court recognizes a responsibility to each party to settle the controversy "fairly." Fairly here means "under law." If the relationship between court and party fails this test, the court is nothing more than a mechanism of coercion applied against an individual.

The identification of fairness with "under law" is a critical part of the definition of the judicial role. Even within the model of private arbitration, there is a reciprocal relationship of obligation and responsibility established by the contract between the parties. In a courtroom, however, the obligation of the citizen runs not to a mechanism of dispute resolution, but to an entire public order. The judge's responsibility to the parties is an expression of the state's equal duty of care that runs to each citizen within the public order. Thus, behind the court's judgment stands the entire coercive machinery of the state.

The court is, therefore, a kind of theatre that puts the private on display, making it simultaneously transparent to and transformable by the public order. For this reason, courts resist the exclusion of the public. This transformation of the private into the public occurs most visibly in the rules that reshape the controverted event into a public narrative. The court is the locus of the construction and display of that narrative. The judicial narrative takes a standard form: every private controversy must be read by the court as a challenge to the public order and the court's decision is the successful resolution of that challenge. Ideally, judicial proceedings are moral tales in which the good guys always win.

The judicial decision operates on that narrative. This is not to deny that the judicial decision has effects outside of the narrative. But those effects can never appear in the court without undergoing a transformation into the public register. The private is the thing-in-itself, outside of and inaccessible to the courtroom.

From this perspective, judicial independence is a condition not just of dispute resolution, but of public narrative construction. Judicial independence from the parties qualifies the court to sit at the transformative point of the private into the public. It allows the confluence of public norms and private controversy. A judge that lacked independence with respect to the parties could never realize this transformation.

The judicial narrative imposes a public order on the private controversy. Construction of that narrative requires a transparency in both directions. The judge must be neutral toward the legal standards that express the rules of public order. Without that independence, the public is transformed into the private order of the judge. He or she must also be independent of the parties. Without that, the private never makes contact with the public order of the community. Judicial independence from the parties is, then, a symbol of the possibilities of the political. The judge is the symbol of the wholly public person, the person whose private being has been eliminated by his or her public role. Being this symbol, the judge can now represent the possibility of such a transformation in every adjudication.

## B. Judicial Independence with Respect to Politics

My argument so far has assumed that the controversy before the court was one between private parties. Frequently, however, the government is one of the parties. This raises a different set of questions about judicial independence.

I have portrayed the courtroom as a mechanism that transforms the pre-political character of the person and event into a dimension of the public order. In the courtroom the public continually asserts its transformative power over the private. By opening the jurisdiction of the court, the state allows every private party to become an agent of the public order. This decentralization of political authority is at least as important as the vote in understanding the structure of democratic government. Through the courtroom, the entire authority of the state, including its diverse mechanisms of coercion, are put at the disposal of the individual citizen. Litigation is the great equalizer within a democratic order. In theory, if not always in practice, it equalizes distinctions of private power and, even more importantly, the distinction between citizen and government. Indeed, the availability of the courts is a better measure of democratization than the availability of the vote. The vote empowers a majority. Only the lawsuit empowers each citizen.

Even if the courtroom is a political theatre, it is not supposed to be the theatre of politics. To understand this requires that we draw a distinction between law and politics. Above, I spoke of the distinction between the private and the public. The distinction of law and politics is a distinction wholly within the public. To draw this distinction is to shift the locus of judicial independence from the intersection of the private and the public to a location wholly within the public order.

We can begin to get at this when we ask why a controversy between the government and a particular citizen would ever come before a court. There are, of course, many such controversies that do not take a judicial form, including many that involve the application of coercion to the individual -- for example, police and military actions. What are we saying about the relationship between citizen and state when such a dispute falls within the jurisdiction of a court?

To take jurisdiction is to engage in a double movement. First, there is a dislocation of government's claim to represent the state. Government loses its privileged place and becomes one of two parties before the court. Simultaneously, the private person, by becoming a party, asserts that it too has a claim to represent the interests of the state. The court, then, reduces the government to a party and raises the private party to a public role. The court drama now becomes a contest of claims to represent the state. The court's decision is the resolution of that contest through the legitimation of one set of claims and the rejection of the other.

The court's role from the first perspective on independence was that of inscribing the private transaction in a public narrative; its role from this second perspective is that of legitimating a claim to speak for the state. These are quite different roles. In the first, the court is itself an agency of government with a defined role. In the second, it allows for the expression of a potentially revolutionary claim against government. Judicial independence now makes possible the delegitimization of the government and the recognition of a new and competing set of representatives of the state.

An independent court, in this sense, is uniquely tied to a theory that distinguishes state sovereignty from the holders of governmental power. We are most familiar with this idea in the form of popular sovereignty, but there is no necessity that sovereignty be linked to "the people." One could, for example, imagine a similar distinction between sovereignty and political office being made in an Islamic nation. This distinction is ordinarily formalized in the contrast between law and politics. Officeholders pursue a political practice; law is the expression of the sovereign. These may or may not intersect in any given case.

Once the idea of sovereignty is detached from the particular officeholders, government exercises only a controvertible claim to represent the state. The private party, in the dispute with government, puts forth a claim to more accurately stand for the state. The court is the locus of that controversy and the decision of the court charts the meaning of sovereignty.

To understand the transformation that the distinction between law and politics works on the idea of sovereignty, it is instructive to consider the trial of Louis XVI. One sees there just this double movement of reduction and equalization. Before the French Revolution, it could make no sense to talk about the government as a party before the court. Rather, the court was itself an expression of the sovereign power of the King. Judicial procedure, a procedure that involved torture as well as the spectacle of the scaffold, was a display of the sovereign's power. Its end was the affirmation of political power against the enemies of the state. "Enemies" included equally the criminal within and the soldier without. Indeed, the courtroom was a drama of battle, different in form but not in kind, from the battlefield. The court had no independent power to legitimate, but only the force of the King's power itself.

The trial of the King only becomes possible when sovereignty has been relocated to the people. At that moment, the King's rule becomes "politics," which can be measured against a rule of law. Thus, the King is tried for "treason" -- again, a claim that was literally inconceivable before the transposition of sovereignty from the King's body to the body politic. To try the King now is to assert that he stands in the same relationship to the sovereign as does each of his prosecutors: all are citizens making contestable claims to represent the state. In locating the law in one of these competing claims, the court locates the "true" representative of the state.

Louis' loss was more dramatic than most instances in which government loses its case, but its significance remains the same. The independence of the court means that the locus of the public interest and the public order is contestable. It means that no one, regardless of position, has a privileged claim to represent the state.

Politics can always be measured against extra-political norms. This, however, is not the same as measuring politics against law. The distinction between law and politics is a distinction between the state and the government. To draw the distinction is to recognize the state as an intergenerational project that has its own integrity and endurance -- the law -- quite apart from the persons who occupy office at any given moment. They are at best "trustees," while the law is the corpus of the trust. Their performance as trustees is always contestable. The courtroom becomes the point at which that intergenerational project that is the state most clearly displays itself.

The distinction between law and politics is not a logical necessity. We can understand a politics that extends its claims into the courtroom. If so, sovereignty would be seen as the power wielded by the institutions of government against potential dissents, whether inside or outside of the state. Such a politicized court could be neutral in the first sense -- with respect to the parties before it -- without being neutral in the second sense -- with respect to political actors. This is a state in which power is personalized, in which the state is the King -- and for "King" one can substitute any number of authoritarian figures in the modern state. But when we ask that our judges be independent in a dispute between citizen and government, we are rejecting this idea of sovereignty.

This second meaning of an independent court, therefore, represents the contestability of power in the name of the sovereign. If the first understanding of judicial independence (independence from the parties) is necessary to see the court as an institution of the public order, the second (independence from politics) is necessary to see it as a forum for the contest over the meaning of the public order. An independent court, in this sense, is the institutional expression of the possibility of perpetual revolution. This is a mild revolution to be sure. The court does not allow a revolution in the idea of the state, but only in the claim to represent that idea. More extreme revolutions must take an extra-institutional form.

## C. Judicial Independence with Respect to Ideology

One way to set about obtaining a neutral judiciary[3] would be to appeal to an idea of diversity. For example, recognizing deep and subtle connections between a judge's personal preferences and his or her attitudes toward the parties and interests that appear before the bench, one could rationally pursue the first form of judicial independence by selecting judges from diverse economic, social, and religious backgrounds. Similarly, recognizing the links between political beliefs and normative values, one could rationally pursue the second form of judicial independence by appointing judges from a broad spectrum of political backgrounds. But this is not a rational strategy with respect to ideology. One does not pursue ideological neutrality by appointing judges representing an ideological mix ranging from liberal to fascist. Why is this so?

Within a university, for example, one often finds just such an effort to achieve ideological diversity. A law school may deliberately appoint professors who bring radically different ideologies to the law. Philosophy departments have deliberately pursued ideological diversity, ranging from analytic philosophers to existentialists. Those who attend to these academic matters are aware that more than one department has experienced a kind of internal self-destruction from the internecine wars that such efforts at diversity may produce. But even with this experience, this ideal of diversity has not died. This risk of paralysis is not sufficient to defeat the value of ideological neutrality that informs the effort to achieve diversity.

That courts are not law schools was made clear in the recent experience of Robert Bork before the Senate.[4] The kind of ideological diversity that he represented, while a virtue at his old law school, was seen as a disqualification for the Supreme Court. We had the seeming oddity of a leader of the legal academy being rejected for a role of judicial leadership. Judicial neutrality, it seems, does not mean ideological diversity in the forum of power. But why not? Why, at the point of ideology, have we reached the limits of the commitment to neutrality? After all, no one suggested that Bork would lack the requisite judicial independence in the first two senses.

Diversity cannot be a strategy for obtaining judicial neutrality when diversity suggests arbitrariness in the judicial decision. Arbitrary decisions are neutral -- the roll of the dice is a neutral decision-making process -- but they undermine the end for which we seek judicial neutrality.

A strategy of diversity here would suggest a lack of normative standards by which to make an ideological distinction. Because we do not know, for example, which philosophical approach is correct, we seek broad representation among philosophical schools in an academic department. If that department then makes practical decisions, we are forced to acknowledge that the decisions are essentially arbitrary. They are the result of the particular configurations of power within the department, which are themselves nothing more than the present effects of past decisions that were themselves based on no principle beyond that of difference. If these past acts had been resolved differently, the decisions could just as easily have come out the other way. Either way, there would be no violation of any normative standard that informs the institution.

But the first two arguments for neutrality suggest that a court plays an important role in the inscription and location of public order. That role cannot survive if the decisions of the court are seen as essentially arbitrary. The court must be committed to the idea that it can decide the case before it on the basis of law. It cannot suggest that it is exercising power in an arbitrary manner. Rather, it must stand for the law against the claims of both private and political life. Legitimation is not dependent upon reaching the "right" decisions in some ethical sense. It is, however, dependent upon the belief that law is something other than the arbitrary configuration of power. This was precisely the point at which Bork failed. He had made an academic career of denying that the law itself carried the weight of the judicial decisions that have served in large part to define the modern public order. If not law, then nothing determines results but the arbitrariness of judicial power. Even if this is true, it is not a truth that the public can hear and remain the same public.

A judge must make clear his or her own ideological commitment to the law, to the idea that the law can decide cases. This leaves some room for ideological diversity, but not a great deal. Differences begin only after the claim of law is acknowledged. We are far less concerned with the theoretical merits of this claim -- what is the law -- than with the expression of the claim within the drama of the courtroom. What rides on it is the very possibility of the drama. Whether it is fiction or nonfiction may be a subject of academic interest only.

## III.
## Judicial Independence and Sovereignty

I am now in a position to return to the puzzle of an internationalized judiciary. Such a judicial corps would seem to possess all three kinds of neutrality. It would have no ties to the parties, no ties to domestic politics or to particular officeholders, and it would be founded on a commitment to the rule of law. What then is the problem?

The answer cannot simply be to repeat what I said above about the courtroom as a scene of political drama. Such a drama could equally be found in an international judiciary's activities. State sovereignty within the courtroom is not a necessary condition for national participation in the judicial drama. For example, the Nuremberg proceedings have been defended by appealing to just such an argument. The proceedings made clear to the German people what their government had been doing and therefore let the German people exercise a kind of collective judgment on past political behavior. The proceedings were a device for simultaneously reestablishing the rule of law and the potential, if not actual, sovereignty of the people. One could easily think of other instances in which this domestic political end would be furthered, not frustrated, by international tribunals managing the trials of human rights violators during periods of transition from authoritarian to democratic regimes.[5] The rule of law, as it emerged in such a courtroom, would go a long way toward legitimating competing claims to represent the state and, conversely, toward delegitimating the claims of certain governmental actors.

The problem, then, is not with the public transparency of the judicial proceedings. Rather, the problem lies in the idea of responsibility. The proposal for an international judicial corps bureaucratizes the judiciary. The judge has no responsibility for the dispute that finds its way into the courtroom. This is justified as a logical outcome of the pursuit of the ideas of neutrality sketched above. The judge can have no contact with the parties and no connection with domestic politics. He or she must have a total devotion to the rule of law. The international judge is responsible only for the future, not the past. While a domestic judge must also be independent from the parties and politics, the domestic judge is part of the society he or she judges. The domestic judge, as a citizen, is responsible not only for the future, but for the past.

I have described the two-fold task of the judge as that of inscribing and locating the public order. Both tasks rest on an ideology of the rule of law, which is expressed in the public narrative the judge produces. Every narrative links the teller with the listener. The judge's authority rests ultimately on the ability of the listeners to see themselves in that narrative. It is a story about who they are. If those beliefs fail, so does the court's power.

This means that the judge's story -- as a story of the public -- is equally the story of each of the listeners. In recognizing the self in that narrative, each recognizes the possibility of changing positions; each could be the teller of the tale. Indeed, a successful narrative will be repeated in just this way, merging roles of teller and listener. The judge may be the originator, but he or she is not the owner of the narrative. The judge says what each of us would say, and will say again, if the judge properly performs his or her role. This is what Alexander Bickel meant when he wrote that the judge "labors under the obligation to succeed."[6] The judge must give expression to principles that will be taken up and repeated by the larger body of citizenry. This is why the judicial narrative is not a story of the court's own power. It is rather the legitimation of a party's claim to power. The more successful the rule of law, the more successfully the court itself disappears from focus. Courts are, for this reason, remedial institutions.

The judge, then, expresses the narrative that is the public order of the state. But has this answered the puzzle? Why is it that the international, judicial bureaucrat cannot express that narrative? A first answer is that an international court would threaten to undermine the relationship of identification between the speaker and the listener. The judge speaks the public speech that each citizen imagines that he too would speak if called upon. For this reason, the public space of the courtroom has traditionally been shared by judge and jury. To defer to an outsider might break this relationship of communal identification.

While this might all be true, it does not yet get to the heart of this relationship between judge and citizen. To speak of the public order as an insider is to express one's own identity in the act of narrative construction. To find one's identity in that order is to take responsibility for the order that we already have. This is the moment that cannot be replicated by the "innocent" outsider. The judge is simultaneously responsible for the public order and at a distance from that order. The judge does not come with clean hands to a controversy. None of us do.

The judge shares responsibility in a double sense. First, there is the sense in which all citizens share responsibility. States and the governments which lead them are tenuous things that depend upon the citizens' beliefs. When those beliefs change, governments fall and they fall rapidly as we saw in eastern Europe. If the change in beliefs is dramatic enough, the state itself collapses and new "publics" emerge. Government is rarely an alien occupation. Instead, we usually get the government we deserve, even if it is not the government we want. Indeed, there is a substantial danger that a judicial proceeding will, by converting the government agent into a party, misrepresent the truth of this relationship of interdependence between citizen and state. This danger would be made even greater by an international tribunal. The danger is mitigated by a court that acts, not as an agent of the government, but with a sense of responsibility for what we already are.

Second, judges, in particular, share responsibility because they are inevitably the product of the organization of political power. They are a part of that power structure, even as they attempt to judge it. Again, in this they are only a more visible instance of the moral ambiguity of all citizens. True, some citizens wholly resist power and are its victims. But most of us willingly take our part in the state. Each of us is both within and without the institutional structure of power.

Despite the fact that the judge is a part of that which he or she judges, the judge must still judge. This is not a clean academic enterprise of applying formal law to controversial facts. It is rather a struggle to balance law against power, to work out the continually shifting line between the state as it is potentially, and the state as it is actually -- the ideal state, against the real historical actor, deploying power for and against particular interests. The judge sits on the same line on which each of us sits: we are simultaneously responsible for the state we have and the state we might have. Past and future intersect at the moment of judgment.

This is not just a struggle between law and politics. It is rather a struggle in the creation of law itself. The law that emerges from the courtroom is inevitably principle modified by compromises with power. It is not the predictable application of abstraction to fact, but the working out of responsibility. Judges cannot be replaced by international bureaucrats for the same reason that they cannot be replaced by machines. When we rule ourselves, we take responsibility for both past and future.

This understanding of the role of the court explains yet another paradox in the institutional structure of an effective judiciary. There are two quite different traditions with respect to the relationship between political and judicial offices. The continental model is to make the judiciary a career path, chosen by a lawyer at the very beginning of his or her career. The American system is to use the political system to select and approve judges, either through a process of nomination and confirmation or by direct popular election.

Despite these differences, I think we would be hard pressed to say that either system has generally resulted in a less effective or less independent judiciary. It is a little bit like trying to measure the difference between presidential and parliamentary systems. Substance does not follow form in these matters. Flourishing democracies, as well as flourishing judiciaries, are found under both of these formal structures -- for example, Britain and the United States. Conversely, no structural system will in and of itself produce a flourishing judicial system. Liberia, a country with which I have had some experience, seemed to give its judges substantial independence through the formalism of life tenure, modeling its system on that of the United States. Yet, that formalism counted for next to nothing when the impeachment mechanism was used freely and quickly for political ends.[7] What matters in each case is not the formal structure, but the informal tradition of norms and expectations that develop around political and legal practices.

Nevertheless, if we examine institutional structure a bit further, we find what looks like a counter-intuitive relationship between the structural independence of the judiciary and the scope of its legal authority. The American system makes judicial appointment dependent upon a political process. But American courts are probably the most powerful courts in the world. This is true not only with respect to their formal jurisdictional reach, but also in the support they receive from informal political norms. Judicial decisions are largely beyond political challenge. They are simultaneously a part of, and apart from, the political process. Those challenges that are politically tolerated must themselves take legal form; for example, a litigation strategy or a long-term plan to appoint judges who one "hopes" will be more sympathetic to a contrary legal claim.

This inverse relationship between political appointment and judicial strength is not accidental. Even in countries with a strong tradition of a professional judiciary, the constitutional courts are more likely to have formal links to the political order, particularly in the process of appointment. There is a suggestion in this that constitutional law is not law in the same sense as ordinary law, that it is somehow more political. But American constitutional jurisprudence rejected this distinction at the very moment that it established an authoritative judicial voice. Simply because the Constitution is law, the Supreme Court announced in *Marbury v. Madison*,[8] it is the appropriate responsibility of the courts.

It is not the political nature of the law that accounts for this linkage. A system that truly believed that law and politics coincide in constitutional adjudication would undermine its courts by subordinating the judiciary to political institutions. The court would then be seen as just another agent of the government. Nevertheless, within a state that maintains informal norms that distinguish law from politics, this establishment of political links gives assurance that a court will not exercise its independence in a way that is substantially at variance with the political beliefs and interests of the country. It gives assurance that the public order set forth in the judicial narrative is the public order of the larger community.

The prevalence of this structure of "independence within limits" suggests something of the symbiotic relationship between courts and political institutions. In a functioning democracy, they support each other. This same relationship of law to politics is replicated in each citizen who must simultaneously understand law from within a structure of power made possible by politics, and politics from within the possibilities opened up by law. The courts provide a kind of legitimacy to the political institutions and the political institutions return the favor to the courts.

At this point, we are well beyond the possibility of judicial independence. A judge loses independence at the moment of decision, if that is also the moment of accepting responsibility. A judge must, therefore, be committed. This commitment, however, is not to an ideology, but to a practice. This is a practice of the morality of citizenship in which responsibility moves simultaneously toward the past and the future. Sharing responsibility for the past, the judge responds sympathetically to the possibilities of the future. In performing this role, a judge is the symbol of popular sovereignty. This is what an international judiciary could never provide.

If this is correct, it says something about the possibility of independence and the meaning of the rule of law. In the dispute between citizens or between government and citizen, the court's role is not to legitimate one claim and reject the other. It is not to measure such claims against an abstract public order -- the law. Rather, the court's role is to take the dispute into itself and thus bring the sovereign out of the clouds and into the struggle for power. The court's role is not to be transparent to the public life we already have, but to represent the possibility of a public life that creates itself anew out of its own past.

This is the drama of the democratic state that is at stake in a properly functioning court room. A court that is not independent from both the parties and politics can never struggle with these issues. But to confront this struggle is to give up independence in any broader sense. It is to make a commitment to accept responsibility, which is just about where each of us should be in our relationship to the state. This, it seems to me, is the important lesson that the courts can teach in the transition to democracy or, for that matter, at any other time.

## Notes

[1]For example, the Permanent Court of Arbitration of the Hague. *See generally* Convention on the Settlement of Investment Disputes Between States and Nationals of Other States, 17 U.S.T. 1270, T.I.A.S. No. 6090, 575 U.N.T.S. 159, *reprinted in* 4 INT'L LEG. MAT. 532 (1965); W. LAURENCE CRAIG ET AL., INTERNATIONAL CHAMBER OF COMMERCE ARBITRATION (2d ed. 1990); Lester Nurick & Stephen J. Schnably, *The First ICSID Conciliation: Tesoro Petroleum Corp. v. Trinidad and Tobago,* 1 ICSID REV. 340 (1986).

[2]For example, the Inter-American Court of Human Rights. *See generally* SCOTT DAVIDSON, THE INTER-AMERICAN COURT OF HUMAN RIGHTS (1992); J. G. MERRILLS, THE DEVELOPMENT OF INTERNATIONAL LAW BY THE EUROPEAN COURT OF HUMAN RIGHTS (1988).

[3]I do not wish to pursue directly the line of inquiry that opens up at this point: What is the meaning of the rule of law? That is too large a topic for this inquiry. Instead, I will focus more narrowly on the idea of ideological neutrality.

[4]Nomination of Judge Robert H. Bork to be Associate Justice of the Supreme Court of the United States, 100th Cong., 1st Sess., 133 CONG. REC. § 9189 (1987).

[5]Argentina is a case in point. In Argentina, of course, a national tribunal oversaw the trials. *See* COMISIÓN NACIONAL SOBRE LA DESAPARICIÓN DE PERSONAS, NUNCA MAS: INFORME DE LA COMISIÓN NACIONAL SOBRE LA DESAPARICIÓN DE PERSONAS (1985) [NEVER AGAIN: THE REPORT OF THE ARGENTINE NATIONAL COMMISSION ON THE DISAPPEARED].

[6]ALEXANDER M. BICKEL, THE LEAST DANGEROUS BRANCH 239 (1986).

[7]*See, e.g.*, Stanton Peabody, *Chief Justice Detained for Accusing Doe of Corruption*, REUTERS LIBRARY REPORT, Dec. 3, 1987 (the impeachment of Chief Justice Chea in December 1987, after accusing the Liberian President Samuel Doe and Justice Minister Scott Jenkins of accepting bribes). The fear of political uses of the impeachment mechanism is an aspect of Nixon v. United States, 938 F.2d 239 (D.C. Cir. 1991), *cert. granted*, 112 S. Ct. 1158 (1992), which is currently before the Supreme Court and raises the question of the justiciability of challenges to Senate impeachment proceedings.

[8]1 U.S. (1 Cranch) 137 (1803).

# 7

# The Judiciary and the Political System in Chile: The Dilemmas of Judicial Independence During the Transition to Democracy

*Jorge Correa Sutil*

## I.
## Introduction

This chapter addresses the question of how, in the transition from dictatorship to democracy, the independence of the judiciary can be preserved and protected from pressures exerted by political powers. I use the case of Chile's Supreme Court as an example. Indeed, Chile is a particularly striking example of the problem because three of the five most common techniques employed to exert such pressures on the judiciary have been or are actually being tried in Chile, either by the president (court packing and the forced retirement of Supreme Court Justices) or by some other major political forces (impeachment).[1]

Some try to justify such actions by claiming that the new government must change the composition of the Supreme Court established under the previous authoritarian regime. This justification is questionable for at least two reasons. First, although Pinochet did make some changes in the Supreme Court -- he increased the number of Supreme Court Justices and offered special retirement pensions to the older justices still in office -- those changes were not made until the end of his reign. Pinochet did not overtly intervene in the Supreme Court when he came to power; he did not replace the justices, he did not threaten them, nor did he, to my knowledge, use corrupt methods to assure the collaboration of the Supreme Court, at least not in the early years of his dictatorship.[2] Second, it was the Supreme Court, composed of justices appointed by democratic presidents, that made no effort to protect human rights during the worst years of dictatorship.

Indeed, it is the ideology and philosophy of those justices that today's democracy must change.

I argue that most of the characteristics of the present Chilean judiciary -- especially those that justify the changes that the democratic government is trying to effect -- have deep roots in Chilean democratic history. More specifically, I look at those characteristics that are rooted in, or express themselves through, a conception of judicial independence. In doing so, I hope to examine several facets of the Chilean legal culture that may be of comparative interest for other Latin American countries and thus stimulate discussion of the concept of judicial independence.

## II.
## The Chilean Supreme Court During the Dictatorship: Should Today's Government Change the Court or the Legal Culture?

When the Chilean armed forces took control of the government in 1973, they claimed legitimacy mainly through the argument that the Allende government had gone beyond constitutional and legal boundaries. The military argued that the rule of law had already been abrogated.[3] To make this argument convincing -- and dictatorships require a legitimating rationale as much as any other government -- the military authorities needed some symbolic link with the past. Nothing could represent that link better than the Chilean Supreme Court. Although the Supreme Court had been under political attack and criticism from the left during the five years prior to the coup, and had responded with "political language" during the last year, the Chilean Supreme Court at the time of the coup still enjoyed a tremendous amount of legitimacy throughout Chilean society.[4] Though poorly paid, the Chilean judiciary was not corrupt. Rather, most Chileans perceived the members of the Supreme Court as a highly professional, honest, and skillful group of civil servants.

Because the armed forces needed legitimate collaborators, they did not intervene in the Supreme Court. The military neither removed any Supreme Court Justice nor threatened the Supreme Court in other ways. Moreover, no one has claimed that the dictatorship used corrupt methods to assure the collaboration of the Supreme Court, at least not during the early years of the dictatorship.

Nonetheless, the Pinochet regime committed gross and grave human rights violations, and the judiciary had no impact on preventing these violations.[5] Of course, a comparative analysis with other nations strongly suggests that it is an illusion to expect too much from the judiciary in such periods.[6] Indeed, it is one thing to be a judge and quite another to be a hero. But I am not concerned with heroic behavior. I am trying to explain why the Chilean judiciary possessed such a highly collaborative and sympathetic attitude toward human rights violations.

This attitude is best exemplified by the words of the Chief Justice of the Supreme Court in his inaugural speech for the 1975 judicial year, during one of the worst and most sinister periods of human rights violations. He chose this occasion to describe the Supreme Court's understanding of human rights violations:

> Chile, which is not a land of barbarians, as it is often said abroad, either by bad Chileans or by foreigners, has made diligent efforts to comply strictly with these rights. As to torture and other atrocities, I can say that here there are no executions or iron walls and any information in that sense is due to a political media compromised with ideas that have not and will not prosper in our country.[7]

This Chief Justice then discounted reports that there were people missing in Chile. He went on to say that both the Appellate Court in Santiago and the Chilean Supreme Court had been pestered by the numerous writs of *habeas corpus* presented to them on the pretext that members of the executive branch ordered the arrests of Chileans. "This has disrupted the work of the courts, interfering with their duty to occupy themselves with the urgent matters of their jurisdiction."[8]

One may attempt to explain this attitude by arguing that the justices were too conservative or that the acts of the Allende regime forced them into the political arena.[9] One must then explain why they were so conservative or why they believed that they had to enter the political arena and stand against the Allende government. One must consider that the justices were middle class lawyers, trained at highly liberal and progressive universities, appointed to their offices by democratically elected presidents, and that they possessed life tenure that the authoritarian government wanted and needed to respect. Indeed, at the time of the coup, Presidents Frei and Allende, both highly progressive politicians, had appointed eight of the thirteen members of the Supreme Court.[10] Some have also claimed that the justices lacked the "moral courage" necessary to defend human rights during the military regime.[11] If one makes such moral statements, however, one must then explain why, if an entire profession shared these same moral characteristics, the people who appointed the justices did not realize or accept this fact and do something about it.

It is clear that, if they desired, the justices could have created more authority for the protection of human rights. They had enough political authority to do so. Even if the justices were conservative or politically involved, one could expect that professional judges would be counted among the moderate forces in government. After all, the social expectations of the judicial profession demand that the judges be prudent people, with the capacity to hear both sides of an issue, reluctant to openly show their political preferences, and with a capacity to revise their individual biases and prejudices.

Thus, my argument is that what the transitional government needs to change is not the Pinochet Supreme Court, but the institutional causes for a judicial culture shaped by previous democracies and merely reinforced by the dictatorship. The transitional government's required response is not, and should not be, an effort to pack the actual court, but an effort to change a pervasive cultural trend deeply rooted in the Chilean democratic tradition. This cultural trend validated the very concept of judicial independence that played a key role in reinforcing the judicial crisis. The judges employed this concept of judicial independence to comfort themselves while they ignored the government's abuses of human rights.

### III.
### The Dominant Notion of Judicial Independence as One of the Factors that Could Partially Explain the Behavior of Chilean Judges Toward Human Rights Issues During the Military Regime

What is this conception of judicial independence that developed under democratic governments yet runs so counter to democratic values? In the inaugural address of the 1975 judicial year, the Chief Justice said: "I declare, with all the truthfulness that a solemn occasion like this requires, that the courts have continued to act with the independence that the law confers to them . . . that the executive branch has taken care not to diminish in the least the autonomy, rights and prerogatives of the judges."[12] An independent observer, aware of the violations of human rights that were taking place at that moment, could ask himself if those words were merely the product of cynicism or a sign of open political support for the de facto military government. My conclusion is different. I argue that this statement is highly consistent with what a Chilean Chief Justice in 1975 could have understood as judicial independence. Indeed, I argue that he could have reasonably believed that the judges could enjoy the best of judicial independence in the middle of a dictatorship that systematically violated the human rights and civil liberties of the people.

### A. *Three Significant Moments in the Relationship Between the Courts and National Politics*
I proceed in my explanation of the Chilean judicial culture and its perception of judicial independence by focusing on three very significant moments

in the relationship between the courts and national politics: the codification movement, the twentieth century trend to preclude judicial involvement in the more important social policies of the period, and the final marginalization of the courts in the social changes of the late 1960s and early 1970s. These three moments helped shape the dominant legal culture, especially the legal culture of judges.

*The Period of Codification.* The codification movement began vigorously in Chile in the middle of the nineteenth century. It brought about all the progress, modernization, and professionalization of the legal culture that one can normally attach to such movements.[13] This movement was full of all the optimism, faith in law and reason, and the conception of sources of law that have been largely described as characteristics of the period.[14] The concept of the judicial role and the nature of its reasoning were no exceptions. If Montesquieu went as far as to say that the judges are nothing but the "mouths that pronounce the words of the law,"[15] our great jurist of the nineteenth century and the most influential man in the Chilean codification movement stated that the judges "are slaves of the law."[16] If Montesquieu said that of the three powers of government "the judiciary is in some measure next to nothing,"[17] Andrés Bello argued that judges were not law givers but only law appliers, and that power and sovereignty were not in the hands of the judges but in the hands of the legislators.[18] This idea -- that judges are mechanical appliers of the law -- is firmly established in our legal culture even today.[19] To prove this point one could cite many statements made by Chilean judges. Probably the clearest statement is one made by the Supreme Court in 1987. This was one of the few occasions where the Supreme Court publicly and officially responded to criticisms:

> It has been said that the judiciary is weak, and that such weakness manifests itself in the incapacity to search for the ethical ideals of the law and the Chilean society. . . Courts are strict and loyal law enforcers, law that continues to be for them the written reason. According to such law, the judges ought to decide the cases . . . and they are not authorized to disdain and deviate from this rule and look for general principles of morality or law which could produce their decisions. . . . The judges are aware that they must be strict appliers of the law.[20]

The Supreme Court further argued that it is the law which orders them to decide the cases in such a way.[21] This view is not only dominant among judges, but is shared by many lawyers and is still very influential in law schools.[22]

*Twentieth Century Social Policies: Successfully Avoiding the Courts.* Another key factor in explaining Chilean judicial culture and its perception of independence can be traced to the political process which marginalized the judges from the most important social changes of the twentieth century. Starting in the early 1920s, the Chilean legislature passed a great deal of social legislation.    This legislation reflected the world-wide tendency towards welfare states.   As in many other places, it was easy to argue that the Chilean judges were ill-suited to understand such changes.

Politicians knew that judges would have difficulty understanding the new philosophy of the legislative trends because judges were trained in the formal conceptions of free trade and freedom of contract.    Politicians thought of many devices to preclude ordinary judges from making decisions in these new areas of the law.   For example, after the government partially failed to establish administrative agencies that would resolve labor conflicts, the Chilean Legislature responded and passed special labor laws.   These laws gave bureaucratic agencies the right to settle such disputes, and some studies show that they handled more cases than the courts.[23]   Moreover, this legislation created a special independent institution to ensure the legality of the administrative acts of the executive and its agencies.   Though the judiciary retained some control over such acts, the ordinary courts did not decide a wide range of administrative law issues.[24]   These administrative law cases, of course, dealt with the multitude of problems that arose because of government intervention in the economic and social order.   The government created many supervisory, anti-trust, and controlling agencies to regulate and control the economic and social activities of the private sector that the government understood to play a public role, for example, private education, banking, the stock market, and so forth.   The enormous amount of legislation passed to regulate such activities created a similar amount of disputes, few of which the courts were allowed to resolve.[25]

Agrarian reform, one of the most controversial issues in Chilean social history, produced the same result.   The government created special courts to deal with the disputes that arose out of the agrarian reform movement. The agrarian reform courts were not considered part of the judiciary.   Only one of the three members of the agrarian reform courts was a member of the judiciary.[26]

Additionally, following the European model, a Constitutional Court was created in 1970.   Though the Supreme Court retained its power to declare an unconstitutional law inapplicable, a power that it exercises very infrequently,[27] the creation of the Constitutional Court was a sign that the ordinary courts should keep their hands off the political process.

Finally, since 1973, the armed forces have increasingly precluded the ordinary courts' involvement in the new major area of social concern -- human rights violations.   Indeed, many of the cases involving human rights violations were put under the jurisdiction of the military courts.[28]   Other examples show how the political process made important efforts to keep the disputes arising from these social developments out of the hands of the judiciary.[29]

In 1970, Eduardo Novoa, a well-respected lawyer and law professor, wrote an article that launched one of the most important attacks on the Supreme Court in its entire history. By analyzing the results of cases, Novoa argued that the Supreme Court frequently ruled in favor of the rich. He accused the Supreme Court of suffering from class-bias. Because of the controversial nature of the article, there was an intense response to it by members of the legal profession. Indeed, articles which discussed this controversy even appeared in the newspapers. The effect on the legal profession was as if a bomb had fallen in the middle of the Supreme Court.[30] What Novoa failed to see in the midst of such highly ideological times, however, is that most of the data he collected came from Supreme Court cases addressing these new areas of law. It seems to me that even if the decisions he analyzes can be explained as class-biased, they can be better explained as the application of old legal principles to new areas of law.

The Supreme Court Justices had been educated in the formal principles of a *laissez-faire* state. As described above, during their career as judges, they were kept away from the new areas of law. These new areas of law had to be construed and interpreted according to new principles that the old justices simply did not understand. The justices believed that they were interpreting the law in the only correct way and according to the only correct principles of law -- formal equality, freedom of contract, and so forth. They believed they were being treated unjustly, that they were the targets of a political battle in which they had played no role. In his inaugural address in 1970, the Chief Justice said, "It is absurd to say that our courts are class-biased. They just apply the laws that apply in the country."[31]

The justices claimed that they were not defending a social order. Their function was only a technical one and their role was and should remain autonomous from politics. They argued that changing the social system was not their business. It was the legislature that should change the law, if necessary, and the justices must merely apply the new law.[32] What the Supreme Court Justices failed to see, however, and I think they honestly did not see it, was that they became an obstacle to social change when they did not apply the new principles in their interpretations of the laws. And it was not their fault; politicians had intentionally kept them isolated from the social changes of society. Explaining their role as mechanical appliers of the law provided the judiciary the mask with which to hide the real problem, even from themselves.

*The Era of Revolutionary Changes: Successfully Forgetting the Courts.*
The third moment I want to emphasize is the one that took place in Chilean
politics from the mid-1960s until the coup by the armed forces in 1973.
This has been called the era of the "global projects," a highly ideological
period where all the political groups fought for mutually exclusionary
programs for major changes and where there was little flexibility for
negotiation. For example, the Frei government (1964-1970) called its program for change: the "Revolution in Freedom." The Christian Democrat
candidate in 1970 used the slogan: "Advance without Compromising" (with
the established order). Allende, the socialist candidate who won the 1970
presidential election, offered to carry out the revolution that the Christian
Democrats had failed to bring about because of their petit-bourgeois links.
The "new man" was the true slogan for the era to come.[33]

During these years, people paid attention to justice, but their concerns
were with social justice, justice with a capital J. No revolutionary had time
to waste with concerns of individual justice, with the "minor problems" of
protecting rights in individual cases. An example of this is the scant attention paid to the courts by the media controlled or sympathetic to the left.
This was in stark contrast to the attention paid to the courts by the media
controlled or sympathetic to the right.[34] It was simply the final and logical
result of a long process in Chilean politics -- the shift from keeping the
courts away from the social process to actually forgetting about them. The
only problem was that the courts suffered. Their salaries decreased. In
1968, the overall budget of the courts was only 0.65% of the national public
budget, an extremely small percentage of governmental spending. For the
first time, the judges went on strike to protest their salaries. This may have
created personal animosity on the part of the judges towards the politicians.
Most of all, however, I think it created a deep feeling in the judiciary that
politicians had no idea of what the role and importance of courts was and
should be.

## B. The Reaction of the Judges
Some similarities can be drawn between the judicial reaction and the
reaction of the armed forces in Chile. Both considered themselves civil
servants, both were composed of individuals from the middle classes, and
both were isolated from social problems by the politicians. They both had
a hierarchical structure and developed similar corporative sentiments against
the politicians who did not understand their "technical role" in society. This
is not the occasion to develop such similarities, but one can hypothesize that
a similar view of the political process developed among them. At this
point, however, I will focus on the reaction of the judges.

*The Corporative Spirit.* A profession must differentiate itself from other professions in order to affirm its role in society. But the Chilean judiciary went further than mere differentiation. It developed a sentiment of ill-treatment. Corporative spirit became very strong. The feeling of isolation and lack of understanding by the society transformed the Chilean judiciary into a highly coherent group that believed it was special and unique.

In the midst of such sentiments, the concept of independence may become a very powerful voice demanding that no other part of the government or society interfere in the business of the courts. Prior to this period and during most of this century, the only demand Chilean judges strongly voiced was the need for financial resources. I have already mentioned that at the beginning of each year, according to the law, the Chief Justice of the Supreme Court is required to make a public address. According to the law, such addresses should focus on the main difficulties that the justices have encountered in their role as interpreters of the law and to signal, for example, the technical problems that the justices may have found with the laws.[35] It is hard to find one such opening speech that does not address the need for more financial resources and better salaries. Indeed, one seldom finds any technical statements about the law.

But during this period the concept of judicial independence also became part of the judicial reaction. In Chile, the judges, including the Supreme Court Justices, are appointed by the President. The President selects his appointees from a list of three to five candidates that a superior court submits to him. In the case of the Supreme Court, it is the Supreme Court itself which selects the five candidates placed on the President's list. Though provisions allow the courts to include people from outside the judicial profession, such an event seldom occurs. The Supreme Court has attacked even this very narrow political intervention in the appointment of judges. In the opening speech of 1925, the Chief Justice stated that he had defended judicial independence when the new constitution was being drafted: "I also indicated the need that the judges should be self-appointed, in order to abort absolutely through this mechanism the political influences and those of any other nature in the selection process; so that judges should only remain subjected to seniority and merit in their work."[36] It is clear that in the Chief Justice's mind, the political beliefs, ideology and values of the candidates had no merit. In 1942, the Chief Justice's annual address reflects the same notion of independence:

> The independence of the judiciary is only a relative one, because the constitution and the law allow another branch to intervene in its generation. Such a mechanism demands of judges and the judicial personnel, whenever they want a position or to ascend in their career, to use influences

that are strange to their role and that run against their dignity and prestige. They should only invoke, to their superior judges, their capacity and merits.[37]

Again, one may appreciate the idea that politicians and the democratic processes have no business in evaluating the capacities and merits of the judicial profession. At the same time, this vision also reflects a highly dubious conception that the superior judges can appreciate the capacity of judges in an untainted and unbiased way.

The judges not only saw themselves at odds with politicians and the political process. They also became, to some degree, insulated from the social changes that the country was experiencing. As already noted, they saw their role as technical and professional. This is evident in their response to the criticism the Court received because of their toleration of human rights violations. In 1986, for example, when Cardinal Fresno voiced his concerns about the actual investigation of a case involving human rights violations, the Supreme Court surprisingly responded. This is remarkable because the Supreme Court rarely responds to criticism. The Supreme Court argued that the priest was wrong and that his criticisms were founded on facts of which he had no knowledge. Two of the Supreme Court justices added in their concurring opinion that the Cardinal

should not invoke his spiritual situation as a priest to talk about the Supreme Court. The Court, in order to achieve justice has no other guidance than the law, or conscience when law authorizes a decision according to it. This does not mean that we are not willing to listen to people that criticize us, *especially when they are men that have knowledge about the science of law*.[38]

The final sentence states very clearly that the priest had no business talking about a science that only some specialists could understand.

Judges not only perceive their role as technical, they also believe it entails no political or moral responsibility. A good example of this occurred when President Aylwin officially sent Chile's national report on human rights violations to the Supreme Court. Such an action required an official response from the Supreme Court. The report of the National Commission for Truth and Reconciliation contained open criticism of the judiciary's role in dealing with human rights violations during the military regime. It stated that the ineffective protection of human rights was due not only to failures of the legal system but also due to the "lack of effort of many judges to fully comply with their obligation of securing due respect for the essential rights of the people."[39]   The Court's answer states that judges are

> and ought to be the strict appliers of the law.  For them laws continue to be written reason, born as a product of the contingencies of a given time and place.  The judges have to decide cases according to the law.  If the legislative activity that took away some of the powers granted to the ordinary courts is now perceived as reprehensible, the blame should not be placed on the shoulders of the judges.[40]

As a Chilean scholar has said, the judges perceive themselves as having no responsibility for the social consequences of their decisions.  The courts perceive themselves as autonomous entities whose role is to apply the law, "independent from the fact that the law is just or unjust, adequate or inadequate for the social circumstances to which it applies and entirely independent from the fact that those laws were created by a Parliament democratically elected or by political power achieved through revolutionary means."[41] Perhaps the best and most dramatic example of such legal formalism is an interview that a Supreme Court Justice gave in 1985.  Asked by the journalist if the Supreme Court's role was to be just or to enforce the laws even when the laws were unjust, he answered, "You are using the words 'even if they are unjust laws.'  I don't believe them to be unjust, because if they are laws that have been duly enacted, they are there to be enforced."[42] Are these statements just the cynical words of a group of judges who are under criticism who do not believe a word of what they are saying?  After analyzing Chilean judicial decisions, one could argue that judges pay only lip service to formalism and to a strict obedience to the letter of the law. In fact, one could plausibly argue that when deciding cases, they deviate from such a formalism.  One could prove that they have filled important gaps in the Chilean legal scheme, that they updated old legal institutions. Stated otherwise, it would not be difficult to discuss decisions that are completely inconsistent with a law that is at odds with prevailing social values.[43]   In that sense, the Chilean laws and the Chilean judiciary are no exception to what occurs in other countries.[44]

Nevertheless, I would still argue that the Chilean Supreme Court Justices are not being dishonest when they see themselves as mechanical appliers of the law.  It is precisely that perception of the judicial role, when deeply rooted in the legal culture, that enables decision-makers to develop a habit of not even recognizing their own biases, values, and prejudices and the role these play in their reasoning.  For someone educated in such a culture, it is the law that decides cases, not the judge.  A judge has no personal prejudices to revise. Even when such biases are decisive in the resolution of a case, all of the past training helps judges deny that reality.

In a judicial culture strongly dominated by legal formalism, judicial independence may become a very narrow concept, and may lead to the isolation of the judiciary. All connection between the judges and the world, and particularly with the world of politicians, means contamination with substances that impair the cleanliness of their technical role.

*Hierarchy.* When such a corporative feeling dominates an organization, its hierarchical structure tends to strengthen itself. There are rules in the Chilean judicial system that have significantly contributed to the Supreme Court's control of all Chilean judges. It is very easy for the higher courts to use the appellate system to control not only the final decision, but also the many minor procedural decisions that a lower court judge may make during the judicial process. But the most important rules give the Supreme Court broad discretionary powers to discipline lower court judges. This control allows the Supreme Court to take measures against lower court judges and strike down decisions that are supposed to be faulty or clearly illegal. These types of decisions represented forty-four percent of all the cases decided by the Supreme Court in 1989.[45] The lower court judges are always under this "Sword of Damocles" when they decide a case.

This power is exercised in other ways. According to Chilean law, the Supreme Court must annually rank all of the judges in the country. This ranking is important for career promotions. Indeed, being ranked poorly in some categories may mean the end of that judge's career. While ranking should be based on merit, the rules to ascertain such merit are vague. Thus, there is a great deal of discretion in the hands of the Supreme Court. Moreover, the military regime amended the law governing judicial ranking so that the Supreme Court's ranking of lower court judges does not need to be explained at all and the voting of particular justices is kept secret.[46]

Finally, the promotion to the Supreme Court or to the appellate courts is dependent on the submission of a list of candidates by the Supreme Court. That decision, of course, is also highly discretionary.[47] As career promotion is very important to any judge because of increases in salary and prestige, loyalty to superior judges is necessary. This, of course, leads to a clientelism in the Chilean system which, in turn, creates a very homogeneous judiciary. Indeed, some of the sanctions exercised by the Supreme Court have been interpreted as punishment of those lower court judges who have gone too far in contesting the Supreme Court's holdings on human rights issues. The Supreme Court, of course, publicly denies such interpretations.[48]

Thus, when discussing judicial independence where the judiciary itself is composed of a hierarchical structure, one must focus not only on the independence of the judiciary from the other branches of government, but also examine the personal independence of each judge. The actions of superior judges may also be a threat to personal independence and to the idea of having an heterogeneous and evolving judiciary.

## IV.
## Judicial Independence

The Chilean situation that I have described may be unique in its particular characteristics.[49] Stated otherwise, I think that the analysis of judicial independence I have sketched out above makes it clear that there are significant dangers in advancing the value of judicial independence without carefully giving it a concrete contextual meaning. Moreover, there are two main questions that must be addressed before judicial independence can be given a concrete meaning: first, how much independence should the judiciary have while still remaining accountable to the people; and, second, from what type of forces should the judiciary be independent. Let me briefly focus on each one.

### A. How Much Independence? Insulation or Isolation?

Judicial independence is not an absolute value. It is an instrument for the protection of people's rights and it makes possible government under the rule of law. If judicial independence is understood in this way, then it is a value that must be balanced against judicial accountability; that means there must be some amount of political and popular control over the judiciary.

Because of this, procedures for political appointment and impeachment exist in almost every constitution. But what are easily forgotten, as a matter of legal culture, are the philosophical reasons for such procedures. It is only when an understanding of the philosophical reasons are deeply rooted in the political culture that the intervention of the other branches of government take their proper place, win social legitimacy and endure. This did not happen in Chile. Instead, Chilean legal culture confused political insulation with social isolation.

The Chilean experience may also show that, in order to have a judiciary that remains accountable to the people, the judges must be active political figures. Though they need some insulation from the political battle, they cannot be isolated from it. Rather, they need to be citizens of the state. A caveat is in order. Where judicial careers start at a very early age, the balance between the need for individual judges to be active citizens and the need for judicial independence from partisan politics may become difficult to achieve.

The Chilean situation may also show that some kind of representative character within the judiciary is needed. To put it another way, judicial decisions, to some degree, need to reflect social beliefs. A restricted political participation in the appointments system may not be enough to ensure such ideological representation between the courts and the people. In a heterogeneous society, a judiciary that is too ideologically homogeneous is also politically dangerous.

### B. *Independent of What? Political Intervention and the Concept of Law*

To be sure, I am not making an argument for judicial dependency upon short term political interests. Yet, on what are judges to be dependent? To say that they should be dependent on the law is not enough. A particular concept of law is needed. If the judiciary understands the law in a highly formalistic way, the Chilean experience shows that the problem of values, and specifically of democratic values, is forgotten. As Jefferson once wrote, "A judiciary independent of a king or executive alone is a good thing; but independence of the will of the nation is a solecism, at least in a Republican government."[50]

If the dominant legal culture is highly formalistic, and if at the same time there is a tradition of judicial independence, the concept of independence may become difficult. All kinds of corporative demands and hidden ideological intentions may win a confused battle against the values for which judicial independence stands.

## V.
## Conclusion

The Chilean experience reveals a paradoxical situation. It is probably the one country in Latin America with a long-standing tradition of judicial independence. Indeed, it is a tradition so strong that a military regime was not able to overtly destroy it. That tradition, now that Chile is recovering its democratic history, is at odds with democracy. It may be time for the new government to intervene with measures that have traditionally, and correctly, been viewed to run counter to judicial independence, in the name of democracy and on behalf of a new concept of judicial independence.

## Notes

[1]The most important changes that the Chilean democratic government is attempting to bring about in the judicial system are expressed in numerous laws and in a series of bills to amend the Constitution. Since July 1992, those proposals have

been discussed in both chambers of the legislative branch. Among them is one that increases the number of Supreme Court Justices from seventeen to twenty-one. At the same time, law number 18.805, published on June 17, 1989, permits the retirement of Supreme Court Justices over seventy-five years of age, and awards those who do retire an extraordinary pension. In March 1991, soon after the publication of a proposal for reform in light of human rights violations committed under the authoritarian regime, the juvenile section of the Christian Democratic Party -- President Aylwin's party and the largest in the country -- proposed to impeach some of the Supreme Court Justices. The idea received little support.

[2]There is very little literature written about what actually happened to the Chilean Supreme Court after the coup of 1973, and certainly no reliable "inside stories." *See, e.g.,* Hugo Fruhling, *Poder Judicial y Política en Chile, in* LA ADMINISTRACIÓN DE JUSTICIA EN AMÉRICA LATINA 84 (Javier de Belaúnde L. de R. ed., 1984). Jorge Correa Sutil, *Formación de Jueces para la Democracia, in* 34/35 FILOSOFÍA DEL DERECHO Y DEMOCRACIA EN IBEROAMÉRICA 271-320 (Agustín Squella ed., 1989/1990). Some questionable inside stories not coming from a Supreme Court Judge may be found in JOSÉ CÁNOVAS ROBLES, MEMORIAS DE UN MAGISTRADO (1989).

[3]*See* EDITORIAL JURIDICA DE CHILE, 100 PRIMEROS DECRETOS LEYES DICTADOS POR LA JUNTA DE GOBIERNO DE LA REPUBLICA DE CHILE 1 (1973-1981). (These arguments are summarized in Bando number five and Decree Law number one, both issued by the "Junta de Gobierno" on the day it took power, September 11, 1973).

[4]*See* Carlos Peña et al., *El Poder Judicial en la Encrucijada Estudios Acerca de la Política Judicial, in* 22 CUADERNO DE ANÁLISIS JURÍDICO 207 (1992); *see* Fruhling, *supra* note 2 (for an analysis of the political behavior of the Court prior to the coup).

[5]*See* 1 COMISIÓN NACIONAL DE VERDAD Y RECONCILIACIÓN, INFORME RETTIG: INFORME DE LA COMISIÓN NACIONAL DE VERDAD Y RECONCILIACIÓN 95 (1991) (a general report on the violations of human rights). *See also supra* at 95-104 (a description and analysis of the attitude of the courts towards those violations). It is said there that the judicial branch did not aggressively respond to the violations. The Supreme Court answered that report; a complete version of that answer is published in DIARIO EL MERCURIO, Santiago, Chile newspaper, May 16, 1991 at c.7 [hereinafter EL MERCURIO. Many articles in this newspaper have no author or title].

[6]*See, e.g.,* FRANCISCO J. BASTIDA, JUECES Y FRANQUISMO: EL PENSAMIENTO POLÍTICO DEL TRIBUNAL SUPREMO EN LA DICTADURA (1986); INGO MULLER, HITLER'S JUSTICE: THE COURTS OF THE THIRD REICH (Deborah Lucas Schneider trans., 1991).

[7]A full version of the speech in Spanish may be seen in DIARIO OFICIAL, March 14, 1975. The translation to English is made by the author.

[8]*Id.*

[9]*See* Fruhling, *supra* note 2 (giving a more complete view of the political involvement of the Supreme Court at the end of the Allende government).

[10]The composition of the Court and the appointment date of each member is published every year in a booklet called ESCALAFÓN DEL PODER JUDICIAL by the Supreme Court Library.

[11]President Aylwin referred to the "lack of moral courage" to describe the attitude of judges towards the protection of human rights in a press conference in March 1991. This comment generated widespread public discussion.

[12]*See supra* note 7.

[13]*See generally* I, II ALEJANDRO GUZMAN, ANDRES BELLO CODIFICADOR, HISTORIA DE LA FIJACIÓN Y CODIFICACIÓN DEL DERECHO CIVIL EN CHILE (1982) (giving a general overview of the process of codification in Chile).

[14]*See* ERNST CASSIRER, EL ESPÍRITU DE LA ILUSTRACIÓN (a description of the optimism and values of the period); JOHN H. MERRYMAN, THE CIVIL LAW TRADITION: AN INTRODUCTION TO THE LEGAL SYSTEMS OF WESTERN EUROPE AND LATIN AMERICA (1985) (providing a short description of the process of codification and its philosophy). *See also* THE CODE NAPOLEON AND THE COMMON LAW WORLD (B. Schwartz ed., 1956); JOHN P. DAWSON, THE ORACLES OF THE LAW (1968).

[15]MONTESQUIEU, THE SPIRIT OF THE LAWS (Thomas Nugent trans., 1949).

[16]Andrés Bello, *Observancia de la Ley, in* EL ARAUCANO (Chilean newspaper 1836) *reproduced in* ANDRÉS BELLO, ESCRITOS JURÍDICOS, POLÍTICOS Y UNIVERSITARIOS 75 (1979).

[17]MONTESQUIEU, *supra* note 15, at 156.

[18]Andrés Bello, *Necesidad de Fundar las Sentencias, in* EL ARAUCANO (Chilean newspaper, 1834 and 1839); *reproduced in* BELLO, *supra,* note 16 at 109 (translation by the author).

[19]Jorge Correa Sutil, *La Cultura Jurídica Chilena en Relación a la Función Judicial, in* LA CULTURA CHILENA 75 (Agustín Squella ed., 1988).

[20]EL MERCURIO, *supra* note 5, July 8, 1987, at A.1, A.10 (translated by the author).

[21]*Id.*

[22]*See* Correa Sutil, *supra* note 19.

[23]Helia Henriquez, *La Crisis del Estado y del Poder Judicial en Chile* 22 (July, 1980) (unpublished manuscript on file with Jorge Correa Sutil) (she reaches this conclusion for the early 1970s).

[24]Generally, the "Contraloría General de la República" ensures legislative supremacy over administrative acts. In the last decade, however, the judicial remedy, known as "Recurso de Protección," has returned the control over administrative agency actions to ordinary courts. *See generally,* EDUARDO SOTO KLOSS, EL RECURSO DE PROTECCIÓN: ORÍGENES, DOCTRINA Y JURISPRUDENCIA (1982).

[25]*See* Hugo Pereira Anabalón, *Unidad de Jurisdicción y Justicia Administrativa en el Derecho Chileno,* 12 REVISTA DE DERECHO PÚBLICO 37-62 (1971).

[26]Henríquez, *supra* note 23.

[27]*See* Gastón Gómez, *Corte Suprema: Análisis de Algunos de sus Comportamientos,* 7 REVISTA EL FERROCARRIL 51-74 (1986) (for a study of the nature of the work

of the Court). *See also* EDUARDO FREI ET AL., LA REFORMA CONSTITUCIONAL DE 1970 (1970) (for a defense of the Constitutional Court).

[28]Centro de Promoción Universitaria, *Reunión de Estudio sobre El Poder Judicial y la Protección de los Derechos Humanos: Situación Actual y Proposiciones, in* PROYECTO DE CAPACITACIÓN, FORMACIÓN, PERFECCIONAMIENTO Y POLÍTICA JUDICIAL, Volume I.C.P.U., 1990. After the democratic government came into power, it promoted several reforms in order to reduce the jurisdiction of the military court. Before the Congress would enact legislation representing these reforms, many changes were made because of necessary compromises with the right wing. These laws are popularly known as "Leyes Cumplido." *See* CRISTOBAL EYZAGUIRRE, LEYES CUMPLIDO (1991) (provides an analysis of these "Leyes Cumplido" and their effect on the military jurisdiction). *See also* COLEGIO DE ABOGADOS DE CHILE, JUSTICIA MILITAR EN CHILE (1990) (for a view of the military court during the military regime); VICARIA DE LA SOLIDARIDAD, 1 JURISPRUDENCIA: DELITOS CONTRA LA SEGURIDAD DEL ESTADO (1990).

[29]*See generally*, Correa Sutil, *supra* note 2. One result, the lack of access to the courts by the poor, may not have been intentional. *See* MIGUEL AYLWIN ET AL., JUSTICIA Y SECTORES DE BAJOS INGRESOS (1988) (provides a general overview of law and poverty in Chile).

[30]Eduardo Novoa Monreal *¿Justicia de Clases?, in* 187 REVISTA MENSAJE 108-18 (Mar./Apr. 1970). Some of the answers may be found in the Chief Justice's inaugural speech of 1971, published in REVISTA DE DERECHO Y JURISPRUDENCIA, Tomo LXIII January-April 1971; *La Corte Suprema Analizó Críticas de la Justicia, in* EL MERCURIO, *supra* note 5, April 15, 1970 at 25; Pablo Rodriguez Grez, *Tribunaleo Populares,* EL MERCURIO, *supra* note 5, April 15, 1970 at 3.

[31]Chief Justice Inaugural speech of 1970. Published in REVISTA DE DERECHO Y JURISPRUDENCIA, tomo LXVII, January-March 1970.

[32]*See* André Cuneo, *La Corte Suprema de Chile, sus Percepciones Acerca del Derecho, su rol en el Sistema Legal y la Relación de Este con el Sistema Político, in* LA ADMINISTRACIÓN DE JUSTICIA EN AMÉRICA LATINA 71 (Javier de Beláund L. de R. ed., 1984) (a general analysis of the chief justices inaugural speeches).

[33]GENERO ARRIAGADA HERRERA, DE LA "VIA CHILENA" A LA "VIA INSURRECCIONAL" (1974).

[34]*See generally* Peña, *supra* note 4.

[35]*See* CODIGO CIVIL art. 5 (Chile).

[36]DIARIO OFICIAL, March 31, 1925, at 749.

[37]DIARIO OFICIAL, March 18, 1942, at 10.

[38]Cardinal Fresno made his criticism on July 26, 1986; the Supreme Court answered it on July 28, 1986 (emphasis added).

[39]I COMISIÓN NACIONAL DE VERDAD Y RECONCILIACIÓN, *supra* note 5, at 104.

[40]EL MERCURIO, *supra* note 5, May 16, 1991, at c.7.

[41]*See* CUNEO, *supra* note 32, at 78-79.

[42]Interview with the Supreme Court Judge, Hernán Cereceda Bravo, published in EL MERCURIO, *supra* note 5, January 20, 1985 at d.4.

[43]For the arguments sustaining this statement in the Chilean case, *see* Correa Sutil, *supra* note 19. *See also* CARLOS DUCCI CLARO, INTERPRETACIÓN JURÍDICA EN GENERAL Y EN LA DOGMATICA CHILENA (1977); FERNANDO FUEYO LANERI, INTERPRETACIÓN Y JUEZ (1976); BERNARDO GESCHE MULLER, JURISPRUDENCIA DINAMICA: LA DESVALORIZACIÓN MONETARIA Y OTROS PROBLEMAS EN EL DERECHO (1971).

[44]There is seldom another topic in the area of jurisprudence that has generated such an amount of literature. *See* INTERPRETING STATUTES: A COMPARATIVE STUDY (D. Neil MacCormick & Robert S. Summers eds., 1991).

[45]Instituto Nacional de Estadísticas, ANUARIO DE JUSTICIA 1989.

[46]DIARIO OFICIAL, Dec. 6, 1973, at 3 (amended by DIARIO OFICIAL, Oct. 13, 1975, at 1).

[47]EDITORIAL JURIDICA DE CHILE, CODIGO ORGANICO DE TRIBUNALES, ART. 275, 279, 281, 283, at 111-120 (1985).

[48]1 COMISIÓN NACIONAL DE VERDAD Y RECONCILIACIÓN, *supra* note 5, at 95. *See also* EL MERCURIO, *supra* note 5, May 16, 1991 at c.7.

[49]It would be interesting to explore whether the underlying causes of the judicial crisis in Chile are based on a legal culture similar to that in other Latin American countries. There are few comparative studies of the judiciary in Latin America. *See* sources cited *supra* note 2. It would be tedious to cite all the national studies. Interested scholars should look at the works of Fix Zamudio in México, Rogelio Pérez Perdomo in Venezuela, Luis Passara in Perú, Bergalli in Argentina. In Colombia, interested scholars should look at the studies done by the *Fundación para la Educación Superior* (F.E.S.) (a non-profit organization created in 1964 whose judicial program is funded by A.I.D.) and the works of Jaime Geraldo.

[50]ROBERT A. DAHL, DEMOCRACY IN THE UNITED STATES: PROMISE AND PERFORMANCE 223 (3d ed. 1976) (letter to Thomas Richie from Thomas Jefferson dated Dec. 25, 1820).

# 8

# Judicial Power and Three
# Conceptions of Impartiality

*Roberto Gargarella*

## Introduction

In this chapter, I analyze three different conceptions of impartiality, all of which have their roots in North American history. I analyze these conceptions in connection with two relevant variables: deliberation and public participation. I begin by analyzing concept (X) where neither public participation nor deliberation are necessary requirements for achieving impartiality. I illustrate this concept by reference to the most traditional interpretation of the Federalists' view of politics. I call this view the elitist conception of impartiality.

I then analyze concept (Y) where deliberation is a necessary requirement for achieving impartiality. In this case, however, as in the former case, public participation is not a necessary requirement of impartiality. I illustrate this concept by referring to a more modern interpretation of the Federalists' view of politics. This, of course, implies a re-interpretation of Madison's political concepts. I call this view the deliberative conception of impartiality.

Finally, I analyze concept (Z) where both deliberation and public participation are necessary conditions for achieving impartiality. I illustrate this concept by referring to the Anti-Federalists' view of politics.[1] I call this view the Anti-Federalist concept of impartiality.

I utilize a four-box matrix (Figure 1) to illustrate these concepts (in the matrix PP = Public Participation; nN = not necessary; and D = deliberation).

|    | PP | nNPP |     |
|----|----|------|-----|
|    | Z  | Y    | D   |
|    | W  | X    | nND |

**Figure 1**

I examine the institutional significance of each of these concepts and, more particularly, their implications concerning the role of the judiciary in a transition to democracy.

The major purpose of this chapter is descriptive. However, I am also interested in showing that only the third concept of impartiality, the Anti-Federalist concept, appears consistent with current intuitions about democracy. Although I do not directly defend this latter idea in this chapter, I do so indirectly throughout the chapter.

## I.
## Impartiality and the Federalists

### A. *Majorities and Factions*

The first concept of impartiality assumes that impartiality is not connected with public deliberation. On the contrary, it is presumed that large bodies of people tend to undermine rather than promote the adoption of correct solutions. I call this the elitist conception of impartiality. In North American politics, this concept dominated the political landscape during the few years preceding the Constitutional Convention. This view, however, contradicted the prevailing view held in 1776, at the time of the American Revolution.[2]

In the 1780s there was a breakdown of confidence in the legislatures. This was probably a result of the economic crisis that followed the American Revolution. At that time, several legislatures, under popular pressure, promoted laws favoring an impoverished majority of farmers and under-class people. Indeed, references to an "abusive legislative power" or an "unchecked majority" became customary in literature describing the political landscape. To some of the Constitutional Framers, Rhode Island was undoubtedly the most dreadful example of unchecked legislative power. John Collins, the governor of Rhode Island, was elected by a large margin for defending pro-debtor laws. These laws were rapidly enacted in 1786. Another significant example of this unchecked legislative power was the reaction of the Massachusetts legislature, after a pro-debtor rebellion (the so-called Shays' Rebellion). Most alarming was the fact that these measures were not the result of the absence of law, but on the contrary, were a product of law.[3] The perceived state of affairs contributed to an association between majoritarian debate and irrational outcomes. That is, the framers believed that outcomes such as the abolition of debts, the issue of paper money and the re-distribution of property were not only incorrect, but also the expected result of popular majorities. To explain this situation, they appealed to the powerful notion of factions.

Particularly in Madison's view, the idea of factions connected these biased and self-interested laws to the will of majorities.[4] The development of the Madisonian notion of factions resulted most directly from the reports he received about the so-called "paper money crisis."[5] Madison clarified his views about factions, "mentioning with special concern *'a rage for paper money, for an abolition of debts [and] for an equal division of property'*" as examples illustrating improper or wicked projects of the factions.[6] All these measures, he believed, were the result of the lack of "wisdom and steadiness" in legislation, which was as he said in 1786, the "grievance complained of in all our republics."[7] According to Edward S. Corwin, it was clear that after the American Revolution Madison reserved his strongest words of condemnation for the legislative evils which he found within the individual states.[8] Included among his "words of condemnation," Madison referred to the "mutability of the laws," a "vicious legislation," the great evil of the "multiplicity of laws"[9] and, worst of all, the clear injustice of the legislation.[10]

## B. Refining the Public View

Not surprisingly, the above-mentioned events greatly influenced the Constitutional Framers. Particularly, those events created a distrust in democracy and, more specifically, a distrust in the virtues of public discussion. Indeed, most of the institutional results of the Constitutional Convention reflected this motivation for separating the "common people" from their representatives.

Consider, for example, the most important work of Madison, *The Federalist No. 10*. In that paper, Madison stated that the first effect of his defended representative government would be "to *refine and enlarge the public views,* by passing them through the medium of a chosen body of citizens, whose *wisdom* may best discern the true interest of their country, and whose patriotism and love of justice, will be least likely to sacrifice it to temporary or partial considerations."[11] The representatives were not assuming their role because of the practical impossibilities of a pure democratic government. On the contrary, their role was to replace the people. The implicit justification of this was the perceived risks of having a citizenry actively involved in politics.

Madison defended this position in numerous other statements.[12] Inherent in all of them was the principle that the larger the number of the people discussing an issue, the greater the possibilities of factionalism.[13] He was not defending representation because of the practical impossibilities of direct democracy; he was doing so because of his distrust of majoritarian participation in politics.[14] Many other Federalists supported the same ideas in diverse speeches and texts.[15]

## C. The Federalists, Impartiality, and the Judiciary

A product of the widespread distrust in the virtues of public discussion (and its reflection in the popular branch of the state legislatures), the judicial power appeared after the American Revolution as a possible remedy for achieving impartiality. As Gordon S. Wood stated, "As early as the 1780s many were already contending that only the judiciary in America was impartial and free enough of private interests to [solve that problem and] defend people's rights and property from the tyrannical wills of interested popular majorities."[16] Gordon S. Wood admits that these ideas were "a long way from the 1776 republican confidence in popular legislative lawmaking and represented a severe indictment of democracy."[17] The judiciary appeared, therefore, as "the only governmental institution that came close to resembling an umpire, standing above the marketplace of competing interests and rendering impartial and disinterested decisions."[18]

This assumed notion of impartiality, then, was independent of any kind of public discussion. That is, impartiality required neither the presence of all those who might be affected by the decision in question, nor any kind of open discussion about the issue in question. On the contrary, the isolated and individual reflection of the judges was considered sufficient to achieve impartiality. Madison affirmed this concept, stating "[the judges] by the mode of their appointment, as well as by the nature and permanency of it, are too far removed from the people to share much in their prepossessions."[19]

## II.
## Impartiality and Madisonian Republicanism

### A. A Wise Deliberation

The second concept of impartiality accepts the importance of deliberation for achieving neutral, unbiased decisions. However, public participation is unnecessary, if not undesirable, for evaluating the neutrality of any specific solution. I call this the deliberative conception of impartiality.

In this conception of impartiality, the importance of deliberation is connected with the necessity to "transform preferences, instead of taking them as given or merely aggregating them."[20]   A deliberative system requires the representatives to present arguments in defense of their proposal. Moreover, these arguments must be public-interested, as opposed to merely self-interested ones. In this sense, the idea of deliberation may be opposed to a concept of representatives as mere "advocates for the respective interests of their constituents."[21]   Through this process of discussion, representatives would have the opportunity to learn other people's arguments; to learn new information; to make comparisons among different arguments; and to improve and change their own arguments. These virtues of deliberation make collective discussion an essential, necessary device to avoid partial, biased outcomes. A deliberative concept, then, is clearly different from the first concept of impartiality, the non-deliberative concept, defended by most Federalists.[22]

Although I remain unconvinced of this possibility, some claim that the most important Federalists did indeed support a deliberative conception similar to this.[23]

## B. Deliberation Without "We the People": The Case of the Constitutional Convention

The Constitutional Convention best illustrates this concept of impartiality. Indeed, it combined a deep process of discussion with the clear exclusion of the people. The doors of the Convention were closed to the people. The defenders of this concept of impartiality agree with Madison's arguments for supporting discussion and secrecy. Madison stated,

> [it was best] to sit with closed doors because opinions were so various and at first so crude that it was necessary they should be long debated before any uniform system of opinion could be formed. Meantime the minds of the members were changing, and much was to be gained by a yielding and accommodating spirit. . . . [B]y secret discussion no man felt himself obliged to retain his opinions any longer than he was satisfied of their property and truth, and was open to the force of argument.[24]

However, this notion of impartiality was neither understood nor accepted in the manner presented by Madison. In fact, most opponents of the Constitution considered the secret character of the Convention, not a device for achieving impartiality, but rather a means to achieve aristocratic results.[25]

The deliberative concept of impartiality raises many important criticisms. Moreover, these criticisms are supported by an analysis of the dynamics of discussion opened or closed to the public. When political discussion is open to the public, the publicity forces the people to argue in terms of the common good. Conversely, when political discussion is closed to the public, the tendency is to switch from a forum of presenting arguments to one of merely defending self-interests.[26] Despite these objections, this concept of impartiality (connected with deliberation, but not necessarily with a majoritarian deliberation), does have some historical and modern support.

## C. Madisonian Democracy, Impartiality, and the Judiciary

The above described concept allows for several different theses when applied to the judicial power:

First, that in order to achieve impartiality, the Judiciary must engage in a discussion with the Executive, and thus destroy the measures of an interested majority and protect a minority in danger of oppression from an unjust populace. At the Constitutional Convention, James Wilson and James Madison explicitly defended this mechanism to combine the Judiciary with the Executive in vetoing legislative acts.[27]

Second, that the Supreme Court, by itself, represents an institution aimed at rational deliberation. In the first notion of impartiality, the judges are not considered to engage in individual and isolated reflection. Rather, the very purpose of the Supreme Court would be to achieve the best decisions, following a period of internal discussion.[28]

Third, that the Judicial Power is involved in a process of permanent dialogue with the other branches. This dialogical interpretation of the Constitution defends the role of the Judiciary as a means of reaching neutrality. The existence of inter-branch struggles serves to "signal the existence of a profound constitutional debate, to refine its meaning, and to provide the People with the means of expressing a rare determination to transform the character of our most fundamental political commitments as a nation."[29]

These three theses are compatible with both a compromise on deliberation and the assumption of a secondary role, if any, of the citizenry's participation in realizing impartial solutions.

## III.
## Impartiality and the Anti-Federalists

The last concept of impartiality that I will analyze is more directly and explicitly connected with public discussion. On the one hand, it is related to the idea that deliberation is necessary for laundering self-interested, ill-informed preferences. On the other hand, this concept assumes that public participation in this discussion is a required condition for achieving impartiality. I call this the Anti-Federalist conception of impartiality. During the origins of North American constitutionalism, opponents of the proposed Constitution, the so-called Anti-Federalists, defended both these principles.[30]

## A. A "Face-to-Face" Process of Deliberation

Legal scholars usually recognize the Anti-Federalist commitment to a "face-to-face process of deliberation and debate."[31] I think this affinity between the Anti-Federalists and public discussion can be further supported by appealing to diverse sources. American history, for example, shows that the majority of Anti-Federalist leaders took a principal role in the radical governments of their time,[32] that is, in those governments distinguished by the promotion of periodic town meetings and local plebiscites. There is also textual evidence of their theoretical defense of public deliberation. For example, Brutus, who claimed it was necessary to guarantee that "the people can conveniently assemble, be able to debate, understand the subject submitted to them, and declare their opinion concerning it."[33] Finally, the institutional reforms they proposed are also good examples of their compromise between open discussion and active citizenry. This is evidenced, for example, by their defense of a more extended use of jury trials, the right to recall representatives, and rotation of the representatives.[34]

## B. A Picture of the People

The Anti-Federalists were also identified with promoting and defending majoritarian governments in the 1780s. In fact, most of them conducted the opposition to the collection of debts owed to Great Britain. According to George Mason, "If we are now to pay the debts due to the British merchants, what have we been fighting for all this while."[35] Anti-Federalists viewed popular movements like the Shays' Rebellion and its consequences much differently than did others.[36]

The Anti-Federalists always distrusted Madison's idea of refining the public views and believed that such a notion would necessarily result in the defense of aristocratic institutions.[37] On the other hand, they considered that, given the practical impossibilities of a permanent and direct democracy, the people should be represented in large assemblies and thereby include the most diverse range of viewpoints. Thus the representatives "ought to mix with the people, *think as they think, feel as they feel, [they] ought to be perfectly amenable to them, and thoroughly acquainted with their interest and condition.*"[38] The Anti-Federalists believed that "professional men, merchants, traders, farmers, mechanics," and the like, should be properly represented in every popular assembly.[39]

The principle that appears inherent in all these views, is: "the more the people discussing, the better."[40] By affirming this principle, the Anti-Federalists were directly confronting the Federalist principle of representation. According to The Federal Farmer, the Federalists feared seeing the popular assemblies transformed into a mere tumultuous mob, and believed that the most respectable assemblies were those which consisted of several hundred members.[41]

These principles are open to several possible criticisms: (1) the non-feasibility of this proposal, given the difficulties in guaranteeing a proper representation of those different sectors; (2) the impracticability of having such a large body of representatives, given the different collective action problems that would make it much more difficult to achieve efficient decisions, foster the formation of minoritarian bureaucracies, and so forth; and (3) the implausibility of having a "corporative" type of representation, that is, to have interest groups, not the people, represented. While these criticisms are valid, the most significant arguments the Federalists advanced in support of their position assumed, instead, an elitist shape, and appeared directed toward creating distance between the government and "We the People."[42]

## C. Impartiality and the Constraints of Public Discussion

As I stated above, the Anti-Federalists appeared to defend not only public deliberation, but also a face-to-face politics of town meetings or, in the worst case, a large representative body which reflected a picture of the people. In this way, the Anti-Federalists made explicit their rejection of the Federalists' concept of impartiality, where the people's claims are biased and those of the members of the learned professions are neutral.

One further example illustrates this point. It is a debate that has been called the crucial moment of American history.[43] In this debate, William Findley, a defender of the debtor-relief and paper-money interests in Pennsylvania, confronted Robert Morris, the wealthiest merchant in the state, in a discussion about the rechartering of the Bank of North America.

> [Findley made it clear that] Morris and the other investors in the bank had every 'right to advocate their own cause,' [in the legislature]. But, Findley then continued, *they had no right to . . . try to pass off their support of their personal cause as an act of disinterested virtue.* The promotion of interests in politics, suggested Findley, was quite legitimate, as long as it was open and aboveboard and not disguised by specious claims of genteel disinterestedness. . . . [Thus], just in a few remarks he

challenged the entire classical tradition of disinterested public leadership and set forth a rationale for competitive democratic politics.[44]

Findley assumed the virtues of an open and public discussion, where all different viewpoints are considered, would be present. There were simply no plausible *a priori* positions. Neither the Federalists nor the Anti-Federalists could presume the relevance or validity of their arguments, if not publicly confronted. Only this process of discussion among all different viewpoints could guarantee impartiality.

To summarize the concept of impartiality inherent in this debate and, more generally, in the Anti-Federalists' position, there are no better constraints for achieving impartiality than those imposed by the rules of majoritarian public discussion. These rules require that each position be shaped in ways that every person can understand and accept. As Jon Elster stated (in terms with which William Findley would have undoubtedly agreed), "Even when ultimately moved by self-interest or partiality, actors are forced by the nature of public debate to argue their case in more general terms."[45]

This concept of impartiality recognizes the impossibilities of assuming, evaluating, and reconstructing other people's beliefs and desires. To say this does not deny that by independent and isolated reflection someone can achieve a non-biased conception. The implication here is that those biases are better avoided by actually considering every different viewpoint. An individual who makes a decision without comparing and contrasting her position with other opinions and criteria cannot presume to have given due weight to the other's preferences.[46] The validity of norms is connected with "the possibility of a rationally founded agreement on the part of *all those who might be affected, insofar as they take on the role of participants in a rational debate.*"[47]

## D. The Anti-Federalists, Impartiality, and the Judiciary

It is easy to identify and understand the Anti-Federalists' view of the judiciary in light of the foregoing discussion of their notion of impartiality. First, they believed that the people could and should be involved not only in politics, but also in administering justice. This was possible, they thought, through the principle of ample political representation and the institution of popular juries. Consider these words in *The Federal Farmer*, "[The situation of the people] as jurors and representatives, enables them to acquire information and knowledge in the affairs and government of the society; and to come forward, in turn, as the centinels (sic) and guardians of each other."[48]

The Anti-Federalists were particularly concerned with the Federalist idea of excluding the procedure of jury trials for civil causes.[49] This particular criticism and others, generally related to the future judicial power. This is evidenced by these Anti-Federalists' statements: "[T]he judicial department will be oppressive,"[50] "The consequence of [establishing the proposed Constitution] will be an absolute confirmation of the power of aristocratical influence in the courts of justice; for the common people will not be able to contend or struggle against it,"[51] and, "The judicial power of the United States, will lean strongly in favour of the general government, and will give such an explanation to the constitution, as will favour an extension of its jurisdiction . . ."[52]

All these statements seem to ratify the Anti-Federalist concept of impartiality. To the Anti-Federalists, impartiality was not a result of a "wise deliberation," but rather a product of a majoritarian deliberation. Therefore, it was important to extend the jurisdiction of the jury trials to include the people in the administration of justice. The creation of correct decisions was not the exclusive task of the selected few, but the task of all the citizenry. Thus, the Anti-Federalists criticized the Federalists' model of justice, because of its isolation from the people.

The Anti-Federalists' model of justice emphasized an existing connection between public discussion and impartial outcomes. I do not think, however, that they would deny the importance of having an institution designed to: (1) control the procedural basis of majoritarian deliberation; or (2) protect a sphere of personal or private morality from majoritarian intrusions.[53]

An example of a useful mechanism to be applied in this context is a general technique of "judicial remand to Congress."[54] As a result of these measures, the Anti-Federalists could coherently defend both their commitment to public deliberation and the necessity of guaranteeing the proper basis for that debate. This criteria, of course, needs more elaboration. However, I think the principles defended by this third concept of impartiality are already clear. In addition, they are clearly differentiated from the Federalists' concept of impartiality (both the more "elitist" and the more "deliberative" Federalist conception).

## IV.
## Conclusion: What Concept of Impartiality Are We Willing to Defend?

In this chapter, I presented three different concepts of impartiality, and analyzed the institutional implications of each. The first of these concepts, the elitist conception of impartiality, endorsed by the Federalists, assumed that there was no requisite connection between impartiality and public deliberation (or, even more radically, that public discussion would undermine impartiality). I explained that this concept was not motivated by practical reasons but by reasons of principle. For example, it is impossible to have all the people assembled or there are collective action problems that make this proposal undesirable. Indeed, the Federalists believed the more numerous any assembly, the greater the ascendancy of passion over reason.[55] By showing the origins and character of this concept, I analyzed the historical meaning of the notion of factions. Moreover, I concluded that it is very difficult to defend the principles embodied in this first concept of impartiality. Currently those principles tend not to be defended in that way, which seems to support this assertion.

A second concept of impartiality, the deliberative conception of impartiality, has in part solved the difficulties mentioned above. That is, this second concept of impartiality assumes deliberation is an essential component of a neutral, non-biased decision. I explained that defenders of this concept believe that some of the framers effectively supported this deliberative idea of impartiality. I did not fully analyze the validity of this historical claim (which I think lacks adequate support). On the contrary, I focused on the validity of the substantive claim of this concept: an impartial decision requires a profound discussion but not necessarily a discussion with all those who might be affected by that decision. Using as an example the Constitutional Convention, I presented some of the criticisms of this concept that were encountered and offered some of the possible current criticisms.

Finally, I analyzed a third concept of impartiality that I believe is clearly compatible with the idea of public discussion. I said that most of the so-called Anti-Federalists defended a concept similar to this. However, I think the most relevant aspect of this third concept of impartiality is that it is the concept that best applies to our present understanding of democracy. We now assume that we all have something to say about the moral problems affecting our societies, problems such as abortion, pornography, racial and gender discrimination, distribution of economic resources, and drug addiction. I do not mean to say that all these problems should necessarily be discussed and decided by plebiscite-like mechanisms. However, for these types of problems I think our current understanding of democracy supports deliberations such as those the Anti-Federalists defended. In this sense, the Anti-Federalists would say that both an active collective participation in politics and in the administration of justice are necessary requirements of democracy. Popular participation as "jurors and representatives, [would enable the people] to acquire information and knowledge in the affairs and government of the society; and to come forward, in turn, as the centinels (sic) and guardians of each other."[56] This Anti-Federalist concept of impartiality would break the protected spheres in which politics and justice are presently contained, and would return both politics and justice to the hands of the citizenry.

## Notes

[1]Because I find it unnecessary for the purposes of this chapter, I will not analyze a concept (W) where impartiality is connected to public participation, but not to deliberation. However, I believe this concept finds historical support in the examples of the radical constitutionalism developed in the 1770s in Pennsylvania and Vermont. This position would have been theoretically supported by Rousseau (and contemporarily by John Rawls). Consider, for example:

> The citizens of Rousseau's democracy do not deliberate, not even with themselves, because Rousseau considers politics to be essentially a simple matter. That is why the process of the formation of the will, individual as well as collective, does not concern him. He is able to identify deliberation with decision making and decision with self-evidence.

Bernard Manin, *On Legitimacy and Political Deliberation*, 15 POLITICAL THEORY 338, 347 (1987).

[2]This is supported by an analysis of the evolution of the idea of "virtual representation," against which most American leaders fought at the time of the Revolution. Consider that in 1776 the English authorities said that "none are actually, all are virtually represented in [the British] Parliament." BERNARD BAILYN, THE IDEOLOGICAL ORIGINS OF THE AMERICAN REVOLUTION 166 (1967). American revolutionaries like John Adams answered that every individual of the community must expressly consent to every act of legislation. Surprisingly enough, the opposition to the notion of virtual representation dramatically changed in the 1780s. Most of the former revolutionaries now defended a representative government, controlled by the wisest people. According to Jennifer Nedelsky, "[T]his emphasis on consent [implied in ideas like that of no taxation without representation] shifted with the grim realization that consent alone was no guarantee against [what they called] injustice or tyranny." Jennifer Nedelsky, *Reconceiving Autonomy: Sources, Thoughts and Possibilities,* 1 YALE J.L. & FEMINISM 16 (1989). The citizenry, then, began to turn "against their teachers the doctrines which were inculcated in order to effect the late revolution." Fisher Ames, *Boston Independent Chronicle* (Mar. 1, 1787), *in* GORDON S. WOOD, THE CREATION OF THE AMERICAN REPUBLIC, 1776-1787, 397 (1969).

[3]James Madison undoubtedly envisioned events like those of Rhode Island and Massachusetts where an unchecked majority had improperly responded to a period of social conflict. Consider, for example, his objection to the legislative process in Rhode Island: "As [Rhode Island's] legislature meets very frequently, and can at any time be got together in a week, it is possible either [they will change their decision by] caprice if [not by] other motive." Letter from James Madison to Thomas Jefferson (June 6, 1787), *in* 10 THE PAPERS OF JAMES MADISON 29 (Robert A. Rutland ed., 1975) [hereinafter PAPERS]. *See also* THE FEDERALIST No. 51 (James Madison). Conversely, after the Shays' Rebellion, James Madison observed with

distrust John Hancock's election in Massachusetts. "His general character forbids a suspicion of his patriotic principles; but as he is *an idolater of popularity, it is to be feared that he may be seduced by this foible into dishonorable compliances.*" Letter from James Madison to Thomas Jefferson (Apr. 23, 1787), *in* 9 PAPERS, *supra*, at 399 (emphasis added). These dishonorable compliances, Madison feared, could be encouraged by the insurgents. "It would seem that they mean to try their strength in another way; that is, by endeavoring to give the elections such a turn as may *promote their views under the auspices of Constitutional forms.*" Letter from James Madison to Thomas Jefferson (Apr. 23, 1787), *in* 9 PAPERS, *supra*, at 399 (emphasis added).

[4]"For Madison, therefore, the defining problem for republics is coping with the danger that a *majority* faction among the people would gain control of the government and proceed to abuse other citizens." Geoffrey P. Miller, *Rights and Structure in Constitutional Theory*, 8 SOC. PHIL. POL'Y 218 (1991) (emphasis in original).

[5]*See generally* 9 PAPERS, *supra* note 3; James Madison, *Vices of the Political System of the United States, in supra* at 345; THE FEDERALIST Nos. 10, 51 (James Madison). The most important reports Madison received came from Henry Lee, George Washington, and indirectly through Washington, from the war Secretary Henry Knox. Lee reported that:

> The Insurgents are taking all the necessary arrangements to prepare for the last appeal. Their ostensible object is the revision of the constitution but they certainly mean the abolition of debts public & private, a division of property & a *new government founded on principles of fraud & inequity,* or re-connexion with G. B.

Letter from Henry Lee to James Madison (Oct. 19, 1786), *in* 9 PAPERS, *supra* note 3, at 144 (emphasis added). Washington conveyed Knox's interpretation of the events:

> 12,000 to 15,000 unprincipled men determined to annihilate all debts by means of unfended paper money, and dedicated to a creed: '[T]hat the property of the United States has been protected from confiscation of Britain by the joint exertions of *all*, and therefore ought to be the *common property* of all.'

Letter from George Washington to James Madison (Nov. 5, 1786), *in supra* at 161 (emphasis in original). Washington concluded,

> *[I]f there exists not a power to check them, what security has a man of life, liberty, or property?* To you, I am sure I need not add aught on this subject, the consequences of a lax, or inefficient government, are too obvious to be dwelt on. Thirteen sovereignties pulling against each other, and all tugging at the foederal (sic) head will soon bring ruin on the whole; *whereas a liberal, and energetic Constitution, well guarded, and closely watched, to prevent incroachments* (sic), might restore us to that degree of respectability and consequence, to which we had a fair claim, and the brightest prospect of attaining.

*Supra* at 162 (emphasis added).

[6]MORTON G. WHITE, PHILOSOPHY, THE FEDERALIST, AND THE CONSTITUTION 221 (1987) (emphasis added).

[7]WOOD, *supra* note 2, at 405 (1969).

[8]*See* Edward S. Corwin, *The Progress of Constitutional Theory Between the Declaration of Independence and the Meeting of the Philadelphia Convention, in* THE CONFEDERATION AND THE CONSTITUTION, THE CRITICAL ISSUES 34 (Gordon S. Wood ed., 1979).

[9]As far as laws are necessary, to mark with precision the duties of those who are to obey them and to take from those who are to administer them a discretion, which might be abused, their number is the price of liberty. As far as the laws exceed this limit, they are a nusance (sic): a nusance (sic) of the most pestilent kind.

James Madison, *Vices of the Political System of the U. States* (Apr. 1787), *in* 9 PAPERS, *supra* note 3, at 353.

[10]The legislative evils included: the States' failure to comply with the Constitutional requisitions; State encroachment on federal authority; the States' violations of the law of nations and of treaties; the States' trespasses on the rights of each other; the States' want of concert in matters of common interest; the lack of a coercive power in the Confederation government; the multiplicity, mutability, injustice and impotence of the laws of the States. *Id.* at 345-358.

[11]THE FEDERALIST No. 10 (James Madison) (emphasis added).

[12]*See, e.g.,* 10 PAPERS, *supra* note 3, at 40; THE MIND OF THE FOUNDER, SOURCES OF THE POLITICAL THOUGHT OF JAMES MADISON 522 (Marvin Meyers ed., 1973).

[13]Madison said "the more numerous any assembly may be, of whatever character composed, the greater is known to be the ascendance of passion over reason." THE FEDERALIST No. 51 (James Madison).

[14]According to Gordon S. Wood, these ideas were based in the notion that "the men holding office in the new central government would by their fewness of numbers be more apt to be disinterested gentry who were supported by proprietary wealth and not involved in the interest-mongering of the marketplace." GORDON S. WOOD, THE RADICALISM OF THE AMERICAN REVOLUTION 253 (1992) (footnote omitted).

[15]*See, e.g.,* WOOD, *supra* note 2, at 512 (James Wilson); *id.,* at 512-13 (John Jay); *id.,* at 508-09 (Jonathan Jackson); FEDERALISTS AND ANTI-FEDERALISTS, THE DEBATE OVER THE RATIFICATION OF THE CONSTITUTION 34 (John P. Kaminski & Richard Leffler eds., 1989) (Francis Corbin); THE FEDERALIST Nos. 31 and 75 (Alexander Hamilton).

[16]WOOD, *supra* note 14, at 323.

[17]*Id.* at 325.

[18]*Id.*

[19]THE FEDERALIST No. 49 (James Madison).

[20]CASS R. SUNSTEIN, THE PARTIAL CONSTITUTION (forthcoming 1993) (manuscript at 14, on file with Cass R. Sunstein) [hereinafter PARTIAL CONSTITUTION]. *See also* CASS R. SUNSTEIN, AFTER THE RIGHTS REVOLUTION (1990); Cass R.

Sunstein, *Interest Groups in American Public Law*, 38 STAN. L. REV. 29 (1985); Cass R. Sunstein, *Legal Interference with Private Preferences*, 53 U. CHI. L. REV. 1129 (1986); Cass R. Sunstein, *Naked Preferences and the Constitution*, 84 COLUM. L. REV., 1689 (1984); JON ELSTER, SOUR GRAPES (1983).

[21]*See* PARTIAL CONSTITUTION, *supra* note 20 (manuscript at 15).

[22]For the theoretical analysis of deliberative conceptions, see MANIN, *supra* note 1, at 15; PARTIAL CONSTITUTION, *supra* note 20; CARLOS S. NINO, THE ETHICS OF HUMAN RIGHTS (1991); Cass R. Sunstein, *Preferences and Politics*, 20 PHIL. AND PUB. AFF. 3 (1991); Joshua Cohen, *Deliberation and Democratic Legitimacy, in* THE GOOD POLITY: NORMATIVE ANALYSIS OF THE STATE (Alan Hamlin & Philip Petit eds., 1989).

[23]Some scholars identify Alexander Hamilton as a defender of a deliberative political concept:

> The popular confidence depends on circumstances very distinct from considerations of number. Probably the public attachment is more strongly secured by a train of prosperous events, which are the result of wise deliberation and vigorous execution, and to which large bodies are much less competent than small ones. If the representative conducts with propriety, he will necessarily enjoy the good will of the constituent.

*Speech of June 21 in the New York Ratifying Convention, in* SELECTED WRITINGS AND SPEECHES OF ALEXANDER HAMILTON 208 (Morton J. Frisch ed., 1985). Such a concept is also evident in Hamilton's references to "the amazing violence and turbulence of the democratic spirit." WOOD, *supra* note 14, at 261. Hamilton clearly emphasized the defects and vices of large deliberative bodies and the importance of deliberation (more properly, a wise deliberation). Other scholars prefer to identify Madison as the strong defender of a deliberative political concept. *See, e.g.,* Cass R. Sunstein, *Interest Groups in American Public Law*, 38 STAN. L. REV. 47-48 (1985). ("Politics rightly consisted of deliberation and discussion about the public good. . . .[Madisonian republicanism] occupies an intermediate position between interest-group pluralism and traditional republicanism.")

[24]3 MAX FARRAND, THE RECORDS OF THE FEDERAL CONVENTION OF 1787, 479 (1911). For a discussion of these ideas, see generally PARTIAL CONSTITUTION, *supra* note 20.

[25]*See, e.g., Letters of Centinel, To the People of Pennsylvania, in* 2 THE COMPLETE ANTI-FEDERALIST 145 (Herbert J. Storing, ed., 1981) [hereinafter COMPLETE ANTI-FEDERALIST]. Thomas Jefferson said that the decision to "close the doors" was an "abominable . . . precedent" based on "ignorance of the value of public discussion." PARTIAL CONSTITUTION, *supra* note 20 (manuscript at 16). One commentator noted, "Federalist attempts to stifle free discussion of the proposed Constitution are an indication of what government under that Constitution would be like." *Essays of Philadelphiensis*, (Philadelphia Independent Gazetter, Nov. 1787-Apr. 1788), *in* 3 COMPLETE ANTI-FEDERALIST, *supra* at 99.

[26]*See, e.g.,* Jon Elster, Arguing and Bargaining 24 (1991) (unpublished manuscript on file with Roberto Gargarella).

[27]10 PAPERS, *supra* note 3, at 25.

[28]*See, e.g.,* KARL O. APPEL, ESTUDIOS ETICOS (1985) (defending the role of the Supreme Tribunal of Justice in Germany).

[29]Bruce Ackerman, *The Storrs Lectures: Discovering the Constitution*, 93 YALE L.J. 1013, 1069 (1983).

[30]The term "Anti-Federalist" has been applied to very different political leaders. A common trait among the leaders is their opposition to the proposed Federalist model of the Constitution. Therefore, it is possible to find among them very elitist representatives, and, at the same time, radicals. *See generally* CECILIA KENYON, THE ANTIFEDERALISTS (1985); STEVEN BOYD, THE POLITICS OF OPPOSITION (1979). Instead, I will take into account a more classical republican version of the Anti-Federalists, and I consider Thomas Jefferson the most prominent representative of them (disregarding the fact that he denied being an Anti-Federalist).

[31]*See, e.g.,* GEOFFREY R. STONE ET AL., CONSTITUTIONAL LAW 5-6 (1986).

[32]*See* WOOD, *supra* note 2, at 516.

[33]*Essays of Brutus, To the Citizens of the State of New York* (Oct. 18, 1787), *in* 2 COMPLETE ANTI-FEDERALIST, *supra* note 25, at 369. *See also The Address of the Minority of the Pennsylvania House of Representatives* (October 1787), *in* 3 *supra* at 14 (stating that, "We are persuaded that a free and candid discussion of any subject tends greatly to the improvement of knowledge. . . ."); The *Letters From the Federal Farmer IX* (Jan. 4, 1788), *in* 2 *supra* at 254 (the idea that "our more numerous state assemblies and conventions have universally discovered more wisdom, and as much order, as the less numerous ones.").

[34]*See, e.g., The Small Republic, in* 1 *id.* at 19 (jury trials); *Essays of Brutus, in* 2 *id.* at 445 (the right to recall); *Letters from the Federal Farmer, in* 2 *supra* at 289 (rotation of representatives).

[35]Letter from George Mason to Patrick Henry (May 6, 1783), *in* 2 THE PAPERS OF GEORGE MASON (1725-1792), 771 (Robert A. Rutland ed., 1970).

[36]Jefferson, in a letter to Madison wrote: "So far as I have yet seen [these rebellions] do not appear to threaten serious consequences." Letter from Thomas Jefferson to James Madison (Jan. 30, 1787), *in* 9 PAPERS, *supra* note 3, at 247. He said that, "a little rebellion now and then is a good thing and as necessary in the political world as storms in the physical . . . a medicine necessary for the sound health of government." *Id.*

[37]"[T]he mode in which [the representatives] are appointed and their duration, will lead to the establishment of an aristocracy." Cato, *Letters in the New York Journal* (Nov. 22, 1787), *in* THE ESSENTIAL ANTIFEDERALIST 160 (W. B. Allen & G. Lloyd Gordon eds., 1985). *See also* George Mason, *Objections to the Constitution of Government Formed by the Convention* (1787), *in id.* at 11; Richard Lee, *Objections* (October 16, 1787), *in id.* at 22; the *Letter of Centinel* (October 5, 1787), *in id.* at 93; John De Witt, *Essay V* (December 1787), *in id.* at 53; *The Address and Reasons of Dissent of the Minority of the Convention of the State of Pennsylvania* (Dec. 18, 1787), *in id.* at 53.

[38]George Mason, Speech in Virginia Ratifying Convention, June 4, 1788 *in* 5 COMPLETE ANTI-FEDERALIST, *supra* note 25, at 257 (emphasis added). A similar idea, that those who become representatives may have extensive political knowledge

yet they must also be aware of the people's common concerns and occupations, appears in Melancton Smith, Speech at the Constitutional Convention (June 21, 1788), *in* 6 *id.* at 155. *See also* CHARLES MEE, THE GENIUS OF THE PEOPLE (1987); CHRISTOPHER COLLIER & JAMES L. COLLIER, DECISION IN PHILADELPHIA (1986).

[39]*Letters From the Federal Farmer* (October 9, 1787), *in* 2 COMPLETE ANTI-FEDERALIST, *supra* note 25, at 230. The same principle is evident in the view of the Minority of the Convention of Pennsylvania. "The other orders in the society, such as farmers, traders, and mechanics, who all ought to have a competent number of their best informed men in the legislature, will be totally unrepresented." *The Address and Reasons of Dissent of the Minority of the Convention of Pennsylvania to their Constituents* (PENNSYLVANIA PACKET AND DAILY ADVERTISER, December 18, 1787), *in* 3 *id.* at 158. *See also Essays of Brutus, in* 2 *id.* at 358.

[40]Note the difference between this and the Madisonian principle: "The more the number of the people discussing, the more the possibilities of factionalism." *See supra* notes 13-15 and accompanying text.

[41]2 COMPLETE ANTI-FEDERALIST, *supra* note 25, at 269.

[42]Richard Hofstadter attributes these types of criticisms to the most notable Federalists: Roger Sherman hoped "the people . . . have as little to do as may be about the government," Richard Hofstadter, *The Founding Fathers: An Age of Realism, in* THE MORAL FOUNDATION OF THE AMERICAN REPUBLIC 74 (Robert H. Horwitz ed., 1977); William Livingston said "the people have ever been and ever will be unfit to retain the exercise of power in their own hands." *Id.*; George Washington, as the presiding officer of the Constitutional Convention, urged the delegates "not to produce a document of which they themselves could not approve simply in order to 'please the people.'" *Id.*; Alexander Hamilton charged that the "turbulent and changing masses seldom judge or determine right and advised a permanent governmental body to check the imprudence of democracy." *Id.*; and Charles Pinckney proposed that "no one be president who was not worth at least one hundred thousand dollars." *Id.*

[43]WOOD, *supra* note 14, at 256-57.

[44]*Id.* at 257 (emphasis added).

[45]JON ELSTER, LOCAL JUSTICE 235 (1992). *See also* Elster, *supra* note 26, at 5 ("[i]n argumentative situations, one has to phrase one's argument in impartial terms, as if one were arguing for the public good and not for one's own self-interest.").

[46]NINO, *supra* note 22, at 252.

[47]Jürgen Habermas, *Further Reflections on the Public Sphere, in* HABERMAS AND THE PUBLIC SPHERE 447 (C. Calhoun ed., 1992) (emphasis added).

[48]*Letters From the Federal Farmer* IV (October 12, 1787), *in* 2 COMPLETE ANTI-FEDERALIST, *supra* note 25, at 250.

[49]*See, e.g., An Old Whig III, in* FEDERALISTS AND ANTIFEDERALISTS, THE DEBATE OVER THE RATIFICATION OF THE CONSTITUTION, *supra* note 15, at 132.

[50]Elbridge Gerry, *Hon. Mr. Gerry's Objections to Signing the National Constitution, in* 2 COMPLETE ANTI-FEDERALIST, *supra* note 25, at 7.

[51]*Dissent of the Minority of the Pennsylvania Convention, in* FEDERALISTS AND ANTIFEDERALISTS, THE DEBATE OVER THE RATIFICATION OF THE CONSTITUTION, *supra* note 15, at 135.

[52]*Essays of Brutus*, XI (Jan. 31, 1788), *in* 2 COMPLETE ANTI-FEDERALIST, *supra* note 25, at 420.

[53]I cannot defend these principles of judicial review in this context. However, for a clear analysis of these issues, see Carlos S. Nino, The Complexity of Constitutional Structures, an Essay on the Philosophy of Constitutional Law (1992) (unpublished manuscript on file with Carlos S. Nino).

[54]*See, e.g.*, JOHN ELY, DEMOCRACY AND DISTRUST 131-34 (1980); ALEXANDER BICKEL, THE LEAST DANGEROUS BRANCH 143-56 (1962); GUIDO CALABRESI, A COMMON LAW FOR THE AGE OF STATUTES 91-119 (1982).

[55]*See infra* notes 13-15 and accompanying text.

[56]*See infra* note 48 and accompanying text.

# PART FOUR

# The Judicial Process: Trial

# 9

## Is It Better to Be Tried for a Crime in a Common Law or Civilian System?

### *George P. Fletcher*

It is generally thought that the common law system offers defendants greater procedural protections than do civil law jurisdictions. In this paper I assay that proposition. As the exemplar of the common law adversarial trial, I will take a United States state court prosecution for felony, say in New York or in California; as the model of the civilian accusatorial trial, I will take the moderate reformed accusatorial proceeding that prevails today in Germany.[1] The first task is to survey some of the procedural and substantive factors that generate advantage for the defense.

### I.
### The Advantages of Common Law Procedure

Let us begin with two factors that dramatically distinguish common law from civilian procedures: the jury system and judge's access before the trial, as finder of fact, to a dossier of evidence prepared by the prosection. In common law trials, the jury determines questions of fact, and the judge has no access to the pre-trial findings of the prosecution. In civilian trials, the judge -- sometimes aided by lay assessors -- decides questions of fact as well as law and has complete access to the dossier of findings made in the pre-trial investigation.

#### A. *The Jury*
It would be difficult to maintain that the use of the twelve or six person lay jury is *per se* better or worse for criminal defendants than standing before a single professional judge, a triad of judges, or a mixed panel of professional judges and lay assessors. A single judge, as trier of fact, could well be more inclined toward acquittal in certain kinds of cases than would a jury of lay people. I recall a rape prosecution that I handled during my

brief career as a prosecutor in California in the early 1970s. The case was to come before a judge who, as everyone in the office knew, had a particular aversion toward convicting in sex cases. The defense wanted to waive the jury trial and proceed before the judge. As the Deputy District Attorney in charge of the case I wanted, of course, to make use of a little known procedural lever: the prosecutor's right to insist on a jury trial.[2] When the higher-ups in the office got wind of my plan, they said no. "Don't insult the judge," they said, "We have to go before him every day. If one of our deputies shows that he has no confidence in him, that will hurt us in more cases than this isolated rape case." It turns out that I won the case anyway, but only because of a fail-safe rule that permits prosecution for sodomy regardless of consent.[3]

It is true that juries can sometimes nullify the law in the case of a popular defendant tried on a charge at odds with community mores. If Dr. Kevorkian is charged and prosecuted for homicide because he supplied his suicide machine to two women who wanted to commit suicide, there is a good chance that a jury will acquit him, no matter what the evidence, no matter what the judge instructs the jury on the law.[4] Indeed in the preindictment proceedings, Kevorkian carried himself as though he had already been acquitted, so confident he was that his message of voluntary exit resonated in public sentiment.[5] To take another example, if after the overruling of *Roe v. Wade*[6] women will be prosecuted and punished for abortion, juries might refuse to convict. Judges, acting alone or with lay assessors they typically control, are in fact much better at enforcing the official morality of the legal system.

Yet the fantasies of lawyers that they can make a few clever moves and induce the jury to nullify the law are grossly exaggerated. Everything I have witnessed and learned about jury behavior suggests that in virtually all cases, juries assiduously seek to apply the judge's instructions on the law. It is true that even most law students do not understand the arcane and convoluted instructions that one finds in the desk books of trial judges, but juries nonetheless make an effort to do their job. Like everybody else, juries are committed to the principle of covering themselves, at least psychologically, by believing that they are merely doing their job in making the choice between two difficult alternatives: committing a human being to jail and sending a probably dangerous suspect back out onto the streets.

I withhold judgment, however, on the difficult issue of racial bias as it affects jury behavior. The once rampant anti-black sentiments that induced the United States Supreme Court, beginning in the 1930s, to intervene in state criminal justice, seem to have subsided. Yet unspoken assumptions about black propensities for violent behavior still inform the thinking of lay people, both black and white. The problem is whether professional judges, also exposed to the same stereotypical thinking, master their biases more effectively. In the prosecution of Bernhard Goetz,[7] the jury of ten whites and two blacks were probably affected by the widespread fear in New York of violence by black youths who look like street toughs -- the profile represented by the four youths who approached Goetz on the subway. There are many who believe that the rape prosecution of William Kennedy Smith[8] differs from that of Mike Tyson[9] as one set of racial and class assumptions differs from another. Alas, there is no definitive way to measure the impact of racial bias on the behavior of jurors, yet it is not clear that the impact on judges would be less severe. It is possible that some professional judges would be more on guard against race-based assessments of credibility, but this a speculative claim.

What seems clear, however, is that defense lawyers regularly demand a jury trial; at least they think resolution of the indictment by jury is better for their clients. There are many reasons why lawyers might favor jury trials.[10] Most defense counsel probably see jury trials as offering more options to derail the prosecution. There is always the possibility of a hung jury -- in most states one holdout is enough -- which would induce the prosecution to give up and turn its energy elsewhere. Also, there is always the possibility of an incident that would "poison" the jury's (but not a judge's) mind and thus generate a basis for a mistrial. These are reasons for favoring a jury trial in the client's interest without assuming that a jury's verdict of guilt or innocence is likely to be more accurate than a judge's.

### B. Implications of the Jury System

For the defendant, the primary advantage of trial by jury over trial by judge (or mixed panels of judges and assessors) may rest not in the decision-making function of the jury, but rather in the implications of the systems for the rest of the trial. Four implications are worth underscoring: (1) the separation of conviction and sentencing, (2) the rules of evidence, (3) the asymmetrical rules of appeal, and (4) the psychological impact on lawyers of separating the functions of jury and judge.

A little appreciated feature of the jury, as we know it in Anglo-American legal systems, is that it leads to the separation of fact finding on guilt and innocence from the sentencing phase of the trial. Juries could conceivably determine sentences in the number of years to be served, as civil juries assign a dollar sign to the defendant's liability. If we had a more clearly retributive system, we might favor the jury's gaining power over sentencing. Yet if the jury were to issue a composite verdict as it does in civil cases --

for example, guilty of an assault worth five years -- there would be a greater danger than now that juries would reach compromise verdicts. Now the compromises are limited to convicting on some counts and acquitting on others. Yet, significantly, the jury is not informed about the gravity of the charges and how serious it would be to convict of one rather than another.

The surprising fact is that civilian courts function without distinguishing between these two phases. Both are lumped together in one determination of guilt and sentence. This interweaving of two questions -- responsibility for the crime and society's response to the crime -- leads to one of the most disquieting features of the civilian trial. As the trial begins, the civilian judges interrogate the defendant about his person: name, residence, occupation, marital status and, believe it or not, prior criminal record![11] Posing this question at the outset of the trial is conceivable only under two assumptions about the administration of justice: first, that sentencing is inseparable from the finding of guilt or innocence and that therefore even at the outset the question about prior record is relevant; and second, that judges are so well-trained that they are not likely to be biased against a criminal defendant just because he or she has a string of prior convictions.

The assumptions that Europeans and Latin Americans are willing to make about their professional judges are fit subject of satire. They would not even consider prohibiting their judges, as we do our jurors, from watching television or reading the newspaper during a highly publicized political trial. It is not surprising that they believe, contrary to every instinct of human nature, that judges can inquire about a defendant's criminal record and then proceed as though the defendant were presumed innocent until proven guilty. German reformers have tried for years to separate the sentencing from the guilt-finding phase of the trial by introducing the *Schuldinterlokut*, a stage akin to a verdict of guilty, but these efforts seem now to have been abandoned.

The great advantage of the jury system is that we build human fallibility into the process. As civilians enthrone their judges on a pedestal of superhuman neutrality, common law lawyers start on the assumption that jurors are imperfect, corruptible, and weak. This seemingly condescending attitude toward the jury accounts for the restrictive rules of evidence. In principle, hearsay, prior convictions, and inflammatory evidence are inadmissible. The *Goetz* jury was not allowed to hear, for example, that prior to the shooting, Goetz was heard to say at a meeting of his neighborhood association, "The only way to clean up [14th Street] is to get rid of the spics and niggers."[12] Had they heard this statement, the jury might have had a different take on the racial dimension in the case.

Of course, this highly complex body of law generates a battleground for lawyers to show their wits. A good trial lawyer shows his or her skill in debating the subtleties of hearsay and its exceptions: spontaneous utterances, states of mind, business records, prior convictions bearing solely on credibility. Although these finely honed rules may restrict the jury's access to material that would be beneficial to the defense (for example, the criminal records of the four youths in *Goetz*),[13] the exclusion of evidence generally helps the defense. The prosecution has a smaller domain of evidence to work with in mustering innuendos of guilt; in principle, all the evidence that is introduced comes under cross-examination. These factors work to the benefit of the defendant.

It would be an exaggeration to say that civilians have no rules of evidence. Using presumptions would violate the Continental principle of "free evaluation of the evidence" and judgment based on the judge's "personal conviction" (*intime conviction*), but the Germans do have well developed exclusionary rules (*Beweisverbote*) that in some respects go further than our own.[14] There is even a preference for direct and immediate evidence as opposed to what we call hearsay. Yet the scope of these debates is far more limited. The assumption behind the free admissibility of evidence is judges can properly assess the relevance of evidence that strikes us as too unreliable, too tangential or too inflammatory to be considered at all.

It is worth noting that in the sentencing phase in state courts, at least in New York, judges put themselves above all the normal rules of evidentiary filtering. They play the role of superhuman civilian judges, capable of gauging the proper weight of all forms of input into their decision, including emotional letters from the community about what should be done with the convicted offender. It may be that the separation of sentencing from the guilt phase in the United States is designed precisely to free the sentencing determination from the evidentiary constraints associated with the jury trial. The nominal justification for the separation is that sentencing has many social purposes other than retributive justice, and presumably judges are in a better position to strike the proper balance among conflicting goals.

The jury system, then, accounts for the common law trial's distinction between the guilt phase and the sentencing phase and it also generates the complicated body of admissibility rules and presumptions called the law of evidence. The third implication of the jury system -- the asymmetrical rules of appeal -- has a paradoxical twist. If the jury cannot be trusted with all the evidence, if it cannot be trusted with sentencing decisions, one would expect appellate courts to exercise close supervision over the jury's finding of fact. The opposite is true. The jury exercises considerable autonomy over findings of guilty. It is difficult, if not virtually impossible, to secure a reversal solely on the grounds that the evidence does not support the verdict. And on findings of not guilty, the jury's autonomy is absolute: there is no appeal, no recourse against the jury's acquitting the defendant. The principle of asymmetrical appeal (appeal from a verdict of guilty, but none from a verdict of not guilty) stands in sharp contrast to civilian modes of appellate review. The first appeal typically gives both the prosecution and the defense the opportunity to retry questions of fact; and even if there is an acquittal after this round, access to the higher appellate courts is open to both sides. Common law deference to the power of the jury to acquit is thought necessary to guarantee the jury's independence; civilians see no reason to defer in the same way to their trial courts.

More than these first three implications of the jury system, I would single out a fourth structural feature of the common law jury trial as generating the most significant advantage for the defense. The division of function between judge and jury liberates common law defense lawyers to be far more aggressive and zealous in their defense than one can expect from civilian defense lawyers. The reason is simple. Civilian lawyers must constantly ingratiate themselves with the judge; in the end the judge renders the low-visibility judgments of fact on which the trial ultimately turns. Alienating the judge by arguing too vigorously means losing the trial. Common law defense lawyers can go much further in their arguments on points of law with the judge. First, these arguments take place outside the hearing range of the jury, and therefore no matter how obnoxious the lawyers become they do not risk losing votes on the jury. Second, if they do alienate the judge, they risk little and they may even gain if they drive the judge into making a prejudicial ruling on a question of law. If the judge makes a mistake, after all, the defense acquires a good ground for appellate reversal.

On the other side of the ledger, it is worth noting that civilian judges have no power of contempt as do their common law colleagues. They can do very little to discipline a recalcitrant lawyer. But this might even be worse for lawyers with *chutspah*, for the frustrated civilian judge has no way to respond except to bury her ill will against the lawyer in her findings of fact. The only control over the judge's fact-finding function is the written opinion on the evidence, which, of course, the judge writes herself.

To review these implications of the jury system, it is worth speculating about what is likely to happen to a common law system in a former English colony that never had the jury system.[15] The first change likely to occur is the abolition of asymmetric appellate rights that favor the defense. The rules of evidence, including the hearsay rule, might well be retained, which in turn would imply that the distinction between the guilt and sentencing phases would survive. I would predict that lawyers, on the whole, would become less aggressive and less willing to risk alienating the judge as trier of fact.

## C. The Dossier

One might be tempted to conclude that the presence or absence of an exclusively lay jury is the most significant factor distinguishing the common law adversarial from the civilian accusatorial trial. The civilian tradition, it might be argued, takes the strong investigative judge as the centerpiece of its mode of trial. Lawyers in the civilian mode have less responsibility for collecting and presenting evidence than does the investigating magistrate prior to trial and the judge during trial. There may be something to this line of thought, particularly in view of the inquisitorial background of the modern civilian trial. Yet there is no necessary connection between the presence or absence of the jury and concentrating the responsibility for running the trial in the hands of a strong investigative judge. One could easily have a jury with a strong judge, and the opposite: trial by a weak judge acting as finder of fact, with the lawyers taking full responsibility for presenting the evidence at trial. One need only think about the permutations with which *voir dire* is conducted in federal and state courts in the United States.

It is a matter of contention in the civilian tradition that the trier of fact is also responsible for structuring trial and examining the witnesses. There have been efforts since World War II, particularly in Germany, to decentralize responsibility for running the trial, with the lawyers taking on ever greater power and independence. Yet as compared with the common law judge functioning as arbiter of the trial, the civilian judge still tries to occupy center stage as the official who must see to it that all the relevant evidence is heard and evaluated.

These variations in the strength and responsibility of the trial judge have no necessary impact on the trial position of the defendant. A strong judge is better for the defendant than a mediocre defense lawyer. Yet behind the institution of the strong investigative judge lies another practice that has a bearing on the procedural power of the accused. And that is the use of the prosecutorial dossier prior to trial. As compared with the common law trial, where the trier of fact knows nothing about the evidence prior to the defendant's "day in court," the civilian judge has full access to the evidence in the dossier and it is part of his task to study the dossier as preparation for trial. This practice, a legacy of the inquisitorial mind, lies at the heart of the civilian mode of trial.

The presumption of innocence at trial presupposes that the jury as well as the judge treat the defendant as though he or she were innocent. They both must engage in an assumption that runs counter to their experience. They may well know -- it would be hard for an experienced trial participant to avoid knowing -- that in most jurisdictions, roughly ninety per cent of the suspects brought to trial are found guilty. Yet they may not infer from this figure that the defendant in the dock is likely to be guilty. It is the nature of things, however, that as the civilian trial begins, the trier of fact has an opinion about the guilt or innocence of the defendant. If he or she has read the dossier, it would be impossible not to have an opinion about the evidence. Accordingly, it is much more difficult for civilians to take the presumption of innocence *at trial* seriously.[16] Of course, the rhetoric of civilian systems now fully endorses the presumption of innocence, but this rhetoric does not amount to much if in fact the judge prepares for trial by studying the evidence before it is introduced.

The purpose of the civilian trial is to test whether the dossier contains a proper case. The only evidence that the judge may properly consider on the question of guilt must be heard in open court. The judge cannot base the written opinion on evidence contained in the dossier but never subjected to public examination. In the sense that it tests the conclusions reached in the preliminary investigation, the civilian trial comes closer to being an appeal from the pre-trial phase than an entirely fresh and independent hearing. The appropriate image for the common law may well be a vise that tightens progressively from arrest, to indictment, to trial and conviction, with appeal representing an opportunity to open a closed vise. The opposing image for a civilian trial is that of a book that grows and grows, from arrest, to preliminary investigation, to trial, to appeal and trial de novo, to appeal on questions of law. The process does not peak in a moment of truth at trial, but rather continually gathers material and weight as it proceeds.

There is little doubt that the use of the dossier at trial severely undercuts the interests of the defendant. He or she loses an opportunity for a totally fresh look at the evidence, firmly rooted in the presumption of innocence, uncompromised by the prestige of the prosecutor's pre-trial findings. The only thing that can be said in favor of the practice is that defense counsel as well as the defendant also have total access to the dossier prior to trial. There are no prosecutorial surprises, no need for pre-trial discovery.

On balance, there is little doubt that common law procedures greatly favor the interests of the accused. This is true, even without considering the panoply of rights offered by current interpretations of the Fourth, Fifth, and Sixth Amendments.[17] If procedure were everything, there is little doubt that a well-advised criminal defendant would choose to stand trial in the United States rather than in a civilian jurisdiction. The question this clear advantage poses is whether all things considered, the criminal law of the United States is relatively favorable to defendants. This requires us to consider whether the substantive law takes away with one hand that which the law of procedure accords with the other.

## II.
## The Advantages of German Principles of Substantive Law

Discussions of substantive criminal law are bound to be superficial, for the details depend so much on the codes and case law of particular jurisdictions. There are tremendous differences, for example, between French and German criminal law. In contrasting civilian and common law theories of liability, all I mean to assert, in general terms, is a general difference between German law and the general principles that constitute the common denominator of jurisdictions in the United States.

There is little doubt that the applicable principles of law in the United States are less favorable to the defense than the principles that have developed in Germany in the last several decades. The most striking differences appear in the law of excuses. American courts are loathe to recognize standard excuses, such as mistake of law, personal necessity, duress in homicide cases and even, in some courts, claims of insanity that go beyond the rigors of the McNaughton test.[18] Denying these excuses imposes a species of strict liability; the defendant is held accountable even though he or she was not at fault in violating the statutory norm.

All these excuses are well developed under German law. There is no strict liability. The fault principle is treated as sacrosanct. It would be unthinkable to convict someone of statutory rape, regardless of his mistake about the age of the girl, simply on the ground that he had an absolute duty to know better. It would be out of the question to convict Dudley and Stevens of homicide,[19] even though no one could blame them for succumbing to the necessity of cannibalism to save their own lives.

It is true that American courts have begun to recognize an excuse of personal necessity in prison escape cases,[20] but in Germany, prison escape is not even treated as a crime. It is true that in some self-defense cases, American courts appear to have become more receptive toward claims of self-defense, particularly in cases of battered wives' fighting back.[21] Yet on several counts, the German law of self-defense is far more favorable to the accused. The way to illustrate this is to take a borderline case, such as the prosecution of Bernhard Goetz,[22] and ask how he would have fared under German law.

Let us assume that when Goetz pulled his gun and started shooting at four young men who surrounded him and asked him for money on the subway, he was responding to a substantial risk of robbery and a low risk of life-endangering attack. On these assumptions, Goetz should have been acquitted of aggravated assault and attempted murder under New York law, for he was using deadly force to repel a robbery. Under German law he would have had a full right of self-defense. Yet let us suppose that the threat was merely of theft without force, rather than robbery. He would lose his right to respond under American law, but not under German law, which recognizes an unqualified right to use all necessary force to defend one's basic rights, including the right to property.[23] The German courts have been slow to recognize a limitation comparable to the common law rule of reasonable force.[24]

The more interesting case arises on the assumption that in fact the youths were not about to rob Goetz but he sincerely believed that they were about to do so. This is the situation that generates the ongoing controversy whether the proper standard for assessing culpability for mistakes is subjective or objective. The New York Court of Appeals decided unanimously that in order to invoke a claim of self-defense, Goetz must have reasonably believed that he was about to be attacked; that is, they adopted the objective standard.[25] Yet although the German code is silent on this point, the theoretical literature has come to the conclusion that the subjective standard should be applied, that Goetz did not attack the youths "intentionally" if he believed sincerely (reasonably or not) that he had to defend himself.[26] Under German law, if he negligently or unreasonably assumed that he was about to be attacked, he could have been liable at most for negligent battery.[27]

This is an instance, however, where procedural and substantive considerations begin to interweave. Even though the jury was instructed to apply the objective standard and assess whether Goetz behaved as a reasonable person would have under the circumstances, the jury in fact, in a simple exercise of common sense, ended up thinking the way German theorists have concluded is correct: if he was trying to defend himself, Goetz did not act or commit assault "intentionally." Thus the procedural form of the jury overcame the less favorable substantive rule.

Even if he had not profited from the explicitly recognized subjective standard of self-defense under German law, Goetz could have invoked a provision of the criminal code that provides a special excuse for those who, under conditions of fright or fear, use excessive force in self-defense.[28] In sum, with all these options available to him, it is hard to imagine how Goetz could have been convicted for anything under German law except illegal possession of the gun. But, one might reply, that is precisely the charge on which Goetz was convicted in New York.[29] How does this show that German law is more advantageous? If the result proved to be the same, the explanation should probably be the procedural advantages of the New York jury and evidentiary system helped Goetz in the same areas that the substantive law hurt him.

Another area in which German substantive law is superior to the common law is the use of the necessity defense. Many states have adopted versions of Model Penal Code § 3.02, which permits the justification of nominally criminal conduct as the lesser of two evils. In New York, which is among these states, the defense is much less at the forefront of judicial and lawyerly consciousness than is the comparable defense in German legal culture.[30] However competent they were, the lawyers in the *Goetz* case did not know how to handle the necessity defense even as to charges, such as unlicensed gun possession, where it might have generated an acquittal.[31]

American criminal law seems to have a knack for retaining substantive offenses that can function, when all other charges fail, as a back-up device. Conspiracy -- which does not exist as a distinct crime in Germany -- has this function, as does the charge of weapons possession. One reason why prosecutors seek to retain a crime of sodomy (decriminalized between consenting adults in Germany) is that it provides a backup charge when rape charges fail. Sodomy is a crime regardless of consent and in many situations of alleged rape, an act of sodomy is also charged. The sodomy count functions very much like the gun-possession charge in self-defense cases. Because it cannot be defeated by the defendant's claims (she consented; he attacked me first), a charge backed up by the victim's testimony and some physical evidence is almost unbeatable.

In engaging in this comparative exercise, I have turned off, for the most part, my normative sensibilities. There are many things wrong with both civilian and common law systems of criminal justice, both at the level of procedure and at the level of substance. The ideal system for the accused would be the combination of German substantive law and American procedure.

The ideal came alive, briefly, in 1980 in Berlin.[32] An East German named Tiede hijacked a Polish airplane over West German airspace and forced a landing at Tempelhof airport, then in the American sector of Berlin. Because the Germans refused to try him, the Americans set up the United States Court for Berlin, called in a federal judge from New Jersey and proceeded to try Tiede under German law (the place of the hijacking) according to federal criminal procedure, including all rights available under the United States Constitution. The result should be no surprise. The jury, consisting of West Berliners, acquitted Tiede of all charges except one minor count; the judge released him on the basis of time served prior to trial.

# Notes

[1]I do not use the word "inquisitorial" in discussing the civilian model. With the advent of oral trials and the separation of the charging and judging functions, the term is no longer appropriate. For comments on the weakness of the "inquistorial" mode of written proceedings, see KARL SCHÄFER, STRAFPROZESSRECHT 249 (1976).

[2]Singer v. United States, 380 U.S. 24 (1965) (a defendant does not have a constitutional right to insist on a bench trial).

[3]For the discussion of the sodomy charge in the text, see text *infra* note 31.

[4]A Michigan court has dismissed criminal proceedings against Dr. Jack Kevorkian on the grounds of insufficient proof of intention to carry out the suicide. *See* Isabel Wilkerson, *Inventor of Suicide Machine Arrested on Murder Charge*, N. Y. TIMES, December 4, 1990, at A1; William E. Schmidt, *Prosecutors Drop Criminal Case Against Doctor Involved in Suicide*, N. Y. TIMES, December 15, 1990, at §1 p. 10.

[5]*See* Wilkerson, *supra* note 4; Schmidt, *supra* note 4.

[6]410 U.S. 113 (1973).

[7]*See generally* GEORGE P. FLETCHER, A CRIME OF SELF-DEFENSE: BERNHARD GOETZ AND THE LAW ON TRIAL (1988) [hereinafter GOETZ]. This book has been translated into Spanish. GEORGE P. FLETCHER, EN DEFENSA PROPIA (Francisco Muñoz Conde & Fernando Rodríguez Marín trans., 1992). Prior to the prosecution, the case went up on appeal to the New York Court of Appeals. *See* People v. Goetz, 497 N.E.2d 41 (N.Y. 1986).

[8]Susan Estrich, *The Real Palm Beach Story*, N. Y. TIMES, April 18, 1991, at A25.

[9]*See* Tyson v. State, 593 N.E.2d 175 (Ind. 1992).

[10]I discount the factor of self-interest. If lawyers prolong the proceedings, they earn more. But if these venal considerations were determinative, profit-hungry lawyers would never plea-bargain on behalf of a paying client.

[11]If you think this is outrageous, recall that in the former Communist lands, the judges would ask the defendant not only to identify his nationality (not exactly a break for Armenians and Jews) but to state his *partijnost*, that is, disclose whether he was a member of the Communist Party.

[12]GOETZ, *supra* note 7, at 243.

[13]GOETZ, *supra* note 7, at 107-09 (discussing the way in which the defense managed to introduce the criminal records of the four youths).

[14]*See generally* SCHÄFER, *supra* note 1, at 271-93.

[15]Typically, the English prevented subject peoples in their colonies, e.g. Palestine, India, from being tried by their peers.

[16]*See, e.g.,* George P. Fletcher, *The Ongoing Soviet Debate about the Presumption of Innocence*, CRIM. JUST. ETHICS, Summer/Fall 1984, at 69.

[17]The Fourth Amendment provides protection against "unreasonable searches and seizures." U.S. CONST. amend. IV. The Fifth Amendment prohibits double jeopardy and provides that no person "shall be compelled in any criminal case to be a witness against himself." U.S. CONST. amend. V. The Sixth Amendment guaran-

tees to defendants the rights of a speedy trial "by an impartial jury," "to be confronted with the witnesses against him; to have compulsory process for obtaining witnesses in his favor, and to have the assistance of counsel for his defense." U.S. CONST. amend. VI.

[18]*See generally* GEORGE P. FLETCHER, RETHINKING CRIMINAL LAW §§ 10.1 - 10.5 (1978).    Modern common law standards of insanity begin with the M'Naughten's Case, 8 Eng. Rep. 718 (1843), which provided that the defendant was insane if at the time of the act, he "was laboring under such a defect of reason, from disease of the mind, as to not know the nature and quality of the act he was doing, or if he did know it that he did not know he was doing what was wrong." *Id.*

[19]Regina v. Dudley & Stevens, L.R. 14 Q.B.D. 273 (1884).

[20]*See* People v. Lovercamp, 118 Cal. Rptr. 110 (Cal. App. 1974).

[21]*See, e.g.,* People v. McGrandy, 156 N.W.2d 48 (Mich. Ct. App. 1967) (holding that battered spouse was not required to retreat from own home to claim valid self defense); Commonwealth v. Johnston, 263 A.2d 376 (Pa. 1970) (ruling that defender may stand ground and meet deadly force with deadly force when threatened in own home).

[22]*See supra* note 7 and accompanying text.

[23]StGB § 32 (F.D.R.).

[24]For commentary on this line of development, see George P. Fletcher, *The Right and the Reasonable*, 98 HARV. L. REV. 949 (1985).

[25]*See* sources cited *supra* note 7.

[26]*See* KARL LACKNER, STRAFGESETZBUCH MIT ERLÄUTERUNGEN 111 (18th ed. 1989).

[27]*Id.*

[28]StGB § 33 (F.D.R.).

[29]GOETZ, *supra* note 7, at 198.

[30]StGB § 34 (F.D.R.).

[31]*See* GOETZ, *supra* note 7, at 159-69.

[32]For additional details, see GOETZ, *supra* note 7, at 160-63.  For a preliminary decision, see United States v. Tiede, 86 F.R.D. 227 (U.S. Ct. for Berlin 1979).

# 10

---

# Persecution and Inquisition:
# A Case Study

## *Ruti Teitel*

*Incident 1:*

> *As he entered his home, he was grabbed by men who handcuffed and blindfolded him. They took him from his home, threw him on to the floor of a car (a Ford Falcon); after a drive they took him out, put him on a table and tied his hands and feet to its four corners. They tortured him with electric shocks to the sensitive parts of his body and beat him systematically with wooden sticks on his back, legs and the soles of his feet. Alternating between electric shocks and beating, the torture went on for days.[1]*

*Incident 2:*

> *The young man was detained by four police dressed in civilian clothes who forced him into an unlicensed Ford Falcon. They tied his feet and hands, drove him to the shores of the Reconquista river where they threatened to throw him in the water. They then blindfolded him with a hood, threw him in the trunk of the car, and drove to a deserted place where they undressed him and beat him, mostly on the soles of his feet. When he was finally let go, the young man was hospitalized, and he may never walk again.[2]*

The two incidents related above occurred during two different periods of Argentine history. The first case occurred during a period of military rule;[3] the second case occurred during civilian rule.[4]

The haunting similarity in the method of abuse in these two cases is reinforced by chilling statistics. Figures collected by leading human rights groups in Argentina reflect a continuous and disturbingly high level of police violence during successive democratically elected administrations. In 1984, the year immediately following Alfonsín's election, police violence resulted in the deaths of 160 civilians.[5] The subsequent year was bloodier still, with the number dead as a result of police violence doubling. Another several hundred were tortured.[6]

A 1990 State Department report documents the excessive use of force by Argentine police dealing with criminal suspects.[7] The 1991 Americas Watch and Centro de Estudios Legales y Sociales (Center for Legal and Social Studies) report (CELS) concludes that the figures for incidents of police violence were high throughout the entire period between 1983-1991.[8] Indeed, these figures include documentation of hundreds of deaths.[9] Moreover, such staggeringly high rates of police violence raise serious questions about the nature of criminal justice in the new democracy. This chapter attempts to explore some of these questions.[10]

With the many recent transitions to democracy, crimes of prior regimes have been publicly exposed, and with exposure, there has been a call for punishment. Proponents of punishment maintain criminal justice is a hallmark of democratic government. The response to the crimes of the military regimes is thought to lie in the criminal justice system. This call has been particularly loud in Latin America's Southern Cone, which is in transition from authoritarian rule to democracy. Indeed, commentators have previously attributed problems in the transitions to the failure to enforce criminal sanctions against perpetrators of past abuses.[11]

The questions I raise here invert the prevailing focus and suggest instead that there is a strong link between the crimes of the military and the inquisitorial system of criminal process prevailing in Latin America. Criminal justice cannot serve as an effective response to lawlessness where there is an ineluctable connection between the criminal process and unlawful actions of the state. I maintain that the inquisitorial criminal justice system is itself a paradigm of the state's expression of the authoritarian exercise of power.

I focus on Argentina as a case study. The persecution that occurred in Argentina during the military period is not a separate phenomenon simply reflecting military culture. Where the military has long shared power with civilian governments,[12] the legal order of the civilian state cannot be considered independent of the military regimes. In turn, the crimes of the military cannot be considered independent of other civilian action. I maintain that the persecution caused by the dictatorship is an extension of the accepted norms of the prevailing inquisitorial system of justice.

I propose a theory of criminal procedure that expresses values outside the criminal system, values which are not part of the general polity. Under my expressive theory, the law of criminal process reflects norms. These norms are not simply a function of societal values but instead constitute an independent factor in the creation of the political doctrine and structure of the state. To put it another way, there is a symbiosis between the criminal process and society's values. Under this view, then, the coincidence of the inquisitorial system in countries with authoritarian regimes cannot be viewed simply as a result of the national culture.[13] Rather, the system of criminal justice is itself expressive of authoritarian norms informing the police state. I term such process a "statist model" of criminal justice.

In Part I, I suggest how my proposed theory and model fit into prevailing criminal procedure theory. In Part II, I offer a case study in the statist model by exploring Argentina's law of criminal process.

# I.
## An Expressive Theory of Criminal Process

In exploring the connection between criminal process and norms of state action, I assert that the law of criminal process ought not be understood simply as a product of culture but instead as an independent factor in promoting an authoritarian ideology conducive to a climate of governmental abuses of rights.[14]

In contrast to this view, the long-standing approach in the literature has been to analyze criminal procedure as it relates to the substantive purposes of the criminal law, as part of a closed system.[15] Herbert Packer's subject of analysis, for example, has been the norms internal to the criminal justice system.[16] Packer writes of "two separate value systems that compete for priority in the operations of the criminal process."[17] He characterizes the two value systems as "crime control" and "due process" models. For Packer, these are dichotomous models. For other commentators, such as John Griffiths, Packer's models both constitute "battle models." Griffiths juxtaposes Packer's models with what he conceives of as a "family model" of the criminal process.[18] Both commentators offer these models to explain values within the criminal justice system.[19] Neither conceives of the models transmitting values from the criminal justice system to the general society.

Commentators writing from a comparative perspective postulate a connection between varying systems of criminal process and systems of government. George Fletcher writes of criminal procedure systems as expressions of national identity.[20] Mirjan Damaska has provided a useful typology of criminal justice systems, and he broadly characterizes these as a function of two governmental systems.[21] Damaska proposes that there are activist and reactive state ideologies that give rise to compatible activist and reactive criminal legal processes, comporting with the inquisitorial and adversarial processes. For Damaska, liberal ideology's preference for limited government leads to electing an accusatorial system of criminal process,[22] characterized by a minimal role for the state, a relatively passive judge, and active private parties. By comparison, such a system can be juxtaposed with the inquisitorial system, characterized by an activist judge and passive private parties. The latter Damaska understands as a reflection of state ideology that favors the concentration of power in public officials.[23] Liberalism is viewed as providing an "arm's length ideology" of criminal justice that contrasts with the "parental" ideology underlying the inquisitorial system. The law of criminal process is, therefore, understood to derive from particular political or cultural ideologies.[24]

Thus the prevailing approaches are either conceptions of criminal justice as an isolated system, expressing norms internal to the criminal justice system, or conceptions of criminal justice as derivative from politics and culture. I disagree with both approaches. I suggest instead that criminal process should itself be considered an independent factor in the creation of political doctrine and national ideology.

## II.
## The Statist Model: A Case Study

Under my proposed analysis, the criminal justice system constitutes a paradigm for coercive state action. I denote a system expressing generous parameters of permissible coercive government action as part of a statist model.

It is clear, after experiencing over a century of the use of the inquisitorial system in Latin America coincident with the founding of the state,[25] that the criminal justice system cannot be viewed as an isolated institution or as a product of ideology. The law of criminal process is in and of itself a critical element in the development of the structure and political doctrine of the state. Moreover, although the system of law ought to be the antithesis of arbitrariness and terror, it is far from this in the case of Argentina. This is perhaps best shown in the most important and longest stage in the determination of guilt, the investigation phase of the process.[26] Indeed, I maintain that the paradigm of the "*incommunicado* suspect" in state custody expresses core elements of authoritarianism.

### A. The Paradigm of the Incommunicado Suspect

In this section, I describe the post-arrest paradigm in Argentina. The virtually unchecked power of the state, acting through the police, juxtaposed with the utter powerlessness of the suspect, is notable at this earliest stage in the criminal case.

The case begins with an arrest which may be triggered by a complaint of the police, a citizen or a judge.[27] Moreover, the police have a duty to arrest.[28] The police also have the power to arrest without any judicial supervision. The code stipulates that suspects must be brought before a magistrate following the arrest.[29] This requirement is routinely satisfied by mere notification to the judge,[30] and many days can pass as the police work on investigating the case.[31] The suspect often spends the entire investigatory period without seeing a judge.

The law contemplates the role of the police as active participants in the investigation. It is the police who define the suspect's status during this period, and who decide whether the suspect is to be rendered "*incommunicado.*"[32]

During the police investigation, the suspect has no right to assistance of counsel. During the post-arrest investigation stage, the police routinely receive so-called "spontaneous" statements or confessions of the arrestee, without judicial supervision.[33] When the suspect finally appears before the judge, the judge will evaluate the charges in light of his or her review of the substantial police report. At the inquiry, the judge's probable cause determination is based not merely on the evidence leading to the arrest, but also on any new evidence obtained by the police in the post-arrest detention, including any "spontaneous statements."[34] The extensive power of the police over the interrogation of the suspect exemplifies the tolerance of unchecked coercive state power at a stage where, according to the Constitution, the suspect is protected by a presumption of innocence.[35]

## B. The Investigating Accused

Under the paradigm of the *incommunicado* suspect, the suspect herself is the chief source of evidence in the investigation.

*Incommunicado Status.* Under the pure inquisitorial system exemplified by the case study, the investigation phase can last indefinitely. Moreover, the suspect/defendant is routinely incarcerated during the entire investigation phase. Argentine criminal procedure contemplates lengthy pretrial incarceration with an outside limit of two years.[36]

From the time of arrest to the time of trial, both the judge and police are authorized to render the suspect "*incommunicado.*" *Incommunicado* status means the suspect is forbidden from having contacts with anyone, including family and counsel, until the presiding judge lifts the status.[37] During the *incommunicado* period, only the police have access to the suspect.

The *incommunicado* practice is designed to break the suspect/defendant and to coerce her to provide information about the crime. Under current law the *incommunicado* period may last for a week, but the period is extendable.[38] In theory, the *incommunicado* status is discretionary but in practice the *incommunicado* defendant has become the rule, usually lasting the maximum period even for crimes that are not serious.

*The Role of Secrecy.* Secrecy in the proceedings is common practice in the Argentine criminal case. In cases of a political nature, it is the rule. But secrecy is not limited to serious cases.[39]

Secrecy is endemic to the investigatory phase. Under the code, there is an official "secrecy" status which closes the proceedings to everyone other than the government.[40] The proceedings can be made secret for extendable ten day periods. The determination to make the proceedings secret is unreviewable.[41] Secrecy in the proceedings means the suspect neither has access to the record being developed in her case nor the right to confront her witnesses. Even the defense attorney often may not know the charges against her client. Access to a suspect's file is exclusively limited to the state.

*The Role of Confession.* The absolute secrecy of the investigatory proceedings, compounded by the practice of holding the suspect *incommunicado* during the investigation, means that as a routine matter in the ordinary case the suspect will be isolated for days, utterly under the control of the police. During the investigation, the police routinely conduct substantial custodial interrogations and delay notifying the judge to request a hearing until they secure a confession.

Though there is a privilege against self-incrimination,[42] the paradigm I have described above encourages confessions. Even if the Federal Code of Criminal Procedure characterizes these confessions as "spontaneous statements," where the suspect is *incommunicado* and has no access to counsel during the investigation phase, it is difficult to imagine how statements made to the police in such situations can be presumed to be anything other than coerced.[43]

Under the inquisitorial process, confessions play a fundamental role in the judicial determination of the legality of the pretrial detention in the *prima facie* case, as well as in the ultimate adjudication of guilt. Allegations of coerced confessions result in little judicial attention.[44] Under the Federal Code of Criminal Procedure, confessions are accorded little probatory weight; however, information obtained from a coerced confession is still allowed before the court.[45]

In failing to exclude the coerced confession obtained through police interrogation in the individual criminal case, the process encourages the interrogation of the *incommunicado* held in police custody. Such statements are extracted from isolated suspects who are often in the dark even regarding the charges against them.

*The Role of Torture.* Prevailing law characterizes police use of torture to be unlawful,[46] yet recent cases reveal that torture in the investigation is not only common practice, but that it is sanctioned within the police culture and by society. Building on the *incommunicado* paradigm set out above, perhaps it is not all that surprising.

Under successive democratically elected governments, the routine use of torture in police interrogations has risen to public attention. About 700 complaints of "illegal coercion" were reported in a two year period of the Alfonsín administration.[47] One case in particular, which rose to public attention, was that of Luis Patti, a provincial police chief, who admitted to torturing two suspects accused of robbery by placing electric shocks to their genitals.[48]

The *Patti* case stands out as one of the few prosecutions of police violence.[49] Yet perhaps more significant, the *Patti* case provoked what in effect constitutes a referendum on torture. The debate over Patti's trial expanded to a public debate over the justifiability of the use of police violence in criminal investigations. A survey conducted by the media concluded that about half of those surveyed supported police use of torture.[50]

## C. Prosecuting the Accused

*The State versus the Accused.* During the investigatory stage there is almost unfettered state control and an absence of accountability. The paradigm of the inquisitorial process depicted in this case study describes a system which, at the critical investigation stage, places maximum power in the state, and allows the suspect minimal power. This power imbalance exists at a stage where the presumption of innocence is thought to protect citizens. Compounding the power imbalance between the state and the suspect is the utter absence of power or access to the criminal justice system for other citizens. Put another way, the suspect cannot be helped because neither she, nor anyone else, has any meaningful access to the system.

The state's power is consolidated in the hands of the police. Though the inquisitorial model contemplates investigation by an "investigating judge," the inquisitorial process, as provided for in Argentine law, contemplates a partnership in the investigation of crimes between the judge and the police.[51] Yet in practice, and as the Federal Code of Criminal Procedure permits, the police play the leading role in the investigation. A *de facto* process has evolved out of the parameters denoted by the text of the Federal Code of Criminal Procedure.[52] In addition to the minimal judicial involvement in the investigation, there is minimal judicial supervision of the investigation.

The shift of control over the case from the "investigating judge" to what I term the "investigating police" has several implications. While conserving judicial resources, it enables the investigation to remain entirely in the hands of the state.[53]

Yet the shift is problematic because to some extent the rules governing the investigatory stage are predicated on at least some minimum judicial supervisory role in the investigation. Further, because the inquisitorial system relies on the written dossier, which is the product of the investigatory stage, police control over the investigation substantially limits the direction of the judicial inquiry. The statist model I describe allows a collusion between the police and the judiciary[54] in a merging of roles as they team up against the accused.

The merging of what I term the "investigating police" with the "investigating judge" expresses values about the proper methods and sources of state fact-finding and state truths. Norms about truth are also expressed in the variety of judicial roles in the case. Even though the judge may have initiated the case in her accusatorial role, the inquisitorial judge picks up where the accusing judge left off, and goes on to control the investigation. Finally, the same judge puts on her adjudicatory hat to determine the defendant's guilt or innocence.[55]

*The Hampered Defense.* In a system where the state controls the investigation, the suspect is *incommunicado*, and the proceedings secret, there can be no meaningful defense.[56] Secrecy in the proceedings means the suspect cannot see the evidence in her own case, nor may she challenge or confront the witnesses against her. Where the proceedings are secret, the suspect's "right" to representation begins and ends at the hearings before the judge.[57]

At the judicial hearing the suspect may have a defense attorney. Yet the right seems utterly academic, as counsel very often will not even know the charges against her client. Furthermore, neither the suspect nor her lawyer has any right of access to the file.[58] The judge controls the contents of the record.[59] During the judicial inquiry, neither the suspect nor her attorney can make arguments,[60] and the judge determines the questions for the suspect.[61] In practice, most suspects become defendants. Though probable cause must be shown to move from the investigation to the trial stage, this judicial decision is not appealable and is usually met by the pretrial detention decree.[62]

## III.
## Conclusion

The statist model I describe above expresses the parameters of permitted state coercive action against its citizens. From the perspective of the criminal justice system, the paradigm raises serious questions about fairness to the accused. But my thesis is that the paradigm of the *incommunicado* suspect expresses values outside of the criminal justice system.[63]

In 1991, for the first time in a century, the criminal process I have described underwent serious scrutiny and some reform. The reform efforts have centered on the trial stage, and more particularly on the publicity of the trial. This focus is exemplified by the holding of the first public trial in Argentina -- the trial of the military commanders.[64] This development is vital. Nevertheless, to effect more substantive change in their criminal justice system Argentines must consider and contest the abuses in the earlier and somewhat hidden investigation stage of the criminal case. Such reform is important not simply to advance the goals of the criminal justice system, but to protect the entire democratic process. Indeed, it is unfortunately a short road from *incommunicado* to *desaparecido*.

# Notes

[1]*See* COMISIÓN NACIONAL SOBRE LA DESAPARICIÓN DE PERSONAS, NUNCA MAS: INFORME DE LA COMISIÓN NACIONAL SOBRE LA DESAPARICIÓN DE PERSONAS (1985) [NEVER AGAIN: THE REPORT OF THE ARGENTINE NATIONAL COMMISSION ON THE DISAPPEARED] [hereinafter NUNCA MAS].

[2]*See* CLARIN (Buenos Aires, Arg. newspaper), Aug. 31, 1990, at 27 [hereinafter CLARIN] (many articles in CLARIN have no title or author listed).

[3]*See* NUNCA MAS, *supra* note 1.

[4]*See* CLARIN, *supra* note 2.

[5]This number accounted for approximately one-fourth of all homicides committed in Argentina during that year.

[6]*See Americas Watch & Centro de Estudios Legales y Sociales, Police Violence in Argentina: Torture and Police Killings in Buenos Aires* 13, 20 (1991) [hereinafter AMERICAS WATCH & CELS] (study of police violence in Argentina between 1983-1991, conducted by Americas Watch and Centro de Estudios Legales y Sociales (CELS), a prominent Argentine human rights group).

[7]U.S. DEPARTMENT OF STATE, COUNTRY REPORTS ON HUMAN RIGHTS PRACTICES FOR 1990, at 492 (1991) ("Informed observers believe that police routinely shoot to kill without cause.").

[8]*See* AMERICAS WATCH & CELS, *supra* note 6, at 11-18.

[9]*Id.* at 17. In 1990, police killings constituted fifteen percent of all homicides. *Id.* at 14. For 1984, the number of police killings accounted for about twenty-three percent of all homicides. *Id.* at 13.

[10]I presented a shorter version of the thesis I propose in this paper at the Center for Comparative Institutional Studies in Buenos Aires, Argentina. Ruti Teitel, Military Crimes and Inquisitorial Criminal Process (Dec. 13, 1990) (unpublished manuscript on file with Ruti Teitel).

[11]*See* Jaime Malamud-Goti, *Punishment and a Rights-Based Democracy*, 10 CRIM. JUST. ETHICS 3 (1991); Emelio F. Mignone, *Boomerang, in* AMERICAS WATCH & CELS, *supra* note 6, at 10.

[12]This is particularly the case in Argentina for its entire national history. *See* Aldo C. Vacs, *Authoritarian Breakdown and Redemocratization in Argentina, in* AUTHORITARIANS AND DEMOCRATS - REGIME TRANSITION IN LATIN AMERICA 15-16 (1987).

[13]My focus is on Latin America.

[14]*See supra* notes 6, 9, 11, 12 and accompanying text. There is a connection between the expression of these norms in the criminal process and unlawful actions of the state, including state crimes and violations of human rights. There is also a historic connection between particular criminal procedure and the prosecution of crimes associated with the police state.

[15]*See, e.g.,* Herbert L. Packer, THE LIMITS OF THE CRIMINAL SANCTION (1968); John Griffiths, *Ideology in Criminal Procedure or a Third "Model" of the Criminal Process,* 79 YALE L.J. 359 (1970).

[16]*See, e.g.* Herbert L. Packer, *Two Models of the Criminal Process,* 113 U. PA. L. REV. 1 (1964) (proposing that the shape of the criminal process has an important bearing on questions about the wise substantive use of the criminal sanction).

[17]*See id.*

[18]Griffiths, *supra* note 15. According to Griffiths' proposed family model, the criminal is seen as an insider; to that extent Griffiths conceives of criminal justice as an isolated part of society.

[19]*See generally,* Packer, *supra* note 15, at 154; Griffiths, *supra* note 15, at 365-66.

[20]*See* George P. Fletcher, *Constitutional Identity,* 14 CARDOZO L. REV. (forthcoming 1993); George P. Fletcher, *Lawmaking as an Expression of Self,* 13 N. KY. L. REV. 201, 205 (1986).

[21]MIRJAN R. DAMASKA, THE FACES OF JUSTICE AND STATE AUTHORITY 10-15, 71-96 (1986).

[22]Mirjan R. Damaska, *Evidentiary Barriers to Conviction and Two Models of Criminal Procedure: A Comparative Study,* 121 U. PA. L. REV. 506 (1973).

[23]*Id.* at 487; Mirjan R. Damaska, *Structures of Authority and Comparative Procedure,* 84 YALE L.J. 480, 532 (1975).

[24]*See generally,* Damaska, *supra* note 22, at 583; Fletcher, *supra* note 20, at 737-38.

[25]*See* JULIO B. MAIER, DERECHO PROCESAL PENAL ARGENTINO 1A (1989).

[26]In my discussion of the prevailing system of criminal process, I will refer to the *Código de Procedimiento en Materia Penal de la Nación* (Argentina's Federal Code of Criminal Procedure). It is worthy to note that some of the Argentine state codes, such as that of the Province of Cordoba, have better individual rights protection than the federal code. Where relevant, I refer to constitutional and other case law. Given the propensity for deviation from prescribed procedure, the text can only be understood as a minimum standard where individual rights violations are concerned. The text is therefore an important threshold for analysis.

[27]CÓD. PROC. PEN. art. 179(4) (a judge on her own motion may have a suspect arrested) (Arg.).

[28]*Id.* art. 3.

[29]*Id.* art. 4. The rules of criminal procedure conflict with article 18 of Argentina's Constitution which requires a written order by a competent authority prior to arrest. *See* CONST. ARG. art. 18.

[30]The practice is to notify the judge by telegram. (Author's interview of Alejandro Carrio, Buenos Aires, Arg., Dec. 1990) (transcribed telephone conversation, on file with Ruti Teitel [hereinafter Carrio]. Though article 326 of the Argentine Federal Code of Criminal Procedure contemplates declarations before the judge, in practice the judge is notified by telegram while police conduct their investigations. *See* CÓD. PROC. PEN. art. 184(8) (Arg.).

[31]The Federal Code of Criminal Procedure says six days. *See* CÓD. PROC. PEN. art. 256, 257 (Arg.). For a discussion of pretrial detention under Continental law, see Abraham S. Goldstein & Martin Marcus, *The Myth of Judicial Supervision in Three Inquisitorial Systems: France, Italy, and Germany,* 87 YALE L. J. 240, 254 n.34 (1977).

[32]*See* CÓD. PROC. PEN. arts. 184(10), 256, 257 (Arg.).

[33]*Habeas* actions have not been helpful in challenges to arrest. Argentina's Supreme Court has been reluctant to intervene. There has been similar judicial review regarding searches and seizures where the Court has abdicated oversight over warrantless searches without a need to show exigent circumstances. *See* CÓD. PROC. PEN. art. 4 (Arg.).

[34]*See* CÓD. PROC. PEN. art. 1197 (allowing the judge to rely on the police investigation) (Arg.). Commentators have suggested that as a practical matter at this point in the investigation, it is difficult for the judge to discern if there was probable cause at the time of the initiation of the case. The dossier of the case constitutes the police file, which is formally validated after the fact. *See* CÓD. PROC. PEN. arts. 236, 365 (Arg.). *See also* Carrio, *supra* note 30, at 46.

[35]*See* CÓD. PROC. PEN. arts. 236, 255 (Arg.).

[36]*See* CÓD. PROC. PEN. art. 379(6) (Arg.). As a practical matter there are no possible challenges to incarceration. The right of bail is completely in the hands of the state as the right is absolutely contingent on the seriousness of the charges. There has been little judicial supervision in this area, reflecting a tolerance for extended pretrial incarceration. *See* MAIER, *supra* note 25. *See also* Todres, 280 Fallos 297 (1971) (the Argentine Supreme Court reversed a finding of the court of appeals regarding a right to bail and upheld a "societal right" to prevent the escape of defendants charged with serious crimes).

[37]Until recently this period could extend for up to eight days. *See* CÓD. PROC. PEN. arts. 184(10), 256, 257 (Arg.). ALEJANDRO J. CARRIO, THE CRIMINAL JUSTICE SYSTEM OF ARGENTINA 54-55 (1989). There is no possibility of appeal from the *incommunicado* determination. Following reforms during the first period of civilian rule after the military period, the *incommunicado* period was limited to six days. *See* CÓD. PROC. PEN. art. 257 (Arg.). In reforms which have been enacted during the writing of this article, the period has been further reduced, but these reforms have not yet taken effect.

[38]*See* CARRIO, *supra* note 37, at 55.

[39]*Id.*

[40]*See* CÓD. PROC. PEN. art. 180 (Arg.).

[41]To renew the period requires a showing of necessity. *See* CÓD. PROC. PEN. art. 180 (Arg.).

[42]Argentina's constitution at article 18 states "nobody shall be compelled to testify against himself." ARG. CONST. art. 18. *See also* MAIER, *supra* note 25 (on the early Argentine history regarding the privilege, and discussing the former obligation to disclose).

[43]*See* Miranda v. Arizona, 384 U.S. 436 (1966) (proposing that there is a presumption of coercion in such instances).

[44]For examples of abdication of judicial review see Romano, 259 Fallos 69 (1964); Chamudis, 235 Fallos 332 (1956); Mansilla, 217 Fallos 1143 (1950) (rejecting defendant's claim of duress).

[45]*See* CÓD. PROC. PEN. art. 316 §7 (Arg.). Under the code, petitions for exclusion can only be brought up very late in the case, at the time of adjudication of guilt. In a recent decision, the Supreme Court limited the effect of exclusion, thus encouraging the police to obtain unlawful confessions. *See* Ruiz, CSJN, R. 424 XXJA, (Sept. 17, 1987) (limiting the exclusionary impact of unlawfully obtained confession to charges not otherwise supported by independent sources).

[46]It is only in a recent case that the Supreme Court held torture during the police interrogation to be unlawful. *See* Montenegro, 303 Fallos 1938, 1941 (1982).

[47]Interview with Jaime Malamud-Goti regarding forty allegations of torture from December 1981 - April 1982, reported at the Palace of Justice. "Illegal coercion" (in Spanish *apremios ilegales*) is a lesser charge than torture. All of the 698 cases initiated between 1984 and 1986 resulted in dismissals. *See* PAGINA 12 (Buenos Aires, Arg. newspaper) [hereinafter PAGINA 12] Oct. 26, 1991. For a discussion of the charges in 698 cases of illegal coercion see CLARIN, *supra* note 2, Oct. 26, 1991, at 9.

[48]*Id.*, Oct. 28, 1991, at 32-34.

[49]*Id.*

[50]*Id.*, Oct. 26, 1991, at 10 (discussing survey). *See also* PAGINA 12, *supra* note 47, at 10.

[51]*See* CÓD. PROC. PEN. art. 184 (Arg.); *See also* Carrio, *supra* note 30, at 30-37.

[52]Goldstein & Marcus, *supra* note 31, at 262. According to Goldstein and Marcus, in the average European case there is no actual pretrial investigation by a judge; instead the power of investigation is entirely in the hands of the police. Germany eliminated its examining judge; in Italy, judicial investigation occurs only in the most serious cases.

[53]*Id.* at 257. Goldstein and Marcus conclude judicial supervision of pretrial investigation in continental practice is a "myth." In the Argentine system, there is no separation of powers between the prosecutorial and the judicial branches.

[54]An example is the evaluation of the practice of telephone and telegram notice. The direction of the collusion seems to be a function of the size of the judiciary as compared to the police.

[55]The accusing judge's discretion to rule on defendant's guilt epitomizes absolute governmental control over the criminal case. Compare the accusatorial model with two different juries -- one for the accusation stage and the other for the fact-finding stage. *See* Pfeifer and Plankl v. Austria, 14 EUR. H.R. REP. 692 (1992) (barring use of the same prosecutor in pretrial and trial stages; construing European Convention of Human Rights section regarding right to be adjudicated by an impartial court).

[56]*See* Carrio, *supra* note 30, at 75.

[57]Antonio, 236 Fallos C.S.N. 657 (1956).

[58]If a suspect's family calls a lawyer, the lawyer finds his client by deducing which judge has been assigned to him. Where the charges are secret, counsel is simply not in a position to challenge an incarceration until long after the arrest.

[59]*See* Carrio, *supra* note 30, at 60.

[60]CÓD. PROC. PEN. art. 180 (Arg.); Carrio, *supra* note 30, at 74.

[61]CÓD. PROC. PEN. art. 198 (Arg.); Carrio, *supra* note 30, at 69.

[62]The courts defer to the police in the determination of whether to release a suspect at the stage of entering a pretrial detention decree.

[63]In developing this thesis in a larger work in progress, I discuss various norms about (1) the power balance between the state and its citizens; (2) secrecy and related truth; and (3) the impact and relation of (1) and (2) on notions of justice and the rule of law.

[64]*See Judicial Proceedings Against Jorge R. Videla et al.*, *in* 5513 REVISTA DE JURISPRUDENCIA ARGENTINA (1987) (originally brought before the Supreme Council of the Armed Forces pursuant to Decree 158 of December 13, 1983). *See* Alejandro M. Garro & Henry Dahl, *Legal Accountability for Human Rights Violations in Argentina: One Step Forward and Two Steps Backward,* 8 HUM. RTS. L.J. 283, 340 (1987).

# 11

## The Latin American Reformer's Stake in U.S. Human Rights Policy

### Jonathan Miller

This chapter focuses on the role of the United States in influencing some of the procedural reforms suggested in other chapters in this section. It argues that lurking behind all of the arguments about these reforms is a democratic transition process profoundly influenced by the United States, even in discrete areas such as procedural reforms, and that the success of such reforms in Latin America depends at least in part on how the United States participates in the process.

Most early Latin American constitutionalism relied heavily on the United States Constitution as a model,[1] sometimes with some benefits, but often with tragi-comic results in cases where countries simply ignored those paragraphs of their constitutions that made no sense in their domestic context -- usually those dealing with states' rights and limitations on the Executive Branch.[2] In the area of criminal procedure, for example, the Argentine Constitution of 1860, which relied so heavily on the United States Constitution that many Argentine publicists claimed that even United States case law should be binding in Argentina,[3] provides that Congress will provide for jury trials in criminal cases.[4] That provision is so unrelated to the Argentine context that, in over 120 years, the Argentine Congress has never instituted anything even remotely like a jury trial.

The process of reform that we see in Latin America today is somewhat different from the vision held by Latin America's nineteenth century liberals. After the forceful attacks on the United States model by the Mexican Revolution and Peronist Argentina, no Latin American liberal can possibly point to United States constitutionalism and United States civil liberties law as a panacea.[5] No mainstream politician today can openly argue for copying the United States. I would argue, however, that Latin American intellectuals have found an alternative guide and objective in international human rights law.

Latin American legal reformers today derive a substantial portion of their authority from international human rights law. That dependency, however, also creates a paradox. For although Latin America no longer blindly follows the United States constitutional model, the prestige and clout of the international human rights movement in Latin America depends in large part on the United States' participation. Thus, the success of Latin American legal reformers will depend at least in part on the United States' attitudes toward international human rights law. To put it another way, Latin American reformers have escaped slavish adherence to American constitutionalism, but their alternative model still leaves them partially dependent on the United States.

Local traditions in most Latin American nations do a poor job of cultivating procedural rights. The procedural reforms proposed by commentators legitimate themselves through universal, humanist values with only weak local roots.[6] Their humanist values derive their political potency from the fact that they cross national frontiers. Rights abuses by police and court officials are built into the procedural system, yet rarely result in widespread protests. What protests there are invariably come from human rights groups and intellectuals who have been nurtured on international human rights law.[7] Some commentators rightly note that Latin America's authoritarian traditions and inquisitorial procedural systems have been mutually reinforcing.[8] It is international human rights law that offers a foundation for activists challenging that tradition. Reformers will not always make their international links explicit, and they will not necessarily cite treaty provisions and United Nations resolutions in their arguments, but they do seek funding from foreign foundations and depend on perceptions that the rights they advocate receive international support.[9]

A comparison of the success and future prospects of the American Convention on Human Rights[10] and the European Convention for the Protection of Human Rights and Fundamental Freedoms[11] illustrates why this internationalist approach also involves some dependence on events in the United States. In the process of enforcing the European Convention for the Protection of Human Rights, the European Court of Human Rights has developed case law on many of the procedural questions that affect the inquisitorial process. To recount just a few criminal procedure precedents with obvious application in procedural systems retaining inquisitorial elements, the European Court has ruled against criminal convictions based on statements by anonymous witnesses to the police or examining magistrates;[12] has ruled that an appeals court with the power to review facts de novo must hear the live testimony of the accused and his witnesses and cannot merely rely on the lower court's dossier;[13] and has ruled that individuals once involved in a case as public prosecutors and investigating magistrates are thereafter barred from involvement in the case as trial judges.[14]  Moreover, the European Court has emphasized that excessive delays violate the Convention whatever the type of proceedings.[15]

Enforcement of the American Convention on Human Rights is still in its infancy, but the rights established in that Convention are similar to those developed in Europe.  The American Convention specifically provides, among other rights, for such rights as the right to a hearing within a reasonable time in both civil and criminal cases,[16] the right to be brought promptly before a judge upon detention,[17] the right to legal counsel of the defendant's choice,[18] and the right to confront witnesses.[19]  Furthermore, the Inter-American Court of Human Rights, which under the Convention has the authority to hand down both monetary and injunctive relief in an action against a state, has emphasized from its very first contentious case the need for effective domestic remedies.[20]  It has also emphasized the duty of the State to undertake a serious investigation when rights are violated, to identify and punish those responsible, and to ensure the victim adequate compensation.[21]

However, while the Inter-American system offers modern day reformers a source of positive authority unavailable to previous generations, the degree to which the Inter-American system will be regarded as persuasive authority depends at least in part on the United States.  It is doubtful whether the Inter-American system can ever approach the success of the European system without much more active participation by the United States.[22] European states respond to the decisions of international tribunals in substantial part because they have cast their lot with European integration generally, and do not want to suffer the broad detrimental effects that characterization as a human rights violator would impose.  One of the lessons of the success of the European human rights system has been the existence of a close relationship between integration in the human rights arena on the one hand, and economic integration and general regional stability on the other.  Relations between Great Britain and Ireland are reasonably friendly today in part because decisions of the European Court of Human Rights, enforcing legal and moral standards which these two states have agreed upon together with the rest of Western Europe, have provided a neutral evaluation of police and prosecutorial conduct against IRA terrorists in Northern Ireland[23] -- an issue which domestic politics in both countries could easily have inflamed into serious confrontation. Similarly, it is highly unlikely Greece could have ever joined the European Economic Community (EEC) without eliminating its military government and rejoining the European human rights system, and Spain under Franco was clearly ineligible for membership.  Further, even aside from the contribution that the protection of human rights makes towards regional stability,

extensive economic integration is simply impossible without common minimum standards on issues such as labor rights, freedom of movement, prison
labor, protection of property and free speech -- issues which directly affect
the price of labor and capital and the flow of goods.[24] Repression of labor
allows artificially low wages, restrictions on freedom of movement within
a country distorts the labor market, and free speech is needed to allow labor
to organize and manufacturers to promote their goods.[25]

For better or for worse, the United States is the country the other nations
of the Americas most respond to, whether on economic issues or in the area
of human rights. To the extent that Latin American nations ceding part of
their sovereignty to international human rights tribunals expect international
dividends, those dividends are paid primarily by the United States. Just as
European nations abide by the European Convention to better reap the fruits
of European integration both in the human rights field and other areas, Latin
American nations are most concerned about how their human rights record
plays in the United States. The United States is far more significant to each
Latin American country then any third country as a trading partner, source
of foreign investment, and political ally or nemesis. This political fact may
condemn the Inter-American human rights system to mediocrity and hinder
the reform process in Latin America. Indeed, the United States still has not
ratified the American Convention on Human Rights and has ignored decisions of the Inter-American Commission on Human Rights regarding the
death penalty for minors.[26] To the extent that the United States finds itself
unable to accept international human rights obligations, it also finds itself
crippled in its ability to influence human rights developments. Certainly the
United States may offer help through technical assistance programs, such as
AID's Program for the Administration of Justice, and through private grants
funding human rights groups, conferences and research, but the importance
of these initiatives is minimal compared with the need for active United
States integration into the Inter-American system. While the United States
may support the Inter-American human rights system without full participation as a party to the American Convention on Human Rights -- cheering
from the sidelines so to speak -- any kind of pressure by the United States
on other countries to comply with the system will provoke charges of
hypocrisy. Without active United States participation in the Inter-American
system the incentives for compliance for the rest of the hemisphere are so
weakened that the long-term viability of the system is harmed and with it
part of the legitimacy enjoyed by domestic Latin American reformers.

Furthermore, while the United States government may occasionally intervene to halt massive human rights abuses, it lacks the ability to intervene
directly in the case of lesser violations. Section 502B of the Foreign
Assistance Act of 1961[27] provides for a cut-off of security assistance to

countries whose governments engage in a "consistent pattern of gross violations of internationally recognized human rights," and Section 116b provides
for a similar general cut-off of economic assistance.[28]  But it is difficult for
the United States to intervene in lesser violations.  It is politically untenable,
for example, for the United States government to apply significant diplomatic pressure on a country because it fails to provide a lawyer for indigent
criminal defendants, because its criminal proceedings take too long, or
because its police engage in intrusive searches and seizures.[29]  That kind
of intervention can only effectively occur through international human rights
tribunals, such as the Inter-American Commission and Court of Human
Rights.

This chapter does not argue that procedural reform in Latin America is
condemned to failure if the United States does not ratify the American
Convention on Human Rights.  That would be a bit extremist, first, because
there are a number of other factors, such as natural solidarity between
newly emerging democracies, which bind the Inter-American system
together in the absence of United States participation, and second, because
the Inter-American system is not the only source of human rights authority
around.  However, broadly speaking, United States funding, ideological
support and governmental participation are vital to Latin American attitudes
toward international human rights law.  Just as the effectiveness of
hemispheric economic integration increases dramatically with United States
involvement, the effectiveness of human rights integration requires United
States involvement.

We are therefore left with a strange quandary.  Many scholars and states-
men have indicated some of the guarantees which they believe must be
provided by a fair procedural system.  Moreover, they speak with authority
because they invoke guarantees which are protected on an international
basis.  However, the most significant factor for stopping human rights
abuses and encouraging reforms -- the active participation of the United
States -- remains outside the process.  The United States is certainly taking
some initial steps to integrate itself into the international human rights
movement -- perhaps the most significant being its recent ratification of the
International Covenant on Civil and Political Rights (and in a condition
which leaves at least some of the articles without major reservations).[30]
But the basic quandary remains.  The roots of any human rights model in
most Latin American countries ultimately lies in the international nature of
human rights law, but the effectiveness of international human rights law in
Latin America, and with it much of the effectiveness of Latin American
reformers, depends on United States participation.

Thus, in answer to the question of what can be done to devise efficient
procedural systems in Latin America which adequately protect due process,

at least part of the answer has to be that the United States participate in international and regional commitments for the protection of human rights so that countries with more politically pressing concerns than procedural rights on their agenda find that more than procedural rights are at stake when these rights are violated. This may seem patronizing, but human rights concerns cannot be isolated from the political realities of the hemisphere.

# Notes

[1]*See* JACQUES LAMBERT, LATIN AMERICA: SOCIAL STRUCTURE AND POLITICAL INSTITUTIONS 267-68 (1967); Robert S. Barker, *Constitutionalism in the Americas*, 49 U. PITT. L. Rev. 891, 894-900 (1988). On Argentina, see AMADEO P. SANTOS, ARGENTINE CONSTITUTIONAL LAW 3-47 (1943).

[2]The classic Argentine work describing the gap between constitutional theory and practice on federalism and on limits on the powers of the Executive in the late nineteenth and early twentieth century is JOSE N. MATIENZO, EL GOBIERNO REPRESENTATIVE FEDERAL EN LA REPUBLICA ARGENTINA 208-11, 225-26, 312-13 (1910).

[3]*See, e.g.,* DOMINGO F. SARMIENTO, COMENTARIOS DE LA CONSTITUCION DE LA CONFEDERACION ARGENTINA 29 (Santiago, Imprenta de Julio Berlin, 1st ed., 1853). For a time this was also the doctrine of the Argentine Supreme Court. De la Torre, 19 Fallos 231 (1877).

[4]CONST. ARG. art. 24.

[5]These events were obviously not reactions to United States constitutionalism. Nevertheless, the rhetoric of these movements in denouncing United States political and economic influence and emphasizing a social view of property, made reference to the United States as an ideal model for Latin America inappropriate.

[6]Perhaps the clearest example of this may be found in procedural reforms presently underway in El Salvador. This author had the opportunity to observe this process first hand on a trip to El Salvador from May 18-30, 1992, to teach a course for prosecutors and public defenders organized by the United States Agency for International Development (hereafter, USAID). USAID is presently funding the Judicial Reform Project of the Ministry of Justice of El Salvador. This project, which relies heavily on foreign advisors and Salvadorans who have studied abroad, has often emphasized the need to bring El Salvador's criminal procedures into line with international standards. For example, the preambles to two key procedural reforms submitted to El Salvador's Congress, one limiting the use of out of court confessions and the second shortening the period of administrative detentions by the police, both indicate the need to bring El Salvador's law into line with international human rights law. Ministerio de Justicia (El Salvador), *Proyecto Reforma Judicial, Componente I: Apoyo Técnico Para Reforma Judicial*, LA CONFESIÓN EXTRAJUDI-CIAL, Appendix (March 6, 1992) (unpublished manuscript on file with the author);

Ministerio de Justicia (El Salvador), *Proyecto Reforma Judicial, Componente I: Apoyo Técnico Para Reforma Judicial,* LA DETENCIÓN ADMINISTRATIVA, Appendix (March 6, 1992) (unpublished manuscript on file with the author). *See also* Victor Hugo Mata Tobar, *El Problema de la Administración de Justicia en Centroamérica y Su Incidencia en al Observancia de los Derechos Humanos,* REVISTA DE CIENCIA JURIDICAS, 1992, at 61, 65-66.

[7]In the United States, large grass-roots civil liberties organizations like the American Civil Liberties Union (ACLU) and the National Association for the Advancement of Colored People (NAACP) only rarely cite international human rights law as a justification for their positions and almost never look abroad for support in trying to end human rights abuses in the United States. By contrast, large membership human rights organizations simply do not exist in Latin America. Instead, human rights work is performed by small groups of activists with strong links to United States organizations like Americas Watch, the Washington Office on Latin America, and the Lawyers Committee for Human Rights. These United States organizations provide their Latin American counterparts with connections to sources of funding, provide assistance in lodging complaints before international organizations, generate international publicity and send fact-finding missions which demonstrate their support.

[8]Ruti Teitel, *Persecution and Inquisition: A Case Study, in* THE TRANSITION TO DEMOCRACY IN LATIN AMERICA: THE ROLE OF THE JUDICIARY 141 (Irwin P. Stotzky ed., 1993).

[9]There are many examples of Latin American human rights groups receiving vital funding from the United States and Europe. Perhaps the most striking is the case of the Center for Legal and Social Studies (CELS), one of the most prominent Argentine human rights groups publicly combating the abuses of Argentina's last military government. As described in IAIN GUEST, BEHIND THE DISAPPEARANCES: ARGENTINA'S DIRTY WAR AGAINST HUMAN RIGHTS AND THE UNITED NATIONS 213-214, n.19 (1990), the impetus for the creation of CELS came from Leonard Meeker, the director of a Washington, D.C. public interest law firm called the Center for Law and Social Policy, and was initially funded with a $40,000 grant from the USAID. When the Reagan Administration came to power and stopped further funding, CELS turned to the Ford Foundation as its principal source of grant support.

There are likewise many examples of international research projects and conferences offering essential legitimacy for the efforts of Latin American human rights reformers. This book and the conference on which it is based is a typical example.

[10]O.A.S. OFF. REC. OEA/ser. L/V/11.23, doc. 21 rev. 6 (1979), *entered into force* July 18, 1978.

[11]213 U.N.T.S. 222 (1950), *entered into force* Sept. 3, 1953.

[12]Windisch v. Austria, Series A, No. 186, Sept. 27, 1990, 13 EHRR 281 (statements made to the police); Kostovski v. Netherlands, Series A, No. 166, November 20, 1989, 12 EHRR 434 (statements made to police and examining magistrate, but not to trial court).

[13]Ekbatani v. Sweden, Series A, No. 134, May 26, 1988, 13 EHRR 504.

[14]Piersack v. Belgium, Series A, vol. 99, Judgment of May 29, 1986, 5 EHRR 169 (later participation by prosecutor); DeCubber v. Belgium, Series A, Volume 86, Judgment of October 21, 1984, 7 EHRR 236 (later participation by investigative magistrate).

[15]*E.g.*, Moreira de Azevedo v. Portugal, Series A, No. 189, October 23, 1990, 13 EHRR 721 (nine year delay in concluding criminal proceeding ); Martins Moreira v. Portugal, Series A, No. 133, October 26, 1988, 13 EHRR 517 (nine year delay in civil action regarding injuries from a traffic accident); Neves e Silva v. Portugal, Series A, No. 153, April 27, 1989, 13 EHRR 535 (delay of over six years before a decision was issued by an administrative court of first instance); Obermeier v. Austria, Series A, No. 179, June 28, 1990, 13 EHRR 290 (nine year delay in action by employee for wrongful termination).

[16]American Convention on Human Rights art. 8.1.

[17]*Id.* art. 7.5.

[18]*Id.* art. 8.2(d).

[19]*Id.* art. 8.2(f).

[20]Velasquez Rodriguez Case, Inter-Am. C.H.R., OEA/ser. C, No. 4., para. 64 (1988).

[21]*Id.* at para. 174.

[22]As a practical matter, governments have frequently ignored requests for information by the Inter-American Commission on Human Rights. Judith K. Furukawa, Comment, *The Death of Dr. Hugo Spadafora: Human Rights Investigative Responsibility is Past Due*, 4 AM. U. J. INT'L L. & POL'Y 377, 387-389 (1989).

[23]Ireland v. United Kingdom, 25 Eur. Ct. H.R. (ser. A) (1979).

[24]*See* Terry Collingsworth, *American Labor Policy and the International Economy: Clarifying Policies and Interests*, 31 B.C. L. REV. 31, 33-34, 45-55 (1989).

[25]In fact links could probably even be drawn between such issues as police repression and the flow of capital. To the extent that income redistribution with higher tax burdens on the owners of capital alleviates social unrest and the "need" for police repression, a decision to keep taxes low to attract foreign investment also implies a decision not to engage in social policy to eliminate the root causes of crime and unrest.

[26]Case 9647, Inter-Am. C.H.R. 147, OEA/ser.L/V./11.71, doc. 9 rev. 1 (1987).

[27]22 U.S.C. § 2304 (1988).

[28]22 U.S.C. § 2151n (1988).

[29]It may be argued that these rights do not even qualify as rights protected under customary international law. They are not listed in the rights included in the Restatement. RESTATEMENT (THIRD) OF THE FOREIGN RELATIONS LAW OF THE UNITED STATES § 702 (1987).

[30]The Resolution of Ratification passed the Senate on April 2, 1992, and the instrument of ratification was signed by the President on June 5, 1992. The text of the Resolution of Ratification may be found in S. REP. NO. 23, 102d Cong., 2d Sess. 21-24 (1992).

# 12

## Some Thoughts on Institutional Structures in the Judicial Process

### *Marcela Rodriguez*

### Introduction

The purpose of this chapter is to attack a caricature of legal theory that has for too long dominated the profession.[1] The caricature suggests that law is impersonal, objective, in the strong sense that its procedures conform to an external truth and that there are correct answers to legal questions because there is an all-encompassing principle for dispute resolution. Moreover, it is claimed that these factors constitute a constraint on judges sufficient to bar their use of personal, political, or policy preferences in the resolution of cases. This mask of neutrality, I argue, is a myth that is used to justify the domination of the powerless by the powerful.

Part I criticizes an assumption underlying the views of important commentators on the judicial process concerning issues of neutrality and impartiality in judicial decision-making. Part II addresses the use of alternative modes of conflict resolution. Part III puts forward a different perspective on the jury trial, one concerned with democratizing the administration of justice and incorporating powerless voices, in particular women's voices, into its processes.

### I.
### Neutrality and Impartiality

Law is a prototype of authoritative discourse. It is a system of power through which meanings are both constructed and reflected. It frames and systematizes cultural practices. Law uses concepts, categories, terms, and a reasoning structure through which it reveals itself, establishes its operations, and constructs its meanings. Law goes beyond merely illustrating thoughts and conceptions. In this sense, law has a special and effective power to mold popular perceptions of social and political conditions. It constructs and reinforces particular world views and understandings. As a result, law is capable of empowering certain voices and perspectives and of silencing others.

In order to appear as a fair method of resolving competing claims, the law poses as a system of universal, objective, and neutral rules. This pretense of neutrality impedes the discussion of how values, structures, and institutions have been constructed. It also conceals the fact that law is a systematic and systemic institutional arrangement of power and domination.

Moreover, substantive norms are presented as independent of procedural rules. Procedure purportedly serves a merely instrumental function. Its role is to ensure efficient and neutral dispute resolution by aiding investigation and application of the substantive rules. According to this conception, procedure is both litigant-neutral and substance-neutral. The ideal of procedural neutrality is paralleled by a vision of judges as impartial arbiters, applying substantive rules to the facts presented by the parties' attorneys.

The traditional theoretical conception of procedure considers the individual's participation in the settlement of private disputes. This conception deepens the split between procedure and substance. It embodies the ideal that the application of uniform and facially neutral procedures is the proper way to guarantee justice. This divorce between substance and procedure and the presumption that these "neutral" procedures are fair, have resulted in the slighting of questions concerning legal outcomes and their social consequences in the domain of substantive law.

Procedure is not, however, value free. In creating or reforming a procedural system, many competing viewpoints must be considered. These viewpoints are not only related to specific procedural rules, they are also concerned with substantive questions and the elemental goals of judicial adjudication. These conceptions frame determinations of the system's scope and adequacy, including its allotment of costs and benefits, which result in the particular structure, methodology, and arrangement of the judicial institution. The procedural dimensions of this arrangement have a significant impact on the substantive order.

This traditional theory of procedure has been challenged by many scholars who have observed that uniform rules of procedure are neither inherently substance-neutral nor litigant-neutral in practice.[2] Accordingly, they have questioned the distinction between substance and procedure, since procedural rules and substantive outcomes are so closely linked. In order to evaluate the operation of a procedural system, it is important to inquire into the question of who makes the rules and who applies them, as well as who gains or loses when they are applied to factual circumstances, both in terms of specific cases and group consequences.

The classical view of the judicial role assumes that judges do not have any personal interest in the cases they decide.[3] Their disengagement and neutrality is considered central to fair adjudication. In this view, judges must be impartial and independent individuals who are neutrally situated in relation to both sides of cases, and will then adjudicate them fairly. Yet these theoretical assumptions of impartiality and neutrality face serious challenge in the current state of the law and the judicial system. The gap between theoretical pretensions and current practice is so large, that to insist on neutrality only stifles the more significant debate concerning the disparity between rhetoric and reality.

Feminism and other critical theories have attacked the idea that judges can adjudicate controversies from some Archimedean viewpoint. A judge, like anyone else, belongs to a particular gender, class, and race, and has a certain social position, religion, and ideology. Thus the appearance of neutrality and impartiality is just that, an appearance.

In this sense, it is obvious that gender-based bias has distorted the justice system. Women are, of course, the ones who suffer most from this distortion. Gender discrimination lies at the core of judicial administration. Eliminating discrimination is not just a question of using gender-neutral language or recognizing the changes in roles and lifestyles. Gender bias affects the very judicial system and its procedures. Taken seriously, sexual equality requires that the integrity of the entire judicial system be questioned.

The legal system and judicial interpretation -- in terms of reasoning, structure, and language -- have been constructed by taking into account only the life experiences of particular groups of dominant men, presenting them as universal patterns. The structure of law and the administration of justice have been framed in accordance with the experiences, values, and interests of this determinate group of males.

To talk about universal patterns and objective reasoning is simply male language. A few intellectually, economically, and politically privileged men form the powerful group that rules society, disregarding any other perspectives. As a result, they present their situation as reality and their point of view as an objective standard. This framework turns abstraction and universalization from a male perspective into the neutral and universal standard that rules the whole domain of the law and the administration or justice.

The institutional arrangements, including the administration of justice, adopts the male standpoint in the relationship it establishes between law and society. The judicial system sees women the way that *some* men see women. Nevertheless, gender has never been considered a relevant category for legal and judicial structures. Indeed, it is claimed that these structures have been framed specifically so as not to recognize such categories. In reality, however, these institutional structures have been designed in the interests of men as a gender, and they portray the male point of view on every issue.

The law fosters the dominance of men as a social group by empowering their perspective while presenting it under the norm of objectivity and neutrality. Neutrality is considered an essential characteristic of judicial decision-making. Judges are supposed to be impersonal and disinterested. Adjudication is considered to be governed by laws, not by the will of men. Judges are supposed to collect factual information and to be limited by the dominion of "neutral" rule-following.

The problem runs even deeper. The "objectivity" norm is the medium through which the legal and judicial systems are legitimated. This helps obscure the fact that these structures simply accept the prevailing social order. In this context, the role of the judiciary is not to impose its view-point on society, but simply to reflect that society. This objectivist stance in legal interpretation ultimately confirms that the law will strengthen the unequal allocation of power, since it both mirrors a social order dominated by males, and reinforces this unequal arrangement. Adjudication institu-tionalizes this "objectivity" norm. The assumption of judicial neutrality conceals the situation of the powerless groups in society. Their positions are simply abstracted into an established hierarchical distribution of power.

Judicial decision-making empowers some perspectives rather than others, but this fact is often concealed. Indeed, its pretended objective stance actually excludes different perspectives. Neutrality is, therefore, impossible when there are so many standpoints determined by gender, race, ethnicity, sexual orientation, social class, and personal experience. Furthermore, neutrality is impossible given a social reality in which discrimination and unequal distribution of power and resources are the norm.

## II.
## Alternative Modes of Conflict Resolution

Professor Raphael Bielsa has referred to the advantages of managerial judging and alternative dispute resolution systems.[4] Professor Julio Maier has proposed to incorporate the will of the parties as a crucial aspect of procedural reform.[5] He sees this as directly related to reaching agreement about the juridical meaning of their conduct, to creating consensual arrange-ments in order to resolve cases, and, on certain occasions, to determining the applicable punishment.

However, to provide judges with this kind of managerial capacity means granting them greater power without implementing sufficient controls in the application of their discretion. For judges to act as managers and mediators broadens the scope of judicial activity to many other issues beyond the mere adjudication of controversies. Managerial judges develop other activities related both to previous agreements between the litigants and to the stages following the resolution of the controversies. Their power extends beyond the trial and the dispute as it was presented by the parties. In this sense, judges are granted the power to shape the litigation and its final results.

This greater power is not accompanied by corresponding controls. Generally, the activities of managerial judges are outside of public control, and often they are not subject to appellate review. Alternative procedures expand judges' substantive power in a way that leaves them unaccountable, because of their imperceptibility and the lack of patterns to guide them.

Professor Bielsa addresses the necessity of re-tooling procedural rules in the name of systemic efficiency. He claims that managerial judges and alternative modes of dispute resolution reduce litigation costs, shorten the resolution of controversies, and encourage consensual settlements. However, this idea of formal efficiency does not take into account the social outcome resulting from these kinds of procedural reforms. Their presumed greater efficiency does not ensure their fairness. It does not necessarily create a more equal framework for the interests of the parties or for the rest of the society.

According to Professor Bielsa's argument, the efficient, economical, and accurate resolution of controversies is crucial to the legitimacy of judicial administration. However, the legitimacy of a judicial system is based primarily on its success in protecting and enforcing individual rights in a democratic society. In this sense, the administration of justice and the legal process are fundamental structures in the process of transition to democracy.

The implementation of alternative modes of dispute resolution does not contribute to this process, because it usually takes judicial decision-making away from public scrutiny. It closes a realm of public debate. Public litigation is an important part of the process of discussion and enforcement of social values. The litigation process is not merely designed to resolve individual controversies. Educative values develop through public litigation. Indeed, this litigation involves debate over diverse conceptions of justice and institutional arrangements. Thus, the litigation process is not the mere confrontation between individual interests -- it also has a social and political dimension.[6]

The democratization of a society is advanced when there is an open adjudicatory process and public debate over norms and processes of dispute resolution. The requirement that judges justify their opinions in an open manner, and the clearness of the rules that guide their behavior, are of the utmost importance for this process. In contrast, alternative dispute resolution and judges with broad managerial powers enlarge the domain of the judicial power in a contrary and, in my opinion, wrong direction.

Moreover, such procedural reforms may mean that minorities -- people who do not belong to the more powerful social and political groups, or those who most suffer from the lack of resources -- have more limited access to the judicial system. Even if they have access to the procedural reforms, the informality of the reforms leaves these people with little protection against discriminatory treatment from judges, arbiters, and mediators. The defense of minorities and powerless people will be undermined, since they will be more exposed to the hidden considerations and perspectives of decision-makers.

Furthermore, these kinds of judicial procedures substantially increase the difficulty of challenging and transforming current legal precepts and the resulting social distribution of power and resources. To put it another way, alternative modes of dispute resolution are often useful for the resolution of disputes presented within the context of unchallenged legal norms. But the proposed reforms simply do not facilitate challenges to the current social and political order, nor do they reallocate the unequal distribution of resources.

Other critical issues for Professor Bielsa's proposals, as well as Professor Maier's suggestions concerning the incorporation of consensual truth into the criminal system, are the social repercussions of translating current social and economic differences directly into the solution of the conflict. This system enhances existing inequalities. Professor Maier does, however, address this issue. He recognizes that equality before the law is undermined when some people commit a crime and are punished, while others, who commit the same crime, avoid punishment. This view relies on a broad conception of the principle of "material legality." "Material legality" precludes punishment where there was no prior law defining the action as punishable. In addition, it requires the state to prosecute every person suspected of committing a crime. Some people see "material legality" as the only way to guarantee equality before the law. Maier's response is that the principle of equality before the law requires only that the law not confer privileges upon, or arbitrarily discriminate against people based on race, religion, or other arbitrary distinctions. He states that this is not the case for the proposal he is suggesting. However, he recognizes that even though the law purportedly does not make arbitrary distinctions, and promises equal treatment for everyone, it is necessary to proceed cautiously; and he suggests that is necessary to provide assistance for disadvantaged people.

In response to Maier's position, it is important to consider this issue not in the abstract, but in structuring, adopting, implementing, and justifying a real and concrete criminal system. This is especially relevant to evaluating the legitimacy of the system in a context where the unequal distribution of power, resources, and social hierarchy have been the rule. Moreover, to find the appropriate meaning of "equality" involves a normative inquiry. Many legal scholars, of course, argue about the importance of the principle of equal citizenship, as well as that of equal respect and concern. Some even believe that the equal protection clause constitutionalizes equality.[7] This means that the equal protection clause confers constitutional protection to the ideal of equality. The equality clause is designed to guarantee that individuals are entitled to equal autonomy and respect as subjects of moral choice, capable of devising and pursuing their own life plans.

When social inequality is the rule, however, one cannot expect that the mere fact that a law does not discriminate explicitly on the basis of sex, race, religion, or other insidious distinctions ensures that it will guarantee equality before the law. There is no equality when some people face overwhelming impediments or when, as a result of a prior unequal distribution of advantages, some individuals end up with almost negligible chances of success. For this reason, the design of a legitimate system requires avoiding choices that severely limit the opportunities of particular individuals based solely on suspect classifications such as gender and race.

More specifically, a justice system framed without considering this fact will be unable to guarantee meaningful equality. The adoption of an abstract and formalistic conception of equality leaves the system unable to identify and provide answers to the needs of the disadvantaged. Because of this abstraction, the law is incapable of taking into account the diversity of people's situations and claims. A doctrine of formal equality cannot ensure real equality where social reality shows that individuals are not similarly situated. Men and women, for example, are differently situated with respect to numerous economic, political, and social circumstances. Thus, the interpretation of this fundamental constitutional standard under the traditionally accepted view of equality often not only does not contribute to the fulfillment of social and legal equality, but even fosters such inequality.

In order to achieve social equality and guarantee equal status and respect to all citizens, it is necessary to recognize that the identification of discriminatory rules and practices, and society's duty to guarantee substantive rights, is more complicated than traditionally conceived. To put it another way, in order to eradicate socially-caused initial disadvantages, it may be necessary to adopt an expanded idea of equality. Otherwise, social and legal equality will remain an elusive ideal.

Another critical point is that these procedural reform proposals assume that any resolution may be justified if the parties accede to it. However, in the present state of law, it is questionable to consider consent as a sufficient justification. Consent is viewed as the exercise of freedom of decision and choice. But this does not take into account the underlying conditions of inequality and disparity that the parties face. Freedom of choice requires fundamental social preconditions to its exercise. A meaningful or genuine sense of consent requires that those who consent are reasonably aware of the consequences of their act, and that they have the option to refuse to consent. This idea of consent relies on a broad voluntarist theory of society which presupposes that individuals are free and equal, and have equally developed capabilities to engage in free commitment.[8] This notion ignores the realities of power and inequality.

In this chapter, I have not undertaken a broad search for alternative procedural reforms. Nevertheless, I do have a particular concern for the persistent animosity towards jury trials. The judicial system is a sphere in which it is imperative to take rights and needs seriously. It is an arena where diverse perspectives may be displayed, in a framework of contextualism and fluid interaction with society. In the context of the transition to democracy, it is necessary to reconceive institutional arrangements in order to reinforce this process. In this sense, it is essential to take into account the need to empower the voiceless. Existing institutions do not reflect a diversity of perspectives. The institutional order delineates a single perspective that is taken as the norm. We have to be very careful not to create new forms of inequality or simply to reshape existing ones when we seek new patterns.

### III.
### Jury Trials and Democracy

I wish to address Professor Fletcher's proposal regarding the jury trial.[9] In addition to the advantages that Professor Fletcher suggests the jury trial presents, I wish to elucidate a feminist perspective on these advantages in the context of the transition to a democratic system.

The restoration of civilian rule and the process of transition and consolidation of democracy offer new opportunities to transform existing institutional structures. This period provides political openings to rethink the structure and the rules of the political game. More significantly, this expands the opportunities for including new issues and new perspectives in the public debate.

In the context of these different opportunities for the transformation of the institutional framework, how can feminists best take advantage of political openings? The opportunity to develop normative, structural, and institutional transformations raises gender-specific consequences, although they may not seem directly related to gender-specific issues. Because there is no adequately developed systematic theory of the state in relation to society from a feminist perspective, there has never been a design of political institutions that takes into account the way in which state power is articulated in a gender-powerful social context in which power is gender-based.

Many social, cultural, economic, and political factors play a fundamental role in the maintenance of women's oppression. But there has not yet been a similar analysis with respect to the role of institutional factors in this oppression. The relationship between the subordination of women and the design of institutions and political processes deserves more attention than it has so far received.

Feminism has described the state's treatment of gender difference, but it has not analyzed the state's role in gender hierarchy. Only recently has the relationship between the state and society been explored from a feminist standpoint. It is necessary, however, to go further in the analysis of the effects of gender on social and institutional relationships. Indeed, because gender is one of the central spheres within which, or by means of which, power is articulated, it is important to study how gender is implicated in the conception and construction of power itself through the design of political institutions.

Institutional structure has been treated as a mere epi-phenomenon of social and economic structure, disregarding its importance as a component in the process of constructing the hierarchical social system. Most feminists focus on those micro-political or individual variables that are crucial for understanding women's subordination. The concept of gender is used mostly in areas involving primary relations between the sexes. Although this use of gender asserts that relationships between the sexes are social and political, it says nothing about why these relationships are constructed in the context of the state. In this descriptive usage, gender has been a concept mostly associated with the study of issues directly related to women's personal relations.

There are few analyses concerning institutional and organizational contexts and their gender-related consequences. We must place gender at the center of the design of institutional structures and mechanisms. We need to explore which structures and procedures of institutions are better in representing women and their claims.

Feminism has shown that women's experiences and perspectives have been disregarded in official views of the world.[10] The description of what is considered reality is constructed from a male viewpoint, conceived as a universal viewpoint. Women's perspectives have been neglected and suppressed. It is a real challenge for the democratization of a society to bring these voices into the public debate.

Assumptions concerning the neutrality and objectivity of legal discourse tend to suppress the points of view of those who have not taken part in its creation. The law reflects and shapes the male dominant point of view while silencing and discounting the voices of the powerless. The power invested in judges may be a means to preserve and reinforce a prevailing arrangement of domination in which one group systematically exercises its power over others. Moreover, in this framework, other voices challenging this supposed objectivity are considered biased.

We must seek to include more experiences, perspectives, and voices into law, in order to empower and legitimate them, rather than insisting on the prototype of impartial judgment. In the context of the administration of justice, one partial solution to this question may be the transformation of judicial procedures. This may prevent the power to legitimate and reinforce some points of view over others from being exercised by only a few persons.

In this sense, the incorporation of the jury trial may be a means to include diverse perspectives. It may be an arena where competing experiences and standpoints could meet. A standpoint is the perspective from which one perceives the world and the social relations in it. It is framed by a diversity of factors such as race, class, gender, and work, as well as psychological characteristics. Diverse people will generate distinct knowledge frameworks according to their backgrounds and situations. These experiences shape a crucible for perceiving, interpreting, and understanding by stirring many of the unconscious facets of experience into the domain of consciousness. The jury trial may help translate the diversity of viewpoints into a meaningful dialogue.

The jury trial may also help to develop a practice where the construction of social meaning by a dominant group can be broken, because the trial provides a forum where the confrontation of realities may take place. A dominant perspective may be recognized as such when confronted with different viewpoints and when challenged by different experiences and realities. The trial may link other people's perspectives because each side must persuade the other in a dialogue over values. The jury trial provides a place for the encounter of realities and the construction of new understandings.

The confrontation of viewpoints challenges both the abstract universalism of the legal language and its presumed neutrality. Once one realizes that any point of view, including one's own, is only a point of view, it is easier to be more open to a process of dialogue that attempts to reach beyond one's own perspective and experiences. There is an opportunity to perceive that what we count as differences are evaluated in comparison to a pattern already accepted from a particular starting position.

Although it is very difficult, and perhaps impossible to understand absolutely the perspectives of others, a confrontation between different perspectives requires that we be aware of the partiality of our own perspective. Before making a decision, jurors face diverse perspectives that challenge their own viewpoints. Isolated judges, however, do not generally have to deal with such diverse perspectives. Instead of seeking impartial or objective judgment, the jury provides a medium through which particular viewpoints become publicly visible.

## Conclusion

Institutional structures are designed and transformed to combat the structural obstacles to democracy. But if the question of the conceptual justification and social prerequisites of democracy is taken seriously, attention must be paid to the voices of the powerless. To fail to incorporate their voices would mean to neglect an essential dimension of democratic social transformation.

The legitimacy of institutional arrangements and their decision-making processes derives essentially from the democratic characteristics of the process generating them. In this sense, equality of access to and participation in the decision-making spheres are essential. It is important that those who are affected by norms and decisions have a real chance to participate in the process on equal terms. The jury trial may contribute to the creation of procedural conditions for legitimacy, fostering the process of social transformation.

A caveat is in order. Context is essential to the process of democratization. No general pattern exists, suitable for every age or culture. Each society possesses its own specific features requiring diverse institutional arrangements to promote the reform of the social and political structure, leading to greater equality of power for the diverse components of that society.

Therefore, institutional design cannot follow a fixed rule for every society or age. In every context, however, institutional design should be a tool to fight against different forms of oppression. Moreover, it is important to assign an heuristic function to the analysis developed here. This means that my analysis should be considered as a means to generate hypotheses and general principles of interpretation useful in orienting further research, rather than a substitute for such research, a posterior analysis, or a specific proposal for reform.

## Notes

[1]For a general discussion of this problem, *see* Irwin P. Stotzky, Book Review, 8 J. ECON. & PHIL. 197 (1992) (reviewing RICHARD A. POSNER, THE PROBLEMS OF JURISPRUDENCE (1990)).

[2]*See generally* ROBERT M. COVER ET AL., PROCEDURE (1988); GEOFFREY C. HAZARD, JR. & JAN VETTER, PERSPECTIVES ON CIVIL PROCEDURE (1987).

[3]Owen M. Fiss, *The Right Degree of Independence in* TRANSITION TO DEMOCRACY IN LATIN AMERICA: THE ROLE OF THE JUDICIARY 55 (Irwin P. Stotzky ed., 1993) [hereinafter TRANSITION]; Paul W. Kahn, *Independence and Responsibility in the Judicial Role, in* TRANSITION *supra*, at 73; Jorge Correa Sutil, *The Judiciary and the Political System in Chile: The Dilemmas of Judicial Independence During the Transition to Democracy, in* TRANSITION *supra*, at 89.

[4]Raphael Bielsa, Authenticity of Independence of Judicial Power and Organization (March 19, 1992) (unpublished manuscript on file with Irwin P. Stotzky).

[5]Julio B. Maier, The Present Penal System: Between the Inquisition and Composition (1992) (unpublished manuscript on file with Irwin P. Stotzky).

[6]Indeed, as Irwin Stotzky has argued, the process of constitutional adjudication helps to determine the quality of our social existence because it defines public values and imposes severe limits on government action. *See, e.g.,* Irwin P. Stotzky, *The Tradition of Constitutional Adjudication, in* TRANSITION, *supra* note 3, at 347; Carlos S. Nino, *On the Exercise of Judicial Review in Argentina, in* TRANSITION, *supra* note 3, at 309.

[7]*See generally* LAURENCE H. TRIBE, AMERICAN CONSTITUTIONAL LAW (1978).

[8]*See* Stotzky, *supra* note 6; Nino, *supra* note 6.

[9]*See* George P. Fletcher, *Is it Better to be Tried for a Crime in a Criminal or Civilian System?, in* TRANSITION, *supra* note 3, at 127.

[10]*See generally* FEMINIST LEGAL THEORY: READINGS IN LAW AND GENDER (Katherine T. Bartlett & Rosanne Kennedy eds., 1991); CATHARINE A. MACKINNON, FEMINISM UNMODIFIED: DISCOURSE ON LIFE AND LAW (1987); Symposium, *Gender and Law,* 46 U. MIAMI L. REV. 503 (1992); Symposium, *Feminist Jurisprudence,* 24 GA. L. REV. 759 (1990); Lucinda M. Finley, *Breaking Women's Silence in Law: The Dilemma of the Gendered Nature of Legal Reasoning,* 64 NOTRE DAME L. REV. 886 (1989).

# 13

## The Judicial Process in Context

### *Stephen J. Schnably*

## I.
### Introduction

In this chapter, I struggle with a question as perplexing as it is important: What is the relationship between the structure of the judicial process and the transition to democracy? To formulate a comprehensive answer would be a daunting task, but three brief observations can profitably be made.[1]

## II.
### The Importance of Context

Attempts to evaluate the implications for democracy of judicial procedures and roles, or to reform the judicial process to make it more compatible with democracy, are of limited usefulness if they overlook the concrete social context in which that process functions. Comparisons of civil and common law systems of criminal law provide one example. Professor Fletcher notes that under the common law the defendant enters the judicial process with a presumption of innocence; at the start of the trial, neither judge nor jury knows what the prosecutor already knows. In civilian systems, on the other hand, the judge reads the prosecutor's dossier before the trial, a practice that saps vitality from the presumption of innocence.[2]

The comparison is telling so far as it goes. When one considers that most criminal cases in the United States are resolved by plea bargain,[3] however, one may wonder how much it tells us about the relative favorableness of the two systems for the accused. Does not the common law prosecutor's function in such a context come to resemble, to some degree, that of the civilian judge? And although the civilian assumptions about judicial impartiality "are fit subject of satire,"[4] we do not, of course, even expect prosecutors to be impartial or to accord the defendant a presumption of innocence.

Moreover, can we always assume that "more favorable to the accused" means "better for human rights"? The assumption is beguilingly easy to make. Professor Fletcher argues that the law of excuses is more favorable to the accused in the civil law system than in the common law. By way of example he says that under German law, Bernard Goetz would have had to show only that "he sincerely believed (reasonably or not) that he had to defend himself," whereas the New York Court of Appeals said that Goetz would have had to have had a *reasonable* belief that he was about to be attacked.[5]

In a society as marked by racial hatred and mistrust as is the United States, however, the question of a subjective versus objective basis for believing oneself threatened cannot be evaluated as a purely abstract matter of state versus defendant. There are many whites who treat any young African-American man approaching them as an imminent threat to their safety.[6] Adopting a standard that, in context, effectively authorizes people to use deadly force based on racist stereotypes would hardly constitute a victory for human rights.

Finally, attention to social context might be useful in evaluating proposals for reforming the management of the judiciary. Speed and efficiency are important components of justice. It is striking, though, that amidst all of Secretary Bielsa's noteworthy proposals to streamline the judicial process and improve the judges who carry it out,[7] there is no mention of race, gender, or class in the composition of the judiciary. That omission is significant, for the experience of the United States surely teaches us that if nearly all judges are white, upper-class males, the courts will be much less likely to hear the voices of the oppressed or marginalized.

## III.
### Government Intervention and the
### Protection of Democracy and Human Rights

A closer look at the context of particular proposals for reform of the judicial process may help us see that protection of democracy and human rights may in some instances require more rather than less government intervention. In fact, while it may sometimes be helpful to speak loosely of "more" or "less" intervention, strictly speaking the question is always what form government action should take.[8]

This assertion might seem surprising, for human rights law has tended to focus on limiting public power over individuals (e.g., preventing torture or disappearances).[9] We might thus be tempted to gauge the contribution of the judicial process to democracy exclusively in terms of how well the courts shield people against the oppressive invocation of state power (e.g., by *habeas corpus* or *amparo*). While that function is indeed important, it would be wrong to focus exclusively on limiting state power or reducing the occasions for its exercise. Moreover, this misconception has concrete implications for our thinking about the role of judicial procedures in securing respect for democracy and human rights.

Consider proposals to take cases out of the courts. Secretary Bielsa suggests that negotiation, conciliation, mediation, and forms of "private justice" be employed, both in conjunction with trials and in place of them.[10] Professor Maier proposes revival of the "composition" -- that is, a procedure by which the disposition of a crime could be handled as a matter of consensual settlement between victim and criminal, with the criminal paying civil damages to the victim. This would at least involve taking matters out of the criminal law system and, as it is envisioned, diverting them into consensual solutions.[11]

The exploration of alternatives is certainly worthwhile. But the judgment as to when to promote non-judicial approaches cannot be made by abstract references to negotiated solutions or the benefits of private justice. Women throughout the world, for example, suffer from ingrained, socially institutionalized domestic violence;[12] gay bashing is another activity that, in the United States at least, often goes unaddressed.[13] Without active state intervention, the violence may well remain "invisible" -- not, of course, to its perpetrators and victims, but to the law and the judicial system.[14] Not surprisingly, then, the exclusive focus on limiting the power of the state is one of the features of international human rights law that renders it most vulnerable to a feminist critique.[15]

Nor would it be sufficient to say that women would have an alternative forum, one that left them free to reach a negotiated solution. On the contrary, our suspicions should be raised all the more by the invocation of the notion of consent -- that is, the idea that parties will voluntarily come to some resolution with which they both agree, rather than having one imposed on them. Consider a particular example of the class of first-time offenders to whom Professor Maier refers:[16] a husband who is, for the first time, accused of battering his wife. Unless the state had already established a consistent pattern of prosecuting batterers, what incentive would he have to bargain seriously with her? Unless the state had helped create safe havens for women (like battered women's shelters), attacked discrimination in employment, and taken other steps to undermine the system of gender hierarchy, how much bargaining power would the woman bring to the negotiating sessions?[17] The very refusal to exercise the power of the state in these ways would constitute support for "private" hierarchy and oppression. There is, in other words, a sense in which state power is constitutive of private power even as it refrains from disturbing it.

One can also make this critique of calls for greater use of "private justice." An alternative dispute resolution system is arguably private only if its costs are paid for by those who use it; if it were open to all, with the state bearing the costs of administration, it would simply amount to another branch of the courts. In turn, people are unlikely to pay for private justice unless they perceive it to be significantly faster, more efficient, and more equitable than the public courts. If, however, the state sets up a system in which the affluent can obtain speedy justice by paying for it, while the poor are relegated to the public -- and inferior -- form of justice, that is a clear case of state-sanctioned discrimination against the poor, one that ends up intensifying inequality by replicating it in still another domain.[18]

These observations can be summarized in two general points, which are really just two different ways of saying the same thing. First, in a society riven by severe inequalities of class, race, and gender -- a characterization true (though of course in different ways) both of the United States and of Latin America -- active government intervention may be needed to protect the full range of human rights. Any particular plan to limit what comes before the courts must be examined very carefully in that light.

Second, careful attention to factors that influence consent is essential for any democracy. Consent, after all, is a bedrock notion for democracy: the government rules with the consent of the governed. One of the most useful things that could be done in the transition to democracy, therefore, would be to begin to think critically about what "consent" means in concrete social contexts -- particularly in societies that are marked by enormous disparities in access to economic resources, the persistence of right-wing ideologies, and significant inequalities of race and gender.

## IV.
### The Relationship Between Social Context and the Possibility of Creating a Fair and Independent Judiciary

The enormous inequalities of some Latin American societies (particularly, though by no means exclusively in Central America) might lead us to wonder whether there is even any point in bothering with such efforts until more basic changes take place. An independent judiciary is often characterized as a bulwark against repression. But is it a key source of support for an emerging democracy, or an institution that becomes possible only in a more established one?

The example of El Salvador is not heartening. Over the last decade or so, the United States made every effort to build up an independent judiciary (including an investigative apparatus), and more generally, respect for the rule of law. Yet the effort failed, as was made clear by the inability of the judiciary to deal effectively even with high-profile cases of state terror, let alone the ordinary run of disappearances and murders.[19] The extreme concentration of land ownership and resulting impoverishment of many Salvadorans, the lack of a democratic culture, and the war of the Salvadoran military against large segments of its own population, only recently brought to a halt,[20] all posed apparently insuperable barriers to the project.[21]

Equally discouraging is the failure of the Chilean judiciary, with its long legal tradition, to stand up to the military regime. On the contrary, the judiciary took refuge in legal technicalities and superficial formalities to avoid any serious confrontation with it.[22] Even in the United States, the last twelve years have seen a concerted effort to pack the courts with judges whose first impulse is to back the state in any confrontation with a citizen.[23]

It may be wrong, however, to think of the judicial process as nothing more than a reflection of prevailing political ideologies and structures. With its sanctioning of near-absolute power of the state over the accused, Professor Teitel argues, the Argentinian criminal justice system does not merely reflect a wider authoritarian ideology, but is "itself . . . an independent factor in the creation of political doctrine and national ideology."[24] This is an extremely suggestive claim, one that would fit well with an understanding of state power as constitutive, to some degree, of social life. It would also bolster one's confidence that attempts to restructure the judicial process have an affirmative contribution to make to the transition to democracy.[25]

One possible direction for future work on the relationship between the judicial process and democracy might lie in Roberto Unger's notion of "formative contexts" -- frameworks of "imaginative assumptions about the possible and desirable forms of human association as well as . . . institutional arrangements or noninstitutionalized social practices."[26] In a society with authoritarian political norms, an authoritarian form of procedure could well help reinforce those norms. Precisely for this reason, real reform of the judicial process might be useful. The example of a more democratic form of criminal process might provide the occasion for people to rethink or question authoritarian norms in other areas of political, social, and economic life. One could view the building up of the judiciary as an instance of "revolutionary reform," in Unger's terms -- a reform that, even if it amounts to less than a sweeping institution of an entirely new order, systematically changes the context of a wide range of routine social disputes.[27]

Thus, one need not assert that reforming the judicial process would necessarily bring about fundamental, democratic changes in other areas of society to see how such reform might still have favorable implications for democracy. Indeed, one need not even assume that it will always be possible to reform the judiciary no matter how undemocratic the social context; the very effort to disturb one of the formative contexts might have eye-opening effects, even if only to show the tenacity of the hold that a military or elite had over a seemingly democratic government. The point is neither to establish a simple model of causation, nor to dismiss efforts to build up an independent judiciary as hopeless without a complete transformation of economic and social relations, but rather to explore in a concrete way the varieties of relationships between the structure of the judicial process and the growth or decay of democratic values.

## Notes

[1] A preliminary word about terminology may be useful. "Human rights" and "democracy" are not synonymous. Even gross and systematic human rights violations are possible in a democracy, and undemocratic governments may respect some human rights; *see, e.g.*, Angela Cornell & Kenneth Roberts, *Democracy, Counterinsurgency, and Human Rights: The Case of Peru*, 12 HUM. RTS. Q. 529 (1990). At the same time, neither are the two disconnected. To undermine democracy is to violate a basic human right, *see generally* Thomas M. Franck, *The Emerging Human Right to Democratic Governance*, 86 AMER. J. INT'L L. 46 (1992); and the absence of democracy is likely to make it more difficult to remedy human rights violations. Further complicating the question, the terms are often given an unduly narrow interpretation. Democracy is equated to elections, and human rights to a few civil and political rights. The relationship between the two thus merits more extended exploration. In this brief chapter, however, I will make the simplifying, but also, I think, generally correct assumption that to the extent that the judicial process bolsters democracy, it also bolsters respect for human rights.

[2] George P. Fletcher, *Is it Better to be Tried for a Crime in a Common Law or Civilian System?*, *in* TRANSITION TO DEMOCRACY IN LATIN AMERICA: THE ROLE OF THE JUDICIARY 133-134 (Irwin P. Stotzky ed., 1993) [hereinafter TRANSITION].

[3] *See, e.g.*, Robert E. Scott & William J. Stuntz, *Plea Bargaining as Contract*, 101 YALE L.J. 1909, 1909 n.1 (1992).

[4] Fletcher, *supra* note 2, at 130.

[5] *Id.* at 136. *See* People v. Goetz, 497 N.E.2d 41 (1986).

[6] *See, e.g.*, *Crime: A Conspiracy of Silence*, NEWSWEEK, May 18, 1992, at 37 (referring to many whites' "unspoken fears about young black men"). The problem is all the more difficult because most racism today is probably unconscious. *See* Charles R. Lawrence, *The Id, the Ego, and Equal Protection: Reckoning with Unconscious Racism*, 39 STAN. L. REV. 317 (1987).

[7] Raphel Bielsa, Authenticity of Independence of Judicial Power and Organization 11-12 (1992) (unpublished manuscript on file with Irwin P. Stotzky).

[8]*See* Stephen J. Schnably, *Beyond Griswold: Foucauldian and Republican Approaches to Privacy*, 23 CONN. L. REV. 861, 930-31 (1991).

[9]The theme of limiting government power may well have particular attractions to those living in a society that has suffered relatively recently from military dictatorship and all the horrors that attend it. Interestingly, Secretary Bielsa expresses a very classic notion of limited government: "The ideal state, without doubt, is that which least needs to resort to its power to obtain the concurrence of its people." Bielsa, *supra* note 7, at 1.

[10]*Id.* at 8-9.

[11]It is not entirely clear to what degree Professor Maier envisages any direct role for the courts. He does speak of "dispensing with the criminal system," Julio Maier, The Present Penal System: Between the Inquisition and Composition (1992) (unpublished manuscript on file with Irwin P. Stotzky) ("El intento de prescindir del sistema penal"), and he speaks repeatedly of a consensual solution between perpetrator and victim. On the other hand, presumably the threat of criminal sanctions would have to be present to induce the perpetrator to bargain seriously.

[12]*See, e.g.*, WOMEN, POLICING, AND MALE VIOLENCE: INTERNATIONAL PERSPECTIVES (Jalna Hanmer et al. eds., 1989); U.N. CENTRE FOR SOCIAL DEVELOPMENT AND HUMANITARIAN AFFAIRS, VIOLENCE AGAINST WOMEN IN THE FAMILY, U.N. Doc. ST/CSDHA/2, U.N. Sales No. E.89.IV.5 (1989); MUJER GOLPEADA (Leonor Vain ed., 1988); NATIONAL CENTER ON WOMEN AND FAMILY LAW, WOMAN BATTERING: THE FACTS (1989). *See also* Nathaniel C. Nash, *Bolivia Is Helping Its Battered Wives to Stand Up*, N.Y. TIMES, March 30, 1992, at A4. For an account of violence of women directly at the hands of the state, see AMNESTY INTERNATIONAL, WOMEN IN THE FRONT LINE: HUMAN RIGHTS VIOLATIONS AGAINST WOMEN (1991) (AI Index ACT 77/01/91).

[13]*See generally, e.g.*, GARY D. COMSTOCK, VIOLENCE AGAINST LESBIANS AND GAY MEN (1991); Kevin T. Berrill & Gregory M. Herek, *Primary and Secondary Victimization in Anti-Gay Hate Crimes: Official Response and Public Policy, in* HATE CRIMES: CONFRONTING VIOLENCE AGAINST LESBIANS AND GAY MEN 289-305 (Gregory M. Herek & Kevin T. Berrill eds., 1992); Donna Minkowitz, *It's Still Open Season on Gays*, 254 NATION 368 (1992).

[14]*See* LA MUJER Y LA VIOLENCIA INVISIBLE (Eva Giberti & Ana M. Fernandez eds., 1989). *See also* Silvia Chejter, *Violentar y Silenciar: Dos Caras del Sexismo, in* MUJER GOLPEADA, *supra* note 12, at 121, 126 ("uno de los factores que más contribuyen a la victimación de las mujeres es el silencio"). For a general critique of the exclusion of women from accounts of international politics, see CYNTHIA ENLOE, BANANAS, BEACHES & BASES: MAKING FEMINIST SENSE OF INTERNATIONAL POLITICS (1989).

[15]*See* Hilary Charlesworth et al., *Feminist Approaches to International Law*, 85 AMER. J. INT'L L. 63 (1991); Renee Holt, *Women's Rights and International Law: The Struggle for Recognition and Enforcement*, 1 COLUM. J. GENDER & L. 117, 129-32 (1991); GEORGINA ASHWORTH, OF VIOLENCE AND VIOLATION: WOMEN AND HUMAN RIGHTS (1988); Karen Engle, *International Human Rights and Feminism: When Discourses Meet*, 13 MICH. J. INT'L L. 517 (1992).

[16]*See* Maier, *supra* note 11.

[17]For a good statement of the relationship in the Brazilian context, see AMERICAS WATCH, CRIMINAL INJUSTICE: VIOLENCE AGAINST WOMEN IN BRAZIL 50-52 (1991). *See also* Carmen Gonzalez, *Violencia en las Instituciones Juridicas, in* LA MUJER Y LA VIOLENCIA INVISIBLE, *supra* note 14, at 171, 181 ("Esta extrema violencia [contra mujeres] es agravada por varios factores: la falta de refugios para mujeres golpeadas y el temor que tal situación genera en aquellas obligadas a convivir con el agresor . . ., y también la política general de los jueces, que consideran este acto como perteneciente a la esfera de la privacidad y la familia y que, por lo tanto, la justicia no debe intervenir."); REGINA GRAYCAR & JENNY MORGAN, THE HIDDEN GENDER OF LAW 306-07 (1990). In earlier times, the law was more explicit in its support of men's power over women. *See* Leonor Vain, *Mujer y Derecho, in* LA MUJER Y LA VIOLENCIA INVISIBLE, *supra* note 14, at 63, 65-66.

[18]*See* Note, *The California Rent-A-Judge Experiment: Constitutional and Policy Considerations of Pay-As-You-Go Courts*, 94 HARV. L. REV. 1592, 1601-06 (1981).

[19]*See* AMERICAS WATCH, EL SALVADOR'S DECADE OF TERROR: HUMAN RIGHTS SINCE THE ASSASSINATION OF ARCHBISHOP ROMERO (1991).

[20]*See* Tim Golden, *Salvadorans Sign Treaty to End the War*, N.Y. TIMES, Jan. 17, 1992, at 1.

[21]Interestingly, Segundo Montes, one of the Jesuit priests murdered by the Salvadoran army in 1989, had despaired of the possibility of democracy in El Salvador in an essay written a decade earlier. *See* Segundo Montes, *Is Democracy Possible in An Underdeveloped Country?, in* TOWARDS A SOCIETY THAT SERVES ITS PEOPLE: THE INTELLECTUAL CONTRIBUTION OF EL SALVADOR'S MURDERED JESUITS 141 (John Hassett & Hugh Lacey eds., 1991). When he came to view the establishment of democracy as at least a possibility -- ironically, in essays published the year he was assassinated -- he apparently did not found his hopes on the judiciary. *See* John Hassett & Hugh Lacey, *Comprehending Reality from the Perspective of the Poor, in id.* at 1, 13 ("Like his colleagues, he held that liberation could be achieved through the movements of the people themselves -- not ushered in by elites, whether local or foreign, whether elected or militarily installed.").

[22]*See* PAMELA CONSTABLE & ARTURO VALENZUELA, A NATION OF ENEMIES: CHILE UNDER PINOCHET 115-39 (1991). As the Inter-American Commission on Human Rights noted, the judiciary rejected large numbers of applications for *amparo*, accepting at face value either the government's denial that it had detained the individual in question or its assertion that the detention was lawful. See Inter-American Commission on Human Rights, Report on the Situation of Human Rights in Chile, OEA Ser.L/V/II.66, Doc. 17 (27 Sept. 1985), at 165. The Chilean judiciary was not alone in this regard. *See, e.g.,* Inter-American Commission on Human Rights, Report on the Situation of Human Rights in Argentina, OEA Ser.L/V/II.49, Doc. 9 corr.1 (11 April 1980), at 231 ("[T]he petition of Habeas Corpus has been frustrated. . . . It is because the organs centralizing control of the state forces are certain that they will be treated with impunity that they answer the judges simply that the beneficiary of the appeal is not under any detention order.");

*id.* at 228-29; Frederick E. Snyder, *State of Siege and Rule of Law in Argentina: The Politics and Rhetoric of Vindication,* 15 LAW. AM. 503, 512-19 (1984).

[23]One result is to make it increasingly unlikely that the federal courts will be receptive to international human rights claims. *See* Howard Tolley, Jr., *Interest Group Litigation to Enforce Human Rights,* 105 POL. SCI. Q. 617, 632-34 (1990-91).

[24]Ruti Teitel, *Persecution and Inquisition: A Case Study, in* TRANSITION, *supra* note 2, at 143 ("I claim the law of criminal process ought not be understood simply as a product of culture, but instead as an independent factor in promoting an authoritarian ideology conducive to a climate of government abuses of rights.").

[25]Though suggestive, Professor Teitel's account appears at first glance incomplete and somewhat contradictory. It is incomplete because she does not say how or to what extent the criminal process serves as a factor in the creation of a national ideology. It seems somewhat contradictory because her references to the criminal process as an "independent factor in the creation" of ideology could easily be read as an assertion of causation; yet she also seems to draw back from asserting any causal relation. *E.g., id.* at 144 ("the paradigm of the *'incommunicado* suspect' in state custody expresses core elements of authoritarianism") (emphasis added); *id.* at 146. In light of her earlier statements, one might have expected her to say "reinforces" or "helps create" rather than "expresses."

Despite these qualms, I think that Professor Teitel is correct not to claim any simple or one-way causal relationship. What remains to be done -- and it is a project well worth undertaking -- is to provide a more concrete understanding of how the expressive aspect of the criminal justice system interacts with wider political norms and institutions.

[26]ROBERTO MANGABEIRA UNGER, SOCIAL THEORY: ITS SITUATION AND ITS TASK -- A CRITICAL INTRODUCTION TO POLITICS, A WORK IN CONSTRUCTIVE SOCIAL THEORY 89 (1987).

[27]*See id.* at 163-64.

PART FIVE

# The Role of the Prosecutor

# 14

## The Function of the Prosecution in the Transition to Democracy in Latin America

*Andrés José D'Alessio*

### I.
### Introduction

This chapter is concerned with those requirements necessary for efficient prosecutions in a transitional democracy. I begin with the assumption that a transition to democracy does not occur instantaneously but rather evolves over an extended period of time. Moreover, the shift from an authoritarian government to a democratic one is not accomplished simply because a dictatorial regime is replaced by an elected government. Fundamental change occurs only with the successful consolidation of the rule of law. Furthermore, the establishment of the primacy of the rule of law occurs only when a large majority of the population becomes convinced that personal well-being and security are more likely to be secured in a democracy, whatever its shortcomings, than in a dictatorial setting. Where the previous authoritarian regime committed gross violations of human rights, the new democratic government must not only prosecute those human rights violations, it must also create an efficient enforcement system to prosecute effectively other types of offenses committed by government officials and deal with common criminal matters. Indeed, an efficient prosecutorial system is a necessary condition for a well-functioning and democratic judicial system. To put it another way, such a system is essential for creating an adjudicatory process that respects individual rights.

In cases of human rights abuses committed by government agents, the prosecutorial arm of the democratic government requires a broad independence in at least two senses -- institutional independence and some measure of independence for the officials who serve that institution.[1] These notions of institutional and intra-institutional independence raise a broad array of

questions. First, at an institutional level, within which branch of government, if any, should the prosecutioner's office be affiliated? Second, should
prosecutors be entitled to exercise discretionary powers? If so, how should
the exercise of these discretionary powers be controlled? Third, at an
individual level, how independent should lower-ranking officials be?

This chapter deals primarily with Argentina, a nation which epitomizes
the deficiencies of the inquisitorial justice system inherited from continental
Europe. More particularly, I discuss the influence of the inquisitorial
system in frustrating public confidence in the administration of the criminal
justice system, and the role of the prosecution in this system. I analyze
these problems through my experience as a federal judge and Attorney
General during the Alfonsín regime, and discuss how the first constitutional
government after many years of military rule faced and attempted to solve
these serious issues.

## II.
## Prosecutorial Function and
## the Inquisitorial Judiciary

### A. A Brief Illustration of Argentine Criminal Procedure

Suppose that while reading the morning newspaper at breakfast, a judge
learns about a crime committed in his jurisdiction. He then calls the police,
inquires about the details of the case and instructs them to begin the investigation. Once at his office, the judge orders the search of the suspect's residence and issues an arrest warrant. The suspect is arrested and remains
*incommunicado*.[2] Next, the judge gathers additional evidence through proceedings that he is entitled to carry out without any input from the suspect's
counsel. The judge may order the suspect held in detention; this detention
may last for months or even years. It may take the judge years before he
or she is convinced that enough evidence exists to move to the accusatory
stage. During this first stage, the investigatory stage or *sumario*, the
prosecutor will only be informed of the proceedings and is entitled only to
suggest to the court what measures she deems conducive to establishing the
truth. The judge is entitled to turn the proposed measures down without
supplying reasons.

On the basis of the available evidence, the judge may decide either to
open the accusatory stage, thereby closing the *sumario*, or simply dismiss
the case. Whatever the judge's decision, the prosecutor is entitled only to
suggest that further investigative proceedings be carried out, or oppose the
closure of the *sumario* should other suspects be indicted. If such opposition
does not take place, the trial is finally ready to begin.

## B. Some Historical Facts

At some point in history, rulers decided to stop the irrational infliction of pain through torture as the primary method of obtaining confessions in criminal matters. The judge emerged as a supervisor over the infliction of pain upon the suspect. In this role, the judge was required to be both unemotional and enlightened. Thus, judges were to question the facts rather than deal with issues of law. This is where the "Court of Inquisition" came into being.

When humanitarian ideals led to the abolition of torture, the judges' role remained unchanged. In some nations, such as Spain, judges were considered semi-gods, believed to remain impartial when pondering evidence they themselves collected. It became clear in other societies that without assigning judges a truly impartial role, humanitarian ideals could not be fully achieved. The judge had to become a third party, essentially devoted to allotting punishment.

## C. Argentina's Institutional Organization and Criminal Procedure

In 1853, a year after the overthrow of Rosas' tyranny, the people of Argentina drafted a new constitution. At the same time, people began to accept progressive ideas. For many politicians, the United States Constitution represented the best political model. Thus, the Argentine Constitution borrowed Article III.[3] Moreover, the Argentine Constitution stated that criminal cases should be decided by a jury, which implies a public and accusatory trial system presided over by an impartial judge.

But the weight of tradition could not be easily replaced. Because many of the ruling elite considered such a scheme too progressive, it was never taken seriously. This can be seen in the following statement made by Manuel Obarrio, who drafted the 1888 Code of Criminal Proceedings: "[O]ne could say that a country like ours which has only recently adopted free institutions and, although it is painful to admit it, is still not accustomed to self-government . . ."[4]

Argentine rulers of that period believed in a slower transition. Thus, the legislative committee that revised Obarrio's proposed draft of the Code of Criminal Proceedings stated:

> Transition would be too fast and too dangerous to attempt to advance from the rudimentary way in which our democratic existence is developing and the reigning chaos in its present criminal proceedings, to the most perfect society and its habits of self-government required by the jury in order to be a viable and effective institution. Large reforms, even more so in newly formed countries like ours, cannot be introduced abruptly; they must spring forth spontaneously, if that expression may be used, as

the result of a gradual and progressive process of evolution, in the pursuit of perfection.[5]

Thus the United States Constitutional model never took root. Instead, through legislative re-introduction, the old Spanish code, which the Spaniards had already abandoned, became the reigning model of criminal proceedings in Argentina.

### D. The Consequences of the Adoption of the Inquisitorial Model on the Role of Prosecution

The drafters of the code tried to prevent the *sumario* from becoming the centerpiece of the criminal procedural system. A century of practice, however, was too difficult to overcome. Thus, the use of the investigatory phase reigns supreme. Indeed, investigations conducted by the judge are extremely long; the *sumario* is the largest part of the Argentine criminal procedural system. Except for very simple cases, the *sumario* invariably outlasts the legal time limit.[6] Most of the evidence to be used against the suspect is gathered at this stage. Only rarely do the parties produce further evidence during the debate stage, called the *plenario*.

Statistics indicate that of all the cases brought to court, ninety-one percent never reach the *plenario*. When a case terminates in the *sumario*, the defendant is acquitted. Nevertheless, a sizeable number of suspects endure extended terms of arrest or curtailment of their freedom during the *sumario*, even if they are acquitted later.

Such a system produces two kinds of victims. The first victims are the suspects, whose rights to due process are only casually respected during the adversary stage. The second victim is the population at large which is adversely affected by the ineffectiveness of the judicial system to prevent crime and punish criminals. When people perform several roles in a system, each different in function and purpose, it is clear they become inefficient. This is surely the case of investigating and deciding the very same cases. To put it another way, judges are not able to accomplish judicial decision-making duties at the same time as they perform prosecutorial duties. Moreover, as often happens in Argentina, the investigation is carried out by the police, with little or no control by the judge,[7] who sits miles away from the place where the offense took place. Giving investigative powers to an independent prosecutor would improve the efficiency of the criminal justice system, and also enhance respect for the rights of the suspects by controlling the police activity.

These reflections suggest that the inquisitorial system harms the performance of prosecutorial tasks. It is clear that no autonomous mission is left for the prosecutor if the judge is entrusted to move the proceedings forward.

Such a system dilutes the prosecutor's role to such an extent that many lawyers refer to the prosecutor as "the fifth wheel of the judicial carriage."

Because of these problems, one conclusion seems certain: the role of the prosecutor can only be properly fulfilled in an adversarial system.[8] Moreover, respect for the principles of the adversary system cannot be achieved without a prosecutor acting independently from the judiciary. Stated otherwise, an impartial criminal judiciary depends on making the prosecutor an exclusive agent of the criminal process.

## III.
## The General Requirements of an Efficient Prosecution

### A. *The Necessity for Prosecutorial Discretion*

Strong objections have been advanced against allowing prosecutors discretion in deciding which cases to prosecute. Indeed, it is often argued that the legislature is the proper government branch to decide which acts warrant criminal prosecution. While there is some truth to this assertion, it is also a sobering truth that "too many criminal laws have been enacted and too many offenses are committed for it to be even remotely possible to prosecute every crime."[9]

In practice, there are two ways in which a legislature may select which acts should be punished. First, it may entrust the prosecution with discretionary powers and provide necessary safeguards to avert abuses of this power (the "opportunity system"). Second, it may require each and every offense be prosecuted (the "legality system"). This latter approach, however, is impossible to achieve. Such an approach makes the prosecution allocate resources so thin that each case cannot be given the effort it deserves. Only an ideal system, provided with unlimited human, technical, and financial resources could reasonably fulfill this principle's ideal. Under present day circumstances, in which the courts are overwhelmed with cases, objections against prosecutorial discretion cannot be seriously maintained unless the society has no serious plan to tackle crime.[10] Crimes which require complicated investigations would remain unpunished and only the simple cases would or could be prosecuted and a conviction achieved.[11]

### B. *Locating the Prosecutors' Office: The Issue of Public Confidence*

In this section, I primarily discuss the problem of public confidence in prosecutorial discretion and popular perceptions of how discretion is put into practice. If the prosecutorial body is not independent from the executive branch, such public confidence would be impossible to achieve today in Latin America. Every plea bargain entered into would be suspect because of political favoritism. Indeed, such plea bargains would be seen as the ratification of the idea expressed in a very popular Argentine poem: "[l]aw is like a spider web that traps the weak but is easily broken by the powerful."[12] This belief constitutes a pragmatic basis for supporting the claim that the "best" or the "natural" system should allow for the independence of the public prosecutors.

## C. Locating the Prosecutorial Body Within the Governmental Organization: The Issue of Affiliation

Once it is desireable for practical reasons to grant prosecutors a considerable degree of independence, the question of where the office should be located becomes a decision about which branch of government should be responsible for the financial support of the office. There are at least four possible locations: the executive branch, the judicial branch, the legislative branch, or an entirely separate department independent of all three traditional branches of government.[13]

*The Executive Branch.* In both England and the United States, of course, the prosecutor's office is located in the Executive branch. I believe that its effectiveness in both countries is due to the merits of their legal traditions, rather than the virtues of the system itself. Nevertheless, problems arise even in the United States. The Watergate affair, for example, posed a serious challenge to the system, and, one may assume, only the pressure of public opinion and the integrity of the second special prosecutor appointed to investigate the case averted a shameful outcome.

Some advocates for locating the prosecutors' office in the Executive branch claim that doing so is a necessary step in the implementation of criminal policies.[14] There are, however, two significant reasons that make this argument unconvincing. First, it is not clear that the Executive branch should establish criminal policy instead of Congress. Second, the Executive branch is more prone than other branches to engender public distrust.

*The Judicial Branch.* The traditional location of prosecutors in Argentina has been in the Judicial branch.[15] This "judicialized" prosecutorial system has rendered prosecutors as independent as judges. Nevertheless, in Argentina, placing the prosecutors within the Judicial branch has had some negative consequences. Ideally, prosecutors initiate the proceedings and pursue the case against the accused, clashing with the defense in their endeavor to reach a conviction. Because the prosecutor is a part of the Judicial branch in Argentina, however, the prosecutor must, like others in this branch, be impartial. To require that the prosecutor be impartial is unrealistic; it is as abnormal as to require the same impartiality from defense counsel. In Argentina, individual members of the Judicial branch are autonomous and thus not required to follow directives from superior judges. Under these conditions, it would barely be possible to organize a well-functioning prosecutors office. Additionally, because it is desireable to keep judges from acting as prosecutors, it must also be desireable to keep prosecutors from acting impartially and emulating judges. Indeed, distinguishing between legal adjudication (judicial rules) and prosecutorial duties is the first step towards attaining a healthy and republican judicial system.

*The Legislative Branch.* No existing political model that I know of has located the prosecutors with the Legislative branch. Although the legislature may be in the best position to control prosecutors, given the number of its members, and the requisite political considerations, it is simply absurd to attempt to do so.

*The Separate Department.* The objections I have raised against the other choices are plausible reasons for favoring a fourth alternative for organizing the prosecutor's office. If adequately organized, I believe that this fourth option has none of the drawbacks previously mentioned. Moreover, it also does not require deviating from the United States and Argentine constitutional structures because traditional republican branches of government are related only to political power in a very broad sense. Consequently, the distribution of governmental power does not preclude the creation of authorities which do not hinge directly on any of the three branches of government, provided they are controlled by at least one of them.

## IV.
## An Outline for the Ideal Prosecutor's Office

I propose the creation of a prosecutor's office whose members are independent because they have life tenured positions. The office should be coordinated by a top official and given the power to investigate all criminal cases. Moreover, the top prosecutorial official must have direct authority over the police. All members of the prosecutors' office should be supervised by an internal control department and a parliamentary committee.

### A. Prosecutorial Autonomy

I have stressed that the prosecutor's office be independent from "outside" control. This is essential to the development of new Latin American democracies. Without such independence, it would be impossible to have an effective prosecutorial system that promotes society's interests.

The prosecutor's office must also have internal independence. By this, I refer to hierarchical relationships within the prosecutor's office. At first blush, if the prosecutor has discretionary powers, she should be compelled to advance a cause only if she is personally convinced of its merits. If we accept this premise, however, we must acknowledge that total independence among the prosecutors will hinder coordinated prosecutorial strategies. Such individual prosecutorial autonomy makes it impossible to upgrade the activities performed by lower ranking officials. To put it another way, every prosecution is a congruous unit in which each party's initial position will normally limit that party's position through the rest of the proceedings. This circumstance, and the fact that in most cases higher ranking officials do not personally participate at the beginning of the investigation, make it extremely difficult to coordinate efforts. Indeed, too much autonomy allows lower ranking officials to make decisions which run counter to those of the higher ranking officials. This, in turn, leads to inefficient organization of the prosecutor's office.

To overcome these obstacles, I advocate a hierarchical organization in the prosecutor's office in which general directives and specific instructions are mandatory and must be followed by all members of the prosecutor's office. However, the system must not restrain the freedom of conscience of individual prosecutors. They must be allowed to express their dissent in writing.

But the congruity of the prosecutorial activity demands that restraints be imposed upon the issuance of general instructions. In this system, the reasonability of the guidelines and the specific directives must therefore be revised by an inside board and, ultimately, by the highest level authorities with competence to control the prosecutors.

### B. Conditions of Independence

This independence must be ensured by practical means. Internally, within the prosecutor's office, life tenure is one of the best devices for assuring such independence. Independence is rendered moot whenever a department is authorized to oust a prosecutor without a formal trial.[16]

Before the judiciary may review dismissals, there must be a set procedure for dismissal in the prosecutor's office. In the case of superior officers, congressional impeachment may be a sensible requirement. However, judicial review should be limited to prevent arbitrariness, not to examine the substantive merits of the dismissals.

While the independence of the members of the prosecutor's office would be protected by life tenure, who will oversee and control the prosecutor's office from the outside? There must be adequate scrutiny of every official decision and a disciplinary board to decide what, if any, penalties should be imposed for specific transgressions. Moreover, decisions made by the top ranking prosecutors, particularly as to questions about the discretionary power to prosecute, must be controlled. The safest way to oversee and control the prosecutor's office is to establish a bicameral congressional committee. This committee should discuss with the Attorney General the general guidelines to be followed, and the correctness of any decisions he may adopt.

## C. Prosecutorial Investigative Powers

The officials empowered to pursue certain criminal cases must be bound by the duty to conduct the investigation. Responsibility comes with power. Thus, debunking and abandoning the inquisitorial judiciary system requires assigning the task of investigating criminal cases to the prosecutor. But there must also be checks on the prosecutorial power. The protection of individual rights is paramount. Thus, to secure these rights, when the investigation requires searches, seizures, the interception of mail, or telephone tapping and the like, the prosecutor must be restrained by judicial oversight.

Even with all of the advantages of my proposal, however, powerful traditions oppose these reforms in Argentina. An inquisitorial conception of a justice system is so deeply rooted in Argentine jurists that they are unable to imagine that any official other than a judge should be allowed to collect evidence.[17] Their motto is: *one who has the prosecutor for a judge needs God as a counselor.* But if a judge's essential task is to adjudicate guilt or innocence and impose punishment, an equally powerful motto can be put forward -- *when the trial judge has collected the evidence by himself, only God can help the suspect avoid conviction.*

Although it is still arguable that justice can be protected through a process which puts the investigative and sentencing decisions in the hands of the same official, Argentine experience suggests otherwise. Indeed, to do so would result in preserving the inquisitorial system in countries like Argentina. Those who favor the *status quo* must also accept the fact that less than nine percent of the cases in Argentina go to trial, that long terms of incarceration are endured by suspects who are later found innocent, and that ninety-six percent of the sentences handed down result in sentences of three years or less.

My position also requires that prosecutors should have authority over the police.[18] Without the latter's human and technical resources, investigative endeavors could not be expected to be run correctly -- according to law -- and successfully.

## D. Prosecutor's Attitude Toward a Case

Supporters of the inquisitorial system agree that there is a need for an independent prosecutor. In their opinion, however, such a prosecutor should act as an impartial party to the interests in conflict. The inadequacy of this view is exemplified by the 1977 Attorney General's instruction to all prosecutors that the principle *in dubio pro reo*[19] was not to be construed as addressed to the prosecutors, but to judges only. The prosecutor's uncertainty, the directive stressed, should be surmounted by gathering more evidence. If in doing so the doubts ended, the case should be pursued so that the decision is left to the judges only.

Moreover, it is also true that prosecutors are bound by certain restraints that do not apply to other actors in the system, such as defense counsel. Although both defense lawyers and prosecutors are bound by the same code of ethics, private attorneys are bound primarily by an oath of loyalty to their clients. Stated otherwise, they are tied to the personal fate of their client. Prosecutors, by contrast, are not personally committed beyond their professional duties, which include, of course, a commitment to truth and justice. Prosecutors must pursue any means of establishing the truth, even if it benefits the suspect. Defense lawyers, in contrast, are forbidden from acting in any way that might jeopardize their client's situation.

## V.
## The Role of Prosecution and the Participation of Private Parties in the Proceedings

### A. *Prosecutors as Society's Representatives*

It is often claimed that public prosecutors originated as a substitute for the private accuser as society made the transition from private retaliation to public punishment. Offenses generally outrage public sentiments. This raises an immediate claim for the punishment of the perpetrator. As representatives of the public, it follows that prosecutors are the conveyors of claims stemming from those sentiments.

Democratic consensus requires that citizens experience the way in which abstract legal provisions are concretely applied in the furtherance of their interests. In authoritarian settings, political practice instills the idea that illegal means are sometimes the more effective way to solve social problems. Indeed, one of the most harmful aspects of a dictatorship is the practice of living with illegality and its Siamese sibling: impunity. Under such circumstances, an efficient and fair prosecution becomes an essential condition of democracy. Prosecutors are meant to represent the interests of the people by protecting citizens within the rule of law.

Generalized tolerance by the populace of a "dirty war" as a method to end terrorism is a particularly dangerous example of the value attached to expediency at the cost of legality.[20] Moreover, in Argentina, this value has not been completely removed from public opinion, even after the exposure of the dictatorial barbarism and the conviction of those political leaders responsible for such acts. It is the responsibility of the prosecutor to change this psychology into one that favors the enforcement of laws enacted by the people's representatives. Under these circumstances, an efficient prosecution becomes an essential condition for democracy.

## B. *The Role of the Victim: Private Parties in Criminal Procedure*

If prosecutors represent both the victim and the public at a criminal trial, there is no sound reason why the victim should remain a party. But unlike most countries, Argentina's federal system allows for the victim to participate together with the public prosecutor.[21]

Modern views of criminal justice have generally criticized this system as contradictory to the state's monopoly of the *jus puniendi*.[22] Except for certain offenses, such as libel, in which the offended party retains the power to prosecute, the victim's power to pursue punishment has been abrogated in most of the provincial systems in Argentina. The victim, however, preserves an essential standing in the criminal procedure on issues that may affect their right to obtain compensation for damages. In spite of the soundness of the reasons to support a very limited participation of the victim, the issue is highly controversial.[23]

Congress, after rejecting Professor Maier's draft proposal,[24] enacted a draft submitted by the current Chief Justice of the Supreme Court, Ricardo Levene. In its original wording, Levene's code bans the victim from participating. Before it was finally approved, however, Carlos Arslanian, then Minister of Justice, introduced some revisions which included a limited role for the victim, who is now entitled to participate when the public prosecutor decides that the case merits being pursued.

Although the exclusion of the victim is the perfect solution from an academic vantage point, practical reasons suggest the convenience of granting the victim some role. For example, the new Code of Criminal Procedure allows the victim to take part in the *sumario* with some limited powers. When the judge decides that this stage must be closed, only the prosecutor has the power to open the trial. If, however, the prosecutor decides there are no grounds for bringing the case to trial, the victim has standing to ask the court of appeals to reverse that decision and order the prosecution to take place through another official. This should help to develop confidence in the system through the assurance that the offense will be adequately pursued. This participation will serve as a means to stimulate the prosecutors to improve their performance.

## C. *The Extent of the Victim's Role*

This intermediate system built into the new code improves Argentina's criminal justice system as it stands today.[25] Unlike the prosecutor, the victim has a personal investment in the outcome of the trial, not only from her goal of having the perpetrator punished, but also because of the decisive bearing of such a conviction on the issue of compensation.

Private criminal actions have often lent themselves to abuses involving significant public expenditures. Criminal charges are often pressed by the (real or alleged) victims of economically unruly practices which may or may not constitute criminal offenses. The purpose of these criminal suits is to pressure the indicted party to compensate the claimant. The sole prospect of a criminal trial is sometimes enough deterrent to reach an agreement to compensate the plaintiff if he drops the charges.

In systems in which only the public prosecutor can pursue the case and the suspect's rights cannot be affected without the intervention of an impartial judge, the described transactions are unthinkable. If the prosecutor unfairly refuses to advance the victim's interests, then the victim will be entitled to report her case to the inside or external control committees.

# VI.
## Some Empirical Verifications of My Proposals

In this chapter, I have argued that confidence in the rule of law is a necessary aspect of any successful transition to democracy, that such confidence cannot possibly be engendered without efficient prosecution of crimes, and that this requires an adversary system of criminal procedure. Moreover, I am convinced that this system requires an independent prosecutors office which has some authority to investigate possible offenses, and to select the cases to be prosecuted. Finally, only an impartial judiciary must be allowed to decide cases.

All of these proposals derive from my personal experiences immediately after the return to constitutional government in Argentina, in December 1983. Massive violations of human rights during the military rule generated a general clamor for severe punishment for those who engaged in kidnappings, torture, and murder. It was also widely asserted that this retribution should be done swiftly and through fair trials.

But a problem confronted us. There were simply too many cases to be investigated and tried in such a short time with the prosecution system normally used in Argentina. The creation of a prosecutor's office, composed of many prosecutors and directed by the Prosecutor of the Federal Court of Appeals in Criminal Matters of Buenos Aires -- which acted as the trial court in those cases -- helped to resolve this dilemma. That office acted responsibly and admirably. It gathered the evidence and, on the basis of the conclusions drawn from its analysis, selected less than 800 cases from a possible pool of ten to thirty thousand cases. The culmination of the prosecutions was the conviction of the top military officials responsible for those crimes.[26]

There were other positive aspects realized from this structural change. General instructions issued by the Attorney General -- using the power conferred to him by these reforms -- allowed successful and efficient prosecutions of a variety of offenses, including drug trafficking, tax fraud, and extradition cases.

Recognition by the Supreme Court that disciplinary power over prosecutors belonged exclusively to the Attorney General,[27] greatly helped to achieve coherence in the actions of all the prosecutors before the federal courts.  Widespread use of prosecuting teams, and the appointment of special prosecutors for difficult cases, also helped in the efficient prosecution of difficult cases.  Even plea bargaining, absolutely unknown in Argentine prosecutorial practice, became a powerful tool to discover the major offenders in cases of petty drug trafficking and in bank fraud, and to obtain financial satisfaction by the government.

Moreover, this reorganization plan enhanced relationships between the prosecutor and the police and other similar agencies.  Indeed, particularly impressive was the willingness of the police to accept supervision from prosecutors.  This in turn helped the police succeed in their investigations when submitted to the scrutiny of judges.  Finally, the investigative activity of prosecutors allowed difficult cases, such as military uprisings and a terrorist attack on the barracks of the Army's Third Infantry Regiment, to be successfully prosecuted without retribution.

## Notes

[1]This does not mean, of course, that each prosecutor should not be under the control of a superior.

[2]The Code of Criminal Procedure of 1888 forbids any suspect under detention from communicating with any person for a ten day period.  In 1985, reforms shortened the time to six days.  The new code, in force since September 1992, reduces it to three days.

[3]Articles 100 and 101 of the Argentine Constitution are a nearly literal translation of Article III, § 2 of the United States Constitution.

[4]*See* CODE OF PROCEEDINGS IN CRIMINAL MATTERS 8 (1988).

[5]*Id.* at 29.

[6]Originally, this was fixed at thirty days.  Nevertheless, this stage rarely ended within this time frame.  In 1980, a resolution over this tension between legal theory and practice occurred.  The system replaced the thirty-day limit and simply required judges to inform the appellate court if more than six months elapsed.

[7]Five years ago, even depositions from the suspect given to the police could be used as evidence. In the Province of Buenos Aires, for example, the police alone conduct the *sumario*. Judges revise and "ratify" these results. Such a system, of course, simply encourages police torture of suspects.

[8]The Regional Course on Public Prosecution organized by Ilanud and held in Lima, Peru in April 1989, unanimously reached the same conclusion.

[9]Abraham Goldstein, *La Discrecionalidad de la Persecución Penal en los Estados Unidos*, 49 LECCIONES Y ENSAYOS 27 (1988).

[10]Indeed, this approach will simply exacerbate a prominent cultural and political problem of many Latin American countries -- the avoidance of rules and processes. Latin American nations are not, however, the only nations facing this issue. Norway's Director of Criminal Prosecution once told me that even if his country had adopted the "opportunity system" more than a hundred years before, and Sweden the "legality system," no one would note any difference in legal practice.

[11]In Argentina, approximately ninety-six percent of convictions have resulted in three-year sentences or less.

[12]José Hernández, *Martín Fierro*.

[13]In countries like Peru, as well as in some Argentine provinces such as Salta, the prosecutors' office is not located in any of the three branches of government. It is instead located in a separate department.

[14]This is, for example, the view of Argentine Minister of Justice Leon Carlos Arslanian. He made this claim in a recent meeting about public prosecution held in Cordoba. *See* Inaugural Speech of the Fourth National Conference on Public Ministries, September 1991.

[15]President Carlos Menem is, however, trying to change this location by putting prosecutors under the jurisdiction of the Ministry of Justice.

[16]President Menem's government has recently taken such steps in the case of Ricardo Molinas, and Argentina's Supreme Court agreed with the President's position (conversation with former Solicitor General Jaime Malamud-Goti).

[17]Many of these jurists opposed such a proposal made by Julio Maier in the 1987 project for a new code of procedure as dangerous to civil liberties. Congress rejected this proposal.

[18]A particularly egregious example of not allowing prosecutors to have this power can be seen in the efforts made by the best part of the Argentine judiciary to inquire about missing people during the military regime. The Supreme Court, modifying previous doctrine from *Ollero*, 300 Fallos 457 (1978), ordered that in *habeas corpus* proceedings every effort should be made to discover what had happened to the kidnapped people. Although many judges willingly followed that rule, their undertakings were rendered unsuccessful by the lack of any help from police, who were under military command.

[19]Any doubt about the facts must be decided in favor of the accused.

[20]*See generally* COMISIÓN NACIONAL SOBRE LA DESAPARICIÓN DE PERSONAS, NUNCA MAS: INFORME DE LA COMISIÓN NACIONAL SOBRE LA DESAPARICIÓN DE PERSONAS (9th ed. 1985) [NEVER AGAIN: THE REPORT OF THE ARGENTINE NATIONAL COMMISSION ON THE DISAPPEARED].

[21]In cases of homicide, the victim's relatives replace the victim.

[22]The power to punish.

[23]Indeed, discussions in Argentina over the past six years on proposals for victim participation reflect this controversy.

[24]*See supra* note 16.

[25]This is so even if I disagree with many other aspects of the code, especially in the maintenance of the *sumario* and its natural consequence, the inquisitorial function of judges.

[26]The case began in October 1985 and ended on December 6, 1986. *See generally, supra* note 20.

[27]Resolution 927787, November 3, 1987.

# 15

---

# Should Prosecutors Be Independent of the Executive in Prosecuting Government Abuses?

*Philip B. Heymann*

## I.
### Introduction

The more I have thought about the implications of the question whether prosecutors should be independent of the executive in prosecuting abuses by the government, the more complicated it seems. My own experience teaches me the importance of context in addressing this question. Having helped establish the Watergate Special Prosecution force to investigate President Nixon's abuses, I began a major project in Guatemala with the assumption that judges and prosecutors could force an end to massive governmental abuses of every sort in that troubled country. I came to see that I was expecting far too much ingenuity of ordinary human beings, that they could not compensate for a lack of enthusiastic cooperation by the highest political figures. Only the President and the Minister of Defense could mobilize the police to provide the investigative resources that were needed when there was a massacre, a political murder, or a well-connected drug deal.

When abuses became particularly troublesome with the murder of ten or twelve students in the late summer of 1989, I went to the Minister of Defense and the President and told them that Harvard Law School would leave Guatemala unless they initiated a vigorous investigation of crimes for which the country's security forces might well bear some responsibility. Each told me that the failure was attributable to the investigative judges and prosecutors who were, they were at pains to remind me, independent and responsible. For successful trials of terrible abuses, Guatemala needed determined efforts by high-level leaders to motivate the police to investigate and to protect judges and prosecutors from violence -- two essentials for a successful prosecution. And, in the case of Guatemala, independence provided an excuse for withholding those efforts.

I have studied prosecutors attempting to deal with governmental abuse in a number of countries. The stories are very interesting. An Israeli prosecutor, traditionally independent, is fired for refusing to suppress a case against the domestic security forces for killing two Palestinian terrorists after they were arrested.[1] The Japanese Ministry of Justice, theoretically very independent, declines to bring an obvious wiretapping case, reminiscent of Watergate, against the official tappers of the phone line of the Chairman of the Communist Party.[2] The quite independent prosecutors of South Africa decline to investigate cases of police violence, including one involving a South African officer who has personally killed dozens of demonstrators or suspects.[3] That the police are in charge of such investigations was the explanation I was given by the Attorney General in Cape Town.

A British investigation of a "shoot-to-kill" policy affecting Irish Republican Party (IRA) suspects in Northern Ireland and as far away as Gibraltar is effectively hushed-up by the government without so much as a peep from the prosecutors in a land we strongly associate with the rule of law. Nor is it the prosecutors who reveal an apparent fabrication of evidence against IRA suspects tried for bombings in England.[4]

Obviously, more is involved than a structural arrangement and a pledge of independence if the object is controlling governmental abuses. For reasons of state, the government of France humiliated its theoretically independent chief prosecutor by having him urge on an unwilling court a trivial sentence for Abdallah, the terrorist murderer of American and Israeli officials. Even the evidence presented by the French prosecutor seemed purposely pared back to accomplish that result.[5]

The answer as to the desirability of an independent prosecutor and what that means seems to me to require a quite complicated analysis. In this chapter, I will try to be the guide for a first exploratory excursion of this subject. My hope is that, after this preliminary excursion, others will build on my analysis to explore further its implications.

There are several major steps to the analysis, but the beginning is to make clear a not very controversial assumption that lies behind it. Like most of those analyzing the subject of the relationship of the prosecutor to the highest governmental officials, I will assume that, because of professional tradition or public expectation, the prosecutor is more committed to equal and unbiased enforcement of the law than is the President or the other governmental powers such as, in Latin America, the Minister of Defense. Otherwise, and "otherwise" was often the situation in Guatemala until the appointment of some recent Attorneys General, structures make no difference. The prosecutor will simply behave as the highest political officials wish, whatever the structural and other guarantees of independence. I will also assume that the law itself is, on its face if not in application, fair, neutral, and respectful of human rights. Substantial pressures from other nations have assured this condition of formal correctness even in very repressive regimes. With those assumptions stated, I begin my analysis.

In Part I, I categorize the types of governmental abuses and discuss the sources of abuse, the motivation for each of the sources of abuse, and the attitudes of high-level officials toward those abuses. In Part II, I analyze the power of the significant actors -- elected officials, police, and prosecutors -- in relation to one another. In Part III, I discuss the relevance of independence for the effectiveness of prosecutions, analyzing the ambiguities in the notion of independence and the inherent complexity about the areas of independence. In Part IV, I explore these ideas as applied to the most difficult cases -- abuses by security forces in the name of security. Finally, in Part V, I look at the steps prosecutors may be able to take that would increase the power of democratically elected leaders to prevent abuses by the military in the name of national security.

## II.
## A Categorization of the Types of Governmental Abuse

### A. *Sources of Governmental Abuse*

Without great loss in generality, we can use a relatively simple framework to classify abuses by their source and by their motivation. As to source, there are at least four possibilities which I shall illustrate with American examples.

First, they may be initiated by the highest government officials, including the elected or unelected leaders. In the United States, the cover-up of Watergate would be a clear example. Second, abuses can be carried out by lower-level officials in the executive branch, without the direction of their political superiors. The claimed independence of North and Poindexter in the Iran-Contra Affair would be an example of the second.

Since the police are the primary investigators of crime and the maintainers of public order, we should consider as a third category, different from the second, abuses by the police. The beating of Rodney King by Los Angeles Police Department officers is a now very familiar example. Fourth, and finally, there is the extremely troublesome case of abuses directed by intelligence or military forces and carried on relatively independently of the elected political leadership. The break-ins to the houses of the families of political radicals in the aftermath of the activities of the Weathermen in the United States, break-ins ordered by top officials of the Federal Bureau of Investigation (FBI), would be a rare example of this in the United States.

## B. Motivations for Governmental Abuse

The source of abuse furnishes only one axis on the matrix of governmental abuse. The other axis is furnished by the motivation, for each of the sources of abuse may be acting out of any of several motivations. Recognizing that any of several categorizations would be useful, I will propose a division into three types of motivations.

First, the purpose of the governmental abuse may be personal enrichment through corruption or extortion. Corruption at the highest level of government has posed serious problems for Japan, Argentina, the United States, and many other countries. The corruption of the military or intelligence forces, for personal gain, is a serious problem in many countries in Latin America -- a problem made far worse by the United States policy of encouraging military involvement in drug suppression. Mexico and Colombia are only two examples. I need hardly provide examples of corruption or extortion at the working levels of the police or the lower levels of other bureaucracies.

A second major motivation for governmental abuse, and one that is particularly threatening to democracy, is the monitoring and control of political opponents.[6] Sometimes the monitoring itself is illegal; examples are Watergate and the wiretapping in Japan. However, in many countries, including Great Britain and France, some political intelligence-gathering on mainline political opponents is believed to be an appropriate activity for the police or intelligence agencies. In other countries, Germany is an example, where gathering intelligence on radical parties of the Left or Right is an authorized activity, the authorization has at times been stretched to reach mainline opponents.

Of course it is not simply the intelligence gathering that constitutes the serious abuse in many cases. Using the intelligence, the government may order the torture, murder, or disappearance of political opponents. That has been true in Argentina, Chile, Uruguay, Guatemala, and many other Latin American countries. In the United States, the Nixon Administration proposed to use such information to penalize by tax audits or, in the case of Daniel Ellsberg, by making public his most personal secrets (which the Administration hoped to find by breaking into the office of Ellsberg's psychiatrist).

When political repression is carried out at a street level, at the direction of a local police commander or even of lower-level officers, we have order maintained through the repression of legal activities that are disapproved by the police. I would include racist forms of law enforcement in this category, although they are of course worse for being based on race. They are an effort to maintain a form of dominance on the street and are thus a low-level abuse motivated by political repression.

Neutrality in the ever-present contest between lawyers and police requires me to note that prosecutors, too, can be the initiators or agents of repression and violence, if they knowingly use false evidence to obtain convictions, either for their own purposes or at the direction of political superiors. Bringing false or weak charges against the political leader's enemies was an abuse perfected by Stalin and his chief prosecutor, Vyshinsky, and then associated more broadly with the former Soviet Union and its satellites.

Finally, I would use a catch-all category of abuse of power where the motivation is neither economic self-interest nor political repression, but simply pleasure in the exploitation of the powers of an office or excessive enthusiasm for one's role. An army that kills its guerrilla opponents even when it would be wiser (not simply more moral) to take them prisoner, a police force that freely provides beatings without trial, an intelligence agency that exploits its access to private information -- these are the more dramatic examples I have in mind. But the same category would cover Kafkaesque abuses of bureaucratic power.

### C. Attitudes of High-Level Officials

As if four sources of abuse and three motivations for each did not create a complicated-enough matrix of twelve boxes, I should add one more variable in terms of types of abuse. As to any abuse, except the obvious case of those directed by the highest-level government officials, it is important to know what is the attitude of those highest political officials. There are several possibilities. The form of governmental abuse may be opposed by the highest political levels in which case it survives only when it is undiscovered. The abuse may be tolerated by the political leaders or simply ignored. This is the case when the political power of those engaged in the abuse or, in Latin America, their military power makes opposition unwise or dangerous. In extreme cases, the governmental abuse may be protected and covered up by the highest political levels. Prime Minister Shamir protected the killing of two Palestinian terrorists by Shin Bet in the Bus #300 Affair.[7] Margaret Thatcher protected the killing of IRA terrorists.[8] On assuming office Ronald Reagan promptly pardoned Felt and Miller, the FBI executives who had ordered illegal break-ins to pursue the Weathermen.[9]

This final distinction is important. If the highest political levels are protecting a form of governmental abuse or, worse, are directing it, any control they can exercise over the prosecutor will be used to prevent successful prosecution of that wrongdoing. If, at the opposite extreme, the highest political levels are opposed to the form of abuse, but simply are unable to discover and control it, they will be a source of support to the prosecutor, particularly if they are his superiors and can claim credit for his activities.    The most interesting category is the middle one, where the highest political officials are tolerating or ignoring abuses because of the political or military power of those responsible.    That situation, so charac-teristic of military-civilian relations in recent decades in Latin America, will require our further attention, but not yet.

## III.
## The Powers of the Major Actors
## (Elected Officials, Police, and Prosecutors)
## Vis-a-Vis Each Other

Since I am assuming that for purposes of our discussion, the sole aim is to strengthen the rule of law and respect for human rights, and since I am assuming that the prosecutor is more committed to these values than the police, the highest political figures, or the security forces, what is needed is to grant the maximum freedom, resources, and influence to the prosecutor.    This description of my objectives is, however, contentious. There are values other than the rule of law and respect for the political and civil rights of individuals.    But if my statements of the tentative objective is accepted -- at least for countries where legality and human rights have not been widely respected -- then the fact that I believe it is significant to grant maximum power to the prosecutor follows from his greater interest in the objectives.

What does *not* follow is that the greatest power comes from the greatest independence.    We would not think that necessarily true of a foreign minis-ter who we know needs the help of the President in dealing with military and intelligence officials as well as domestic organizations.    It is not necessarily true of an Attorney General.    It is of course true that being subject to the direction of political figures less committed to the rule of law and human rights results in their power to deflect him from pursuing his, and by hypothesis my, objectives.    But being subject to some control by the highest political figures may also provide powers that the prosecutor needs.

Let me be precise.    Preventing governmental abuses may require the cooperation, at the prosecutor's request, of any or all of the following groups which are independent of him: police, courts, and the authorized managers of government agencies.    The first is obvious.    To find the facts, the prosecutor is likely to need the cooperation of the police.    In many countries the formal arrangement puts the prosecutor in charge of the investigation and directs the police to follow his directions; but rarely if ever is this scrupulously or even generally followed in practice.[10]    The relationship between the prosecutor and the police, whose support he badly needs, is always problematic.

The prosecutor needs the support and trust of the court that will adjudicate any cases he brings. Countries vary in this area. The support of the judiciary is so clear in Japan and China and was so clear in the Soviet Union that many western nations questioned whether the system is one of administrative determination by the prosecutor rather than adjudication by a court. At the opposite extreme, the skepticism of judges in many Latin American countries about evidence produced by the police makes conviction on such evidence very difficult. The same is true, for example, in the Bronx in New York City.

The prosecutor may need the cooperation of the highest government officials if he is to get the cooperation of lower-level officials in furnishing information and evidence about governmental wrongdoing and if he is to get the cooperation of the police in investigating such cases. The prosecutor may also need the cooperation of the highest government officials in establishing systems and mechanisms to reduce the possibility of governmental abuse in the future: review boards for police brutality or procurators or inspectors general to detect corruption.

To handle governmental abuse the prosecutor must put together an effective cooperating team out of this group of independent actors. To enlist the support of these actors, the prosecutor has several powers at his disposal. He can call upon the courts to adjudicate guilt or innocence if he has the necessary evidence and independence from contrary orders by superiors. He can call upon the police to gather the needed evidence relying on their subordination to the highest political or military officials, if the highest political or military officials are willing to assist the prosecutor. He can call on the police on his own if the police have developed a tradition of independence and want convictions (rather than summary punishment of offenders or immunity), but only if the police also see the work of the prosecutor as helpful in convincing the court to convict. That helpfulness may take the form either of advising what evidence is necessary on what elements of the crime or of obtaining the court's approval for certain investigative steps such as a search, arrest, or wiretap.

If the political leaders are recalcitrant and the police uncooperative, the prosecutor can call on the public to use its political pressure to support the prosecutor.[11] Whether the public will respond to the call depends upon the role it assigns to the prosecutor, the police, and (to a lesser extent) the courts in dealing with two crucial issues: the danger of violence by private groups and the danger of lawlessness by government officials.

How the public responds, which is often a crucial variable in terms of the power of the prosecutor, also depends upon the relative importance influential segments of the public attach to order and safety on the streets, on the one hand, and governmental abuses, on the other. If the danger of street violence is very great, the prosecutor may not be able to generate public support in demanding police cooperation or increased police lawfulness; the public is likely to support the police instead. If concern about government illegalities is great, the prosecutor may not be able to generate public support in any conflict over his authority vis-a-vis that of the courts.

Finally, the power of the prosecutor to invoke public support in order to control the other agencies necessary to eliminate government abuse depends upon the reputation of the prosecutor's office. If the prosecutor is thought to be a forceful representative of personal security and order and a strong opponent of street crime, he need worry less about quarreling with the police even in a situation of substantial public apprehension about law and order. The same is true, of course, if the police are thought to be totally ineffective in providing safety. If the prosecutor is thought to be wholly committed to law and human rights, he need worry less about the complaints of judges.

Most important, perhaps, if the prosecutor is thought to be much more committed to enforcing lawfulness among government officials than the highest political officials, he will enjoy a substantial political advantage in mobilizing those who are very concerned about this issue. They in turn may be influential with an elected political figure and yet themselves have very little influence on the leaders of the military.

The result of all this is to create a complicated set of forces, the strength of which depends upon public attitudes and organizational reputations and capacities. This set of forces determines the relative powers of the prosecutor, the police, the judiciary, the highest elected officials, and the security forces. The extent of these relative powers determines the capacity of the prosecutor to generate the cooperation he needs to deal with government abuses. And what cooperation he needs depends upon what governmental abuses we are talking about, as does what cooperation he will get from others.

It may seem that there is too much complexity in this description. Nevertheless, that happens to be the way this world actually works. Perhaps this complexity helps explain why it is so difficult to say that independence helps or harms a prosecutor in dealing with the whole array of forms and contexts of governmental abuse.

## IV.
## The Relevance of Independence for the
## Prosecutor's Effectiveness

There is more ambiguity in the notion of an independent prosecutor than at first appears. Prosecutors in Germany, the United States, and Japan are formally subordinate to justice ministries, but tradition guarantees them substantial independence. It was a scandal for Prime Minister Shamir to remove the Attorney General of Israel. Firing the specially-appointed Watergate prosecutor, Archibald Cox, led very directly to President Nixon's near-impeachment and resignation. There is also complexity about the areas of independence. The highest political figures may be authorized by tradition as well as delegation to make prosecutorial policy at a general level and forbidden to interfere in individual decisions.[12]

So what we are talking about is a continuum between very substantial independence and very substantial dependence on the orders of political superiors who are not entrusted with prosecutorial responsibilities. Few prosecutors' offices have the independence of the United States' "Independent Counsel" in setting their own budgets. Few prosecutors' offices are subject to direct orders to bring or drop a case. Most prosecutors fall somewhere between these extremes. The question is, what is to be said for a closer or more remote relationship between the prosecutor and the highest political figures in a country? I think the answer is contextual; it is different in different situations. Let me illustrate.

### A. Abuses Committed or Protected by the Highest Political Figures

The case that comes most readily to mind and as to which the answer seems straightforward is one in which abuses are committed or protected by the highest political actors. To whatever extent the prosecutor can be given orders by the very officials whose corruption or acts of political repression should be stopped, the prosecutor will be disabled from bringing those leaders into court even where the force of public opinion is strongest in its demands for equal treatment of the powerful with the most ordinary citizen. For that reason the United States has had a statute appointing an independent prosecutor in any such cases.[13] Japan has an even older tradition that involves a similar procedure for similar reasons.[14]

### B. Abuses Committed by Other Governmental Officials

If we turn from the highest political figures to the other possible sources of governmental abuse, several questions become crucial. For example, how important to the prevention of the abuse are steps that only the highest political figures can take? What is their attitude toward the particular combination of the source of the abuse and the type of abuse (for example, brutality by police or corruption by middle-level department officials)? What is their freedom to act with regard to those sources and types of abuse? Are the highest political figures more likely to act in support of a prosecutor who is known as their agent or in support of a prosecutor who is known to be independent?

The last question demands special attention. Depending on the costs and risks, political figures will support a prosecutor if they see that to be in their interests. To be precise, they will do more than they otherwise might do because of the requests or actions of the prosecutor only if they see that to be a route to greater domestic or international support for them and their goals by the public or influential organizations or nations.

If the prosecutor's position is a highly respected one and the occupant shares in that respect, political figures may be brought to support the prosecutor simply because of the losses in political or international support that would come from his publicizing their lack of cooperation. The clearest and most extreme example of this was the ability of Archibald Cox as the first Watergate Special Prosecutor to bring the very powerful President of the United States to deliver incriminating documents and tapes to the courts. The position of Justice Goldstone as head of a judicial commission on violence in South Africa is analogous.

If, on the other hand, the prosecutor's position is not greatly respected or if there is widespread cynicism about the neutrality of application of the criminal law, political figures are not likely to fear the consequences of failing to cooperate or of refusing to order other members of the executive branch to cooperate with an investigation. In that situation the greatest effectiveness of the prosecutor may lie, as in the case of other executive branch officials, in his ability to persuade the highest elected officials of what is in their interest. A prosecutor known to be loyal to the president or prime minister is likely to be more persuasive than one thought to be entirely independent.

Consider an opposite extreme from corruption or abuse by the president, the prime minister, or closely associated colleagues. The police in many countries are corrupt and brutal for their own purposes, not exclusively or largely for the purposes of the administration. A prosecutor cannot successfully investigate this or take steps that will bring it to a stop without the cooperation of friendly or at least supportive police commanders. The Serpico scandal in New York would not have ended in substantial reforms without the appointment of a new, reforming police chief, Patrick Murphy. Reforms in Los Angeles after the beating of Rodney King depended on finding a police chief more supportive of reform than Darrell Gates.

If the chief political figure is embarrassed by police abuse of governmental power and if he could be persuaded to take strong steps, I would rather see the arguments and the proposals for reform made by a prosecutor closely tied to the executive branch than by an independent prosecutor. Only in the former case will the arguments have the force of coming from a loyal supporter and an informed insider. Only in the former case will the recommendations be fully informed and will there be the potential of police cooperation with the prosecutor in carrying them out. Only in the former case will remedial action redound to the credit of the administration and not look like the response of those who were caught failing in their duties of supervision. All or much of the same could be said of crimes of corruption carried on, without high-level approval, by the middle ranks of other government agencies.

## V.
## The Hardest Case: Abuses in the
## Name of Security by Security Forces

The hardest question arises with regard to the most frightening form of governmental abuse in Latin America and South Africa -- abuse sponsored or supported by leaders of the military against a political element they consider dangerous even when it is not involved in armed resistance. Many months after the conversations I had with the Minister of Defense and President of Guatemala in 1989, most people think that the situation is not greatly changed. The assassination in early 1992 of a professor of history at Guatemala's major university in front of his house is still not an unusual event. He had been working on the organization of internally displaced people. The leaders of human rights organizations and trade unions still receive serious death threats. Some are carried out. The student organization, the murder of whose leaders had led us to confrontation and our departure, was bombed in the same early days of 1992.

There is never proof of who is responsible for such events; there never has been in Guatemala or in many other countries, although in Argentina they stopped abruptly with the coming of civilian government. The Attorney General of Guatemala now investigates publicly, but no cases have been brought. This is surely the hardest category to deal with as well as the most important form of governmental abuse, both because of the horror of its consequences and because of its impact on democracy.

## A. *The Many Reasons for Pessimism*

As to this crucial category of governmental abuse, the central question is not about the independence of the prosecutors or even the courts. It is simply this: Why should anyone think that independent prosecutors or courts could help deal with abuses in the name of internal security carried out by a quite independent military? If the highest *political* authorities had the power to control the security forces, they would do it *if* they wanted to. If leaders enjoying popular legitimacy lack either the power or the will, of what possible relevance are independent courts and prosecutors?

The reasons the highest political authorities in Latin America often lack the power to control the security forces are clear enough. Middle and lower military ranks will not follow the direction of political authorities when they conflict with military orders, at least with regard to matters that are very broadly considered matters of internal security. Civilian supremacy is not established among security forces. The tradition is otherwise; the training is otherwise; political authorities are often regarded as corrupt or naive; and the risks of disobedience to military superiors are far greater than the risks of disobeying elected leaders. All this is different in western democracies.

What is more, the risks to the political authorities of mounting a broad based political challenge to this -- as Yeltsin did in Moscow in the Summer of 1991 -- are extremely serious. There could be a coup, supported in Latin America (as it would not be in western nations and was not in France at the time of the Algerian solution), by powerful and politically influential economic forces. Democracy is held in too little repute and coups are too frequent to count on a popular uprising against them in many countries. And even if a coup is out of the question -- because coups have become politically reprehensible in international society with the wave of democracy -- selective assassination remains a powerfully inhibiting threat. Compared to these risks, allowing the military to control substantial but bounded areas of the nation's policy seems a small price for elected political leaders to pay in terms of insurance.

Faced with such a confrontation of extremely powerful political and military forces -- the one supported by an elected mandate and an ideology of democracy, the other by a loyal army and an ideology of national security -- what can be expected of the relatively weak claimants to an ideology of law, the courts and independent prosecutors? Exclusive military jurisdiction over adjudication of alleged military abuses is jealously guarded in many Latin American countries, although often civilian prosecutors may at least initiate cases in military courts. The police are generally under the control of the military, and without police support the resources for investigation of murders when bodies are found in remote areas is slight. The police will also not cooperate in protecting prosecutors, judges, and witnesses from the risks associated with investigating crimes by security forces. Even if the police were willing to cooperate and to protect, evidence of crimes committed on military bases or evidence that could only be obtained there would be inaccessible.

To all these reasons to doubt the efficacy of independent judges and prosecutors in situations where the highest elected officials find themselves unable or unwilling to prevent government abuse by military forces, one more reason for doubt should be added. Nowhere is the legitimate domain of law more vigorously contested even in the most lawful of western countries than where its boundaries confront claims of national security or internal security. It was in this area that the Prime Minister of Israel refused to allow the trial of apparent murders by the intelligence forces,[15] where the Prime Minister of England took active measures to prevent the exploration of responsibility for the killings of IRA agents,[16] where the French tampered with the trial of a murdering terrorist,[17] and where the Japanese prevented the trial of officials for illegal wiretapping.[18]

I could extend the examples to the United States and many other countries. This point is straightforward, however, without more examples. No one knows the precise boundary between the ideology of national security and the ideology of law in most countries, although the boundary is surely located far more favorably to the rule of law in the United States than in, for example, Guatemala. Each of these ideologies claims passionately jurisdictions that are as vigorously claimed by the other. For our purposes, what is important is that the contested areas are the least secure domain for those insisting on the rule of law. Carter acted on behalf of law to try high FBI officials, Miller and Felt, for illegal break-ins to the homes of family members of Weathermen.[19] Reagan immediately returned the territory -- hard-won by a successful conviction -- to the hands of those responsible for internal security by pardoning the FBI officials.[20]

## B. The Grounds for Hope

An elected President, who finds himself pushed by the military or some elements of the military to tolerate forms of brutal political repression that he personally despises, may find his bargaining position strengthened by pressure from the other side. Look for a moment at why death squads are chosen. A government could go about repression, as the Soviet Union or East Germany did, using law as its tool. The system is simple enough. You create new political crimes and crimes of association. You censor and punish for unauthorized speech. You strengthen your capacity to enforce these laws by weakening familiar judicial protections: the burden of proof, access to counsel, guarantees of privacy, rights not to be tortured, freedom from surveillance by a mass of paid or terrified informants, opportunity to confront hostile witnesses and evidence. Judges may be subjected to pressure by the political leadership, perhaps using prosecutors for this purpose. The Nazis did this. Alternatively, military courts or special secret courts can replace regular and open trials. If all these options remain too cumbersome, internment without trial is still available wherever the British colonial tradition survives.

But instead of using these forms of legality, with their accompanying publicity, Latin American governments have relied on death squads for repression and they have done this despite a set of special risks that come with this secret use of violent repression. The likelihood of making mistakes increases rapidly; the Mossad brought to an end its assassination of Black September assassins when it mistakenly killed a Norwegian waiter.[21] Those who operate the secret system tend over time to turn it to their own personal purposes, seeking money, power, or sex. That was true in Guatemala and in Argentina. And the absence of the notice that even repressive laws give, and of the opportunity to remain safe by obeying such laws, increases fear and resentment even in those who might support the repressive regime.

The primary reason for bearing such costs is that those who are operating the system want deniability at home and abroad. Deniability requires effective control of any authoritative fact-finding system, such as the criminal justice system. In the words of a scholar of the South African death squads, deniability requires a "user-friendly" criminal justice system.[22] The form of government abuses we are looking at is not simply a death squad, it is a secret death squad. Very few countries operate open death squads. The cost is too high in terms of international opprobrium and domestic disdain.

In this context, the "deal" between elected leaders and the military in a country tolerant of brutality by the military against dissident leaders and organizations, generally assumes that there will be no scandal caused by open revelation of what has been done. The President agrees to do nothing, perhaps because his hands are tied, but only so long as it is politically and internationally tolerable to do nothing; and that is only so long as there is a substantial measure of ambiguity as to who is responsible for any killings, disappearances, or torture. The military must deliver unaccountability as part of the bargain under which the President delivers silence or excuses rather than pointed denunciations and personal support of organized opposition to the repressive role of the military.

## VI.

## What a Prosecutor Can Do About Military Abuses

In the final analysis the crucial questions about independent prosecutors, like those about independent investigation or trial are these. What could a prosecutor do that would strengthen the hand of democratically-elected leaders in preventing abuses by a powerful military in the name of internal security; and what resources would the prosecutor's office need to provide that support? I do not think the prosecutor can act alone. Even in Israel the prosecutor who insisted on investigating killings of terrorists by the intelligence forces was fired without bringing about fundamental changes.[23] The same was true in Spain where a prosecutor, together with the investigating judge, insisted on pursuing killings of ETA terrorists by a special police unit.[24] The results have been the same with an occasional brave investigating judge in Guatemala.

Some answers are indirect. To the extent that prosecutors can strengthen the capacity of law enforcement to bring cases for violation of laws -- by improving the performance and credibility of the police in the eyes of courts and the courts in the eyes of the police -- they reduce the justification for secret death squad activity. The Minister of Defense of Guatemala responded to my question about illegal assassinations by describing the hopelessness of trials in Guatemala; colonels in the countryside said the same thing when asked why they took no prisoners.

To the extent that prosecutors can make high-level corruption more costly and can make more credible claims that corruption is not riskless, they will help to build the popular support that the President needs in dealing with a powerful military. After the first coup attempt of President Cerezo's tenure in Guatemala, no crowds had appeared in support of democracy as they later did in the streets of Moscow. Rumors and allegations of massive corruption were a major reason for this dangerous show of democratic weakness. Credibly establishing the independence of a strong prosecutor in handling corruption allegations would have served President Cerezo well in terms of his power vis-a-vis the military.

But what of more direct attacks on repressive violence? As we have seen, what is necessary is simply that the truth be brought out in an authoritative way for, in many circumstances, neither the elected officials nor military leaders will choose death squads whose activities are made public. Secrecy has been crucial to the maintenance of trade and aid relationships and to a general level of acceptance in the world community -- matters which are frequently more important than the rather limited benefits of buying insurance in the currency of violent repression.

The military has several ways to prevent an investigation that would make the deal with political authorities intolerable: It can control the police by demanding the appointment of military men as the police leaders, by establishing an understanding and a custom that certain cases will not be investigated, and by using threats or violence to discipline police who may mistake their primary responsibility, thinking it is to law enforcement.[25] Instead of controlling the investigators they can control the evidence, destroying or denying access to it and intimidating or killing witnesses; and they can limit the jurisdiction of independent, civilian courts in cases against active duty officers or use less formal means, intimidating or corrupting prosecutors or judges or other fact-finders.

Each of these was familiar in Guatemala. Each is familiar elsewhere in Latin America, Africa, and Asia. The question is: in light of these powers of the military to block investigations, how can a prosecutor or investigative judge help break the chain on which impunity for military abuses depends? How can they defeat the secrecy which provides unaccountability to domestic and international audiences? Indeed, this unaccountability is a crucial condition of elected officials tolerating military abuses. If a prosecutor or investigative judge could help elected officials "trump" the three military devices for maintaining a user-friendly criminal justice system, she could help prevent the most dangerous form of governmental abuse. But how? The answer is by carefully building institutional and public support for honest and fearless investigations and prosecutions.

Picture a prosecutor's office that is widely respected both for the role it plays in dealing with ordinary crime and for its commitment to fair application of decent laws. Assume that office has learned to work closely with police investigators and has won their trust, creating at the same time a shared commitment to enforcing the law. That would bring an enviable reputation to the police as well. Imagine that the relationship of the prosecutor's office is close enough to the highest elected officials that they can win domestic and international support by defending its independence and yet providing it with political support and resources. With these characteristics, what could a prosecutor's office do to deal with the hardest form of governmental abuse?

We have seen that the first military guarantee of a "user-friendly" criminal justice system is control of the police. Defeating "user-friendliness," on the other hand, requires the prosecutor providing leadership to the police. She needs their support. Credibility in placing responsibility for deaths or disappearances requires information, and information requires independent investigators with whom it is safe to cooperate and whom it is risky for others to obstruct or even to ignore. Those investigators in turn must feel safe. These conditions, and the fact that repressive violence may take place in any corner of the country at any time, all suggest that the independent investigators cannot be a small handful of people assigned to the prosecutor's office. Nor does it suffice merely to place the entire police investigative force *formally* under the jurisdiction of the prosecutor; the leadership that appoints, promotes, transfers, and assigns must be behind the investigation, not blocking it.

These are well-known relationships. Military leaders demanded the removal of the Minister of Government in Guatemala for the crime of obtaining outside financing that was building the independence of the police. Similarly, I caused immense fear of a military response by recommending that the prosecutor's office be given a handful of investigators to handle investigations of serious government abuse including, prominently, by the military. The reluctance of the military in many countries to recognize and accept a truly civilian chief of police is further evidence of the centrality of this issue.

How can a prosecutor build support in the police? Not quickly is one answer. He must be effective enough in cooperating with the police in fighting ordinary crime and spreading the credit. He must understand that the police feel torn between loyalty to honest investigations and responsiveness to military superiors. He must be popular enough domestically or enough of an international symbol to be relatively safe from threats and attacks, and he must be able to spread that net of safety over those working for him on important cases. He must speak up with the elected officials for police needs for resources and openly condemn police abuses. He must encourage police relationships with the best of police elsewhere and police training by the best of foreign departments.

What about the second capacity of the military: to deny access to information or to obstruct investigations of otherwise accessible information? The prosecutor must be clever enough to generate outside demands for steps the President would otherwise be reluctant to take. Relations with the media are central here. He must be honorable enough so that his conclusions provide public credibility to his resolution of questions *either* about the responsibility for violence *or* about the responsibility for failure to solve violent crimes. (If so, he can himself generate outside demands for effective investigative steps, honestly performed.) He must be political enough to build a domestic and international constituency that the President must respect and can tell the military he must respect -- thereby lending Presidential prestige to independent investigations.

And what of the final recourse of a military determined to block investigations? In Guatemala, the Chief of the National Police gathered evidence that the Chief of the separate Treasury Police and a number of his agents were engaged in death squad activity. He brought the evidence to an investigating judge, Judge Trejo. Judge Trejo was kidnapped and, the same day, one of his close associates was murdered. When he was released, Judge Trejo promptly dismissed the charges against all the Treasury Police. Similar stories are told of Chile under Pinochet and elsewhere.

Is this a hopeless final obstacle to serious investigations of repressive violence? No, not if the prosecutor and police choose from among the sets of steps that the Italians learned in dealing with the Red Brigades, the French learned in dealing with Lebanese and domestic terrorists, and the Colombians learned in dealing with Pablo Escobar and the Medellin Cartel. There are steps, such as spreading responsibility for dangerous investigations to make intimidation difficult, and they must be taken.[26] The same is true of corruption in the judicial system. Dealing with repressive abuses by the military will require a program to deal with corruption among police, prosecutors, and judges, too. Indeed, corruption and intimidation joined together, as drug dealers have learned to use them in Mexico and Colombia, is the most potent "medicine" for police, prosecutors, or judges straying toward honesty. But even this combination can be combatted, as President Salinas has sometimes shown in Mexico.

## VII.
## Conclusion

In the final analysis an upright and courageous prosecutor can make a difference in dealing with governmental abuses. Even in areas where the police fear to tread, the press or legislators may provide the investigative support that is necessary. That happened in the case of the Spanish GAL and its assassinations of ETA members. It was true in the United States of the first stages of Watergate and of the Iran-Contra Affair.

Still, it is a mistake to think that uprightness and courage alone are enough. Nor is independence the only missing ingredient. Independent prosecutors without appropriate powers can be a dumping ground to provide political cover to leaders. Investigative help of the sort that only the police can furnish is necessary in many cases. The cooperation of others in the government is often necessary. Evidence must be accessible and preserved; witnesses cannot be too frightened to speak. Judges and other participants in the process must be free of fear or of hope of promotion engendered by those whose actions they are judging. For some of these, the help of the President is very useful and may be more readily available if the separation of the prosecutor from the executive branch is not exaggerated.

For the most difficult type of governmental abuse, violence by the security forces in the name of internal security, the picture is complicated. A strong prosecutor enjoying the trust and respect of the public and the police could provide a substantial and desired incentive for elected leaders to stop the abuse. But overcoming the capacity of the security forces to prevent investigations, deny evidence, and influence tribunals requires far more than independence. What is needed is a process of building trust and spreading a belief that the prosecutor is crucial to the two matters that are of central public concern: the control of crime and the control of governmental abuse.

# Notes

[1] The incident involved here was the "Bus #300 Affair," in which Israeli security officers killed two Palestinian bus hijackers while they were in custody. For a comprehensive discussion of this case, see Pnina Lahav, *A Barrel Without Hoops: The Impact of Counterterrorism on Israel's Legal Culture*, 10 CARDOZO L. REV. 529 (1988).

[2] Setsuo Miyazawa, *Scandal and Hard Reform: Implications of a Wiretapping Case to the Control of Organizational Police Crimes in Japan*, 23 KOBE U. L. REV. 13 (1989).

[3] The South African case is considered in Nico Steytler, *Policing Political Opponents: Death Squads and Cop Culture*, in TOWARDS JUSTICE? CRIME AND STATE CONTROL IN SOUTH AFRICA (D. Hansson and D. van Zyl Smit eds., 1990).

[4] *See World in Action In the Interests of Justice* (Granada television broadcast, Oct. 28, 1985) (transcript on file with Philip B. Heymann); *A Surprise Witness* (Granada television broadcast, Jan. 12, 1986) (transcript on file with Philip B. Heymann). One of our triumphs in Guatemala was to bring the prosecutors and investigative judges to the point where they would attack such an effort to fabricate evidence.

For general examinations of British responses to IRA activities, *see* William R. Nelson, *Terrorist Challenges to the Rule of Law: The British Experience*, 13 TERRORISM 227 (1990); R.J. Spjut, *The "Official" Use of Deadly Force by the Security Forces Against Suspected Terrorists: Some Lessons from Northern Ireland*, 1986 PUB. LAW 38 (1986). (These articles do not discuss the role of prosecutors specifically, but rather focus on the governmental response in general).

[5] The Abdallah trial, particularly its implications for multilateral cooperation in combatting terrorism, is explored in Philip B. Heymann, *International Cooperation in Dealing with Terrorism: A Review of Law and Recent Practice*, 6 AM. U. J. INT'L L. & POL'Y 1, 31 (1990).

[6] Intelligence investigations give rise to a serious dilemma for democratic societies, even if those investigations are conducted through legal channels. On the one hand, monitoring may be a necessary tool for combatting domestic violence or terrorism. Yet, on the other hand, since people who advocate political views in line

with terrorists and in opposition to the government are the ones most likely to join or aid terrorists, intelligence agencies will seek surveillance of those political groups, thereby threatening democratic values by discouraging dissent. *See* Philip B. Heymann, Intelligence Gathering and Processing (1992) (unpublished manuscript on file with Philip B. Heymann).

[7]Lahav, *supra* note 1, at 533-34.

[8]For an account of the killings in Gibraltar, see Ian Jack, *Gibraltar*, 25 GRANTA 15 (1988).

[9]Francis J. Martin, *Leveling,* N.Y. TIMES, May 11, 1981, at A19. In 1972 and 1973, L. Mark and Edward S. Miller, F.B.I. officials, authorized secret searches of homes of individuals associated with the Weathermen, a violent faction of the anti-Vietnam War movement.

[10]*See* Thomas Weigend, *Criminal Procedure: Comparative Aspects*, *in* ENCYCLOPEDIA OF CRIME AND JUSTICE (Sanford H. Kadish ed., 1983).

[11]An independent media can greatly enhance the prosecutor's ability to draw on the power of the public to pressure high government officials, the courts, or the police to aid the prosecutor. On this topic, consider David M. Kennedy, *Exposing Police Terrorism in Spain, in* PHILIP B. HEYMANN & ROBERT KLITGAARD, DEALING WITH CORRUPTION AND INTIMIDATION IN CRIMINAL JUSTICE SYSTEMS: CASES AND MATERIALS (1991). As Kennedy notes, "The Spanish public, spurred onward by a scoop in the Spanish press, wanted to know much more. Late in August, reporters for the newsweekly *Diario 16* had received a tip and discovered a GAL cache in the south of France. . . ." David M. Kennedy, *Exposing Police Terrorism in Spain,* [Cambridge, MA: CASE PROGRAM, JOHN F. KENNEDY SCHOOL OF GOVERNMENT, HARVARD UNIVERSITY, 1990, CASE NO. C16-90-956.0].

The media can play a role by either investigating government abuses on its own, or by urging the public to demand an official investigation. The key to keeping a system from being "user-friendly" is to preserve avenues which would reveal -- or insist on the revelation of -- information the government may not want published. An independent media is one such avenue.

[12] In a way that is not relevant to our discussion, prosecutorial independence may also be affected by various schemes of judicial or public review of a decision not to prosecute. That is true in Germany and Japan, for example.

[13]Ethics in Government Act of 1978, Pub. L. No. 95-521, 92 Stat. 1820 (codified as amended at 28 U.S.C. §§ 49, 591 (1988)).

[14]Miyazawa, *supra* note 2.

[15]Lahav, *supra* note 1, at 543-47.

[16]Jack, *supra* note 8.

[17]Heymann, *supra* note 5, at 3.

[18]Miyazawa, *supra* note 2.

[19]Martin, *supra* note 9.

[20]*Id.*

[21]*See Appendix I: Court Judgment Published After the Trial of the Israeli Secret Service Agents Accused of Complicity in Wael Zuaiter's Assassination, in* FOR A PALESTINIAN: A MEMORIAL TO WAEL ZUAITER (Janet Venn-Brown ed., 1984).

[22]Steytler, *supra* note 3.

[23]Lahav, *supra* note 1, at 543.

[24]Kennedy, *supra* note 11.

[25]The military may also have to use threats or violence to discipline members of the press who seek to investigate governmental abuse.

[26]*See, e.g.*, LEONARD B. WEINBERG & WILLIAM L. EUBANK, THE RISE AND FALL OF ITALIAN TERRORISM (1987).

# 16

# Human Rights Abuses in Fledgling Democracies: The Role of Discretion

*Jaime Malamud-Goti*[1]

## I.

In the early 1990s, Argentine society exhibits two odd and striking characteristics. The first one is the extremely fragmented views of the citizenry on what happened during the 1974-1983 period in which state-sponsored human rights violations took place. As a consequence, the significance of the human rights trials set up during the Alfonsín administration is also controversial. The second peculiarity is a clear inconsistency between the fervent popular support of those trials of human rights abuses and present indicators that the populace is ready to elect authoritarian rulers and acquiesce again to police brutality. A new campaign of police abuse has met with few public reactions, and in the 1991 elections candidates representing extremely authoritarian views had an astonishing appeal. Military officers running for provincial governorships and seats in the Lower House captured a substantial portion of the electorate. This appeal was not diminished by the fact that these candidates had either represented the delinquent military dictatorship in the same jurisdictions where they were running in 1991 or had stood up against the elected government of President Raúl Alfonsín to have the trials terminated.[2]

The most surprising event was the success of ex-Lieutenant-Colonel Aldo Rico, who ran for governor of the Buenos Aires Province (Argentina's largest province) in the September 10, 1991 elections. Rico had been cashiered during the Alfonsín administration for leading military rebellions against his commanders in April 1987 and January 1988. Pardoned by President Menem in 1989, few considered that Rico or his newly-founded party, MODIM, had a chance of obtaining over two percent of the electorate in Buenos Aires. Identified with a staunchly undemocratic faction of the army, Rico's party obtained three seats at the National Congress when almost eleven percent of the province's population voted for his ticket.[3] This is particularly astonishing considering that Rico headed revolts that were aimed at removing the army's commanders for not having stopped the trials of officers accused of violating human rights. According to Rico, such failure jeopardized the dignity of the army.[4] After the elections, most political observers conjectured that Rico's party's success was a desperate move by the Buenos Aires province's urban poor. Recent polls demonstrate, however, that the ex-officer's voters were mostly middle class.[5]

Another striking example involves General Domingo Bussi. In Tucuman, Bussi obtained forty-three percent of the vote, but still lost to the Peronist Party candidate whom Menem backed personally, pop singer Ramon ("Palito") Ortega. Bussi challenged the elections claiming they were rigged.[6] This opinion is shared by many observers who suspect this occurred because of the federal government appointee who supervised the elections in Tucuman.

My own conclusion is that if genuine (institutional) authority is not asserted in Argentina, democracy cannot be expected to be more than formal, and strong leaders will maintain their appeal to large sectors of society. Immunity, and the pardon decrees of 1989 and 1990 in particular, undermined the reliability of Congress and the judiciary. The theory of punishment presented in this paper is intended to contribute to a change in this authoritarian trend.

In 1991, few Argentines question the premise that human rights violations carried out during the 1976-1983 dictatorship deserved to be brought to trial. Setting aside the views of ultra right wing civilians and army officers as well as a sector of the populace that suffered personal losses at the hands of insurgent terrorism, almost everybody agrees that trying *some* human rights violators was appropriate. There is, however, no consensus as to *why* the trials were suitable (or necessary) and, even less accord, as to *what* category of wrongdoers warranted criminal punishment. Interviewing military officers, I found that very few of them think that trying human rights abuses was per se unjust. Other than that, opinions as to why vary considerably. For some of these officers, the rigidity of military discipline renders prosecutions of lower ranking subordinate personnel unwarranted, as long as they had acted in the furtherance of superior orders,[7] whatever content these orders may have had.[8] Others thought it was irrelevant what officers had ordered or done, provided they had acted for King and Country. For these officers, acting on personal motives was the distinctive feature of the abuses that made punishment justifiable. Greed and egotistic passions were the impermissible goals that some officers believed warranted criminal sanctions.

Except for a handful of staunchly democratic officers who had overtly opposed their comrades' methodology during the 1976-1983 dictatorship, the rest think that, as the trials were actually conducted, prosecutions and convictions were essentially "political."[9] Further, they believe that these proceedings had broken down the army's discipline and eroded its stability. No military institution, they claim, is able to withstand internal disputes and mutual accusations.[10] By allowing junior officers to stand trial, the generals passed on their own responsibility and thus broke a basic loyalty on which the spirit of the armed forces is grounded.[11]

Officers are not alone in their lack of consensus on the trials. Advocates of human rights' opinions also vary sharply as to the width, reach, and severity the human rights trials should have had. At one end of the spectrum, some activists, such as the *Madres de Plaza de Mayo*, staunchly claim that everyone connected to repression should pay her or his due. They consider that lawyers and clergymen, among the host of civilians who either aided or abetted the army's criminal campaign of ideological repression, should also be punished.[12] At the other end of this spectrum, more cautious groups understand there were narrow constraints within which the Alfonsín administration could maneuver, and that the cause of human rights would have to make do with the punishment of the designers of the criminal campaign and its most conspicuous protagonists. Wide disagreement today is not only a consequence of different conceptions of the role of criminal justice, but also reflects incompatible versions of the facts. There is, for example, confusion as to the size of the left wing terrorist organizations operating before and during the military takeover in 1976,[13] the number of victims of state terrorism,[14] the independence of subordinate officers to torture and assassinate, the existence of paramilitary gangs operating with and without the consent of the authorities, and so forth.

Argentine society is riddled with disagreement about its recent tragedy. As frustration and anger soared, the Alfonsín administration became a target of harsh criticism from a vast portion of the citizenry. For some, the government failed to do enough about past human rights violations. For others, including a sizeable number of military officers and right wing civilians, President Alfonsín and his group of acolytes were determined to destroy the country's traditions, and the armed forces in particular, by having brought the whole military apparatus to trial indiscriminately.[15] The most perplexing feature about this fragmentation of public opinion is that hardly anybody, including lawyers, ground their positions on the December 1985 decision[16] of the federal appellate court of Buenos Aires concerning the responsibility of the military juntas that ruled the country between 1976 and 1982. The verdict of the Supreme Court,[17] delivered one year later, is equally irrelevant to the citizenry's view of its recent political history. This shows that in Argentina judicial decisions lack authoritativeness both in establishing the facts brought to trial, and in evaluating these facts. Thus, controversies about what should have been done about past human rights violations continue unabated, with no hope that any arbiter will bring them to an end.

There are many reasons for the Argentine judiciary's lack of authority, one of them being general distrust in the impartiality of the courts in trying politically related cases which arise during dictatorial periods. I wish to entertain two reasons specifically connected to the human rights trials. First, the absence of a clear idea of how the human rights trials may have contributed to the democratization of the Argentine polity. Second, the lack of an adequate system of prosecutorial discretion. In this chapter, I set out first to provide new grounds for conceiving the usefulness of punishment to democratize society, and second, to characterize the role of the prosecutors in accordance with the primary rationale for punishing state crimes.

## II.

Conscientious advocates of human rights expected Argentina to undergo deeper changes after 1983 than those the country actually experienced. Since then, Argentine citizens have regained their right to elect their public officials and enjoy some limits on state power imposed by a republican system of government. This situation, however, falls short of the aspirations that advocates of individual rights pursued in supporting the 1985 trials of the army commanders charged with planning the systematic violation of human rights during the 1976-1983 dictatorship. As exemplified by the extreme cases of El Salvador and Guatemala, formal democracies may turn their backs on human dignity by excluding popular participation and trampling on individual liberties.[18]

As far as a general belief in the importance of individual rights is concerned, the political scenario in Argentina falls short of the expectations that the trials inspired abroad. For many, the value attached to the human rights trials was a quest for a rights-based society. The nature of the human rights crusade rendered irrelevant the personal aspiration of campaigners who did not pursue respect for rights, as such, but rather the satisfaction of personal goals, such as vengeance and political aspirations. The public outcry, largely kindled by the human rights organizations, was not targeted at the military takeover of 1976 itself. What triggered a widespread demand for justice was the systematic brutality deployed by the *de facto* regime. Although the members of the first ruling junta were indicted for overthrowing the elected government, the case for rebellion would probably have been overlooked had it not been for an isolated lawyer who formally requested an investigation.[19] Even after the proceedings were underway, only a handful of citizens, most of them lawyers, strove to see the culprits sentenced for overthrowing an elected government. Widespread public desire to have military officers tried was not for overthrowing a civilian administration,[20] but for their contempt for human rights.[21] The battle for punishing the military revolved around the need to enforce these rights whether or not human rights organizations were pressing the case for individual rights as a genuine principle. Massive disregard of individual rights may obtain under formal democratic systems.[22]

A rights-based democracy stands for the participation of citizens in political decisions and for consensus in the acknowledgment of a cluster of fundamental individual rights and liberties.[23] In this sense, a democratic community may for the sake of simplicity be equated with a pluralist arrangement; that is, one in which individuals pursue their own ideals and values and respect other individuals' preferences and choices. I will presuppose that a rights-based democratic society constitutes the requisite environment in which individuals can flourish most positively. Members of such a society are masters of their own existence.[24] What makes this mastery possible is that individuals value their own -- and other people's -- plans of life and are confident that institutions will protect their pursuit of personal ideals from the interference of third parties,[25] including the state itself. I claim that punishing state criminals may constitute a decisive contribution in attaining such a democratic society.

## III.

In broad terms, the utilitarian and retributivist traditions have competed for the title to the moral justification of punishment. For the former, punishment is warranted by virtue of the forceful reasons it furnishes citizens not to break the law.[26] But for the latter, a just state order must treat individuals according to their merits and demerits.

Like the violations tried in Nuremberg, the nature and extent of the abuses committed by the Argentine criminal bureaucracy against basic rights promoted renewed debates about why, who, and how to punish. Argentina, being currently in the midst of its "transition," invites a re-examination of the justification of legal punishment from a new perspective. This perspective requires that we explore how legal punishment has to be conceived to contribute to the establishment and maintenance of rights and respectful practices among members of society. The situation in which the country finds itself at present indicates that only by attaching a special retributive meaning to criminal sanctions will punishment serve the purpose of fostering a rights-based democracy. The inability of the Argentine community during this "transition" to uphold the very values essential to a pluralist society is the strongest possible evidence for this argument.[27]

Indeed, insurmountable difficulties arise when standard utilitarian and retributivist justifications are applied to state crimes. In the following section I will draw on the Argentine experience to demonstrate the unsatisfactory solutions that derive from the claims of full-blooded retributivists and advocates of deterrence.

## IV.

Given the choice between setting up institutions that ensure pluralism and sentencing human rights transgressors, one would predict that a vast majority of true democrats would elect the first option. I claim, however, that this choice is non-existent, and that failure to impose certain modes of punishment on state criminals will itself undermine attempts to "de-authoritarianize" society. A rights-based community is unlikely to emerge from populations where persecution and fear compelled individuals to give up their personal values and ideals. To limit the category of victims of repression to the disappeared, the tortured, and the jailed ignores the social repercussions of state crime. Protracted repression not only caused pain and anguish to those who were related to or associated with the murdered and the disappeared, it also debased the large majority of the population.[28] Brutality brings about a culture of fear and insecurity that pervades the community at large. The notion that almost everybody qualifies for state abuses penetrated most aspects of social life.[29]

Fear demands adjustment. Afraid that, by the most whimsical criteria, they will become victims of repression, individuals break social ties and throw away any possibly "incriminating evidence," such as books, that could link them to the left.[30]

In dictatorial regimes, the state systematically represses the pursuit of individual ideals and values it considers undesirable. As members of the community abandon walks of life that make existence meaningful to them, they surrender self-respect and esteem.[31] This feature of dictatorships represents one of the heaviest legacies for transitional governments to overcome, and often leads to an inescapable paradox. Prospects for impartial justice depend on a community's sense of moral responsibility, and this sense is determined by individuals' perception of their own worth and by authoritative institutions that ensure and promote that perception. Minimally, state repression blurs such perception.[32]

As an argument against prosecuting military officers, a sizeable number of Argentine politicians claimed, from 1983 on, that allotting resources to avert future violations was the state's priority.[33] But the choice of not trying human rights violators and securing respect for individual rights in the future is non-existent. The failure to exact punishment on state criminals will, in and of itself, frustrate attempts to lessen society's authoritarian tendencies. Citizens who bore -- or feared to bear -- state persecution are not likely to spontaneously develop self-respect once the dictatorship is over.[34] Incapable of self-respect, they will also deem other people's choices unworthy.

The oppressor kills our ideals, our self-respect, the perception of our rights. Compromising our goals makes us feel shame; deserting our principles and loyalties instills guilt in us. Our sense of worthlessness, of shame and guilt demands a "political remedy."[35] Only public admission by political institutions that we were wronged will legitimize us in our own eyes. Punishment of the violators of our rights is the clearest and strongest statement an authoritative institution may issue to that effect.[36] Citizens need to *learn* that they have rights, not only to be able to act on these rights, but to respect other people's liberties as well. As an authoritative institution, punishment must play this role,[37] but to do so a conception of punishment is required that is not "perpetrator centered," such as deterrence and full-blooded retributive theories are, but rather "victim centered."

Authors who believe in the deterrent effect of punishment will find that convicting state criminals hardly supports their theoretical claim. Punishment may deter officers from staging a *coup d'état*. Being exposed as criminals at home and before the international community is a bitter experience, as some Latin American dictators have discovered. Few would like to share Massera's or Videla's reputation. Following the court's convictions, not many officers would have liked to be in the shoes of the Argentine commanders.[38]

At their best, dissuasive consequences would be applicable only to the generals at the top. For the rest of the officers, the deterrent impact of convictions would be neutralized by the immediate benefits that violating others' rights would bring about: within the armed forces, support from their comrades and superiors. Hypothetical, remote punishment was counterbalanced by immediate rewards from the transgressor's immediate circle. The approval or disapproval of members of their inner circle produced a stronger impact on human rights transgressors than did the threat of possible punishment or, for that matter, a future moral condemnation of society at large. Once an adequate climate had been created, fear of future suffering from a criminal conviction is highly unlikely to carry sufficient weight for an officer who, within an authoritarian bureaucracy, is instructed to assassinate or torture.[39] Those who deviated from this trend out of moral qualms were labeled complacent, cowards, or even traitors. Officers who founded the CEMIDA in support of democracy found that hostility from their comrades was surprisingly strong.[40] Considered disloyal by their colleagues, these officers suffered bomb attacks and endless death threats. Moreover, in 1991, after Menem pardoned the few officers who were still serving in jail, retired army Colonel Juan-Jaime Cesio was barred from wearing his uniform for having endorsed human rights organization complaints.[41] Perhaps the clearest message against the deterrent argument were the four rebellions staged in Argentina since its return to democracy. These mutinies were largely aimed at restoring the army's dignity which, for the rebels, had been damaged by the trials and convictions of human rights abusers since 1985.

Age, and the more stringent discipline younger officers are subject to, allows one to formulate the hypothesis that the lower the rank of these officers, the stronger their loyalty becomes to their comrades, superiors, and force. This phenomenon weakens the effects of criminal convictions as one descends the military hierarchical pyramid. Unstable institutions and political fickleness in Argentina make the dissuasive effects of punishment even weaker. Officers assume that, in the worst of all cases in which punishment is actually imposed, the armed forces will retain enough clout to secure amnesties or pardons in the short or the long run.

Full-blooded retributivists are not any more convincing than defenders of deterrence. Retributivists who have advocated the punishment of state criminals have generally disassociated such punishment from consequentialist considerations. The message to the wrongdoer is: "this is how wrong what you did was."[42] Retributive factors -- the harm done or the culpability of the actor -- are seen as constraints on the treatment of individuals, and as tools for the promotion of social and the state's interests. Full-blooded retributivists will ignore all possible consequences of the criminal sanction as relevant to its justification. The value of retribution is simply that by disregarding the effects of punishment, it places constraints on society against using individuals as mere tools for promoting other people's interests. For a full-blooded retributivist, punishment is demanded of every military officer who participated in violations of human rights, even if it unleashes a new military revolt.

For full-blooded retributivists, an individual is treated according to a specified set of conditions, in this case, the Argentine criminal law; every person who satisfies these conditions warrants an established consequence. For supporters of such a thesis, punishment must be imposed on all officers who had ordered, perpetrated, or aided a violation, on those who failed to avert or report the transgression, and on the civilians who aided and abetted the regime in various ways. In accordance with this view, the *Madres de Plaza de Mayo*, for example, campaigned to have every officer who participated in human rights infringement punished.[43] Although there is an appeal to consequences in the *Madres* rhetoric, this appeal is not based on social effects, but rather on moral or evaluative consequences. In demanding that their children be returned alive and that all those responsible for the violations -- whatever these violations may be -- be punished, the *Madres* are claiming that societies, as such, require minimal justice. Furthermore, as long as this justice is not carried out by punishing the abductors and torturers, they cannot consider that their children are dead. If they did, they would be admitting that human rights abusers are accepted by society, and such society would become non-existent.[44]

I admit that it is plausible to maintain that those officers and their civilian advisers deserved to be punished by standard criminal law criteria. But the consequences of such a policy would surely have been a political and logistic disaster. Indeed, approximately 2000 individuals were directly implicated in tortures and assassinations. A high proportion of the rest were responsible for aiding and abetting the former, and almost every officer in the armed forces was responsible for not averting or at least reporting the deeds. As an army general expressed to me in August 1991, in fighting "subversion" the Argentine armed forces adopted the same methodology employed in Algeria.[45] The French command made sure that not a single soldier remained alien to brutal repression. Every member of the army serving in Northern Africa was forced to participate in torture and assassinations. The hands of numerous Argentine officers were equally bloodied so that, within certain units, no one, if possible, would be able to accuse the rest.[46]

Retributivists stand essentially for equality and for constraints upon the state's power to repress individuals. A central feature of a system of constraints is generality: a person P under circumstances C warrants treatment T even if, as Kant postulated, the sky falls. But this disregard for consequences disqualifies the full-blooded retributivist's answer to the question of "why punish?" First, as H.L.A. Hart has pointed out, such a position cannot appeal to considerations of social usefulness.[47] Taking account of the social advantage of convictions would make the justification of punishment depend in part on its consequences, thereby abandoning the full-blooded retributivist's basic tenet.[48] Second, it is not self-evident that the wrongdoing to which we attach a criminal sanction demands that the offender be made to suffer. If no particular desirable consequences are associated with the violator's suffering, we may prefer to refrain from punishing wrongdoers and elect to impose upon them a duty to compensate the victim instead.  Third, in overlooking the effects of the criminal sanction, a full-blooded retributivist must believe in the intrinsic value of the rules that render the act criminal.  Just punishment presupposes that the rules that render an act punishable are also just.  But the full-blooded retributivist cannot discriminate between rules that are or are not authoritative without looking at the consequences of enforcing such rules as the ultimate reason for their existence.  It makes no sense to elect to punish certain conduct as criminal without considering the consequences of this conduct and the expected effects of making them criminally relevant.[49]

I do not claim that the examined utilitarian and retributivist approaches do not contribute to the justification for punishing state criminals.  Utilitarians are correct to expect criminal convictions to have dissuasive effects.  But, at their best, these effects are, as I have explained, limited to a few officers at the top.  Retributivists also provide a cogent argument for protecting individual rights: persons who are not guilty of a wrongful act ought not be punished.[50]  This negative aspect of retributivism is modest; it refers solely to restraints on the utilization of punishment.  It does not offer a (positive) justification for criminal convictions.  I have argued that punishment should contribute to the making of a rights-based democracy.  I have also suggested that institutional regard for the victims of crime is crucial to the furtherance of that goal.  In that respect, utilitarianism and full-blooded retributivism, as "perpetrator centered" theories, are intrinsically inappropriate.  I propose a "victim centered" theory of punishment as an independent ground for justifying convicting state criminals.

Redress for victims is not essential to a utilitarian justification.  By giving key significance to the deterrence of potential offenders, utilitarians will have no qualms about overlooking the plight of those who have suffered degradation as a consequence of having their basic rights infringed or threatened.  The notion of "justice for the victims" would be excluded from the utilitarian calculus when exercising discretion.  Full-blooded retributivists invite a similar criticism.  By disregarding all consequences of punishment, proponents of this version of retributivism focus only on the wrongdoer's facing the consequence of his deeds.

But there is another variant of retributivism -- a goal-oriented variant.  According to this version, punishment ought to be directed at redressing the valued sentiments of those who are wronged.  I am not referring to vindictive sentiments, but rather to the victim's loss of purpose and sense of worth.  As I have explained, those who endured unwarranted actual -- or potential -- chastisement from the oppressor experience shame and lack of self-respect for renouncing the personal ideals that made their life meaningful.[51] Goal-oriented retributivists will attach to punishment the function of restoring this lost trust.

There is a salient pragmatic difference between full-blooded and goal-oriented retributivists. While the former are compelled to impose punishment given the presence of a set of conditions that render an act criminal, such generality does not apply to goal-oriented retributivists. In seeking redress for the victims, they may consistently choose to forego punishment or content themselves with merely condemning the offender, or solely the offender's deed. If they believe that imposing pain upon the perpetrator will do nothing substantial to improve the victim's sense of self-respect and confidence, punishment will lack warrant. So if the victims of certain forms of state crimes have already regained self-respect and are confident that they will be protected against future violations because the heads of the criminal organization have been convicted, goal-oriented retributivists may refrain from punishing other members of the group. There is room for considerable discretion.

There is no clear way to establish the degree to which the 1985 Argentine human rights trials have attained that effect. Social reaction to recent cases of police torture and other flagrant abuses of individual rights,[52] and the visible success of the electoral campaigns of military officers who participated in the dictatorship of 1976-1983,[53] seem to demonstrate the opposite. If the thesis I have so far laid out is correct, by overriding respect for people's dignity and basic rights on the grounds of security and expediency, citizens reflect that they themselves have not recovered from the harms inflicted upon them by the past dictatorship. Only an insufficient perception of our own rights may explain the appeal of violent solutions to social conflicts. The trials of the generals in 1985 failed to teach the Argentine citizenry the value of their own worth as individuals.[54]

Some clarification is required as to the reach assigned in this paper to the role of punishment. My view of the role of the criminal sanction is not intended to be an exclusionary justification of punishment and, consequently, does not attempt to displace other justifying reasons. A victim-centered view may exhibit the futility of imposing a criminal sanction on a certain offender yet punishing this offender may still be suitable. For example, it may be important to punish a perpetrator simply to deter potential imitators. The applicability of a victim-based justification of punishment is not limited to establishing a rights-based democracy. It may also play a key role in improving the state of individual liberties in already existing rights-based societies.[55] Since the approach is strongly connected with the offender shaming his victim, the thesis may also serve the purpose of justifying punishment of particularly humiliating transgressions, such as rape and blackmail. What I do contend is that a "victim-centered" theory of punishment is a significant means to the democratization of society.

To attach such democratizing effect to punishing state criminals presupposes, however, that judges' decisions are authoritative -- that a large enough portion of the citizenry believes in the impartiality of the courts. The nature of the trials of state criminals and the lack of provisions that institute the practice of prosecutorial discretion made the attainment of such authoritativeness almost impossible.

## V.

Like the criminal justice systems of most Latin American countries, Argentina's adopted the so-called principle of legality. According to this principle, neither the prosecutors nor the courts are entitled to dismiss cases which are required to be brought to trial. In line with the full-blooded retributivist tradition, actions defined as crimes create the duty to prosecute and convict. This feature of the country's law poses a serious obstacle to the judges' credibility when trying state sponsored human rights violations. In such situations, the perpetrators who must stand trial -- usually a large number of people -- and the corporatist powers lying behind them, impose overwhelming pressure upon the judiciary. In Argentina, while the military and their supporters pressed for acquittals, vast sectors of the population demanded convictions. Under such circumstances, bringing the judiciary under the spotlight turned the judiciary itself into the centerpiece of one of the country's most critical political struggles. The military pompously called this struggle, "the judicial battle."[56]

During the transitional period in the establishment of a democracy, judges play the key role of instilling among the citizenry a sense of self -- and other people's -- respect by making rights an essential part of the political arrangement. This idea, I think, should be sufficient as a reason to refrain from passing amnesty laws or any other impediments to the verification of the truth. Placing the judges at the center of the transitional process by having them bear the weight of such significant political conflict, however, threatens to jeopardize the impartiality of the judiciary, given the intensity of the debate taking place outside the courtroom. During my tenure in office, a day did not pass when I did not receive numerous telephone calls or visitors with strong views on these issues. Indeed, they often expressed concern, if not alarm, about the reigning upheaval the human rights trials were causing within the armed forces, the negative impact that trying certain officers would bring about among their comrades, or the "senselessness" of confronting the most powerful sector of society.

Army officers and numerous politicians were apprehensive. Presidential military aides did not miss a single occasion to convey their alarm. High officials and an array of sympathizers with the military regime, and even personal friends among the civilians, shared concern for what the trials could bring about. Directly or indirectly, there were thousands of officers implicated in human rights abuses. The reasons for urging restraint in the scope of the trials or for giving them up altogether ranged from practical grounds to ideological allegiances. The opinion of one judge who had tried the military commanders is an excellent example of one extreme. In late 1991 he confided to me that, although he was convinced of the criminal responsibility of the generals he had convicted, the exclusive concentration on army officers left him unsettled. After all, what had made the military terrorist campaign possible in the first place was the vast sectors of society which had granted them a blank check to reinstate order.[57] If criminal law was the answer to political violence, he reasoned, then the Argentine society would have to try itself for what had happened.

The pressure placed on the judiciary by the trials of human rights violators rapidly became unbearable for the judges. As a consequence of the permanent pressure exerted by different sectors of society with direct interest in the outcome of the trials, the members of the Buenos Aires Federal Court gradually abandoned their life-tenured positions. By the end of 1987, that Court had been entirely replaced by newly appointed judges. For many observers, their resignations severely undermined the credibility of the human rights trials. The military and their sympathizers viewed their move as an admission that the trials were politically biased,[58] and that once their mission of convicting a few generals was accomplished, the members of the tribunal would seek to aggrandize themselves by obtaining important government positions in the Alfonsín regime. While I do not think there are serious grounds for defending such a thesis, the fact that one of the judges was appointed Secretary of the Interior and another one, Andrés D'Alessio, Attorney General, by President Alfonsín himself, made it difficult to argue convincingly for the impartiality of the court.

Human rights organizations also believed that the court's decision had been tainted by an allegiance to the administration in power. They claimed the sentences imposed upon some commanders were extremely light and the acquittal of others were signs that the court had set out to help President Alfonsín in his undeclared effort to please the armed forces by creating a facade of an impartial trial. History confirms however, that it was impossible for the judges to have borne the burden imposed by the duty to try a sizeable number of officers brought to trial.

It is arguable that the pressure could have been ameliorated had the judges been conferred the power to select the cases to be tried. This, however, would have been no solution since the pressure to impose sentence one way or another would have simply shifted to the point of deciding who would be tried, and suspicions would have been equally drawn from both quarters. The military would have still accused the court of turning those indicted into scapegoats. Human rights activists would have raised the objection that the exercise of discretion was but a masquerade of justice. The authoritativeness of the justice system depends to a great degree, then, on prosecutorial discretion.

## VI.

The suitability of discretion is strongly tied to the reasons upon which we ground punishment. For full-blooded retributivists, generality excludes the idea of selective punishment and, consequently, of discretion altogether. In contrast, utilitarians, especially advocates of deterrence, find discretion necessary to optimize the dissuasive effect of the criminal justice system. They claim that not only the harshness of the threatened punishment, but also the frequency with which it is imposed, is essential to effective dissuasion. If instead of severely punishing the most serious offenders, a large sector of the armed forces were sentenced to serve a few months in jail, the deterrent ideal would be better served: chances of conviction would make up for the decrease in severity of the sentences. Under this theory, prosecutors should be encouraged to make as many deals as they can to make the threat of punishment more efficient.[59] For advocates of deterrence, it is indifferent to them whether light sentences may have little affect on the victims' sentiments. For them, criminal sanctions should convey a message, not to the victims, but to those who may imitate the culprits; in the process, our sense of justice and confidence in democratic institutions is irrelevant.

From a victim centered view of punishment, discretion, like deterrence, is also desirable, but the topic is more delicate. Prosecutors will not be able to content themselves with getting as many convictions as possible. A victim centered theory will seek to punish those cases that are crucial to the victims' recovering self-respect and dignity. Making the right choices from this perspective requires an extremely careful analysis of the cases to be brought to court. Essential to this appraisal is the power exercised by the wrongdoer, his sense of omnipotence and immunity, the intensity of the deprivation of the victim's autonomy, and the moral and psychological sequels of the act. These and other such topics acquire decisive relevance in electing who should be punished. Establishing the intensity of a power-subduance between the perpetrator and his victim becomes essential. The issue is too complex and far reaching to be dealt with by prosecutors on the basis of casuistry.

## VII.

For a victim centered theory of punishment, selective justice becomes a very delicate matter with deep moral and political underpinnings. Creating consciousness of individuals' rights by punishing those who most harshly trampled on people's dignity requires more than simply that those who make the decision to punish understand the long term purpose of the policy. Essential is their awareness of the subtleties that making the adequate distinctions demand.

The 1985 Argentine trials were an example of inadequate discrimination. On the one hand, some officers, such as the members of the last Junta, were known to have had no direct responsibility over the scattered abuses perpetrated shortly before government was handed over to elected authorities. On the other hand, generals whom overwhelming evidence singled out as the protagonists of the worst acts of repression, were also tried for forgery and usurpation of property.[60] These offenses have no connection with gross human rights abuses and are not comparable in either nature or moral gravity.

An adequate selection of cases cannot be made by individual prosecutors. Moreover, the issue is too critical to be left to the temptations of quick political solutions adopted on the basis of expediency by the administration in power. Although practical reasons such as political necessity and limited resources make it crucial that the government have a say, it seems indispensable to merge short term political views with far-sighted policy making. Professors Julio Maier[61] and Andrés D'Alessio[62] suggested to me that a criminal policy department should be created in Argentina, and that such department should be headed by what were, until the Menem administration, two life-tenured officials and a high ranking government official. Thus, the Attorney General (or the Solicitor General) as a member of the judiciary, and the ombudsman or special prosecutor,[63] would integrate this office together with the Minister of Justice. While the latter would embody the government's immediate priorities, the former would represent society's long term interests. Maier suggested that a board headed by the three officials may serve the purposes of exercising discretion.

## VIII.

I have now broached the two issues proposed in Section I of this chapter. Both topics (the rationale for trying human rights violations and prosecutorial discretion) are not only inter-dependent, but also tied into the broader context of setting up a rights-based democracy. Disregard for the victims as a reason to punish state criminals has been an important factor in the failure to transform an authoritarian society in a rights-based community. But the dismal path the case for individual rights has taken in Argentina in the 1990s is also a consequence of not taking the judiciary seriously.[64] Blatantly neutralizing convictions for human rights violations, Menem's pardons of officers undercut the nascent authority of the judiciary.[65] Until such authority is restored, a rights-based society will never flourish in Argentina.

# Notes

[1]This chapter is a part of a larger research effort the author is carrying out under the sponsorship of the United States Institute of Peace and the John D. and Catherine T. MacArthur Foundation.

[2]Despite his reputation for having ordered a ruthless political repression as a military delegate in the province of Tucuman, General Domingo Bussi received forty-three percent of the votes in the very same province. David Ruiz Palacios, deputy minister of the interior during the military dictatorship, was favored by the polls to win the elections in the Chaco province. When Ruiz Palacios was barred from running because he lacked the requisite years of residence in the state, he named his own substitute who managed to win the elections by a landslide. *See* PAGINA 12 (Newspaper, Buenos Aires) Aug. 16, 1991, at 7 [hereinafter PAGINA 12] (many articles in PAGINA 12 have no author or title listed).

[3]In the province of Buenos Aires alone, 500,000 citizens voted for Rico. *See id.*, Sept. 10, 1991, at 4; Raúl Kollman, *El Identikit de los Votantes, id.* Sept. 15, 1991, at 2.

[4]*See* HORACIO VERBITSKY, CIVILES Y MILITARES 360 (1987) (provides an account of Aldo Rico's revolts); IAIN GUEST, BEHIND THE DISAPPEARANCES: ARGENTINA'S DIRTY WAR AGAINST HUMAN RIGHTS AND THE UNITED NATIONS 555, n.22 (1990).

[5]Kollman, *supra* note 3; *supra* at 3.

[6]*See id.* at 6; HERALD (newspaper, Buenos Aires) Aug. 26, 1991, at 7.

[7]Article 514 of the military justice code exempts from punishment subordinate personnel acting under superior orders, except when this personnel has exceeded itself in the furtherance of such directives. When orders are manifestly illegal, the courts dismiss the defense on the ground that such directives are not binding on subordinate officers. This decision was reached in 1909 when a colonel who barred a congressman from going into Congress entertained the defense that his commanding officer had ordered him to do so. *See* CARLOS FONTAN BALESTRA, TRATADO DE DERECHO PENAL 352 (2d. ed. 1980). To decrease even more the number of prosecutions, Congress passed Law 23.049, which prescribed that military personnel who had lacked "decision capacity" would be benefitted by the presumption that they had acted on the basis of an excusing mistake, except for "atrocious and aberrant"

offenses. Nevertheless, the systematic perpetration of torture and assassination rendered over a thousand officers liable for prosecution.

[8]Among those officers who held this view was General Raúl Ramayo, the former legal adviser of the Army during the early stages of the transition. Personal communication, August 1991.

[9]It is not clear what "political" means in this context. Each officer apparently has his own position on what is "political."

[10]On a television show on Buenos Aires channel 7 held on August 30, 1991, General Jorge Arguindegui, the first chief of staff appointed by President Alfonsín in 1983, stated that the country had been rendered defenseless. The Alfonsín administration had destroyed the armed forces by bringing military human rights violators to trial thus creating an unbearable atmosphere between commanders and subordinate officers. He placed responsibility for this state of affairs mainly on me. General Arguindegui believes that President Alfonsín too strongly and frequently followed my advice.

[11]In his statements as a witness at the trial of rebel Colonel Mohamed Ali Seineldin, ex-Colonel Aldo Rico, the head of the mutinies staged against the Alfonsín administration in 1987 and 1988, made this point clear: "I would have never allowed my subordinate officers to stand trial." He continued, "The cornerstone of an army is not obedience but loyalty to one's own personnel. Command without leadership is clearly insufficient."

[12]"We are talking about the crime of genocide. All three branches of the armed forces accompanied by many civilians organized this crime. The church was another accomplice. Testimonies have proved the extent of the complicity of the church and these so-called priests cannot be allowed to walk free." JO FISHER, MOTHERS OF THE DISAPPEARED 137 (1989) (quoting Elsa de Becerra). In the same vein, the head of the *Madres*, Hebe de Bonafini declared:

> We're going to continue in the same way because we still haven't got justice. They've tried to convert us into the mothers of dead children and put an end to the problem of *desaparecidos*. We will never accept they are dead until those responsible are punished. If we accepted that, we would be accepting that murderers and torturers can live freely in Argentina. They can't negotiate with the blood of our children. *The Madres de Plaza de Mayo* are never going to permit that.

*Id.* at 158. *See also* Mark Osiel, *The Making of Human Rights Policy in Argentina: The Impact of Ideas and Interests on a Legal Conflict*, 18 J. LATIN AM. STUD. 135-78 (1987).

[13]One of the most reputable Argentine human rights activists, Emilio Mignone, claims, for instance, that after the 1976 military coup, left wing combatants were virtually non-existent. EMILIO FERMIN MIGNONE, DERECHOS HUMANOS Y SOCIEDAD: EL CASO ARGENTINO 52, 54 & n.26 (1991). Opposed to this view stand the expressed opinions of former members of the ERP (People's Revolutionary Army), who recalled in an interview with the author in July 1992 that, though considerably weakened, they were still operating until late 1977 or early 1978.

[14]COMISIÓN NACIONAL SOBRE LA DESAPARICIÓN DE PERSONAS, NUNCA MAS: INFORME DE LA COMISIÓN NACIONAL SOBRE LA DESAPARICIÓN DE PERSONAS 16 [NEVER AGAIN: REPORT OF THE ARGENTINE NATIONAL COMMISSION ON THE DISAPPEARED] (1985). While the *Comisión Nacional para la Desaparición de Personas* (CONADEP), registered about 8,960 disappearances, some human rights activists maintain that the number should be increased to approximately 20,000.

[15]For a good example of this confusion see JORGE GRECCO & GUSTAVO GONZALEZ, ARGENTINA: EL EJERCITO QUE TENEMOS 140 (1990) (Despite the groundlessness of many assertions contained in the investigation, the book was successful to the extent of being awarded the first prize in "Essays and Journalistic Investigations" in that same year).

[16]Judgment of December 9, 1985, CFed., 8 HUM. RTS. L. J. 368 (1987) (Arg.).

[17]Judgment of December 30, 1986, CSJN, 8 HUM. RTS. L. J. 430 (1987) (Arg.).

[18]Argentina was, in the 1970s, another example of a formal democracy where numerous human rights violations were perpetrated. State criminality in Argentina has been referred to as a creation of the military after their 1976 takeover. However, situating the massive violations of human rights between March 1976 and December 1983 when the military were formally in power, is a misleading version of recent history. Numerous state sponsored human rights violations in Argentina began in 1974 when a para-police organization called the "Triple A" (Argentine Anti-Communist Alliance) waged an intense campaign of political abduction, torture, and assassination. Allegedly led by ex-police corporal José Lopez-Rega, appointed Minister of Social Welfare by the Peron administration, the "Triple A" was backed by limited factions within the military and acted with the blessings of President Isabel Peron. After the 1976 military coup, assassinations and torture were stepped up under the command of the armed forces, now operating as an institution. Thus, in Argentina, violations of human rights began earlier than 1976, while the country was run by elected ("democratic") authorities. The reason that most political activists and officials in the Alfonsín administration, like myself, have invariably referred to the "1976-1983 state crimes" period, is simple. We wished to avoid confrontations with the Peronist Party, the largest opposition party during President Alfonsín's tenure.

[19]MARCELO A. SANCINETTI, DERECHOS HUMANOS EN LA ARGENTINA POST-DICTATORIAL 20 (1988).

[20]*See, e.g., id.* Sancinetti points out that article 652 of the military justice code strips officers who rebel against their superiors from authority over their subordinates. Despite the accuracy of this legal account, it is worthwhile mentioning that only two officers disobeyed their superiors' orders in the course of the 1976 uprising. The chains of command remained, *de facto*, as if the legal right to disobey had not been an option.

[21]Disdain for human rights was connected with a variety of demonstrations of military omnipotence. This omnipotence, which led to the brink of war with Chile (1978) and to the armed conflict over the Falkland Islands (1982), emerged in everyday life. There are innumerable stories of officers wielding their army supplied guns to solve traffic disputes. It is impossible to draw a distinction between the

adverse sentiments triggered by these harassers among the populace, and the more reasoned defense of individual rights against torture, abduction, and assassination. Stated otherwise, one factor was the conscientious defense of civil liberties, and another one the resentment and rage caused by constant aggravations.

[22]In this paper "formal democracy" contrasts with a "rights-based democracy." The term is not utilized in the same way that some Marxist writers do when criticizing the bourgeois democratic system as "formal" for not taking the interests of the working class into account on a par with those of the dominant class. *See, e.g.*, Agnes Heller, *A Formal Democracy*, in CIVIL SOCIETY AND THE STATE: NEW EUROPEAN PERSPECTIVES 129 (John Keane ed., 1988).

[23]I could add other properties, like equality, but such extension would complicate rather than clarify the basic scheme. For some conceptions of equality, countries such as the United Kingdom or the United States do not satisfy the conditions required to become a substantive democracy. Today's disappearance of affirmative action in the United States, for example, poses an example of inequity that some authors would consider incompatible with democracy in a substantive sense.

[24]John Rawls, *Social Unity and Primary Goods*, in UTILITARIANISM AND BEYOND 159 (Amartya K. Sen & Bernard Williams eds., 1990).

[25]JOHN BRAITHWAITE & PHILIP PETTIT, NOT JUST DESSERTS: A REPUBLICAN THEORY OF CRIMINAL JUSTICE, Ch. 7 (1990).

[26]Although I have deterrence primarily in mind, the utilitarian definition I supply also encompasses reformation and rehabilitation. The deterrent ideal promotes fear of punishment as a reason for refraining from violating the law. By changing the moral character of the convicted offender, reformation and rehabilitation seek to implant a new set of reasons that will keep criminals from breaking the law again.

[27]Argentine acceptance of torture in the 1990s is revealed not solely by reports of brutal police procedures. A large portion of the citizenry accepts the inhumane treatment of suspects when such treatment is employed to protect the security and property of "decent citizens from a growing street criminality." For example, a crowd staged a demonstration in the suburbs of Buenos Aires in support of police officer Luis Patti when Patti was indicted for torturing prisoners under investigation. PAGINA 12 Sept. 14, 1990, at 7. When the court arrested Patti for torturing two detainees, the community at large stood up in defense of the police officer. The forensic experts declared on Patti's behalf that some detainees would harm themselves -- "even with electrified wires" -- to blame their captors. Another Buenos Aires journal reports that the country's public opinion was split between those who considered Patti a torturer and those who considered him a defender of security. AMBITO FINANCIERO (Journal, Buenos Aires) Oct. 19, 1990, at 4. In districts where he had served, Patti's reputation for brutality earned him the blessings of a vast sector of the population. Turned into a public figure, the policeman became a frequent guest at social events, including a television show where he danced the tango before millions of spectators. Patti declared that he ". . . [N]ot only makes people dance but also dances himself." (To "dance" means in Argentine jargon to suffer inflicted pain). He made this statement when asked to dance on a television show (Channel 9, Silvio Soldan's show in Buenos Aires). Argentina's vice-

president, Eduardo Duhalde, pointed out that Patti was a "model for policemen." *See* BUENOS AIRES HERALD, Aug. 8, 1991, at 11. *See also* PAGINA 12 Sept. 14, 1991, at 7. Furthermore, Patti's reputation induced Argentine President Menem to choose him for a special assignment, namely to investigate a case of rape and murder of a young woman, Maria Soledad Morales, in the northern province of Catamarca. *Id.* The case had become the focus of public attention throughout the country because of the personalities implicated in Morales's death. Among them were high police personnel, members of Catamarca's governor's inner circle, and a national congressman, Guillermo Luque, now under indictment. PAGINA 12, Sept. 9, 1991, at 7. An overwhelming majority of distant Catamarca's population enthusiastically welcomed Patti's arrival.

The case of Santos is another example of the inclination to approve brutality. A respectable engineer from Buenos Aires, Horacio Santos, killed two young men for having stolen his car stereo. The victim of previous attacks on his property, Santos engaged in a frantic car chase that ended in the death of both robbers at the hands of their pursuer. Santos literally executed the thieves by shooting the youngsters in the head at point blank range once they had stepped out of their car and offered to return the stolen stereo. Journalists, politicians, and a vast sector of the Buenos Aires public opinion declared that Santos had done the right thing. Like Patti, Santos' assassination incited heated arguments. His supporters, however, were astonishingly numerous. Well known television journalists stood up to justify the killer, blatantly stating that they would have acted in the same way had they been in his shoes. When queried by television journalists, Santos' neighbors praised his action as a contribution to cleansing the vicinity of potential thieves. Lawyer Antonio Troccoli, President Alfonsín's Minister of the Interior, stopped short of applauding Santos by blaming the occurrence on the state's inability to curb street crime. If ordinary citizens are forced to bear arms from want of security in the streets, Troccoli reasoned, unsavory episodes like that of Santos' are likely to occur.

Argentina's renewed contempt for human rights has had international repercussions. Current violations of human rights in Argentina were brought to the attention of the Spanish public when a Spanish police officer was convicted of torture after the tribunal rebuffed his claim that he had acted under his superiors' directives. A journalist commenting on the case wrote that it was unfortunate that the officer had performed torture in Spain instead of Argentina, the "kingdom of impunity." *See* Juan Carlos Martinez, PAGINA 12, Oct. 30, 1990, at 4.

An illustrative analysis of police abuses is reflected in Paul G. Chevigny, *Police Deadly Force as Social Control: Jamaica, Argentina, and Brazil*, 1 CRIM. L. R. 389 (1990). *See also* AMERICAS WATCH & CENTRO DE ESTUDIOS LEGALES Y SOCIALES, POLICE VIOLENCE IN ARGENTINA: TORTURE AND POLICE KILLINGS IN BUENOS AIRES (Dec. 1991) (Report).

[28]The military governor of the province of Buenos Aires, General Iberico Saint-Jean, reflected the South American dictators' conception of society's potential enemies when he said: "We will first kill all the subversives, later, we will kill those who collaborate with them, then we will kill those who remain indifferent and, finally, we will kill the shy." *See* Carlos H. Acuna & Catalina Smulovitz, Ni

Olvido ni Perdon: Derechos Humanos y Tensiones Civico Militares en la Transicion Argentina (1991) (paper submitted at the XVI International Congress of the Latin American Studies Association). Consistent with this view, one of the head officer's in the repression campaign in the province of Buenos Aires, Colonel Roberto Roualdes, stated to human rights campaigner Emilio Mignone that it was worthwhile killing a hundred suspects if just five of these suspects proved to be actual subversives. *See* MIGNONE, *supra* note 13, at 67.

[29]The fact that the military's enemy was designated as the "subversives" instead of "terrorists," "guerrillas" or "insurgents" was the cause for greater confusion. The fact that "subversion" is more linked to ideological antagonism than the direct or indirect exercise of violence implied in "terrorism," developed an environment in which the military divided allies and enemies. In the "if you are not with us you are against us" approach, there is no room for neutrality. Those who do not spontaneously march with us, who are not our friends are our actual or potential foes. Jon Elster, *Active and Passive Negation: An Essay in Ibanskian Sociology, in* THE INVENTED REALITY: HOW DO WE KNOW WHAT WE BELIEVE WE KNOW? CONTRIBUTIONS TO CONSTRUCTIVISM 175 (Paul Watzlawick ed., 1984).

[30]Corradi describes the general adaptive behavior of the population under the military rule: people abandoned, first, their political activities, and second, their political beliefs; they reduced associational activities and denied any evidence that inhumane practices were being carried out. Members of groups that were potential targets of state terror developed ignorance about what was going on. Selfish strategies of survival, like competition and speculation, were adopted. *See* Juan E. Corradi, *The Culture of Fear in Civil Society, in* FROM MILITARY RULE TO LIBERAL DEMOCRACY IN ARGENTINA 113 (Monica Peralta Ramos & Carlos H. Waisman eds., 1987).

[31]In this paper I treat "self-esteem" and "self respect" indiscriminately. I endorse, however, Waltzer's version according to which "self-esteem" consists of the opinion we have of ourselves, while "self-respect" is the "proper regard for the dignity of one's own person or one's own position." Democratic citizenship is thus narrowly related to the self-respect all individuals enjoy as "full and equal members" of the community. *See* MICHAEL WALTZER, SPHERES OF JUSTICE 227 (1983).

[32]Constructivist authors have insisted on the pervasiveness of our adaptive behaviors. Once a strategy has been developed to protect us from a hostile environment, we return to reconfirm the usefulness of this strategy even once the external danger has disappeared. *See* Gregory Bateson, *Conventions of Communication: Where Validity Depends Upon Belief, in* COMMUNICATION: THE SOCIAL MATRIX OF PSYCHIATRY 212 (Juergen Ruesch & Gregory Bateson eds., 1951).

[33]There were many members of the cabinet and other high officials who opposed the trials on pragmatic grounds. The President strongly defended the view that human rights violaters should be tried.

[34]Amartya Sen points out that subjugated people will abandon their belief in their own and other persons' rights in order to accommodate themselves to the attainment of "small mercies." AMARTYA K. SEN, ON ETHICS AND ECONOMICS 45 (1990).

[35]*See* LAWRENCE WECHSLER, A MIRACLE; A UNIVERSE: SETTLING ACCOUNTS WITH TORTURERS 241 (1990).

[36]A former political prisoner told me that the pardoning of the generals made him feel the same way that a raped woman in a *machista* society sees herself. If the rapist is not convicted, she is likely to feel guilty as a blameworthy participant in the wrongdoing. She needs an institutional response to the wrongdoing to support her dignity.

[37]Though narrowly linked to power, punishment also reflects authority, particularly if we want to be able to discriminate between this institution and other forms of state coercion. *See* RICHARD E. FLATHMAN, THE PRACTICE OF POLITICAL AUTHORITY: AUTHORITY AND THE AUTHORITATIVE 157 (1980).

[38]This consequence of convictions often backfires. If the military should take over the government in the future, the deterrent effect of punishment will discourage them from surrendering their power to a democratic successor. According to some experts, after the Argentine trials were underway, the Chilean and Uruguayan military became reluctant to call for elections and, when they did, they took the necessary steps to commit politicians to grant them immunity. As Przeworski points out, even if the heads of authoritarian power apparatus are able to safeguard the continuity of their economic and political trends through democracy, the issue of personal accountability is still a fence against transition to democracy. Adam Przeworski, *Democracy as a Contingent Outcome of Conflicts*, in CONSTITUTIONALISM AND DEMOCRACY 59 (Jon Elster & Rune Slagstad eds., 1988).

[39]Jaime Malamud-Goti, *Transitional Governments in the Breach: Why Punish State Criminals?*, 12 HUM. RTS. Q. 1 (1990).

[40]Colonel Jose Luis Garcia, one of the founders of the pro-human rights military group called CEMIDA, confessed to me that he cannot say how he would have acted had he been in active duty during the worst years of repression. Military peer pressure is too strong to act contrary to it; it requires one to risk the possibility of being left entirely isolated (personal communication, July 12, 1992).

[41]A sanction with such strong moral connotations was never imposed upon officers indicted for atrocities who later benefited from the Full Stop and the Due Obedience laws. Interview with General Ernesto Lopez-Meyer, at the CEMIDA.

[42]ROBERT NOZICK, PHILOSOPHICAL EXPLANATIONS 370 (1981).

[43]*See* claims of the *Madres de Plaza de Mayo*, *supra* note 12.

[44]*Id.*

[45]The term "subversion" was introduced to the Argentine military by General Carlos Rosas in 1955. Rosas had come back from a mission with the French troops in Northern Africa and gave a series of lectures at military academies on the doctrine the French had developed in Algeria. (Conversation with writer Enrique Garcia Lupo, a close friend and comrade of General Carlos Rosas, Buenos Aires, June 1992).

[46]As a former officer of the Third Army Corps recalls, its commander, General Benjamin Menendez, had every officer under his orders assassinate a "subversive" suspect (July 1992).

[47]H. L. A. Hart, *Prolegomenon to the Principles of Punishment, in* PUNISHMENT AND RESPONSIBILITY: ESSAYS IN PHILOSOPHY OF LAW 1 (1968).

[48]"All ethical doctrines worth our attention take consequences into account in judging rightness. One which did not would simply be irrational, crazy." JOHN RAWLS, A THEORY OF JUSTICE 30 (1971).

[49]BRAITHWAITE & PETTIT, *supra* note 25, at 29.

[50]*See* John Mackie, *Morality and Retributive Emotions, in* 1 CRIM. JUST. ETHICS 3 nn.1-4 (1982).

[51]RAWLS, *supra* note 48, at 446.

[52]*See* SANCINETTI, *supra* note 19. *See also* AMERICAS WATCH, *supra* note 27.

[53]*See* SANCINETTI, *supra* note 19; POLICE VIOLENCE, *supra* note 27.

[54]I wish to point out that my critique of the Federal Court of Buenos Aires is clearly an ex post facto appraisal. Scholarly discussions unleashed by the 1985 trials provide an empirical and conceptual acumen that was not available at the time the trials took place.

[55]The state in which some Indian ethnicities live in the western United States may be a good example. Experts on the Cheyenne, for example, have argued that members of this Indian nation in the 1990s are not only deprived of the material means of existence, but are also compelled to live against their own religious creed and ethos.

[56]*See* BALESTRA, *supra* note 7.

[57]It must be admitted, much to many Argentines' chagrin, that the bloodless March 1976 military takeover enjoyed widespread consensus within the population. *See generally* ROSENDO FRAGA, EJERCITO: DEL ESCARNIO AL PODER (1973-1976) 261 (1988). I agree with this view.

[58]Interview with cavalry army Colonel Federico Toranzo, Buenos Aires, September 29, 1991. Colonel Toranzo reflected the opinion of ninety percent of his comrades.

[59]*See, e.g.,* Franklin E. Zimring & Gordon J. Hawkins, *An Agenda for Research in Deterrence, in* DETERRENCE: THE LEGAL THREAT IN CRIME CONTROL 339 (1973).

[60]*See Sentencia de la Camara Nacional de Apelaciones en lo Criminal y Correccional Federal de la Capital Federal (December 9, 1985), in* PROCESO A LOS EX-INTEGRANTES DE LAS JUNTAS MILITARES 46 (with the collaboration of Guillermo Palombo, no date, Buenos Aires).

[61]Julio B. Maier, The Criminal Justice System Today: Between the Inquisition and the Composition (1992) (unpublished manuscript on file with Irwin P. Stotzky).

[62]Andrés J. D'Alessio, *The Function of the Prosecutor in the Transition to Democracy in Latin America, in* TRANSITION TO DEMOCRACY IN LATIN AMERICA: THE ROLE OF THE JUDICIARY 187 (Irwin P. Stotzky ed., 1993).

[63]Before Menem's cashiering of the head of the administrative affairs' prosecutor in 1990, this official enjoyed life tenure for obvious reasons. The Attorney General was by law a member of the Supreme Court and therefore also a tenured official. Menem, however, issued a decree removing Andrés D'Alessio and appointing a political sidekick in his place, thus ending the life tenure of the Attorney General.

[64]In July 1992, Menem confronted a strike to improve the impoverished state of public education by stating that "subversion" had permeated the ranks of the protesters, and that parents now supporting the dissent campaign should be wary that they may become the future *Madres de Plaza de Mayo* striving to establish their children's whereabouts; *see e.g.*, HERALD (newspaper, Buenos Aires, Arg.) July 10, 11 and 12, 1992.

[65]On October 6, 1989, President Menem signed three decrees pardoning almost 400 officers indicted for human rights violations. On December 29, 1990, Menem signed two more decrees pardoning the rest of the officers charged with torture and murder, including the commanders who had been convicted by the federal courts. He also pardoned a few civilians, including Mario Firmenich, the leader of the Montoneros, convicted for murder by the democratic courts.

# 17

## The Role of the Prosecutor in the Transition to Democracy in Latin America

*Diane F. Orentlicher*

### I.
### Introduction

The most difficult issues related to the role of the prosecutor in transitions to democracy arise with respect to abuses by security forces that operate with relative autonomy, and my own observations will focus on the challenges posed by those situations. To be more specific, I will address the peculiar challenges that a prosecutor confronts when investigating such abuses during the volatile period of transition from military rule to democratic governance and will consider the prosecutor's dilemma from the vantage point of international law and policy.

Issues relating to prosecution of military abuses are at the heart of the broader dilemmas surrounding transitions from prolonged periods of military dictatorship to democratic government. Whether the military can be brought under the rule of law is a central measure of the success of that transition. Yet any effort to prosecute security forces, long accustomed to impunity, is fraught with peril when the military can credibly threaten violent resistance. Like the hypothetical seafarer who rebuilds his entire boat while he is in it, proceeding plank by plank while he is supported by the very structure he seeks to replace, the prosecutor attempting to restore the rule of law operates within the constraints imposed by the very system -- one characterized by military lawlessness -- that her work, if successful, will supplant.

Issues surrounding the prosecutor's dilemma have been framed most sharply in the debate over accountability for human rights violations committed during the recently concluded period of military rule. In many instances, the outgoing government committed grave violations of human rights -- forced disappearances, torture, and political killings -- on a massive scale. Typically, these violations were committed with wholesale impunity, leaving the burden of justice at the doorstep of the successor government.

While issues surrounding the question of retrospective justice have demanded urgent attention in the period immediately following the end of military governance, challenges surrounding the prosecutor's role in a transitional period are scarcely confined to the question of prosecuting violations of the past. In countries where the military has grown accustomed to impunity, any effort to bring the armed forces under the authority of the law requires a rearrangement of entrenched relations between civilian and military institutions. That the military often continues to retain residual power following the formal transition necessarily makes this process complicated and, indeed, perilous.

Internationally, the response to these dilemmas has been characterized by a striking evolution over a relatively short period. At the policy level, the international human rights community has moved from a widely-shared position of deference to the judgments of transitional governments to a generally assertive stance opposing wholesale impunity for massive violations of physical integrity. There has been a parallel evolution in international law, as enunciated by international tribunals that interpret major human rights conventions and by authoritative publicists.

This chapter will consider the role of the prosecutor from the perspective of these recently developed principles of law: What, precisely, does international law have to say about the exercise of prosecutorial power during periods of transition? And how do the international obligations themselves help address -- or, perhaps, exacerbate -- the unique dilemmas associated with the prosecutor's function during periods of transition from dictatorship to democracy? In addressing these issues, I will focus in particular on the impact that international law may have on the exercise of prosecutorial discretion and on the prosecutor's independence -- both perceived and actual -- from political influence.

## II.
## Transitional Justice: Goals and Perils

Before turning to these issues, it is necessary first to consider several preliminary questions: What are the central goals, and what are the peculiar challenges, relating to the prosecutorial function during a transition to democracy? These questions must, in turn, be addressed against the backdrop of two broader questions, one descriptive and one normative: What is the transition "from"? And what is the transition "to"?

For present purposes, a chief characteristic of the circumstances from which many Latin American countries are emerging is a breakdown of the rule of law. In Argentina and other countries governed by military juntas, the former regimes used extra-legal forms of violence against perceived or actual political opponents, and did so as a matter of policy, whether or not the violence was officially acknowledged to be a state policy. A corollary to this systemic violence was the collapse of the judicial system as a bulwark against abuses of citizens by the state. Perpetrators of torture, disappearances, and summary executions operated in a climate of general impunity and they were not criminally punished. Typically too, the civilian judiciary failed to provide other effective protections against arbitrary state action, such as *habeas corpus*, and often lost substantial jurisdictional ground to military courts.

A second attribute shared by many pre-transitional governments in Latin America is, of course, that they were not democratic. Beyond the lack of formal democratic institutions, such as free elections and other institutional arrangements designed to assure public accountability, the former military regimes typically suppressed the political culture and habits of a functioning democracy. As Jaime Malamud-Goti points out, the systematic repression of political opposition to the military government in Argentina had the effect of inhibiting citizens from engaging in a broad spectrum of political activities, as well as other associational activities.[1] Civil society, an essential ingredient of a vibrant democracy, was severely crippled. Further, the general impunity enjoyed by military forces for human rights violations eroded public confidence in the institutions of civilian government, and in this sense human rights violations and the impunity that allowed them to persist further damaged the political culture that sustains democratic government.

These answers to the question "what is the transition from?" suggest several obvious answers to the question, "what is the transition to?" or, more precisely, "what should it be to?" Above all, a key objective of the transitional government should be to restore the rule of law -- in particular, to restore the machinery of justice necessary to secure freedom from torture, disappearance and summary execution.

The independent, and paramount, importance of this aim is underscored by the staggering levels of state violence in a number of countries that are now democracies. In Latin America, where freedom from punishment for violations of outgoing military regimes has been the general rule among fledgling democracies, serious violations by security forces have persisted on a wide scale in several countries. In recent years, the largest number of political killings have occurred in countries whose political processes are democratic.

Beyond the formidable challenge of restoring the rule of law in the wake of its wholesale collapse, transitional governments face the broader challenge of establishing a viable and genuine democracy, with all of the complexity that the term entails. While most dimensions of that challenge are beyond the scope of this paper, I would like to note briefly several respects in which the role of the prosecutor may either contribute to or imperil the consolidation of a democratic transition.

First, as I have already noted, enforcement of legal safeguards against arbitrary state action is indispensable to the free exercise of political rights. Citizens cannot fully exercise the right of political participation if agents of the state are free to abduct, torture, and murder them because of their perceived or actual political activities. Whether the military's human rights violations are prosecuted also has significant implications for the political culture in which a nascent democracy will develop. Because law "is located in our myths and stories as a powerful attribute of legitimate authority,"[2] failure to enforce the law may undermine a new government's legitimacy and breed cynicism toward civilian institutions. Conversely, by demonstrating that no sector is above the law, prosecutions of military violations can foster respect for democratic institutions and thereby deepen a transitional society's democratic culture.[3] Further, by establishing the supremacy of civilian institutions over the military, a civilian government's successful effort to hold members of the armed forces accountable for their crimes helps shift the balance between military and civilian centers of political power in favor of the latter.

But, of course, transitional justice carries risks as well as benefits. Most obviously, prosecutions of military abuses may be destabilizing if they take place during periods when democratic institutions are still competing with military sectors for *de facto* power. In the worst-case scenario, efforts to bring security forces to court may provoke military rebellions, as happened in Argentina. Even short of a coup attempt, prosecutions may provoke confrontations that weaken the authority of the elected government and reinforce the military's propensity to operate as an autonomous sector. Further, prosecutors may undertake criminal proceedings against military personnel at considerable peril. In several countries, prosecutors, potential witnesses, and judges risk assassination in cases against military or paramilitary forces.

The values associated with prosecutions outlined above presuppose that substantial progress has already been made toward consolidating a democratic transition -- in particular, that the civilian government has acquired enough power to institute prosecutions of military defendants without provoking its own overthrow. When that precondition does not yet exist, however, prosecutions may be impossible, dangerous, or counterproductive.

Additional risks are particularly likely to come into play when prosecutions are instituted in respect of violations committed by the previous regime. Such trials may be undertaken as a form of political revanchism. And the risk of *appearing* to dispense revanchist justice is present, to one degree or another, whenever a successor government undertakes prosecutions of systematic violations by a prior regime. Even when the charges are confined -- as of course they always should be -- to discrete crimes, such as murder, prosecutions of these crimes may be perceived as a surrogate for prosecuting the prior regime itself.

This factor was at play to some extent during the human rights trials instituted by the government of Raúl Alfonsín in the mid-1980s. Military opposition to the Alfonsín government's prosecution of former junta members was fueled in part by the military's perception that the trials tarnished the armed forces institutionally. Further, the military's opposition to the trials has to be understood as part of a broader contest between the military and the civilian government over their competing versions of the military's "dirty war against subversion." The point is that the reasons for the Argentine military's opposition to prosecutions was more complex than a predictable desire by potential defendants to elude criminal punishment, coupled with their ability to bring force to bear in asserting their claim to impunity. This disposition was, to be sure, a significant, if not paramount, factor behind the military's opposition to the trials. But military opposition was exacerbated by the perception that the prosecutions represented a judgment on the military itself, and on its political agenda during the 1970s.

While increasing the risk of military opposition, the perception that trials are politically motivated also vitiates their capacity to advance public respect for the rule of law. In this sense, transitional justice can retard the development of public confidence in judicial institutions at a time when society is poised to reassert its commitment to the rule of law.

The various risks relating to the exercise of prosecutorial power during periods of transition from military dictatorship to democracy can be summarized along the following lines: three distinct types of risk can be identified. One is that prosecutions will be undertaken -- or will be perceived to have been instituted -- for political or otherwise inappropriate reasons, thereby undermining public respect for the rule of law and intensifying the military's disposition to oppose the prosecutions.

A second type of risk is that a fledgling democracy will *fail* to prosecute the military's crimes for reasons that reflect, and in turn may exacerbate, enduring weaknesses in democratic institutions. Within this category, two distinct reasons for failure -- both aspects of the legacy of military dictatorship -- should be distinguished. First, the government may fail to bring military forces to trial because of a failure of political will. This failure is, predictably, common among the military leadership itself, and all too often is shared by civilian leaders. Second, the civilian government may tolerate military impunity because the government has, or believes that it has, insufficient power to bring security forces to trial. As I will argue more fully below, in practice the two factors often operate in a relationship of mutual reinforcement. Governments legitimately concerned about challenges posed by autonomous military sectors have often overstated the risks to avoid any challenge from the military, however remote or speculative, to their own authority. In the inexorable logic of the self-fulfilling prophecy, the resulting failure of political will may further embolden the military to assert autonomous power.

Finally, there is the risk that a government committed to the rule of law will undertake prosecutions that provoke harmful consequences. The most obvious case in point is that of Argentina, where prosecutions for human rights violations undertaken by the Alfonsín government eventually provoked military rebellions.

## III.
### International Law Relating to
### the Role of the Prosecutor

### A. *Is This a Proper Subject of International Law?*

The dilemmas sketched above are readily conceived as a conflict between two incommensurable realms: the realm of law and the realm of political reality.[4] In this conceptual framework, the realm of law, represented in the role of the prosecutor as enforcer of the law, is constrained by its antithesis, the realm of political power, embodied in the enduring strength of military sectors that operate above the law and whose paramount control of coercive state power enables them effectively to veto the exercise of prosecutorial power.

Several years ago, when the dilemmas confronting Latin America's growing roster of nascent democracies first engaged the attention of the foreign policy and international human rights communities, this framework dominated the international community's policy debates. Sympathetic to the challenges confronting fragile democracies, human rights organizations, such as Amnesty International, and governments with significant human rights policies tended to regard resolution of the dilemmas surrounding transitional justice as a matter for each society's internal consideration. While this stance may seem the most natural and appropriate response to determinations that have, after all, long fallen within the province of nations' domestic prerogative, in fact it represented a significant departure from the approach typically taken by the professional human rights community. Organizations like Amnesty International have not hesitated to press upon governments recommendations of domestic legal action that would help secure greater respect for human rights, and prosecution of human rights violators has long figured prominently among the measures urged upon governments by the professional human rights community.

In recent years, however, the position of the international human rights community has shifted markedly. From a former position of deference to the domestic judgments of transitional societies, influential organizations like Human Rights Watch and Amnesty International have moved to a policy that favors enforcement of law and which presumes that the most effective and responsible means of addressing the dilemmas of transitional societies is through law, rather than outside law.[5] These organizations have reached a judgment, based upon their experience in countries where civilian governments avoided confrontations with the military by allowing impunity for past violations, that the bargain was too costly. As elaborated below, a similar judgment is evident in recent pronouncements of international bodies that enforce human rights treaties.

## B. Parameters of Current Law

That international law has something significant to say about the exercise of prosecutorial power is itself somewhat surprising. Traditionally, this has been an area that international law has left to the broad discretion of states. But, like the policy positions of the international human rights community, the law as enunciated by international tribunals and authoritative publicists has evolved substantially in a relatively short period. Although mirrored in the jurisprudence of other international bodies, this shift is especially pronounced in the case law of the two bodies that monitor compliance with the American Convention on Human Rights[6] ("American Convention").

Like other comprehensive human rights treaties, the American Convention ensures protection of a range of substantive rights, but nowhere explicitly mentions an obligation to prosecute violations of the rights it assures. Nevertheless, in recent years both the Inter-American Commission on Human Rights ("Commission") and the Inter-American Court of Human Rights have interpreted the Convention to require States Parties to investigate serious violations of physical integrity, such as torture, disappearances, and summary executions, and to bring the wrongdoers to justice.

Still, as recently as 1986 the Commission expressed a general inclination to allow national authorities to determine the validity of amnesty laws enacted by previous governments, subject to the qualification that the truth about past violations must be fully known.[7] Again, this view effectively established an exception to the Commission's general rule that atrocious human rights crimes must be punished -- an exception for new democracies precariously emerging from prolonged military dictatorship. By 1989, however, the Commission's Chairman voiced strong opposition to amnesty laws that foreclose prosecution of atrocious crimes.[8]

By that time, the Inter-American Court of Human Rights ("Court") had issued a landmark decision interpreting the American Convention to require States Parties to investigate certain violations and punish the perpetrators. The decision was rendered in the *Velasquez Rodriguez Case*,[9] which was brought before the Court by the Commission against the Honduran government for the unresolved disappearance of Manfredo Velasquez in September 1981.[10]

The Court found the Honduran government responsible for multiple violations of the American Convention, basing much of its analysis on States Parties' affirmative duty to "ensure" rights elaborated in the convention:

> This obligation implies the duty of the States Parties to organize the governmental apparatus and, in general, all the structures through which public power is exercised, so that they are capable of juridically ensuring the free and full enjoyment of human rights. As a consequence of this obligation, *the States must prevent, investigate and punish any violation of the rights recognized by the Convention* and, moreover, if possible attempt to restore the right violated and provide compensation as warranted for damages resulting from the violation. . . .[11]

Significantly, the Court found that Honduras' duties under the Convention persisted even though the government in power at the time of its decision was not the same one that had presided over the practice of disappearances whose victims included Manfredo Velasquez.[12]

This past year, the Commission has for the first time squarely faced the question whether amnesty laws enacted by transitional governments breach the American Convention. In cases challenging amnesty laws covering military crimes in Uruguay and Argentina, respectively, the Commission has resolved that the laws are inconsistent with the states' obligations under the American Convention.[13]

The bodies that monitor states' compliance with two other comprehensive human rights treaties have interpreted those treaties to require investigation and punishment of grave violations of physical integrity. For example, the Human Rights' Committee, which monitors compliance with the International Covenant on Civil and Political Rights,[14] has repeatedly expressed the view that States Parties must investigate torture, disappearances, and extra-legal executions and attempt to bring the wrongdoers to justice.[15]

Although the European Court of Human Rights has had comparatively few occasions to elucidate the role of punishment in securing rights set forth in the European Convention for the Protection of Human Rights and Fundamental Freedoms,[16] its decisions make clear that punishment plays a necessary part in Contracting States' fulfillment of certain duties under the Convention. In *X and Y v. Netherlands*,[17] for example, the Court found the Dutch government in breach of the European Convention by virtue of a gap in Dutch law that had precluded a victim of sexual assault from instituting criminal proceedings against her attacker, who escaped punishment. Thus, despite their textual silence about punishment, each of these three major conventions has been interpreted to require States Parties to investigate and prosecute serious violations of physical integrity.

Customary law imposes a similar, though less demanding, duty on all governments. The *Restatement (Third) of the Foreign Relations Law of the United States* adopts the view that a state violates customary law "if, as a matter of state policy, it practices, encourages or condones" torture, murder or disappearances,[18] and suggests that "[a] government may be presumed to have encouraged or condoned [these] acts . . . if such acts, especially by its officials, have been repeated or notorious and no steps have been taken to prevent them or to punish the perpetrators."[19]

If international law generally requires states to punish serious violations of physical integrity, must a newly-elected government attempt to prosecute every such violation committed with impunity during a recent dictatorship? Applying the *Restatement* rule, customary law would be violated by an amnesty that established complete impunity for systematic violations of the rights against torture, extra-legal executions, and disappearances, but would not appear to require prosecution of every person who committed such an offense. Limited prosecutions, focusing in particular on those who were most responsible for designing and implementing a system of human rights atrocities or on especially notorious cases that were emblematic of past violations, would seemingly satisfy governments' duties under customary law, provided the criteria used to select defendants did not appear to condone or tolerate past abuses by, for example, cynically targeting a handful of low-level scapegoats. Moreover, criteria used to limit prosecutions should not justify commission of atrocious crimes on the basis that the perpetrators were executing "superior orders," although this circumstance can legitimately be considered in mitigation of punishment or as a defense if the perpetrator had no "moral choice."[20]

More complex issues are raised by the question whether a successor government of a state that has ratified the International Covenant, the European Convention or the American Convention must attempt to prosecute all serious violations of the right to physical integrity committed by or with the acquiescence of a previous regime. Decisions interpreting these conventions include some indications that States Parties are in general expected to investigate every violation of the rights to life, freedom from torture and freedom from involuntary disappearances, and to prosecute those who are responsible.[21] A rigid application of the general rule that a state's international obligations persist despite a change in government[22] might, then, seem to require successor governments to prosecute virtually every violation of these three rights that has not yet been punished.

Yet in a country like Argentina, where from 9,000 to 30,000 persons are estimated to have disappeared during the military juntas' "dirty war against subversion,"[23] such a requirement could place impossible demands on the judiciary. Even a well-functioning judicial system would be incapable of discharging such a burden; much less can this be expected following the wholesale collapse of the rule of law.

Further, open-ended prosecutions could exacerbate military opposition and strain an already fragile social fabric. I believe that a chief lesson of the Argentina experience is not, as some suggest, that prosecutions are destabilizing per se, but that prosecutions of indefinite duration and scope are likely to be destabilizing. Although the Argentine military opposed prosecutions, it was prepared to allow the government to prosecute top military commanders. But some factions rebelled when prosecutions began to sweep more broadly, believing this tarnished the military institutionally. Moreover, public support for prosecutions, strong at the outset of the Alfonsín government, waned as time elapsed and the trials' importance was eclipsed by worsening economic conditions.[24] In contrast, human rights trials of finite scope and duration undertaken in Greece in the mid-1970s provoked military discontent, but were far less disruptive and helped consolidate the country's transition to democracy.

The contrasting experiences of Greece and Argentina suggest that the demands of legal accountability and political stability may be best reconciled through prosecutions that have defined limits. Exemplary trials can vindicate the authority of the law and deter repetition of human rights crimes, provided the trials comport with popular conceptions of justice.

But is selective prosecution compatible with states' duties under the international conventions discussed earlier? I believe that they are. In reaching this conclusion, my starting point is the general canon of construction pursuant to which international treaties should be interpreted in a manner that avoids imposing impossible obligations or duties whose discharge would prove harmful.[25] A functional analysis[26] of the rule requiring prosecution of torture, extra-legal killings and disappearances provides a principled basis for such an interpretation.

The duty to punish serious violations of physical integrity is squarely grounded on a deterrence rationale.[27] Believing criminal sanctions to be the most effective means of securing rights deemed of paramount importance, bodies such as the Human Rights Committee and the Inter-American Commission have found investigation leading to punishment to be the most appropriate response to any particular violation of those rights. This rationale would not, however, compel prosecution by a successor government of every violation committed by a previous regime. While the deterrence model supporting the general rule might require the new government to investigate and seek to punish each violation committed thenceforth, it would simply be too late to apply that model to prevent the violations that have already occurred.

But a failure to punish any of the past violations would frustrate the deterrence objective underlying the general duty to punish. If the new government established complete impunity for atrocious crimes committed on a sweeping scale, its action would, as the Restatement reasoned, have the effect of tolerating or condoning the violations and thereby encouraging similar ones. This result is plainly incompatible with the convention-based duty to undertake affirmative measures to prevent violations. But even a limited program of exemplary punishment could serve a deterrent function and thus achieve the aim justifying the general duty to punish atrocious crimes.

## IV.
## Resolving the Prosecutor's Dilemma Through Law

In this final section, I return to the issues outlined in the first section of this chapter -- the peculiar challenges that converge in the role of the prosecutor during transitions from military dictatorship to democracy -- and consider what impact the international legal duties outlined above may have on those dilemmas. In addressing this question, it is useful first to consider a preliminary issue: the manner in which the international obligations outlined in the previous section are, or might be, enforced.

### A. *Modes of Enforcement*
A general analysis of the nature of enforcement of international human rights law is beyond the scope of this chapter. I would, however, like to note several examples of the manner in which the law summarized above is brought to bear on the choices of national governments.

At the level of bilateral relations, efforts to compel foreign governments to prosecute human rights crimes have ranged from diplomatic initiatives to the use of sanctions. The United States government has successfully pressed several countries to institute prosecutions against persons responsible for grave violations of human rights. In some instances, the United States Congress has enacted legislation that explicitly prohibits disbursement of foreign aid to a country until its government has prosecuted particular human rights cases. This device has, for example, been used with respect to cases in El Salvador and Chile.

Complaint procedures established under human rights conventions provide another venue for enforcement of duties relating to prosecution. As the discussion above suggests, various treaty bodies have rendered decisions finding that states are legally required to bring perpetrators of human rights crimes to justice. Typically, however, these bodies have limited power to enforce their judgments. The European Court of Human Rights has the power, which it has utilized, to order States Parties to provide compensation for the harm suffered in consequence of their failure adequately to provide for criminal prosecution of individuals who infringe rights protected by the European Convention for the Protection of Human Rights and Fundamental Freedoms.[28] The Inter-American Court of Human Rights has similar powers, and can also order States Parties to the American Convention to institute prosecutions. But the Court has little effective power to enforce compliance with such orders. Various treaty bodies can promote friendly settlements of complaints lodged before them. At times, a State Party's agreement to institute criminal proceedings has been part of such a settlement.

In practice, the enforcement "power" most commonly used by human rights treaty bodies is that of declaratory judgment -- issuing a decision finding that States Parties are required to institute criminal proceedings in respect of particular human rights violations. While this "power" may seem limp, the fact is that, as international human rights standards have acquired strong legitimacy and moral authority in recent years, the power of such declaratory judgments to induce conforming behavior has increased correspondingly. Within the Council of Europe, whose member states share a generally high regard for the authority of international law, declaratory judgments are routinely obeyed by states found in breach of the European Convention. In contrast, decisions rendered by the human rights bodies of the Organization of American States have commanded varying levels of respect by member states, some of which have openly flouted rulings of the Inter-American Court.

Resolutions by the General Assemblies of the United Nations and the Organization of American States urging states to prosecute atrocious human rights crimes have also become a source of genuine, if limited, pressure. Another source of pressure has come from a range of special mechanisms established by the United Nations Commission on Human Rights to respond to particular types of violations, such as torture and forced disappearance, or violations in particular countries. Special Rapporteurs and Working Groups appointed by the Commission to examine and respond to such violations have repeatedly pressed governments to pursue prosecutions of human rights crimes. These actions have built cumulative international pressure in support of legal accountability for grave violations of human rights.[29]

One of the most effective sources of pressure for compliance with the legal standards enunciated by authoritative bodies has been the work of influential non-governmental organizations ("NGOs") like Amnesty International. Although these organizations have no power to compel governments to take any action, some have acquired considerable moral authority and, with it, effective power to induce governments to change their behavior. I know of numerous instances in which NGOs have successfully pressed governments to institute criminal proceedings against persons responsible for particular human rights violations.

Let me be clear; I do not believe that international efforts to enforce states' duty to punish atrocious human rights crimes have been adequate or sufficiently effective. My claim is more modest. I believe that the international law requiring states to punish human rights crimes can, and sometimes does, make a difference in governments' behavior.

When governments enforce that law by applying sanctions to states that have failed to prosecute human rights crimes, as the United States government has occasionally done, the coercive power of international law is obvious. Less obvious, but no less important, international law protecting human rights has acquired sufficient legitimacy in recent years that governments can sometimes be shamed into compliance when public pressure is mobilized.

## B. The Law Applied

In this final section, I would like to consider how the legal standards outlined in Section III can help advance the goals of transitional societies identified in Section II and address the peculiar dilemmas surrounding the role of the prosecutor in those societies.

To the extent that a government's failure to prosecute human rights crimes is due to a lack of political will, international law can successfully be brought to bear to assure that prosecutions are instituted.[30] If the resulting prosecutions appear fair and the outcome just, they can help restore respect for the rule of law and deter repetition of the types of violations that are prosecuted.

In situations where a democratic government is inclined to refrain from prosecuting military abuses because it lacks sufficient power, rather than will, to bring the military to court, international law may be less effective in addressing the underlying problem. Still, international pressure to institute prosecutions can help shift the balance of power between civilian and military sectors in situations where that balance is relatively fluid and where civilian institutions already possess significant, if limited, power *vis-a-vis* the military.

Recent progress in a case in Chile exemplifies this process. The case I have in mind is the 1976 assassination in Washington, D.C. of Orlando Letelier, a Chilean exile and prominent critic of the Pinochet regime, and Ronni Karpen Moffitt, a United States citizen and colleague of Ambassador Letelier. Some participants in the crime have been prosecuted in United States courts, but the alleged authors of the crime, military officials who held top positions in Chile's secret police agency, eluded justice for fifteen years. Although resolution of this case has long been one of the most important issues in United States-Chile relations, as recently as April, 1991 high-level officials in Chile privately conceded that there was little likelihood that the Aylwin government would successfully bring the authors of the crime to justice. In their view, although the government was committed to prosecuting the authors of the Letelier-Moffitt assassination, it would be unable to do so in light of the enduring power of the armed forces in the post-Pinochet transitional period.

Five months later, the two principal suspects were indicted, and their trial set to begin in the near future. What happened in the intervening period? Significant pressure was brought to bear on the Chilean government by the United States government and by NGOs. In July 1991, a delegation representing the New York based International League for Human Rights visited Santiago, where they pressed for progress in the Letelier-Moffitt case on behalf of the families of the victims. Their visit received considerable publicity in the Chilean press and, according to one account, the visit itself "changed the political climate" in Chile with respect to the Letelier-Moffitt case. One week after their visit, Chile's Supreme Court designated one of its own members to investigate the case, and he later indicted the two principal suspects. Recent progress in the case is, to be sure, the result of a confluence of various sources of pressure, including concerted efforts by influential Senators such as Edward Kennedy. Clearly, however, external pressure made a difference, providing a counterweight to the internal pressure emanating from a recalcitrant military.

Significantly, too, the very act of indicting the two suspects -- an act that not long ago was thought likely to provoke military unrest -- instead helped enhance the Aylwin government's power *vis-a-vis* the Chilean armed forces.[31] One lesson that Eastern Europe's human rights revolutions brought home is that legitimacy is itself a basis of political power, and that a government's commitment to human rights is a powerful basis of legitimacy. To the extent that a government succeeds in meeting public demands for the rule of law, it enhances this base of power relative to military sectors that occupy a realm of autonomous power. As the Letelier-Moffitt case suggests, international pressure for prosecutions can help advance this process by bolstering the positions of governments that wish to bring human rights violators to account.

Conversely, a civilian government's capitulation to military demands for impunity can enhance the military's relative power. I believe that this happened in the Philippines during the period of transition following the ouster of former President Ferdinand Marcos. At that time, advisors to Marcos' successor, Corazon Aquino, privately expressed the view that efforts to prosecute the military for violations committed during the Marcos era would be destabilizing, and in fact the military enjoyed *de facto* impunity for virtually all of those violations. Several years later, the same officials told me that, in retrospect, they wished that the government had been pressured by the international community to institute prosecutions. Its failure to do so had, in their view, emboldened the military to assert autonomous power (the government has survived half a dozen rebellions), and to persist in lawless behavior.

The correlation of political forces in each country is unique, of course, and the government of Corazon Aquino had considerably more power *vis-a-vis* the Philippine military in the period immediately following the ouster of Ferdinand Marcos than many governments in Latin America have had following the formal transition from military to civilian government. International efforts to assure prosecution of a recalcitrant military must be sensitive to the peculiar constraints that each government faces. In some countries, there may be periods when there is virtually no possibility of successfully prosecuting the military.

Still, it is important to recognize that, in many transitional societies, the correlation of political power between a civilian government and the military is constantly shifting, and to some degree may be susceptible to realignment as new factors are introduced. One source of effective political power is public support, based upon perceived legitimacy. (Indeed, such support has generally been crucial to the success of military coups in recent Latin American history.) Increasingly, respect for human rights has become a crucial aspect of a government's legitimacy, both domestically and internationally. In this setting, international opposition to impunity for human rights violations can bolster the efforts of a prosecutor seeking to bring the military under the rule of law.

When external pressure is explicitly based upon duties imposed by international law, such pressure can, I believe, further minimize certain risks associated with human rights trials. By identifying crimes that must be punished, international law diminishes the risk that prosecution of those crimes will be perceived as politically-motivated revanchism -- and opposed on that basis. When international law insists upon punishment of atrocious crimes, the prosecutions can, as Otto Kirchheimer said of the Nuremberg prosecutions for crimes against humanity, "define where the realm of politics ends or, rather, is transformed into the concerns of the human condition."[32]

The constraints on prosecutors' discretion imposed by international law can, in effect, help insulate the decision to prosecute human rights crimes from the charge that the trials were the product of political manipulation. In this sense, international law can serve a function somewhat analogous to the role served in our national system by such devices as the grand jury, or in other national systems by laws requiring prosecutors to institute proceedings in respect of certain crimes.

While setting outer limits on the exercise of prosecutorial discretion, international law allows governments considerable latitude to fashion policies appropriate to the complexity and diversity of their domestic circumstances. Consistent with a state's obligations under international law, prosecutors can, for example, fashion plea-bargaining arrangements that increase the likelihood of convicting those who are most responsible for a system of atrocious crimes, while incidentally diminishing the cohesiveness of the military. In this respect and others, the flexibility that is characteristic of the law outlined above is one of its strengths.

## V.
## Conclusion

In recent years, the requirements of international law have been added to the complex mix of constraints operating on the prosecutor's exercise of discretion. Recent authoritative interpretations of international law have carved out a narrow exception to the traditionally broad discretion of governments in respect of prosecution: when it comes to atrocious crimes against personal integrity, governments must make good faith efforts to investigate the alleged violations and bring to justice those who are responsible.

Paradoxically, international efforts to enforce these duties may actually enhance the power of prosecutors in situations where their position is most precarious -- when they seek to prosecute autonomous military sectors for politically-motivated human rights violations. In these circumstances, international support for prosecutions can confer a measure of legitimacy on the role of the prosecutor that enlarges her power *vis-a-vis* the military.

At best, the contribution of international law in advancing democratic transitions is limited. The one certainty is that restoring the rule of law in the wake of its wholesale collapse will be a protracted process. Still, international law requiring governments to enforce their own domestic law can play a constructive part in this process by enhancing the legitimacy of institutions and individuals committed to the rule of law.

# Notes

[1]Jaime Malamud-Goti, *Human Rights Abuses in Fledgling Democracies: The Role of Discretion, in* TRANSITION TO DEMOCRACY IN LATIN AMERICA: THE ROLE OF THE JUDICIARY 225 (Irwin P. Stotzky ed., 1993).

[2]Robert M. Cover, *The Folktales of Justice: Tales of Jurisdiction*, 14 CAP. U. L. REV. 179, 180 n.7 (1985).

[3]The relationship between prosecution of a prior regime's human rights violations and consolidation of a democratic transition are addressed in greater depth in Diane F. Orentlicher, *Settling Accounts: The Duty to Prosecute Human Rights Violations of a Prior Regime*, 100 YALE L.J. 2537 (1991).

[4]I am grateful to Professor Paul W. Kahn of the Yale Law School for suggesting this conceptualization.

[5]*Id.*

[6]Jan. 7. 1970 O.A.S. Official Records, OEA/ser. K./XVI/1.1, doc. 65, rev. 1, corr. f, (1970).

[7]Inter-Am. Ct. H.R., OEA/ser. L./V1.11.68, doc. 8 rev. 1 (1986).

[8]Ambassador Oliver H. Jackman, Speech Before the First Committee of the XIX Regular Meeting of the General Assembly to Present the Annual Report of the Inter-American Commission on Human Rights (November, 1989).

[9]Inter-Am. Ct. H.R. (ser. C) No. 4 (1988) (judgment).

[10]The principal findings of the Inter-American court in the Velasquez Rodriguez Case were reaffirmed in the Godinez Cruz Case, Inter-Am. Ct. H.R. (ser. C) No. 5 (1989).

[11]Velasquez Rodriguez Case, Inter-Am. Ct. H.R. (ser. C) No. 4, para. 166 (1988) (judgment) (emphasis added). *See also id.* paras. 174; 176.

[12]*Id.*, para. 184. The Court stressed in particular that the duty to clarify the fate of someone who has disappeared, and to inform the victim's relatives of the results of these efforts, persists as long as the victim's fate remains uncertain. *Id.*, para. 181.

[13]Cases 10.147, 10.181, 10.240, 10.262, 10.309, 10.311, Report No. 24192 (Arg.), Inter-Am. Ct. H.R., DEA/ser. L./V.11.82, doc 24 (1992); Cases 10.029, 10.036, 10.145, 10.305, 10.372, 10.373, 10.374, 10.375, Report No. 29/92 (Uru.), Inter-Am. Ct. H.R., DEA/ser. L./V.11.82, doc. 25 (1992).

[14]G.A. Res. 2200A, U.N. GAOR 21st Sess. Supp. (No. 16) at 52, U.N. Doc. A/6316 (1966), 999 U.N.T.S. 171, 6 I.L.M. 368 (1967).

[15]*See, e.g.*, Human Rights Committee, General Comments under Article 40, para. 4 of the Covenant, U.N. GAOR, 37th Sess., Supp. No. 40, Annex V, U.N. Doc. A/37/40, U.N. Doc. E/CN.4/Sub.2/Add.1/963 (1982) (complaints of torture "must be investigated effectively by competent authorities; [t]hose found guilty must be held responsible"); Dermit v. Uruguay, Comm. No. 84/1981, 38 U.N. GAOR Supp. (No. 40), Annex IX, para. 11, U.N. Doc. A/38/40 (1983) (government responsible for victim's death-in-detention is "under an obligation to take effective steps . . . to establish the facts of [the victim's] death [and] to bring to justice any persons found to be responsible. . . ."); *to similar effect* Baboeram, et al. v. Suriname, Comm. Nos. 146/1983 and 148-154/1983, U.N. GAOR, 40th Sess., Supp. No. 4, Annex X, para. 13(2), U.N. Doc. A/40/40 (1985); Bleier v. Uruguay, Comm. No. R.7/30, 37 U.N. GAOR Supp. (No. 40) Annex X, para. 14 U.N. Doc. A/37/40 (1982); Quinteros v. Uruguay, Comm. No. 107/1981, 38 U.N. GAOR Supp. (No. 40) Annex XXII, para. 16 U.N. Doc. A/38/40 (1983) (respondent government should take effective steps to clarify fate of victim who had disappeared and to bring to justice those found responsible).

[16]Adopted Nov. 4, 1950, 213 U.N.T.S. 221, Europ. T.S. No. 5 (entered into force Sept. 3, 1953).

[17]91 Eur. Ct. H.R. (ser. A) (1985) (judgment).

[18]RESTATEMENT (THIRD) OF THE FOREIGN RELATIONS LAW OF THE UNITED STATES, § 702 (1987).

[19]*Id.*, comment b.

[20]That an individual acted pursuant to "superior orders" was explicitly rejected as an absolute defense to crimes against humanity and other Nazi violations of international law prosecuted at Nuremberg, and its rejection as a valid defense was subsequently ratified by the Untied Nations.  Since then, this principle has been incorporated into numerous human rights instruments and into the municipal law of virtually all major legal systems.

[21]For example, in the Velasquez Rodriguez Case, the Inter-American Court repeatedly asserts that a State Party to the American Convention must investigate and punish "any" and "every" violation of the rights protected by the convention. *See* Velasquez Rodriguez Case, *supra* note 11, at paras. 166, 174, 176. In X and Y v. Netherlands, 91 Eur. Ct. H.R. (ser. A) (1985) (judgment), the European Court found the Dutch government responsible for violating the European Convention because a gap in Dutch law prevented the applicant from instituting criminal proceedings against her attacker, even though Dutch law generally provided for such a procedure and, more generally, for prosecution of sexual offenses.

[22]*See* LOUIS HENKIN ET AL., INTERNATIONAL LAW 266 (2d ed. 1987).

[23]*See* Irwin P. Stotzky, *The Fragile Bloom of Democracy*, 44 U. MIAMI L. REV. 105, 109 n.17 (1989).

[24]Telford Taylor, who led the United States prosecutions of Nazi war criminals in Nuremberg following the joint Allied prosecution of Major War Criminals, reached similar conclusions about the United States prosecutions. Writing of the effect of delays that prevented the beginning of those prosecutions by almost one year, he wrote:

> In retrospect, it can be seen that the loss of this year was costly. The complexion of international events changed with surprising rapidity, and German affairs rapidly . . . sank into relative obscurity in the press and, one must assume, in the public mind. . . . If the trials . . . had started and been finished a year earlier, it might well have been possible to bring their lessons home more effectively.

Telford Taylor, *Final Report to the Secretary of the Army on the Nuremberg War Crimes Trials Under Control Council Law No. 10* (Brig. Gen., U.S.A., Chief of Counsel for War Crimes, Washington D.C.) August 15, 1949, at 105.

[25]*Cf.* [1978] 2 Y.B. Int'l L. Comm'n (pt. 1) 75, para. 33, U.N. Doc. A/CN.4/ 315/1977 (quoting Schwarzenberger's view that treaty obligations "are likely to be interpreted in a manner which circumscribes them so as to exclude situations of both absolute and relative impossibility from the very scope of such duties"); *id.* at 133 (quoting assertion by Prof. Alfred von Verdross that "international duties must not be taken so far as to result in self-destruction").

[26]By "functional analysis," I mean an analysis of the application of a general rule of law to a particular situation in light of the rationale supporting the general rule.

[27]This is implicit in the fact that the duty to prosecute is consistently identified with, and based upon, states parties' obligation to "ensure" or "secure" the full enjoyment of rights set forth in the conventions.

[28]The Court did this, for example, in X and Y v. Netherlands, *supra* note 21.

[29]One measure of the growing strength of legal norms requiring states to punish human rights crimes is the incorporation of these standards into major peace accords negotiated by the United Nations. Human rights guarantees set forth in the accord signed by the parties to the El Salvador conflict in San Jose, Costa Rica on July 26, 1991 include the following:

> All necessary steps and measures shall be taken immediately to avoid any act or practice which constitutes an attempt upon the life, integrity, security or freedom of the individual. Similarly, all necessary steps and measures shall be taken to eliminate any practice involving enforced disappearances and abductions. *Priority shall be given to the investigation of any cases of this kind which may arise and to the identification and punishment of persons found guilty.*

U.N. GAOR, 44th Sess., Annex, U.N. doc. no. A/44/971-S/21541, 1990 (accord between the government of El Salvador and the FMLN, in Costa Rica on July 26, 1990) (emphasis added).

[30]Such pressure can be effective -- although experience suggests that the effects are likely to be limited -- even when the failure of will lies chiefly with the military. In these circumstances, the threat of sanctions directly affecting the military, such as a cutoff of military aid, may supply the necessary incentive for military sectors to allow prosecutions to go forward.

[31]*See* Diane F. Orentlicher, *Chile Awakening From Pinochet Nightmare*, NY TIMES, Oct. 2, 1991, at A22 (letter to the editor).

[32]OTTO KIRCHHEIMER, POLITICAL JUSTICE 341 (1961).

# 18

## Designing the Institutional and Legal Structure of Prosecutorial Power in the Transition to Democracy

### Elizabeth M. Iglesias

### I.
### Introduction

In responding to the question whether the prosecutor should be independent or aligned with the government when investigating abuses of the government, I draw on two experiences. First, as research associate with the Center for Criminal Justice at Harvard Law School, I worked on the Guatemala/Harvard Criminal Justice Project where I was responsible for investigating political violence, witness intimidation, and judicial corruption, and for developing proposals to combat these problems in and through the Guatemalan criminal justice system. This work involved numerous interviews with representatives of virtually every sector of Guatemalan society from the most endangered, including human rights workers, labor leaders, student activists and church leaders, to the most privileged, including members of CACIF, Guatemala's most powerful business association. During these interviews, representatives of each sector expressed serious complaints about the Guatemalan criminal justice system and offered competing visions of the role criminal justice should play in ensuring that the democratic opening survived in Guatemala.

Political opposition groups reported that their members were followed, harassed, and abducted often within view of police officers who failed to intervene; that the Guatemalan police offered little protection, which could not be trusted even when offered; and that the courts provided no recourse for the violations they suffered. According to these groups, democracy would remain a facade in Guatemala as long as the government remained implicated in the practices of repression, and the government would remain implicated until at least some of the individuals responsible both for past violations as well as for the ongoing repression were identified, prosecuted, and convicted.

By contrast, for members of the business class, common crime and the civilian government's inability to deter it were the biggest threat to the new democracy. To preserve democracy, the criminal justice system would have to become more efficient and the police would have to be better trained and better equipped with patrol cars, radios, guns, and even computers. Corruption in the courts was the other major threat to democracy. It enabled common criminals to escape punishment, justified resorting to private vengeance, and would ultimately require a return to military rule. In short, while the representatives of these various sectors expressed different visions of how the criminal justice system should function, all were adamant in demanding aggressive enforcement against law breakers, whose violations they perceived to threaten their particular interests, and leniency, indeed, even impunity for law breakers with whom they identified.

The second perspective I bring is as a Professor of American Constitutional Criminal Procedure and Civil Rights Law. Use of the state's law enforcement apparatus by dominant social groups to repress the political mobilization of socially subordinate groups and silence their demands for change is not unique to Guatemala or to Argentina. In 1965, for example, the United States Commission on Civil Rights published a report graphically documenting events implicating State law enforcement officials in conspiracies to deprive black citizens of their constitutional rights. This included the failure to investigate and solve incidents of racially motivated violence against blacks, the failure to protect blacks, as well as official acts aimed at obstructing black citizens in the exercise of their constitutional rights of free assembly, freedom of speech, and the right to vote.[1]

Like racial minorities, American women of all races have faced enormous obstacles obtaining redress through the criminal justice system for crimes committed against them by men, in large part because law enforcement officials have routinely exercised their discretion *not* to arrest, prosecute, and convict the men who abuse them.[2] Victims of police misconduct and brutality face similar obstacles, particularly when police misconduct is directed at criminal suspects, street people, and members of other low status groups.[3] Like police officers, corporate executives routinely escape criminal prosecution even in cases which involve knowing and willfull violations of law resulting in numerous deaths, serious physical injury, and property loss.[4]

Thus, impunity is not unknown in the United States; however, impunity in this country is not primarily attributable to rampant and blatant corruption, nor to the intimidation of state officials charged with enforcing the law, though both do occur and not infrequently. Instead, impunity results from the presumption of respectability and credibility afforded the socially privileged as cases proceed through the succession of discretionary decision-making points at which complaints are investigated, charges filed, and judgments rendered.[5] In short, in the United States, impunity is more a reflection of ideological bias, social privilege, and prejudicial stereotypes operating through the discretionary decision-making structure of the criminal justice system than a result of inadequate police resources or limited prosecutorial power.[6]

The history of the American civil rights and other grass roots social movements is, in part, the history of this country's effort to wrest state power from the control of dominant social interests, based on class, race, and gender privilege, and to submit that power to the rule of law. A small part of this struggle has focused directly on developing the legal doctrines and institutional arrangements necessary to render prosecutorial discretion accountable to the values of due process and equal protection. It is the legal doctrines and the institutional structures developed in response to the vision projected by these broad based social movements that informs my proposals for constructing an independent prosecutor's office as part of the transition to democracy in Latin America.

The account I offer here is based on my perception that any effort to design a prosecutorial office for a democracy must attend, first and fundamentally, to the question of whose interests that office is to serve. It is not enough to say that the prosecutor will serve "the law," for, as we all know, not every law can be enforced. The question is really which laws will be enforced and how much effort the prosecutor will expend to ensure that unpopular laws are enforced against powerful interests. Conversely, real democracy requires principled limits on the use of prosecutorial power to target only those with the least resources and and the lowest social status, as often happens in the United States.[7]

From this perspective, an independent prosecutor's office with discretionary charging authority is not a simple solution to the problem of establishing an effective criminal justice system consistent with democratic values. Nor can we build an adequate prosecutorial structure on the bald assumption that the prosecutor's objectives are coextensive with the goal of fair and equal enforcement of the law.[8] On the contrary, establishing effective controls on prosecutorial discretion is crucial in securing the state's respect for the due process and equal protection values upon which any real democracy is based. Thus, assuming that prosecutorial discretion is an unavoidable reality,[9] the ultimate question is this: what legal rules and institutional arrangements will best ensure that this tremendous power is exercised in a manner consistent with the values of due process and equal protection of law?

In the following sections, I examine some of the more significant concerns raised by proposals for an independent prosecutor's office. I begin by focusing on two legal doctrines established to control the exercise of prosecutorial discretion in the United States, namely, the doctrines of presumptive vindictiveness and selective prosecution.[10] My purpose in discussing these doctrines is two-fold: first, to challenge any proposal which categorically rejects the critical role of judicial review in controlling the exercise of prosecutorial discretion, and second, to raise questions about the advisability of importing the plea bargaining system as a means of increasing prosecutorial effectiveness in the emerging democracies of Latin America.

In the final section of this chapter, I examine the problem of designing prosecutorial structures from an institutional perspective. I argue that any prosecutorial structure will be fundamentally inadequate if it fails to include institutional arrangements that secure the accountability of prosecutorial discretion to the community of actual and potential victims. Such accountability is crucial not only for successful prosecutions, but also to ensure the democratic integrity of prosecutorial policies. Accordingly, I propose a prosecutorial arrangement, which secures accountability through the creation of an office I will call the Victim-Witness Advocate. I also provide a general account of how such an office might function, focusing particularly on its role in the regulation of prosecutorial discretion.

## II.
## The Legal Limits of Prosecutorial Power

### A. A Critical Appraisal of Judicial Review by Way of the Doctrines of "Presumptive Vindictiveness" and "Selective Prosecution"

In making the case for prosecutorial charging discretion, some commentators have categorically rejected the appropriateness of any judicial review of prosecutorial decisions.[11] This rejection appears to derive, in part, from a perceived need to secure the prosecutor's institutional independence in the transition from an inquisitorial to an accusatorial system of prosecution. Indeed, judicial review, if institutionalized in a manner that is routine and pervasive, would certainly obstruct any hope of establishing an accusatorial system. Nevertheless, even in the United States, judicial review of prosecutorial decisions performs important functions.

By elaborating and enforcing specific legal limits on prosecutorial discretion, judicial review ensures that prosecutorial power is exercised in conformity with the constitutional requirements of due process and equal protection. Just as prosecutorial autonomy checks the power of the judiciary, judicial review operates to check the power of the prosecution. To bar judicial review of prosecutorial decisions is to thrust the organization and deployment of prosecutorial power beyond the restrictions imposed by law. The only remaining controls are necessarily and blatantly political.[12]

In the United States, the evolution of the doctrines of presumptive vindictiveness and selective prosecution provide a fruitful perspective. The doctrine of presumptive vindictiveness derives from the due process requirements of the Fourteenth Amendment and is applied in cases where adverse decisions made by state officials against a criminal defendant, for example decisions imposing a harsher sentence or filing more serious charges after the successful invocation of a procedural right, appear to be based on the state's interest in deterring the individual from exercising an established right.[13]

In our context, the doctrine of presumptive vindictiveness illustrates the role judicial review can perform in enforcing constitutional limits on the exercise of prosecutorial discretion. Under this doctrine, prosecutors retain broad discretion in making their charging decisions and directing the prosecution. Judges perform no general oversight. On the contrary, review is triggered only when the defendant files a proper motion and the scope of judicial intervention is limited to invalidating the particular decision at issue in cases where the circumstances surrounding the decision suggest a reasonable probability of impermissible retaliation.

By invalidating judicial sentencing and prosecutorial charging decisions in such cases, the doctrine of presumptive vindictiveness does no more than impose rational limits on the use of state power. As the Supreme Court has repeatedly noted, the doctrine of presumptive vindictiveness is based on the "uncontroversial principle" that "[t]o punish a person because he has done what the law plainly allows him to do is a due process violation of the most basic sort."[14] The Court's reasoning is simple: if the state can punish individuals for asserting their rights, then those rights are no rights at all. Consequently, "for an agent of the State to pursue a course of action whose objective is to penalize a person's reliance on his legal rights is 'patently unconstitutional.'"[15]

The doctrine of selective prosecution operates in a similar manner; however, this doctrine derives from and is intended to enforce the requirements of the equal protection clause of the Fourteenth Amendment, which prohibits discriminatory enforcement of the criminal laws.[16] Under this doctrine, courts will dismiss the prosecutor's case if the defendant can overcome the usual presumption of good faith nondiscriminatory prosecution and prove the following three elements: (1) that other similarly situated individuals have not been prosecuted; (2) that the defendant was consciously and deliberately singled out; and (3) that the basis upon which the defendant was singled out was arbitrary and invidious.[17]

As these cases demonstrate, judicial review is an important mechanism for enforcing constitutional limits on the use of prosecutorial power. In the United States, however, judicial review is both a procedural mechanism and a forum in which the doctrinal content of constitutional norms is articulated in and through the interpretative practices of judges. These two functions converge in the United States judiciary as a result of our common law tradition; however, they can and arguably ought to be separated in any prosecutorial system designed as part of the transition to democracy in Latin America.

In the United States, judicial review of prosecutorial decisions is most open to attack, not because it places legal limits on prosecutorial autonomy, but because the substantive contours of those limits reflect the "ideological blindness" of the group which judges,[18] to the detriment of women, as well as racial and ethnic minorities and other socially subordinated groups.[19] In countries where the judiciary lacks the traditions of professionalism, independence, commitment to the rule of law, to the objectivity and impartiality of principled decision-making and most fundamentally to the principles of equal protection and due process of law, reliance on judicial review to preserve the democratic integrity of prosecutorial discretion is potentially even more problematic.

Accordingly, Latin American countries considering a transition to an accusatorial system of prosecution must recognize that while prosecutorial independence from the judiciary is not inherently inconsistent with judicial review of prosecutorial charging decisions under explicit legal standards, the power to articulate these legal standards need not be entrusted to the judiciary. Legal limits on prosecutorial power could be ensured as well in a system which codifies the legal rules proscribing selective, retaliatory, and arbitary prosecution, so long as there is an effective mechanism for enforcing these rules. What the United States experience does suggest is that judicial review of prosecutorial conduct, upon motion by an interested party, with the dismissal of the prosecutor's case as a potential sanction, is the most effective mechanism for ensuring that the norms restricting prosecutorial power are routinely respected in individual cases.[20] Consequently, while I have no quarrel with efforts to move from an inquisitorial to an accusatorial system and while I recognize that the law-making aspects of judicial review are highly problematic, claims that judicial review has no role in the regulation of prosecutorial discretion are simply misplaced.

## B. Plea Bargaining: The Prosecutor's Power to Bargain

Some scholars have advocated the formal introduction of plea bargaining in Latin America. The power to offer reduced sentences and even immunity from prosecution in exchange for cooperation of various sorts is, indeed, a powerful resource for law enforcement. This practice enables prosecutors to induce individuals to break ranks with co-criminals and thereby enables prosecutors to penetrate organizational structures that might otherwise remain impenetrable. Moreover, the power of selective prosecution may be crucial for maintaining the prosecution of human rights violations within workable limits.[21] Nevertheless, the practice of plea bargaining is problematic, particularly when it becomes, as it has in the United States, a routine practice for bypassing a formal trial as well as the requirement that the state prove its case "beyond a reasonable doubt."

In the United States, the plea bargain has been institutionalized as an alternative avenue for obtaining "cheap" convictions at the expense of procedural rights, which are themselves designed to protect the falsely accused and to ensure that prosecutorial power is exercised in conformity with the requirements of due process and equal protection of law.[22] The result is that convictions are not only easier, but more frequent, and they are often obtained despite the lack of sufficient admissible evidence to win at trial.[23] The acceptablity of this result is not uncontroversial. At least some would argue that more convictions are better than less, even if the standard of proof is lowered in the process. However, the issue cannot legitimately be debated without a close look at the differential impact the plea bargaining system has had on the rich and the poor, that is, on those who can afford private defense counsel and those who must rely on the state's public defender system.

According to Professor Bond, "All studies of how present processes actually work indicate that the poor, the black, and the 'least criminal' defendants get worse 'deals' than the affluent, the white and the inveterate criminal defendants. Indigents enter a greater percentage of guilty pleas than do defendants with retained counsel."[24] These results are not surprising given the circumstances under which indigent defendants obtain their legal advice. The state's failure to adequately fund public defender offices, despite the large volume of cases, creates pressures to process cases quickly, while the need to maintain long-term working relationships with prosecutors and judges induces public defenders to curb the zeal with which they press their clients' interests.[25] Moreover, while the client who pays can expect to call the shots and, ultimately, may dismiss an attorney who refuses to conduct the case as the client wishes, the indigent defendant has very little option, but to rely on the advice of her appointed defender.[26] That advice will almost invariably be to plead guilty,[27] and the likelihood that the defendant will follow that advice has less to do with the defendant's guilt or innocence, than with the supposed value of the offer measured against the burden of facing prosecution and the risks of conviction.[28]

Thus, while the authority to offer reduced sentences is a powerful resource for investigating criminal organizations, like drug cartels and death squads, Latin Americans should think carefully before importing a system of routine plea bargaining. In Latin America, particularly in those countries which lack any public defender system, the introduction of prosecutorial plea bargaining is likely to produce an assembly line of convictions even more unjust and oppressive of the poor than the ones we have in the United States.

## III.
## Prosecutorial Power: The Structural Alternatives

### A. *Toward a Better Statement of the Issues*
The question whether the prosecutor should be independent or aligned with the government when prosecuting governmental abuses presupposes an either/or situation: either governmental abuses are most effectively prosecuted by an independent prosecutor,[29] or they are best prosecuted by a prosecutor closely aligned with and hence privy to the resources and support of the Executive.[30] What is missing in this debate, however, is a vision of the importance of community involvement in the prosecutorial effort.

Successful prosecutions of powerful persons like high level government officials depend first and fundamentally on the willingness of witnesses to furnish information and otherwise to assume the risks of cooperating with the prosecutor's office.[31] From this perspective, the location of the prosecutor's office seems less significant than the institutional arrangements established to ensure the prosecutor's communication with and accountability to the relevant communities of actual and potential victims. If the prosecutor's office is not operationally aligned with and institutionally accountable to these community groups, then it is ultimately irrelevant whether the prosecutor's office is located within the Executive or independently situated. In either case, the office will lack the informational and political resources necessary for successful prosecutions.

Community accountability and participation is also crucial for assuring the democratic integrity of prosecutorial discretion. We have already discussed the fragmentation of public opinion over the appropriate limits on the state's use of violence. Some commentators, who have noted this phenomenon, nevertheless fail to recognize its full implications for designing a prosecutor's office. If the fragmentation of public opinion is based ultimately and fundamentally on a deep-rooted contempt among the various groups in a society for the rights and interests of *other* groups, then the way prosecutorial discretion is exercised and the categories of cases that are deemed worthy of expending prosecutorial resources translates directly into a statement about who owns the democracy. If democracy belongs to all citizens, irrespective of their race, gender, or social and economic status, then prosecutorial power is legitimately exercised only when it is neutral and applies equally to the crimes of the privileged and powerful as well as the crimes of the deprived and depraved. This means that institutional arrangements must be devised to combat the ubiquitous tendency (shared by prosecutors as well as police) to divide victim groups into the "worthy" and the "unworthy."[32] Structural arrangements that increase prosecutorial accountability to the communities of actual and potential victims of governmental abuses help to ensure that prosecutorial power is exercised in the interest of *all* victim groups and not primarily in the interest of victim groups with whom the prosecutors identify.

## B. Institutionalizing a Solution: Victim-Witness Advocates

In this section, I sketch out a general description of one institutional arrangement that might be used to achieve a variety of objectives, including the supervision of prosecutorial discretion. Initially, it is important to distinguish two levels of prosecutorial discretion. The first level involves the determination of the prosecutor's institutional priorities, that is, the catagorization of crimes pursuant to some standard and a determination that prosecutorial resources will be channeled into those cases deemed most pressing under the established standard.[33] The second level of discretionary decision-making occurs when the prosecutor decides whether to prosecute an individual case within one of the priority categories.[34] The important task is to establish arrangements which render discretionary decisions at each level responsive and accountable to the community of actual and potential victims. The arrangement proposed below centers on the creation of a Victim-Witness Advocate's office and an elaboration of its various functions.

The idea for a Victim-Witness Advocate derived from efforts at the Center for Criminal Justice to design an official institution within the Guatemalan criminal justice system whose purpose would be to represent the perspectives and further the interests of victims and witnesses. This effort drew upon the positive experience of various Victim Rights programs in the United States. These programs have received broad support from prosecutor offices, police departments, and trial courts across the country because the programs, in many ways, further these actors' own institutional objectives.[35] At the same time, many Advocate programs in the United States are community based efforts. As independent organizations, victim advocates work to combat the lack of concern, abuse of power and corruption that victims and witnesses often face in their interactions with police officers, prosecutors and, at times, even judges.

The Advocate was envisioned as an organization, governed by a Board of Directors with representatives from a diverse range of community organizations,[36] with an operating office comprised of staff attorneys and social workers. The Board of Directors would be responsible for establishing policies to coordinate three types of activities.[37]  First, the Board would coordinate a system of direct services to individual victims and witnesses. These services would be performed by social workers (or individuals under their supervision) and would focus on easing the trauma of victimization and assisting individuals through the ensuing police investigations and legal proceedings.

Second, the Board would coordinate the implementation of educational programs. Some of these programs would aim at educating police, prosecutors, and judges about the consequences of victimization and training these officials to better interact with victims and witnesses.  Other programs would focus on educating community organizations on the functions of the criminal justice system and the appropriate procedures for seeking redress in and through that system.

Finally, and perhaps most important, the Board would coordinate legal work at two levels.  Legal work, at the first level, would involve staff attorneys (or volunteer attorneys under their supervision) filing and prosecuting individual complaints against government officials.  For example, staff lawyers might file complaints in cases where an individual alleges that a police officer refused to investigate a reported crime or arrest a suspected individual, that a prosecutor refused to prosecute a particular case, or that a court official requested a bribe.  These complaints might be filed initially in the official's own internal disciplinary office.  For example, if the complaint was against a police officer, the complaint might first be filed in the police department's office of internal affairs.  Alternatively and ultimately, the attorney might file a legal complaint in the courts.

The second type of legal work would involve research efforts to draft and lobby for legislative reforms that would make the system, as a whole, more responsive to the needs of crime victims.  For example, staff would design proposals for changes in the rules of evidence or new civil rights laws that provide effective remedies for police misconduct and incentives for individuals to file complaints.  The information and insights acquired in the process of filing individual complaints and through the implementation of educational programs for justice system personnel as well as community organizations would provide a valuable source of information for identifying the types of reforms that would be most needed and most practical.

Ideally, the Board should have a formal role and participate directly in the determination of prosecutorial priorities at the first level of discretionary policy-making.  Just as the work of the Advocate's operating offices would provide an informational base for proposing legislation aimed at systemic reform, it would also generate a wealth of information about the impact of prosecutorial and police priorities upon the communities of actual and potential victims. Thus, the Board would have the informational base from which to contribute to a more accurate and fairer assessment of prosecutorial priorities.

If the Board were denied a formal role in the determination of first level prosecutorial priorities, it should at the very least be afforded advisory status. As an advisor, the Advocate would have access to information relevant to staff researchers working on legislative proposals for systemic reforms. At the same time, since the Board would have direct information on the number and nature of complaints filed against prosecutors and police officers, the Board's advisory status would give officials at the highest level of the criminal justice system easy access to important information about how lower level officials are doing their jobs. The value of such information increases directly in proportion to the superiors' desire to control and ensure the integrity of their subordinates.

In short, then, the idea is to create institutional arrangements that ensure that individuals with close ties to community organizations participate in or at least have available effective procedures through which to challenge the exercise of prosecutorial discretion at both the institutional policy-making level and at the level of individual cases. A Victim-Witness Advocate's office would have the potential to do both and would thereby contribute to the practical success and the democratic integrity of prosecutorial efforts.

## Conclusion

A state's power to investigate, prosecute, and convict criminals plays an important role in strengthening the rule of law to the extent it ensures that no individual, regardless of his or her economic, political, or social status has the power to violate the law with impunity. However, in the struggle to combat the impunity of the powerful, we must not forget the vulnerability of the powerless nor the fact that, even in democracies like the United States, the criminal process is more often, easily, and successfully invoked against powerless suspects and in favor of powerful victims, while the socially privileged escape criminal sanction and low status victims are denied justice.

## Notes

[1]UNITED STATES COMMISSION ON CIVIL RIGHTS, LAW ENFORCEMENT: A REPORT ON EQUAL PROTECTION IN THE SOUTH (1965).

[2]Jalna Hanmer & Elizabeth A. Stanko, *Stripping Away the Rhetoric of Protection: Violence to Women, Law and the State in Britain and the U.S.A.*, 13 INT. J. SOC. L. 357-374 (1985). Numerous accounts have been offered to explain why the criminal justice system remains unacceptably unresponsive to the claims of rape victims, battered women, and prostitutes. In one influential account, women's inability to obtain protection and retribution through the state apparatus is attributed to the fact that state power as well as substantive criminal law and law enforcement practices are defined and operated from a male point of view. *See* Catherine A. MacKinnon, *Feminism, Marxism, Method and the State: Toward Feminist Jurisprudence*, 8 SIGNS 635-58 (1983). *See generally Mandatory Arrest for Domestic Violence*, 11 HARV. WOMEN'S L.J. 213 (1988); Barbara K. Finesmith, *Police Response to Battered Women: A Critique and Proposals for Reform*, 14 SETON HALL L. REV. 74 (1983).

[3]*See* Roger L. Goldman & Steven Puro, *Decertification of Police: An Alternative to Traditional Remedies for Police Misconduct*, 15 HASTINGS CONST. L. Q. 7, 59-60 (1987) (prosecutors are reluctant to prosecute police because they depend on police to make arrests and conduct investigations and convictions are hard to obtain).

[4]RUSSELL MOKHIBER, CORPORATE CRIME AND VIOLENCE: BIG BUSINESS AND THE ABUSE OF THE PUBLIC TRUST (1988).

[5]*See* GARY D. LAFREE, RAPE AND CRIMINAL JUSTICE: THE SOCIAL CONSTRUCTION OF SEXUAL ASSAULT (1989). LaFree describes the criminal justice system as a network of discretionary decisionmaking points. At each step in the process, decisionmakers make judgments whether to move the case forward, based on assumptions about the credibility of the complainant, the believability or feasibility of her story and other equally subjective intuitions about what is likely to have happened and how seriously it should be treated. *See generally* ARTHUR I. ROSETT & DONALD R. CRESSEY, JUSTICE BY CONSENT: PLEA BARGAINS IN THE AMERICAN COURTHOUSE 4 (1976).

[6]*See generally* J.M. Balkin, *Ideology as Constraint*, 43 STAN. L. REV. 1133 (1991).

[7]According to the New York Times, "most women prosecuted for using illegal drugs while pregnant have been poor members of racial minorities. . . even though drug use in pregnancy is equally prevalent in white middle-class women." Gina Kolata, *Bias Seen Against Pregnant Addicts*, N.Y. TIMES, July 20, 1990, at A13. Similarly, the Los Angeles Times reports that although about 80% of cocaine users are white, the majority of those arrested have been black. Ron Harris, *Blacks Feel Brunt of Drug War*, L.A. TIMES, April 22, 1990, at A1.

[8]*See, e.g.*, Philip B. Heymann, *Should Prosecutors Be Independent of the Executive in Prosecuting Government Abuses?*, in TRANSITION TO DEMOCRACY IN LATIN AMERICA: THE ROLE OF THE JUDICIARY 203 (Irwin P. Stotzky ed., 1993) [hereinafter TRANSITION].

[9]While full enforcement of *every* criminal law is clearly made impossible as much by limited prosecutorial resources as by distaste for the kind of society such an effort would be likely to create, full enforcement statutes have served an important function in controlling unacceptable patterns of official discretion. Thus, a number of states have adopted mandatory arrest statutes, which require police to arrest the batterer in domestic abuse cases. *See Mandatory Arrest, supra* note 2, at 214 n.9.

[10]*See generally* JOSEPH F. LAWLESS, PROSECUTORIAL MISCONDUCT 156-181 (1985).

[11]*See, e.g.,* Andrés J. D'Alessio, *The Function of the Prosecution in the Transition to Democracy in Latin America, in* TRANSITION, *supra* note 8, at 187.

[12]For example, efforts to control the exercise of discretion by individual prosecutors through the articulation of internal standards by top level prosecutors presupposes that the standards devised by these officials will be constitutionally adequate. Absent judicial review, however, these standards are likely to reflect the priorities and interests of the sectors which are best positioned to influence the top prosecutorial officials. Whether these agents of influence are members of the Executive Branch, congressmen, police officials or the press, the bottom line is that the articulation of prosecutorial standards will appear to be grounded in political factors rather than constitutional norms.

[13]*See* North Carolina v. Pearce, 395 U.S. 711 (1969) (applying doctrine of presumptive vindictiveness to invalidate a harsher sentence imposed after retrial of a criminal defendant, who had successfully appealed his first conviction); Blackledge v. Perry, 417 U.S. 21 (1974) (invalidating a prosecutorial decision to obtain a felony indictment after defendant appealed for a denovo trial from a six month sentence imposed on misdemeanor charges tried before an inferior court).

[14]United States v. Goodwin, 457 U.S. 368, 372 (1981) (quoting Bordenkircher v. Hayes, 434 U.S. 357, 363 (1977)).

[15]Bordenkircher, 434 U.S. at 363 (quoting Chaffin v. Stynchcombe, 412 U.S. 17, 32-33, n.20 (1973)).

[16]*See, e.g.,* Yick Wo v. Hopkins, 118 U.S. 356, 373-4 (1886). *See generally* LAWLESS, *supra* note 10, at 156-172.

[17]Thus, while prosecutors are permitted the "conscious exercise of some selectivity" in making their charging decisions, such selectivity may not be based on "an unjustifiable standard such as race, religion, or other arbitrary classifications." Commonwealth v. King, 372 N.E. 2d 196, 205-6 (1977). Judicial precedents also prohibit prosecutorial selectivity which infringes upon fundamental constitutional rights. Prosecutions based on an individual's associational activities such as union organization are prohibited. *See, e.g.,* Murguia v. Municipal Court, 540 P.2d 44 (Cal. 1975) (court dismissed prosecutions against members of the United Farm Workers because they were targeted for prosecution on account of their union affiliations. Prosecutions initiated as a result of an individual's exercise of free speech are also prohibited). *See* United States v. Falk, 479 F.2d 616 (7th Cir. 1973) (en banc); *cf.* Wayte v. United States, 470 U.S. 598; 105 S.Ct. 1524 (1985) (such prosecutions are ordinarily impermissible).

[18]*See* Balkin, *supra* note 6.

[19]For example, the scope of prosecutorial activities that can be challenged through the doctrine of presumptive vindictiveness depends heavily on the courts' willingness to recognize a probability that retaliatory motives underlie the state's action. As judicial interpretation may vary with the political ideology that dominates the Court, the doctrine may become an increasingly ineffective vehicle for restraining prosecutorial misconduct. *See, e.g.*, United States v. Goodwin, 457 U.S. 368 (1981).

[20]Other possible alternatives, such as civil rights law suits, have proven to be inadequate substitutes for the dismissal of the prosecution's case. *See* Commonwealth v. King, 374 Mass. 5, 372 N.E.2d 196 (1977) (holding that dismissal of the prosecutor's case is necessary to deter sex based discrimination in the enforcement of the State's prostitution statute, which, if proven, would establish claim of selective prosecution). Similarly, relying on the internal disciplinary proceedings of the prosecutor's office will be inadequate precisely to the extent selective or arbitrary prosecutions reflect prejudices or interests widely shared within the prosecutor's office and perhaps even by the department superiors.

[21]*See, e.g.*, Jaime E. Malamud-Goti, *Human Rights Abuses in Fledgling Democracies: The Role of Discretion, in* TRANSITION, *supra* note 8, at 225; Diane F. Orentlicher, *The Role of the Prosecutor in the Transition to Democracy in Latin America, in* TRANSITION, *supra* note 8, at 249.

[22]*See generally* William F. McDonald, *The Prosecutor's Domain, in* THE PROSECUTOR 28-40 (William F. McDonald ed., 1979).

[23]*See generally* JAMES E. BOND, PLEA BARGAINING AND GUILTY PLEAS (2d ed. 1982). Prosecutors will often plea bargain in cases where the evidence is weak or inadmissible because obtained by the police in violation of the accused's constitutional rights.

[24]Professor Bond cites "[o]ne Chicago study [which] showed that 42% of white defendants with retained counsel secured some kind of non-guilty disposition, but only 8% of black defendants with public defenders secured non-guilty dispositions." *Id.* at 2-38.

[25]*See generally* Abraham S. Blumberg, *The Practice of Law as Confidence Game: Organizational Cooptation of a Profession*, 1 LAW & SOCY. REV. 15 (1967).

[26]ROSETT & CRESSEY, *supra* note 5, at 117-144.

[27]*Id.* at 137-38. "An individual public defender may be firmly and unalterably convinced that he is an adversary defender of the poor and at the same time accommodate to the needs of an organization that requires him to persuade most defendants to plead guilty."

[28]*Id.* at 147-150. *See also*, Peter Westen & David Westei, *A Constitutional Law of Remedies for Broken Plea Bargains*, 66 CAL. L. REV. 471 (1978) (the more attractive the prosecutor's offer, the greater the likelihood that a false conviction will be obtained by plea bargain because prosecutors are likely to make the best offers to those against whom they have the weakest cases and because the better the offer (for example, release on time served), the more likely even an innocent defendant will accept the offer, rather than suffer the anxiety of extended prosecution and the risk of erroneous conviction).

[29]*See, e.g.*, D'Alessio, *supra* note 11.

[30]*See* Heymann, *supra* note 8.

[31]PETER FINN & BEVERLY N.W. LEE, SERVING CRIME VICTIMS AND WITNESSES 2 (1987). According to this report,

. . . a staggering proportion of crimes are never reported, and that one probable cause of this silence is the dread of 'getting involved' with the criminal justice system. Police failures to address victims' personal problems may reduce the quality of the evidence victims provide to investigating officers -- an alarming consideration, when the single most important determinant of whether a case will be solved may be information the victim supplies to patrol officers. Finally, many witnesses are so inconvenienced or distressed by their involvement with the courts, or so afraid they will suffer reprisals from the defendant if they appear, that they fail to testify. As a result, cases are dismissed for lack of 'prosecutability.'

[32]*See* LAFREE, *supra* note 5 and accompanying text.

[33]For example, a prosecutor's office might choose to prioritize cases according to the likelihood of obtaining a conviction, cases, for instance, in which there is an identified suspect and reliable witnesses. Alternatively, cases might be prioritized according to the seriousness of the crime (rather than the likelihood of conviction). In any event, at this level, discretion is used to define the policies which will govern the prosecution as an institution.

[34]In the United States, individual prosecutors have varying degrees of autonomy over the cases they prosecute. Some prosecutors, for example, in large urban offices, have little autonomy and usually work on specific stages of different cases (for example, the pre-trials). On the other hand, individual prosecutors, in smaller local offices, may have very broad discretion over their caseload. *See generally* McDonald, *supra* note 22.

[35]For example, programs run out of prosecutor offices often aim at facilitating the victim's and/witness's participation in legal proceedings against the accused. By explaining the nature of the procedures, securing transportation and providing other assistance, Advocates decrease the likelihood of non-cooperation, and thus increase the likelihood of conviction. Similarly, police may perceive the various ways in which the Advocate's activities can facilitate their own investigative and "crisis intervention" objectives. For a fairly comprehensive account of the various program models *see* FINN & LEE, *supra* note 31.

[36]For example a representative might be chosen from each of the following sectors: the labor unions, women's groups, peasant groups, university teachers, business leaders, members of the private Bar, and church leaders.

[37]While these three activities were chosen because they operate interactively and are mutually reinforcing, the Advocate's most crucial functions are in the second and third activities (namely, educational programs and legal advocacy). Furthermore, as a matter of organizational structure, the technical aspects of the Advocate's work would be designed and implemented by individuals with the relevant expertise (for example, social workers and staff attorneys); however, the Board would receive regular reports from the operating offices and have ultimate policy-making authority and coordinating responsibilities.

# PART SIX

# Judicial Review and Remedies

# 19

## Judicial Independence and Constitutional Democracy: Lessons from the U.S. Experience[1]

### *Robert A. Burt*

The United States has made two distinctive contributions to the science of politics: the ideas of a written Constitution as the basic charter for government and of a life-tenured judiciary as the interpreter of the constitutional guarantees. The United States is also distinctive in another way: It is the longest continuously functioning democracy in the western hemisphere (depending on definitions, the longest in the world). It is therefore understandable that many people, seeking to learn from the United States experience, would conclude that democracy was causally related to constitutionalism and an independent judiciary. These elements are indeed related -- but only in a very complex way.

Let me briefly summarize some of the complexities as I see them.[2] The starting point for understanding the United States experience is to define what we mean by democracy. I take as my text the definition offered by Abraham Lincoln: "No man is good enough to govern another man, without that other's consent. This is the leading principle -- the sheet anchor of American republicanism."[3] This conception of democracy is different from, and much more demanding than, majority rule. By this definition, democracy exists only insofar as the minority consents to its governance by the majority. In practical terms, this consent is likely to exist only if the minority regards its electoral defeats as relatively insignificant or even merely temporary. If the minority views itself as permanently powerless or if the minority views some particular political issue as so urgently important that it cannot tolerate electoral defeat on this issue, then the minority has not consented to its governance by the majority; and democratic principle is thereby violated.

With this understanding of the consensual basis of democracy, it becomes clear that no formal Bill of Rights is sufficient to protect the minority against majority tyranny. To be sure, some formal provisions are necessary protections -- especially rights to free speech, free press, and free access to the political process generally in order to ensure that the minority is capable of seeking redress for its grievances. These rights to political expression and organization are, in effect, guarantees that the defeated minority will be given a fair opportunity to persuade others so that they might be transformed into a majority. But it is possible that after the most free and open political debate imaginable, the minority still loses. Unless the minority is truly prepared to accept this conclusive defeat, then the democratic consent principle is violated.

Imagine -- to make these abstractions more concrete -- that the majority treats the minority as slaves, forcing them to work without compensation, and taking custody of their children. Imagine further that the slave minority is permitted to protest their enslavement in the media and in public demonstrations and that the slaves are also given full voting rights; and that, after a heated political campaign, the majority votes to perpetuate the minority's enslaved status. The democratic rules of free debate and of "one man/one vote" would have been satisfied; yet the basic principle of self-governance would surely be violated.

But here we can turn to an independent judiciary -- or so it is claimed by many students of the United States constitutional experience -- to protect this minority against its enslavement. The United States courts have themselves made this claim, not only that they protect the procedural rights of the minority to electoral participation but that they guarantee that the minority is not enslaved but is treated as equals by the majority. This -- so the supporters of judicial authority claim -- is the command of the Fourteenth Amendment to our Constitution, guaranteeing "equal protection of the laws" to every person. There is, however, a problem, a deep paradox, in the judicial enforcement of the equality ideal. The problem is that if the judiciary reverses the electoral defeat suffered by the enslaved minority, at the very least the majority is now entitled to complain that the judiciary itself has violated the democratic principle, as Lincoln enunciated it, "that no man is good enough to govern another, without that other's consent." Even more powerfully, the majority is now itself likely and entitled to view itself as enslaved by the minority and its judicial allies.

Again, let me give a concrete example to illustrate the abstract problem. Let us say that in the original electoral campaign, the majority imposed a steeply progressive income tax amounting to ninety-five percent of the gross income of the wealthiest ten percent of the population and only five percent of the income of the rest of the citizenry. The losing minority then claims -- understandably enough -- that the majority has forced them to work without compensation. At the same time, the majority votes to draft all children between the ages of fourteen and eighteen into a national service corps to work on agricultural improvement projects in poor, rural areas, receiving no compensation except food, lodging, and clothes. Again the losing minority claims -- understandably enough -- that the majority has taken custody of, indeed has enslaved, their children.

Has the minority in fact been treated unequally, been enslaved, by this high tax or compulsory national service corps? What if the majority claims that even retaining five percent of their gross income, the wealthy minority still retains resources much greater than the rest of the population and, indeed, has obtained these greater resources only by long-standing exploitation of the laboring class? What if the majority claims that the four-year compulsory national youth service is a patriotic obligation or, more narrowly, is justified as repayment for free, public education that the majority provided to all children from four to fourteen years of age? From the majority perspective, the high tax and the compulsory service is necessary to assure that the minority does not take unfair, uncompensated advantage of the majority -- to avoid, that is, a form of enslavement of the majority by the minority.

In my view, there are no objective criteria by which these competing claims of equal treatment or enslavement can be adjudicated. Unless the contending parties can come to some agreement between themselves, any resolution -- whether by majority rule or judicial enforcement of minority rights -- violates the basic democratic principle of rule by the consent of the governed. Stated in other words, democratic principle is protected only when the entire society is committed to an ethos of mutual accommodation -- only when no one is satisfied with any political outcome unless everyone is more or less satisfied.

No written Constitution can guarantee the existence of this democratic ethos. No judiciary can enforce it. But unless this ideal of basic mutual respect is cherished and practiced in a society, then democracy cannot exist. The society will be governed by coercion -- whether the form of this tyranny is majority or minority rule.

A Constitution can, however, provide formal institutional mechanisms that are likely to facilitate this ethos of mutual accommodation. And the judiciary in particular can actively promote this ethos by careful, skillful use of its authority to declare majoritarian laws unconstitutional. The formal constitutional mechanisms can create multiple opportunities for discontented minorities to protect their interests; this is the effect of the scheme of "checks and balances" in the United States Constitution in the complex relationships between the President and the Congress; within the Congress, between the Senate and the House of Representatives; and between the national and state governments.

The judiciary's role in promoting mutual accommodation is less obvious. And for much of its history, the United States Supreme Court has not seen its function in this way but has instead been prepared to impose its will on an unconsenting majority. The Court violated democratic principle in this way before our Civil War, when it ruled in 1857 that Congress could not ban slavery from national territories that had not yet been organized as states.[4] The Court similarly violated democratic principle in a series of decisions from the 1890s until the 1930s overturning a wide range of economic regulatory laws providing, for example, maximum hours and minimum wages for workers or forbidding child labor.[5] More recently, the Court violated democratic principle in its 1973 ruling that states could not restrict the availability of abortion in the first trimester of pregnancy.[6]

There have been other instances in United States history, however, where the Court has been more attentive to the democratic ethos and its role in fostering that ethos instead of attempting simply to impose its will on political adversaries. The clearest modern example of this judicial action is the Supreme Court's response in the 1950s and 1960s to racial segregation laws. In *Brown v. Board of Education*,[7] the Court ruled that segregation laws were unconstitutional but, at the same time, it refused to dictate immediate enforcement of this ruling. The Court instead purposefully initiated an extended deliberative process in order both to enlist other governmental institutions -- especially the federal Congress and the President -- and to prompt the immediate adversaries, southern whites and blacks, themselves to reach a new and mutually acceptable political relationship.

In my recently published book,[8] I consider these various judicial decisions -- those that violated and those that fostered the democratic ethos of mutual accommodation -- in considerable detail. One generalization emerges from my extended discussion of the role of the judiciary in constitutional interpretation: that it is wrong to conceive of the judiciary as supreme and as independent of other governmental institutions in interpreting the Constitution. This view of the judiciary, as supreme and independent, is the dominant conventional conception today. When observers from other countries draw lessons from the United States experience about the judicial role in preserving democracy and constitutional government, supremacy and independence are the elements they imagine to be characteristic. But this is erroneous. Both in principle and in actual practice, it is more correct to conceive of the United States judiciary not as supreme but as the *equal* of other governmental institutions in interpreting our Constitution; and not as independent of but as *interdependent* with these other institutions.

Judicial equality with other institutions does not mean that courts are subordinate to the elected institutions. Many contemporary United States constitutional theorists argue for a subordinated status on the ground that judges are obliged to defer to majority rule and can invalidate legislation only in the very limited cases where a majority of voters in the past has enacted an explicit, specific constitutional prohibition.[9] This conception of the judicial role erroneously identifies majority rule with democratic principle. As I have already suggested, however, democratic principles rest on an egalitarian conception of consensual self-government, not on majority rule as such. The United States Constitution itself endorses this conception, most explicitly in the Fourteenth Amendment guaranteeing equal protection of the laws to all persons; and this democratic principle applies to *all* laws, not simply to a few particular circumstances specifically intended by the authors of the Constitution (such as relations between blacks and whites).

But how can the judiciary apply this democratic principle of equality without falling into the paradoxical trap I have already identified, of protecting the minority by enslaving the majority? *Brown v. Board of Education* shows the way. The judiciary should invalidate majority-enacted laws that the minority views as intolerable enslavement; but the effect of this invalidation should be carefully limited not to impose the minority's will on the majority but to force the majority and minority to work toward a different, more mutually respectful and therefore more equal relationship. The court applies this force not by imposing *its* will on the parties or dictating *its* definition of equality in their relationship. The court instead reopens the dispute and imposes at least a temporary stalemate between the parties. By giving this added advantage to the previously defeated minority, the court enhances the minority's public moral stature and its practical legislative bargaining capacity. In this way, the court acts to promote democratic principle by pressing political adversaries to reach mutually satisfactory accommodation, principally through their interactions in other, electorally responsive institutions.

In this complex intervention, the court has a relationship neither of supremacy nor of subordination to the other institutions. Like the democratic relationship between the political minority and majority that the court intends to protect, the court is equal to -- but no more than equal to -- the other institutions. That is, the court cannot impose its will on the others but neither can they coercively impose their will on the court. Each party instead -- court and legislature, minority and majority -- is able to impose a stalemate on the other and thereby persuade (or cajole or bully) the other party to agree to a mutually satisfactory outcome.

This is not the kind of tidy relationship that most lawyers and constitutional scholars are comfortable in describing. There are no clear lines of hierarchical authority in this relationship. The separate and distinct powers of the different branches of government cannot be portrayed on a formal organizational chart. But the very messiness, the competitiveness of overlapping authority, the sheer complexity of these institutional relationships are its defining characteristics as democratic. It is possible to define political relationships in clear-cut terms of hierarchical command authority; but such definitions are authoritarian, not democratic (whether the ultimate command authority clearly rests with a majority of voters, a majority of judges, or a majority in a military junta).

In the United States experience, as I have indicated, courts have often ignored democratic principle by speaking as if they had ultimate command authority, as if they possessed supreme rather than merely equal authority in constitutional interpretation. The United States Supreme Court has typically indulged in this conceit when a majority of Justices believed that political conflict was so intense that the adversaries could not possibly reach mutual accommodation and were instead intent on coercively subjugating one another. The Justices believed this in 1857, when they attempted to award preemptive victory to one side in the dispute between the North and South regarding territorial slavery; the Justices believed this at the end of the nineteenth century when they tried to award victory to employers in their conflicts with laboring classes; and the Justices believed this again in the 1970s regarding the clash over the morality and legality of abortion. In all of these disputes, the Justices may have been correct. The Civil War may have been inevitable in 1857, as with class warfare subsequently and with moral warfare in our own time. And by using constitutional litigation to impose the will of one adversary over another, a court might succeed in averting open violence between the parties. But whatever the possible arguments may be in favor of forced judicial resolution of hotly disputed political issues, it must be acknowledged that such forced resolution -- like subjugative warfare itself -- necessarily violates democratic principle.

The United States experience, moreover, does not demonstrate that in practical terms a supreme, independent judiciary can deter open civil warfare and thereby preserve democratic values. This is not because of the Court's obvious failure in 1857 to avert the American Civil War. There have been other occasions when the United States judiciary has had greater success in dampening civil conflict or in upholding democratic values (two goals, incidentally, which are not identical and may often be in conflict with one another). But whatever success United States courts have had in these efforts, their accomplishments do not rest on the constitutional supremacy or independence of the judiciary. This is for one simple reason: because under the United States Constitution, the judiciary is neither supreme nor independent regarding the other branches of the national government. By the terms of the constitutional document, the judiciary is clearly dependent on the other branches in at least three ways: its composition, its jurisdiction, and its practical enforcement capacity.

As to composition, the Constitution requires only the establishment of one supreme court; it does not, however, specify the number of Justices on the Court. Accordingly, in the nineteenth century, Congress used its authority on several occasions to enlarge or contract the size of the Court in order to accomplish overtly political goals; in the twentieth century, President Franklin Roosevelt threatened to do the same and nearly succeeded -- before the Court itself gave him adequate reason to withdraw his threat.[10] Beyond guaranteeing the existence of this one supreme court, the Constitution gives Congress authority to create as many or as few lower federal courts as it might choose. This gives Congress considerable capacity to exert control over judicial conduct, particularly by creating specialized federal courts to deal with particular subjects, staffed by judges specially appointed because of their political affiliations or ideology. At various times in this century, Congress (working cooperatively with the President) has used this authority to create special federal courts to enforce economic regulations or civil rights laws, thus bypassing the life-tenured federal judges who generally were known to be hostile to such enforcement.[11]

The Constitution also explicitly authorizes Congress to control the jurisdiction not only of the lower federal courts it might create but also of the Supreme Court itself. In the nineteenth century, Congress used this authority to withdraw jurisdiction from the Supreme Court over a case then pending on its docket that raised questions about the constitutionality of military occupation laws after the Civil War; and the Court, in an opinion that has never been overruled, agreed that Congress had this authority.[12] In both the nineteenth and twentieth centuries, Congress frequently limited federal court jurisdiction generally and Supreme Court jurisdiction specifically on substantive matters -- and it has even more frequently threatened to do so.[13] The Supreme Court might someday challenge the extent of congressional authority to control its jurisdiction; but it has not yet done so and, in this sense at least, remains dependent on the Congress for its capacity to issue virtually any substantive rulings.

But even if federal courts generally or the Supreme Court specifically takes jurisdiction over some substantive matter, the Constitution gives no assurance that these rulings will be enforced. Federal courts themselves have acknowledged that they have no authority to direct the President to enforce any law.[14] Even if the Supreme Court might someday claim this enforcement authority, it is difficult to imagine how the Justices might give practical content to this claim against determined opposition from the President (with his constitutionally clear authority to command United States armed forces) or from the Congress (with its constitutionally clear authority to control all government expenditures).

The institutional dependence of the federal judiciary is thus extensive and clearly visible in the very text of the United States Constitution. Nevertheless, throughout United States history, there have only been a few occasions when Congress and the President have joined forces to take advantage of the Court's institutional vulnerabilities and try to force it into submission. On those few occasions, the Court has itself backed away from confrontation with the other branches -- thus preserving the appearance of its stature as supreme and independent by "supremely and independently" surrendering. The defining characteristic of the relationship between the Court and the elected branches is not, however, truly found in these few moments of high crisis. Its true character is found in the fact that these moments of crisis, and of virtually overt judicial surrender, are so rare in United States history. The Justices' awareness of their institutional vulnerability has most often prompted them to seek at least rough accommodation with the other branches. At the same time, the Justices' rhetorical claims for supremacy and independence have most often inclined elected officials toward reluctance against engaging in all-out warfare against the Court. Like the Justices, that is, elected officials have tended to look for paths of mutual accommodation and to avoid ultimate confrontations between mutually inconsistent demands.

In one sense, this extended history of reciprocal institutional respect -- though often wary, grudging, and accompanied by angry rhetorical exchanges on all sides -- is simply an expression of the persistent strength of the democratic ethos of mutual accommodation among political adversaries in United States social relations. In this sense, the Court is not responsible for this ethos but is its beneficiary. In another sense, however, the existence of the Court and its historical tradition of inflated, unrealistic claims for independence and supremacy are contributing causes to the persistent strength of this democratic ethos. The Court, that is, serves as a continual reminder in United States political relations of the tradition of mutual accommodation. Indeed, the very visibility of the Court's institutional weakness symbolizes the basic requirement of the democratic ethos -- that even though the vulnerable minority (like the Justices themselves) can easily be coerced into submission, the majority is obliged to withhold its superior force based not on fear of effective retaliation but on respect for the equal status of its weaker adversary.

The United States Supreme Court served as a vivid reminder of this fundamental democratic principle at a crucial early moment in our national history -- in a way that, in particular, has a suggestive parallel in recent Chilean and Argentinean experience. The first contested presidential election in United States history was held in 1800, when Thomas Jefferson's Republicans narrowly defeated the incumbent President John Adams and his Federalist Party. Before the election, Adams and his Federalists waged a campaign of intimidation against the opposition, including imprisonment of Republican newspaper writers for "sedition" simply based on their political criticisms of President Adams. After Jefferson won the election but before he took office, Adams took advantage of his temporary tenure to fill the judiciary with last-minute Federalist appointees (including the appointment of John Marshall as Chief Justice). When Jefferson was finally inaugurated, many Republicans -- scornful of Adams' "lame-duck" appointments and eager to retaliate against the Federalist Party for their past political oppressions -- resolved to impeach all of the Federalist judges, including Marshall. Between 1801 and 1803, the new Republican majority in Congress did impeach one lower federal court judge, effectively removed sixteen appellate court judges by abolishing their judicial offices, and began impeachment proceedings against one Supreme Court Justice (intending to reach Marshall next).

In 1803, Marshall's Court agreed in one case that the Republican Congress had authority to abolish the sixteen judicial offices.[15] But in another case -- the now-famous decision in *Marbury v. Madison*[16] -- Marshall announced that Jefferson was constitutionally obliged to honor one of Adams' last-minute appointments even though the formal commission of office had not been delivered before Jefferson took office. In an ironic twist, however, Marshall ruled that the Supreme Court did not have jurisdiction to issue this order against the Executive branch because the jurisdictional statute enacted by Congress was unconstitutional.

*Marbury v. Madison* is famous today because it was the first Supreme Court decision to invalidate a congressional act. The political significance of Marshall's decision in 1803 -- and its strategic brilliance -- was not, however, in this invalidation. The most important aspect of the decision, as contemporaries viewed it, was Marshall's claim that President Jefferson was obliged to respect the tenure of the judicial office-holders previously appointed by his political opponents. Marshall's refusal to issue a direct judicial order against the Executive to enforce this respect was in effect a strategic concession to the newly dominant Republicans. The underlying implication of Marshall's decision was that Jefferson also should disavow the use of force and should instead observe "the rule of law" in his actions toward his political opponents.

For whatever reasons, the impeachment effort against Marshall's colleague subsequently failed (though only by a narrow margin in the Senate).
Marshall himself was spared (and remained Chief Justice until his death in
1836). The principle of judicial independence thus won its first victory in
the United States constitutional tradition. This principle, as Marshall
presented it to his political opponents in 1803, was not a claim for judicial
supremacy. It was a claim for the equal status of the judicial and executive
branches. Underlying this claim was an offer of mutual respect and an
implicit appeal that, regardless of past oppressions that the Federalists might
have inflicted, nonetheless the victorious Republicans should not now
engage in retaliatory inflictions. Marshall in effect appealed for mutual
accommodation between old enemies in order to establish a reliable "rule
of law."

Drawing comparisons across different historical eras is always difficult;
and comparing different cultures is even more complicated. I was, however, struck by apparent similarities between the events around 1800 when
the principle of judicial independence was first tested in the United States
and recent events in Chile and Argentina. In particular, I saw parallels
between President Adams' actions packing the judiciary with his political
allies after he had been electorally defeated, and the similar actions of
President Augusto Pinochet regarding the Chilean Supreme Court in the
year following his plebiscite defeat. And, like Jefferson's newly victorious
Republicans in 1800, many of Pinochet's opponents were concerned that the
Chilean Supreme Court would obstruct their efforts to remedy past oppressions and, in any event, they regarded the last-minute Pinochet judicial
appointments as illegitimate. For these reasons, like Jefferson's
Republicans, many Pinochet opponents saw powerful reasons for them to
use their newly won authority to remove these judges or substantially to
curtail their authority. But like Jefferson, President Patricio Aylwin refused
to endorse wholesale subjugative retaliation against the judiciary, notwithstanding its partisan identification with his opponents. Thus Aylwin, like
Jefferson, not only respected the principle of judicial independence but --
more significantly, I would say -- openly acknowledged the importance of
working toward mutual accommodation rather than using immediate political
power to subjugate political opponents.

Recent events in Argentina provide a sharp contrast to the Chilean (and
much earlier United States) experience. In 1990, a short time after the
Peronist Party won electoral command of both the Presidency and the
Congress, President Carlos Menem signed legislation enlarging the membership of the Supreme Court in order to take control away from the Justices
who had been appointed by his predecessor, Raúl Alfonsín.[17] This court-
packing action not only directly assaulted the principle of judicial indepen-

dence but -- again, I would say, more significantly and ominously -- rejected the proposition that social relations should be based on the pursuit of mutual accommodation rather than disrespectful subjugation of political opponents.

The restraint demonstrated by President Aylwin was even more remarkable because of the provocation presented by his predecessor in packing the Chilean Supreme Court with his appointees notwithstanding his lame-duck status -- a provocation that was not present in the Argentine context when Menem succeeded Alfonsín. President Aylwin's restraint was an application of the proposition that, because democratic principle rests ultimately on an ethos of mutual accommodation among political adversaries, it follows that even victims of wrongful oppression are obliged to seek mutual accommodation with -- rather than vengeful subjugation of -- their oppressors. If newly elected leaders accept the continued tenure of judges appointed by their oppressive opponents, this acceptance in itself signifies the new regime's willingness to break the cycle of retaliatory vengeance and to pursue the democratic path of mutual accommodation.

Judges must also understand that they too are obliged to respect and to facilitate the democratic principle of mutual accommodation. Toward this end, judges themselves must exercise considerable restraint. They must not confuse their claims for independent tenure with a demand for unquestioning obedience to a supreme judiciary. Though the United States judiciary has frequently fallen into this confusion, their claims for supremacy cannot be reconciled with democratic principles -- any more than majority rule or legislative supremacy can simply be reconciled with democracy. If properly understood and if adroitly put into practice, the equal status of the judiciary with other governance institutions and the acknowledged interdependence of these institutions can work to protect the political equality of all citizens. This is the lesson that I would draw from the experience of the United States over the past two centuries from the moment in *Marbury v. Madison* when the principle of judicial independence, and its relationship to the ideal of the rule of law, was first established.

## Notes

[1]Previous versions of this chapter were delivered as lectures at the University of Chile Law School on July 30, 1991, and at the University of Buenos Aires Law School and Centro de Estudios Institucionales in Buenos Aires on August 7-9, 1991. This essay was published in Spanish. *Independencia Judicial y Democracia Constitucional: Lecciones de la Experiencia Norteamericana, in* 1 REVISTA DE DERECHO Y HUMANIDADES 15 (May 1992) (Chile).

[2]This summary is drawn from ROBERT A. BURT, THE CONSTITUTION IN CONFLICT (1992).

[3]Address by Abraham Lincoln (Oct. 16, 1854), *in* 2 COLLECTED WORKS OF ABRAHAM LINCOLN 266 (Roy P. Basler ed., 1953).

[4]Dred Scott v. Sandford, 60 U.S. (19 How.) 393 (1857).

[5]Lochner v. New York, 198 U.S. 45 (1905); Hammer v. Dagenhart, 247 U.S. 251 (1918); Adkins v. Children's Hospital, 261 U.S. 525 (1923).

[6]Roe v. Wade, 410 U.S. 113 (1973).

[7]Brown v. Board of Educ., 347 U.S. 483 (1954) (Brown I); Brown v. Board of Educ., 349 U.S. 294 (1955) (Brown II).

[8]*See supra* note 2.

[9]*See, e.g.*, ROBERT H. BORK, THE TEMPTING OF AMERICA: THE POLITICAL SEDUCTION OF THE LAW (1990); Antonin Scalia, *Originalism: The Lesser Evil*, 57 U. CIN. L. REV. 849 (1989).

[10]*See* Robert A. Burt, *Inventing Judicial Review: Israel and America*, 10 CARDOZO L. REV. 2013, 2054 (1989).

[11]*See* Yakus v. United States, 321 U.S. 414 (1944) (specialized court with sole jurisdiction over Emergency Price Control Act); South Carolina v. Katzenbach, 383 U.S. 301 (1966) (jurisdiction over Voting Rights Act restricted to District of Columbia Court).

[12]*Ex parte* McCardle, 74 U.S. (7 Wall.) 506 (1869).

[13]*See generally* HART AND WECHSLER'S THE FEDERAL COURTS AND THE FEDERAL SYSTEM 309-75 (Paul M. Bator, et al. eds., 1973).

[14]*See* Robert A. Burt, *Constitutional Law and the Teaching of the Parables*, 93 YALE L. J. 455, 475 (1984).

[15]Stuart v. Laird, 5 U.S. (1 Cranch) 299 (1803).

[16]5 U.S. (1 Cranch) 137 (1803).

[17]*See Argentina: Controversy Surrounding the Judiciary*, 45 INT'L COMMISSION JURISTS REV. 1, 4 (1990).

# 20

---

# The Opinion-Writing Function of the Judiciary of Latin American Governments in Transition to Democracy: *Martinez v. Provincia de Mendoza*

## *Joseph Goldstein*

With the close of the twentieth century has come the hope and expectation that constitutional democracies will take secure root in the countries of Latin America. Following what appears to be the end of a series of military coups that since the 1930s had plagued these countries, civil democracy began to be restored by popular elections. Such was the election in 1983 of Raúl Alfonsín to the Presidency of Argentina. The judiciary plays many important roles in a country's transition to democracy. Below is a fictitious opinion recently drafted by Justice Jose Pierdoro, a fictitious figure in the reconstituted *Corte Suprema de Justicia de la Nacion* (the Supreme Court of Argentina) in the case of *Martinez v. Provincia de Mendoza*. This opinion reflects the communications function of judicial opinions, an important judicial function in the transition to democracy. Justice Pierdoro delivered the opinion of the Court.

*Martinez v. Provincia de Mendoza*
___ Fallos ___ (1992)

[PART ONE is omitted here.]

PART TWO

Having decided the substantive issues before us we now consider, for the guidance of the lower courts as well as this Court, the essential ingredients of judicial opinions in the service of democracy.  Our goal is to foster a tradition of judicial review and of respect for and of good-faith compliance with judicial judgments.

Early in the life of the United States Constitution (on which, in fundamental ways, the Constitution of Argentina is modeled) Chief Justice Marshall in *McCulloch v. Maryland*, a unanimous opinion of the United States Supreme Court, wrote "we [,as judges,] must never forget that it is *a constitution* we are expounding."[1]  What are the implications of an admonition such as Marshall's for the opinion-writing obligations that we, as judges, must meet when expounding -- explaining, interpreting, teaching -- the Constitution of Argentina, as well as the laws enacted under it?[2]  Put somewhat differently, by what criteria are we to assess opinions as communications about what is law and what the law is?

## I.

We must not forget that the Constitution of Argentina, like that of the United States, derives its authority from the people of the nation and that it is meant to secure "the blessings of liberty for them and their posterity."[3]  The judiciary's contribution to the fragile enterprise of building and stabilizing a democratic system requires that we remember, and that we not let the legislature, the executive and the people forget, that the Constitution adopts a republican and representative form of government for the Nation and requires the same for the Provinces,[4] and specifically guarantees the equality of all inhabitants before the law[5] and guarantees, as well, their right to petition the authorities, to publish ideas through the press, to freely profess their religion, and to teach and learn.[6]  Furthermore its "Declarations, Rights and Guarantees" article provides that such enumerated rights "shall not be construed as a denial of other rights . . . which rise from *the principle of the sovereignty of the people* and from the republican form of government."[7]  Finally, the People of Argentina are to govern, not by armed force, but only "through their representatives and authorities created by this Constitution."[8]

To take the Constitution seriously means that we, as judges, must take seriously the principle of popular sovereignty.  To take seriously in our opinion-writing that the people are sovereign is not to suggest that the idea embedded in this constitutional principle is fully realizable.  Like "free elections," "equal application of law," "separation of powers," "law and order," and "liberty," -- the principle of popular sovereignty points the governors and the governed toward the democracy to be achieved.  Taken seriously it invigorates our efforts, as well as those of the executive and legislative branches, to recognize when as a Nation we may falter.

## II.

We are now ready to address how the principle of popular sovereignty should guide the judges of this Court, as well as those of the lesser National and Provincial courts, in writing opinions. At its minimum this principle means that the judiciary has, in its interpretations, a duty to maintain the Constitution (as well as National and Provincial statutory law) as something "We the People" of Argentina can understand. If the government is to become and continue to be a democracy -- indeed an intelligent democracy -- it must be based on the never-ending consent of "We the People." If the people are to be and to remain sovereign their consent must be kept current. Like a good battery, consent must be rechargeable. It must be of a people enabled to comprehend the *what* and *why* of an opinion -- whether it be unanimous, majority, concurring, or dissenting.

This Court's communications to, and on behalf of, the People of Argentina should enable the People to decide whether or not to seek statutory, regulatory or even constitutional change. We see our Constitution as did United States Supreme Court Justice Roberts when he observed, "[t]he Constitution was written to be understood by the voters."[9]

The entire judiciary thus has an important part to play in widening the base of informed people. We know that keeping our readings of the Constitution comprehensible -- within reach of "We the People" -- cannot ensure Constitutional literacy. But we also know that our opinions must not become obstacles to popular understanding. We must not write like, nor only for, the law-trained specialists, who discourse in jargon-bound language in journals of limited circulation. We must not leave to the specialists the task of explaining what the Court has decided and why. Without condescension and without oversimplification, the courts must strive to use language that will enable the People to understand what they mean and do not mean to say -- especially when expounding the Constitution.

The case at bar does not require the Court to define democracy, nor to consider the many variations a republican form of government may take. We need only to recall what Thomas Jefferson declared 200 years ago: that under our Constitution there is "no safe depository of the ultimate powers of the society but the people themselves; and if we think them not enlightened enough to exercise their control with a wholesome discretion, the remedy is not to take it from them, but to inform their discretion."[10] To inform *their discretion* then is a fundamental obligation of the Court -- as ideally it ought also to be of the legislative and executive branches. Otherwise the Constitution's explicit recognition of the principle that the People of Argentina are sovereign will be thwarted. The judiciary will have failed to play its role in fostering the development of a constitutional democracy. One totalitarian government will have replaced another, albeit in the name of the People.

## III.

The Argentine Constitution of 1853, like the United States Constitution of 1787, was made for an "undefined future"[11] -- "for securing the blessings of liberty to ourselves [and] to our posterity."[12]  Likewise, to safeguard these constitutionally protected liberty interests and to promote reasoned court opinions, unencumbered by political considerations, the Constitution of Argentina provides that the judiciary is, and must remain, independent of the will of the executive and legislative branches. We, its judges, have lifetime tenure and non-diminishable salaries.[13]  We, in the judicial branch, are not and must never become beholden to those in power or to those who may threaten to take power. Inevitably, what we decide will be controversial. Often it will have important political consequences. But our decisions are not to be driven by politics,[14] or determined by the power other branches may seek to exert. If ours is to be a constitutional democracy, a tradition of good-faith compliance with our decisions and of orderly challenge by the governed and the governors, must develop. Our rulings must remain free of any suspicion that we have abused and thus sacrificed our constitutionally protected independence.

If the work of the judiciary is to be taken seriously it must rest on more than the constitutional or legislative authority that empowers it to decide cases and controversies. Good-faith compliance and trust must be continually nurtured through the reasoning we, as judges, provide for the results we reach. The judiciary must have more than a "command-obedience" relationship with the people.[15]  The relationship must rest on the authoritative, as distinguished from authoritarian, quality of court opinions.[16]  It must rest on the integrity and trust, that we, as independent judges, earn by taking competing claims seriously and by making reasoned responses to them.

What we hope will develop, if this Court remains true to its opinion-writing obligations, is the kind of trust that is reflected in the declaration, familiar in the United States: "If need be -- I will take my case all the way to the Supreme Court!" There is in that refrain a belief shared by the people that the highest court can be trusted to make an honestly reasoned decision, and that "even if I do not prevail I will be satisfied that I have been given a fair hearing." It is an acknowledgment that "if I lose in a court of last resort I will abide by its decision until I am able to change the law by urging the legislature to rewrite it, or by persuading the Court in another case or controversy to reconsider it, or by setting in motion the process for amending the Constitution."

The acquisition of respect for the work of the judiciary -- for the legitimacy of its rulings -- will not come overnight. It must be built day by day on the opinions that this and other courts give. It must rest on a growing consensus among the people that the judiciary is a fair arbiter of their conflicts -- that it is independent of the other branches as well as free of any allegiance to a particular party. This has led us to fashion opinion-writing canons to guide the judges of this Court and other National and Provincial courts in their work.

## IV.

The goal of the set of canons that we have developed is to ensure that each opinion is coherent by itself and that when there is more than one opinion in a single case all of them -- majority, concurring, and dissenting opinions -- taken together constitute a single communication about the reasons for our agreements and disagreements about the meanings we attribute to the Constitutional or statutory provisions that we expound.

Four canons of comprehensibility provide the essential ingredients for meeting our opinion-writing obligations.[17]

### A. Use Simple and Precise Language "Level to the Understanding of All"[18]

United States Supreme Court Justice Hugo L. Black captured the essence of this canon when he suggested that opinions should be written "so your Mamma [and Papa] can understand it."[19] The goal of this canon is to ensure that the Constitution is accessible to the people. It is to accept our responsibility for helping our government become a democracy. It recognizes, as United States Law Professor Eugene Rostow once observed, that judges "are inevitable teachers in a vital national seminar."[20] This seminar must be never-ending if our nation is to become, as Leon Botstein would say it, a "government by free people through the use of reason and communication and not through the use of violence."[21]

### B. Write with Candor

United States Supreme Court Justice William O. Douglas captured the principle that animates this canon when he wrote, "a judiciary that discloses what it is doing and why it does it will breed understanding. Any confidence based on understanding is more enduring than confidence based on awe."[22] Likewise, Joseph Vining, marking the distinction between authoritarian and authoritative decisions, rightly asks:

> Why does the judge write an opinion if not to justify his decision and his statements? And why would anyone read the opinion if it made no difference whether one was persuaded by it or not? The authority of a legal text is in this sense not automatic. Its authority must be earned too.[23]

This canon recognizes that, as judges, we are obligated to disclose fully our reasons for what we decide. We have an even greater responsibility for speaking with candor than do the executive and legislative branches. Unlike them, though rascals we may be, we cannot be voted out of office. We are not subject to periodic review by election. We have tenure. If our opinions do not speak with candor and clarity we deprive the People -- the governed and the governors -- of much that is important if they are to participate fully in government. The governors will be deprived of guidelines for meeting their constitutional responsibilities and the governed will be denied a basis for holding their governors accountable.

## C. Acknowledge and Explain Deliberate Ambiguity

With this canon we recognize, as did United States Supreme Court Chief Justice Marshall early in the life of the United States Constitution in *McCulloch v. Maryland*, that such are the frailties of human language and human perception "that no word conveys to the mind, in all situations, one single definite idea."[24] But it also recognizes that some phrases and words are clearer than others, and it expresses a strong preference for avoiding the use of those that are more rather than less ambiguous. Within the margins of unavoidable ambiguity, the Court's opinion-writing task is, after all, to give understanding to laws that have conveyed different meanings to different minds at different times and in different circumstances.

Candor requires that ambiguity be unambiguously acknowledged. We should be willing to explain, for example, that we have been unable to find or fashion a clearly graspable principle or set of reasons on which to rest our judgment. Thus we recognize the continuing nature of the process by which courts develop constitutional doctrine and statutory meanings. We deal forthrightly with ambiguity by acknowledging the extent of our differences, especially in unanimous opinions, not only in division evidenced by majority, concurring, and dissenting opinions.

The purpose of this canon is to make visible the basis, however limited, on which the judgment that we share is reached in the opinion that we join.

If we acknowledge our own uncertainty, deliberately ambiguous opinions can then be written in good faith and be taken seriously as the Court continually seeks to refine the reasons behind the constitutional law it articulates. We cannot deny the complexities we confront in the issues we seek to address.

### D. Be Accurate and Scrupulously Fair in Making Attributions to Another Opinion in the Case or to Prior Opinions of This and of Other Courts

This canon recognizes that concurrences and dissents are meant to disclose and clarify important differences within the Court. It recognizes that all the opinions in a case taken together ought to constitute a single communication and that therefore we, as judges, have a common obligation to give in our opinions fair and accurate readings of those whose views we challenge or share. We must take each others opinions seriously. We must avoid making ambiguous that which is not. United States Supreme Court Justice Jackson has noted,

> the technique of the dissenter often is to exaggerate the holding of the Court beyond the meaning of the majority and then to blast away at the excess. So the poor lawyer with a similar case [not to mention the People,] does not know whether the majority opinion meant what it seemed to say or what the minority said it meant.[25]

United States Court of Appeals Judge Frank M. Coffin has described what we believe must become characteristic of the way in which we do our work. "If I am taking a position that differs from what I think one of my colleagues would prefer, I will . . . state his position as fairly and strongly in the opinion as I can and proceed to deal with it."[26]

Separate status for this canon, despite its overlap with the other canons, is meant to underscore the importance of our need to assess (before making a decision public) all of the opinions in a case as a single communication.

A judiciary's contribution to the delicate enterprise of building a democratic government requires the opinions of its judges be comprehensible and worthy of trust. Each canon takes seriously that the People are ultimately sovereign and are, therefore, entitled to know that what the Court says -- it means to say.

## V.

Candor requires me to address one more matter before bringing this opinion to a close. Can I, a bogus and alien judge, have anything relevant to say about the opinion-writing functions of the Argentine judiciary, not to mention the judiciary of other South American constitutional governments? I have drawn upon Anglo-North American, not Latin-South American, sources for the canons. Even my reading of the Argentine Constitution has relied on an English translation. I do not know Spanish. I know almost nothing about the people of Argentina, about the history of their country, and about their life, their customs, and their legal culture.

Yet I decided to write this opinion believing that what it proposes would not need to be accepted, adopted, or even fully understood to serve a useful purpose. I want merely to promote deliberations by the judges of Latin American countries about their own opinion-writing obligations.

However, I do not deny that a part of me believes that the canons rest on a body of knowledge about written communications that is generally applicable to opinion-writing by courts of republican governments, wherever they are. Furthermore, I was encouraged to believe this because the design, language, and structure of government in the Argentine Constitution calls to mind (at least in its English translation) the United States Constitution and its Bill of Rights. Thus, I almost convinced myself that I could rely upon what the two constitutions seem to have in common, particularly with regard to the judicial branch and its relationship to the executive and legislative branches, in fashioning illustrative guides to opinion-writing.[27]

But I continue to have some doubts. I wonder whether I am so bound and tied to peculiarly United States notions about the meaning of "democracy" and "popular sovereignty" and whether we are bound to cultures so different that what I propose cannot be relevant to the role the judiciary must play in Latin American countries if their constitutional democracies are to be realized. The judiciary of the Latin American governments in transition to democracy should therefore consider my admonitions and prescriptions with caution.

Inspired by the popular elections that brought their governments into being, the courts of these countries now have a magnificent opportunity to breathe life and longevity into the constitutions of their fledgling democracies.

# Notes

[1] 17 U.S. (4 Wheat.) 316, 407 (1819) (emphasis in original).

[2] Expound also means "to lay open the meaning . . . as of a text." WEBSTER'S NEW INTERNATIONAL DICTIONARY UNABRIDGED 899 (William A. Neilson et al. eds., 2d ed. 1961).

[3]The Preamble to the Constitution of Argentina of 1853 (as amended) provides "We, the representatives of the people of the Argentine Nation, . . . with the object of . . . securing the blessings of liberty to ourselves, to our posterity, and to all men in the world who wish to dwell on Argentine land: . . . do ordain, decree, and establish this Constitution for the Argentine Nation." CONST. ARG. pmbl. Unless otherwise noted, the translation of the Argentine Constitution can be found in MARIO A. CARRANZA, CONSTITUTION OF THE ARGENTINE REPUBLIC (1925).

The Preamble to the United States Constitution provides: "We the People of the United States, in order to . . . secure the blessings of liberty to ourselves and our posterity, do ordain and establish this Constitution for the United States of America." U.S. CONST. pmbl.

[4]CONST. ARG. art. 1 and 5.

[5]*Id.* art. 16.

[6]*Id.* art. 14.

[7]*Id.* art. 33 *(emphasis added).*

[8]*Id.* art. 22.

[9]United States v. Sprague, 282 U.S. 716, 731 (1931).

[10]Letter from Thomas Jefferson to William Charles Jarvis (Sept. 28, 1820), *in* FAMILIAR QUOTATIONS 389 (John Bartlett & Emily M. Beck eds., 15th and 125th anniversary ed. 1980).

[11]Hurtado v. California, 110 U.S. 516, 530-31 (1884) ("The Constitution of the United States . . . was made for an undefined and expanding future, and for a people gathered and to be gathered from many nations and of many tongues.").

[12]CONST. ARG. pmbl.; U.S. CONST. pmbl.

[13]CONST. ARG. art. 96.

[14]*See* Moshe Etzione, *The "Jewish Wars" in the Law-Courts, in* REUBEN R. HECHT, FESTSCHRIFT 238 (1979).

[15]Hannah Arendt, *What Was Authority?, in* AUTHORITY: NOMOS I 82 (Carl J. Friedrich ed., 1958).

[16]JOSEPH VINING, THE AUTHORITATIVE AND THE AUTHORITARIAN 30 (1986).

[17]The canons are drawn from JOSEPH GOLDSTEIN, THE INTELLIGIBLE CONSTITUTION (1992).

[18]Letter from James Wilson to the Speaker of the Pennsylvania House of Representatives (Aug. 24, 1791), *in* 1 THE WORKS OF JAMES WILSON (Robert G. McCloskey ed., 1967) (emphasis in original).

[19]GOLDSTEIN, *supra* note 17, at 112.

[20]Eugene V. Rostow, *The Democratic Character of Judicial Review,* 66 HARV. L. REV. 193, 208 (1952).

[21]Leon Botstein, *Damaged Literacy: Illiteracies and American Democracy,* 119 DAEDALUS SPRING 1990, at 61.

[22]William O. Douglas, Stare Decisis, Eighth Annual Benjamin N. Cardozo Lecture delivered before the Association of the Bar of the City of New York (Apr. 12, 1949), *in* 4 REC. ASS'N B. City N.Y. 31 (1949), *reprinted in* 49 COLUM. L. REV. 735, 754 (1949).

[23]VINING, *supra* note 16, at 30.

[24]17 U.S. (4 Wheat.) at 414.

[25]ROBERT H. JACKSON, THE SUPREME COURT IN THE AMERICAN SYSTEM OF GOVERNMENT 18-19 (1955).

[26]FRANK M. COFFIN, THE WAYS OF A JUDGE: REFLECTIONS FROM THE FEDERAL APPELLATE BENCH 181 (1980).

[27]CONST. ARG. § 3; U.S. CONST. art. III.

# 21

## On the Exercise of
## Judicial Review in Argentina

### *Carlos S. Nino*

In a democratic society, judicial review is a controversial power that must be justified. The purpose of this chapter is to describe and analyze some aspects of the ways in which courts have performed the function of judicial review in Argentina in light of a specific theory regarding the courts' basis, scope, and power.[1] I proceed by presenting a brief sketch of this theory and then, in light of it, I analyze and evaluate the use of judicial review in Argentina.

### I.
### A General Theory of Judicial Review

The first element of any plausible theory of judicial review is to take seriously the so-called "counter-majoritarian difficulty."[2] The seriousness of this difficulty arises from the manner of justifying democracy.

There are two important categories of justificatory conceptions of democracy in the marketplace of philosophical ideas: those conceptions which justify democracy regardless of how it transforms people's interests and preferences, and those which depend on the transformation itself to assign value to democracy. The first category is defective because it disregards the difference between personal and impersonal preferences, treating the latter in a way that is only appropriate for the former. Personal preferences endorse things that enhance the life or the well-being of the agent. They can be the object of actions which aim at their aggregative satisfaction, without determining their respective validity. Preferences for states of affairs which are supposedly valuable from an impersonal point of view -- such as slavery or its abolition -- are not deemed to be satisfied in an aggregative way. They are adopted or rejected as the basis for action only after their validity is determined. Democratic theories that oppose the marketplace rely on contesting and determining the validity of impersonal preferences. However, I endorse a specific theory which assigns value to democracy based on a processing of preferences, and puts the greatest emphasis on the practice of deliberation.

In my view, the democratic process is an imperfect substitute for the informal practice of moral discussion.[3] The practice of moral discussion has epistemic value for discovering correct moral solutions to intersubjective issues. The validity of interpersonal moral principles, which evaluate actions based on their effects on the interests of people other than the agent, rests on a viewpoint of impartiality, rationality, and knowledge of the relevant facts. The discussion and interplay of ideas, when they successfully conclude in a unanimous consensus, are contributing factors to the achievement of impartial, rational, and knowledgeable moral intersubjective solutions. Unanimity is a functional equivalent of impartiality when it results from discussion among all the concerned parties. This is based on the assumption that each one is the best judge of her own interests.

Democracy, as a system in which the majoritarian opinion is binding insofar as all the people concerned have participated in both discussion and in a collective decision, is the natural substitute for the mechanism of informal discussion and unanimous consensus. This system allows for the adoption of new decisions at particular times; otherwise, the status quo would prevail, even if it were favored solely by a minority. Of course, majority rule is not the functional equivalent of impartiality: the majority of a group may be openly biased against a minority. However, when all the people concerned freely and equally participate in the process of deliberation and decision, democracy preserves some of the epistemic value inherent in the process of informal discussion and unanimous consensus. Democracy, based upon this process, includes a dynamic of collective action and tends towards the adoption of impartial solutions.

This does not mean, of course, that democratic solutions are always right; it only means that they are generally more likely to be right than solutions adopted by any other procedure. Stated otherwise, the democratic method of collective decision-making is more reliable than the procedure of isolated individual reflection in reaching morally correct solutions to intersubjective moral issues. Dictators have acted on the basis of their own reflections on intersubjective moral matters, and have had more power than others to enforce their decisions. But, however wise and well-meaning an individual may be, it is unlikely that he could represent the real interests of others better than they could by participating in the process of discussion and decision.

The epistemic value of democracy varies with the degree to which its underlying conditions are satisfied. Those conditions depend upon the openness of the debate, and the degree to which people equally participate in and support the final decision. Of course, there is a threshold at the lowest degree of satisfaction of those conditions beyond which the epistemic value of the process is so feeble, that it begins to be surpassed by the value of the process of individual reflection.

Nevertheless, there are many cases in which one may be absolutely certain that the majoritarian opinion is wrong, and that the result of our individual reflection is closer to the requirements of impartiality, rationality, and knowledge of the relevant facts. But if we accept that this is not the case *in general and in the long run,* and that the democratic process is more reliable than individual reflection, we have a derivative reason for observing the results of the democratic process even when they are wrong. Otherwise, our individual reflection would always be the final court of appeal and the democratic process would be superfluous. This would contradict our assumption that such reflection is less reliable than the democratic process. For this system to be operative, we must rely on it even in those cases in which we are sure that it is misguided, unless of course the underlying conditions which determine its epistemic value are not fulfilled.

The rules enacted in a democratic way provide the epistemic reasons for adopting the action they prescribe. This solves the paradox of the moral superfluousness of law, which seems to lead us towards anarchism: if law, as I think, is not self-justificatory, but only provides reasons for actions when it is endorsed by autonomously accepted moral principles, why not rely directly on those principles in order to justify decisions and actions? The epistemic vision of democracy provides an answer. We simply cannot determine which valid intersubjective moral principles are the basis for action until we express them in legal rules adopted after a process of collective deliberation and decision. Thus, legal rules are not original reasons for actions, but are reasons for discovering the reasons for action. *Veritas non auctoritas facit legem.*[4]

At this point, it becomes clear that the counter-majoritarian difficulty of judicial review is that judicial review is a piece of moral epistemic elitism. Stated otherwise, it rests on the assumption that a small group of wise people, who are neither directly involved in the democratic process nor directly responsible to those whose interests are at stake, decide that their decision-making process is better at acquiring impartiality than one in which the stake holders determine the outcome of the conflict.

Several attempts at overcoming this difficulty do not do the trick.[5] Justice Marshall, for example, contends that the Constitution is the supreme law of the land and determines which other rules are laws; therefore it provides a logical basis for judicial review. This argument ignores that the supremacy of the Constitution does not logically require that courts are its final guardians. It might just mean -- as it is the case in Britain, Holland, and some Scandinavian countries -- that Parliament is prohibited from enacting certain laws, even if there is no remedy for a violation of this prohibition. Dworkin's distinction[6] between rights established by principles, and collective goals determined by policies, overlooks the fact that a robust conception of rights (such as that endorsed by egalitarian liberalism) covers almost the whole moral realm. Therefore, conceptions which confine democracy to the definition of policies are controversial because they regard it as a procedure for aggregating personal preferences, rather than for establishing the validity of impersonal ones. Ackerman's dualist vision,[7] which confers democratic legitimacy to the enactment of the Constitution and to its formal or informal modification, does not sufficiently take into account the democratic deficits of the process of enacting Constitutions, such as those of the United States and Argentina. It also ignores the difficulty of transferring that supposed legitimacy over time, notwithstanding that a simple majority of the present generation usually does not have the power to impress formal or informal changes on the Constitution.

I think that the only way of overcoming the charge of moral epistemic elitism in ascribing some scope to judicial review is by relying on the conditions under which the democratic process has epistemic value. This leads to three important exceptions to the denial of judicial review which follows from this justification of democracy.

## A. The Guardianship of the Democratic Process

I believe that John H. Ely[8] is correct in claiming that judges must guard the procedures which are inherent in the democratic process. The conditions which allow for the equal and free participation in public deliberation and collective decision must be satisfied to a significant degree for the outcome of the democratic process to have epistemic value. These conditions include understanding the interests, idiosyncracies, and predicaments of other groups, finding a rational justification for a balance of interests, and avoiding distortion at the primary level of deliberation. If those conditions are not satisfied to a certain degree, citizens and judges may not be justified in deferring their own individual reflections to the outcome of the "democratic" process. Therefore, judges do not need a special reason for justifying their power to disqualify rules when their enactments do not minimally satisfy the conditions which grant epistemic value to the democratic process. Indeed, one of the most important tasks of the judiciary in democratic systems is that of strengthening the epistemic power of the process of deliberation and decision, by way of disqualifying those enactments that either impress distortions upon it or are the result of those distortions. The apportionment cases in the United States are typical of the courts' role as a referee of the democratic procedure.[9] But more important, though bearing a more indirect relationship with the political process, are decisions which touch on underlying social conditions for the proper working of the democratic system. For example, *Brown v. Board of Education*[10] was a luminous signpost along the path of understanding that, without the integration of people of very different backgrounds at an early age, the epistemic quality of democracy is undermined where there is no understanding or acceptance of opposing views.

## B. The Guardianship of Personal Autonomy

Another basis of judicial power to review democratic enactments is the fact that the epistemic value of democracy is controlled by intersubjective moral standards. As I stated briefly above, the validity of those standards depends on their acceptability from an impartial standpoint, and the democratic process of discussion and decision relies on a dynamic of collective action which tends towards the adoption of impartial solutions. This does not apply to philosophical or scientific matters (which is why the value of democracy itself cannot be decided democratically), to factual issues (where judges should have the last word in determining the occurrence of individual facts), or to moral questions, which depend not on intersubjective standards but on ideals of human excellence, virtue, or conceptions of the personal good. I do not know what the relevant criteria are for determining the truth of these ideals or conceptions which evaluate actions according to their effect on the life or character of their agent. However, their validity does not depend on their acceptability under conditions of impartiality, since they do not deal with the interests of different people. Public deliberation on personal ideals -- such as the ideals of the good patriot, the good *pater familias*, and the religious devout -- may enhance our understanding of these ideals, but the unanimous or majoritarian consensus about their validity has no more authority than our own reflection to guide our judgment. This is one reason why democratic enactments cannot be based on reasons which are constituted by ideals of personal excellence.[11] Therefore, citizens and judges should not defer their judgments and actions to a democratic enactment which is based on an ideal of personal excellence. Observe that the enactment's lack of epistemic value does not depend on the class of actions it regulates, but on the kind of *reasons* on which the enactment is based.

The same action may also be evaluated by an intersubjective moral standard, which takes into account its impact on other people's interests, and by personal ideals, which evaluate the action's effect on the agent's character and life. For example, abortion may be prohibited on the basis that it frustrates another individual's right to life -- an assumption which is, of course, highly debatable -- or on the basis that it is normally the result of a disorderly sex life which degrades the people who practice it. The judge may disagree profoundly with the first rationale, but if it were the outcome of a democratic consensus about how to balance the supposed value of a fetus with the autonomy of women, she would probably not thwart that consensus but would provoke the re-opening of the democratic debate by highlighting how callous the former consensus had been. Instead, if the prohibition is based on the second rationale, it must be deemed void since there is no reason to rely on it. This is what justifies the decision of the United States Supreme Court in *Griswold v. Connecticut*,[12] on the one hand, and shows that the decision of the same Court in *Bowers v. Hardwick*[13] has been profoundly wrong, on the other.

## C. The Guardianship of the Rule of Law

There is a third source of judicial review which is less obvious than the former two, though perhaps it is of a more transcendental character. Democratic and judicial decisions and enactments are not individual actions. They are contributions to collective actions; their outcomes, which make them relevant as legislative, executive, or judicial commands, are the result of a complex combination involving the expectations, attitudes, and behavior of citizens and other officials in the past, present, and future. A legislative enactment or a court's decision is efficacious as part of a general practice or convention which coordinates the actions and attitudes of many actors over long stretches of time.[14] There are certain salient factors which serve as focal points and allow for the evolution of this practice or convention. A successful constitutional enactment may transcend the foundational event of that practice or convention, which in turn may allow the democratic process to develop even when that enactment has not been democratic. Without this collective action, expanded over time through legal practice and incorporated into the purported ideal of the rule of law, the democratic process will be ineffectual for much of the epistemic value that its outcome may bear. Yet a legal practice does not justify itself: it is only justified insofar as it protects procedures and substantive principles which conform to autonomous moral requirements. But we should not evaluate those requirements based on isolated actions or decisions taken within that practice. We should examine the whole practice which that action or decision involves. This is important because the proper alternative to an action that reinforces an objectionable practice is not another action which reinforces a better practice, but no effective action at all, or an action which undermines or destroys the present practice without creating a new one in its place.

This often leads to the application of criteria of second best rationality. More precisely, it shows that legal reasoning must be developed in two stages. In the first stage, the practice which a decision may reinforce or undermine must be evaluated in light of autonomous intersubjective moral principles -- like those which may be illuminated by the working of the democratic process. If the result of this examination is categorically or conditionally positive, the second stage of legal reasoning is addressed. This stage determines which action or decision contributes to bringing the practice closer to the former moral principles and, at the same time, to strengthening its continuity through the rule of law. Of course, these two goals are often in tension, and the legal actor must necessarily strike a balance between them, but there is no *a priori* precise formula for doing so.

This is very important for the justification of judicial review, since its exercise can be seen as attempts by judges to preserve the continuity of a morally legitimate legal practice against threats coming from either the democratic process or the judicial activity itself. Many decisions of legislatures or courts may well undermine the continuous preservation of the rule of law that makes them effective. The Supreme Court or a Constitutional Tribunal may defend the conventional interpretation of a constitutional text that founds a legal practice even when it has no democratic legitimacy, or when the principles it endorses are less than morally ideal. The court may defend such interpretations in order to preserve the salient factor of the underlying collective action and to prevent its self-frustration, assuming the dynamics of the prisoners' dilemma or any of the other structures of inefficient collective action. Many court decisions in the exercise of judicial review are to be seen in this light when they stress the offensiveness of the democratic or judicial decision under review against the clear meaning of the Constitution under current interpretive conventions, and they cannot be seen as preserving either the democratic process or personal autonomy. But the preservation of the legal practice depends not only on the observance of the document which was successful in founding it, but also on the fulfillment of political and social conditions which are conducive to the strengthening of that practice. Some tokens of judicial review may be seen as far-reaching operations, which aim at handling social and political circumstances so as to strengthen the continuity of the rule of law.

This theory of judicial review converts judges into the triple custodians of democracy, personal autonomy, and the existing legal practice, which by and large is congenial with procedural and substantive values which endorse an ideal constitution of power, rights, and a positive or real constitution. If we assume this theory, then we are prepared to evaluate the use that courts, particularly the Supreme Court, have made of this power in Argentina.

## II.
## The Exercise of Judicial Review by the Argentine Supreme Court

In Argentina the power of judicial review is based upon Article 31 of the Constitution of 1853/60, which establishes the supremacy of the Constitution, the laws enacted under its authority, and treaties with foreign powers. In its turn, Article 100 of the Constitution establishes the competence of the Supreme Court and the inferior courts to deal with all the points regulated by the Constitution. Nevertheless, it is not absolutely clear from these texts which entity should have the final voice about the constitutionality of laws.[15]

However, from the earliest days of the Constitution, the Supreme Court exercised this power. In *Rios*,[16] the Court declared void a decree of the federal Executive Power ascribing judicial functions to the administrator of the port of Rosario, alleging that only Congress may ascribe those functions. In *Calvete*,[17] the Supreme Court held that it is the final interpreter of the Constitution and, consequently, each time that a court questions the interpretation of one of its clauses, its decision is subject to review by the Supreme Court.

But it was only in *Sojo*[18] that the Supreme Court dealt with the constitutionality of a federal legislative enactment, and, for this reason, the case is considered to be the equivalent of *Marbury v. Madison*[19] in Argentina. The case dealt with the editor of the newspaper "Don Quijote," who was imprisoned for contempt by the Deputies Chamber for the entire period of its ordinary sessions. Sojo presented himself to the Supreme Court pleading a writ of *habeas corpus*, pursuant to a statute regulating the organization of the judiciary. The Supreme Court maintained that its main mission was to see that the different federal and provincial powers acted within proper limits; therefore it had to be careful not to surpass its own limits. It held that the statute in question did not grant the Supreme Court the power to act on a writ of *habeas corpus*, and that any such action would be unconstitutional, because the Constitution does not grant the Supreme Court the power to act as a first tribunal on ordinary cases.

The case which definitively consolidated judicial review is *Munipalidad de la Capital c/ Elortondo*.[20] That case concerned the application of a law that permitted the Municipality of Buenos Aires to expropriate land in order to broaden a central avenue, without specifying the land to be taken. The Court held that "Congress cannot depart from the rules which constitute the fundamental notion of the right of expropriation,"[21] and with regard to the power of judicial review maintained that courts have the duty and power to

> examine the laws in the concrete cases which are brought to their decision, compare them with the text of the Constitution . . . and abstain from applying them if they oppose the Constitution. This moderating attribution is one of the fundamental ends of the federal judiciary and one of the greatest guarantees with which constitutional rights are deemed to be secured against possible and involuntary abuses of public power.[22]

Historically, however, the Supreme Court has been relatively restrained in the exercise of this power. Nevertheless, by action and omission the Supreme Court has defined the scope of the power of judicial review which may be subject to scrutiny according to the guidelines which emerge from the above theory.

## A. *The Argentine Supreme Court as Custodian of the Democratic Process*

Perhaps it is unjust to measure the record of the Argentine Supreme Court in protecting the democratic process because democracy did not exist in Argentina for much of its history. One may say, in an obvious oversimplification, that during the first fifty years of the nation's evolution, the country was immersed in civil wars between unitarists and federalists, and between the Province of Buenos Aires and the rest of the Provinces, including the Rosas' dictatorship which lasted for more than half of that period. During the following half century, after the enactment of the final Constitution, a restricted and fraudulent democracy was in force until an electoral law established universal, obligatory, and secret suffrage. Open and genuine democracy lasted only from 1916 to 1930; then another half century of instability ensued with continuous *coup d'état* and the populist democracy of Peron, which was based on wide popular support but had no guarantees for the opposition and public opinion. Open and pluralist democracy re-established itself again at the end of 1983, and continues today. Therefore, the country enjoyed only a bit more than twenty years of full democracy, as against almost 160 years of anarchy, dictatorship, and restricted and populist democracy.

What could a Supreme Court have done in such a context? It is obvious that it could hardly have been more than a victim, not a factotum, of the absence of democracy. However, there has been a constant trend in the exercise of judicial review by the Supreme Court which has contributed to the enfeeblement of democracy. Moreover, this trend continues today.

The most obvious contribution to the impairment of the democratic process on the part of the Supreme Court through judicial review has been the

so-called "doctrine of *de facto* laws." This is the doctrine ascribing validity
to the laws enacted by regimes which came to power by force. The Court
recognized this doctrine as soon as the country reorganized itself after the
battle of Pavon, and the winner -- the Province of Buenos Aires -- joined
the rest of the country under General Bartolome Mitre, who provisorily took
over the national government. In *Martinez y otro*,[23] the Supreme Court
maintained that

> the governor of Buenos Aires and general in chief of the army was a
> competent authority to decide issues relating to the nullification of a
> payment to a government creditor, for he exerted all the national power
> after the battle of Pavon, had the right of the triumphant revolution
> assented to by the peoples, and exercised his authority by virtue of the
> serious duties that victory imposed on him.[24]

The Supreme Court confirmed this crude recognition of rights grounded
on force through the decree it issued on September 10, 1930, in reaction to
the first of the chain of *coups d'état* of this century. In this decree the
Court said that the government of General Uriburu was in possession of the
necessary force to insure the peace and order of the Nation, and consequently, the life, liberty, and property of its people. It added that this fact
constituted a *de facto* government with the power to perform validly those
acts necessary for the preservation of its ends. The Court cites
Constantineau (an obscure Canadian jurist who wrote about the validity of
acts of officials whose appointments were vitiated), in order to argue that
both national and international doctrine grants validity to the acts of *de facto*
officials, and that such a government cannot be questioned in law because
it is based on force.

In later decisions, the Supreme Court broadened its recognition of the
validity of these *de facto* powers. During Peron's first government, the
Supreme Court maintained in *Arlandini*[25] that the power of a *de facto*
government to enact legislation cannot be judicially reviewed. In *Ziella*,[26]
the Court broadened this doctrine by holding that "the decrees-laws enacted
by *de facto* governments are valid on the basis of their origin, and because
they have the value of laws, they are valid even when not ratified by
Congress; once Congress is re-established, they may only be abrogated by
other legislative enactments."[27]   After this, even greater powers were
granted to military regimes.

After 1983, things began to take a positive turn. In the last year of the
military regime, I wrote an article[28] arguing that the doctrine of *de facto*
laws was an expression of an ideological variety of positivism -- quite
different from the conceptual one defended by authors like Kelsen, Ross,

and Hart -- which commits the naturalistic fallacy of supposing that the mere fact that a law exists provides reasons for justifying actions and decisions. Given the lack of the epistemic presumption of validity that attaches to rules enacted democratically, there was no reason for judges to defer their judgment of values such as justice, order, and security, to that of a group that usurped power by force. Therefore, when a law is enacted in an authoritarian way, it is the judge's duty to appraise the substantive value of its content, and to dismiss the law when it is so obnoxious as to outweigh whatever value of order and certainty its dismissal could effect.

When the military regime enacted the so-called self-amnesty law to cover the abuses of human rights, several scholars, including myself, resorted to these kinds of arguments in an epistolary debate published by *La Nación* against other scholars, including the Peronist candidate for the Presidency, who defended the validity of the self-amnesty law on positivist grounds. When Alfonsín took office on December 10, 1983, the first project he sent to Congress and the first law it approved of unanimously, number 23.040, was the nullification of the self-amnesty law on the above basis. The Court of Appeals and the Supreme Court accepted this nullification, opening the gates for the famous trials for human rights violations. The Supreme Court also gave explicit articulation to the new doctrine in decisions like *Aramayo*,[29] and *Dufourq*,[30] where it maintained that *de facto* laws were invalid if they were not ratified, or if they were rejected explicitly or implicitly by the ongoing constitutional entities.

Unfortunately, the Supreme Court, in the new integration produced after the packing of the Court by President Menem in 1990, returned to the old doctrine in *Godoy*.[31] There, the majority of the Court held that *de facto* laws should be deemed as valid as the laws enacted by Congress, regardless of the "affective or ideological evaluation" that we can make of military regimes. It added that, because the country lived under democratic rule for only a short time, the Court's refusal to recognize the validity of *de facto* laws would lead to legal uncertainty. The majority opinion ignored the fact that the Court's previous doctrine, in its former integration, did not produce any such uncertainty, and failed to consider that the recognition of a law unavoidably requires evaluation, particularly as it applies to the values of security and order. The Court, by refusing to recognize the positive evaluation of democracy as affective or ideological, ignores the fact that it is always necessary to resort to moral reasons to justify the application of the law, since positive law, depending on mere facts, cannot justify itself. What the Court has done, in re-establishing continuity with the deleterious tradition of the judiciary, has been to replace that evaluation with non-democratic values.

There were other less direct ways in which the Supreme Court, and of course other tribunals, failed in their task of guarding the democratic process. For instance, the Court expanded the so-called "doctrine of political questions" to the extent that it practically abstained from undertaking this whole dimension of judicial review.

It extended this doctrine in successive decisions to such issues as the state of siege, the electoral regime, and impeachment. For instance, in *Sofia*,[32] the majority of the Court supported the broad interpretation of the doctrine in order to validate the Administration's prohibition of a public meeting under a state of siege. The Court refused to review both the enactment of the law of state of siege, and its application to the particular case; moreover, it found that the Administration's report that the organizers of the meeting were people of the extreme left was enough to legitimize its discretionary power.

Fortunately, there also has been a positive reaction against this broad interpretation of the doctrine of political questions during Alfonsín's administration, and this reaction has not yet been overturned by the expanded Court. On December 3, 1985, the Court decided *Granada*,[33] establishing that courts may revise the method of the enactment and application of the state of siege, maintaining that the existence of a brief term is a condition for the validity of the measure, and that its application implies limitations of time and object. In *Frente Justicialista de Liberacion Nacional*,[34] the Court abandoned the tenet of the irrevisability of electoral and party questions. On April 23, 1987, the Supreme Court decided *Sueldo de Polesman*.[35] There the Court reviewed the impeachment procedure of provincial legislatures against provincial judges, on the basis of Article 5 of the Constitution, which guarantees the Provinces a Republican form of government. This decision opened a gate to the possibility of courts complying with their function of being referees of the democratic process, a gate which we should hope will not soon be closed.

Finally, as a further illustration, we can look at one other aspect of the supervision of the operation of the democratic process: the judicial protection of freedom of expression. The Argentine Constitution establishes the right of freedom of expression and protects it with two guarantees: the prohibition of previous censorship and the prohibition against subjecting the press to federal jurisdiction. The Supreme Court has applied these guarantees in an extremely wayward fashion. On the one hand, it recurrently repeated that "among the freedoms that the Constitution consecrates, one of the greatest is that of the press, and without its due protection democracy would be degraded or purely nominal."[36] But, on the other hand, the Court acquiesced to the Executive's actions against the press, maintaining that the government's closing down of a periodical under a state of siege without a fixed term is not a constitutional violation if it has no punitive character. For instance, in *Bertotto*,[37] the Supreme Court upheld as constitutional the chief postmaster's refusal to distribute the newspaper "Democracy" for containing supposed apologies of crimes, on the basis that freedom of the press is not absolute and that "its employment is irreconcilable with ends contrary to the Argentine political organization, public morality and the good customs of the land."[38] However, during Alfonsín's administration, the Supreme Court, in *Verbitsky s/denuncia*,[39] refused to allow censorship of a publication which may have committed the offense of apology of a crime, because such censorship was the object of an absolute prohibition.

The Supreme Court's recognition of the guarantee against subjecting the press to federal jurisdiction has also varied. Until 1970 the Court interpreted this guarantee as requiring that the federal judiciary should not intervene in questions concerning the press, although it recognized an exception, valid since 1932, when the federal state is affected. It also stated that the provinces should enact legislation regulating issues such as crimes committed by the press, notwithstanding that the Constitution establishes that the Penal Code should be enacted by the Federal Congress. However, in 1970 the Supreme Court decided, in *Batalla*,[40] that the Federal Congress is competent to enact laws concerning the press, since otherwise there could be many crimes which are overlooked by the provincial legislation. This decision seems to be wholly unjustified because it ignores Article 32 of the Constitution.

The Supreme Court has not protected the positive side of freedom of expression; that is, the provision of accessible resources to people to allow them to communicate their opinions. For instance, the Inter-American Convention of Human Rights establishes in its Article 14 the right of reply and rectification, which provides the procedure by which a person harmed by inexact or offensive disclosures may answer through the same means. In a consultive opinion of August 29, 1986, the Inter-American Court of Human Rights held that the obligations contained in the treaty are binding, and that if the member States do not guarantee the right of reply and rectification they are violating the Convention.[41] However, in *Costa*,[42] the Supreme Court held that the right in question is not incorporated in the Argentine legal system, because the law mentioned by the treaty was not enacted. With a bit more imagination, the Court could have devised ways of dealing with cases in which the State is not complying with its international obligations.

In sum, the Supreme Court and in fact the judicial system as a whole, fell short during most of Argentina's history of realizing its responsibility as custodian of the democratic system. A possible hypothesis for this failure is that most of the time the Court was appointed by the government of the day (the military regimes appointed their own judges and the civilian governments ignored those appointments), and, therefore, was too dependent to have the necessary legitimacy to hinder the endeavours of the incumbent government, or to be respected as an impartial arbiter of the political process.

### B. *The Argentine Supreme Court as Custodian of Personal Autonomy*

The task of guarding personal autonomy through judicial review, as imposed by the limitation of the epistemic value of democracy to intersubjective moral issues, is greatly facilitated by the fact that the Constitution contains an exceptional clause. In effect, all the projects and Constitutions of the country, beginning with the one of 1815 (and suggested by a Jesuit priest), included a clause that in the words of Article 19 of the Constitution in force reads: "Private actions that do not offend public morals and orders, nor harm third parties, are only reserved to God and are exempt from the authority of magistrates."[43] There are two interpretations of this clause: a narrow one, which assumes that each description of the protected actions is independent from the other and construes "public morals" as referring to the dominant morality, whatever its contents; and a broad interpretation, which presupposes that the descriptions "private actions," "actions that do not offend public morals and order," and "actions that do not harm third parties," are all equivalent because private actions are those that do not offend public morality, and public morality deals with the harm to people other than the agent. The historical background (the fact that the norm was inspired by Articles 4 and 5 of the French Declaration of Rights of Man, and that at the last moment the phrasing was changed so that public qualifies both "morals" and "order"), favors the broad interpretation. Moreover, this interpretation provides a magnificent opportunity for the Constitution to endorse the so-called "principle of Mill," which is a derivation of the principle of personal autonomy.[44] This allows the courts to see that the democratic process does not overstep the ambit in which its decisions have epistemic value.

Some early decisions of the Supreme Court displayed the broad construction of Article 19; for instance, a decision in 1928 maintained that the norm protects the internal forum of consciousness.[45] However, the Court and other tribunals generally adopted the narrow interpretation, leading to perfectionist decisions; that is, decisions which assume that the State's mission is to make people conform to what it deems to be virtuous ways of life.[46] For example, in the decision of *Ibarra v. Zoria*,[47] the Court maintained that the Constitution protects only the intimate sphere of the person, and that the State may interfere with an action that has a communitarian projection, even though it does not cause harm to third parties.

Another significant issue related to personal autonomy is the criminalization of drug possession. In 1974 Congress enacted law 20.771, which in its Article 6 made punishable the possession of drugs for personal use. This norm was the object of different judicial reactions until March 1978, when the Supreme Court decided in *Colavini, Airel O.*,[48] that the statute was constitutional on the basis that the possession of drugs is "vicious" conduct, leading to criminal activity, moral and economic harm, and the destruction of the family; therefore, any activity directed at containing such risks is proper.

This doctrine held sway during the whole period of the last military government. But the view changed radically after the re-establishment of democracy in December 1983, until President Menem expanded the Court. A decision of enormous transcendence in this respect is *Bazterrica*.[49] The opinion of Justices Bacqut and Petracchi explicitly adopted the broad interpretation of Article 19. Justice Patracchi said that this period in the evolution of the country is an excellent opportunity to reconstruct the constitutional practice according to democratic and republican principles. He held that

> [P]rivate actions of men must be understood to mean those that do not interfere with legitimate actions of third parties, that do not harm others, or do not injure feelings or evaluations shared by a set of people, and in whose protection the whole community is interested. There is thus a series of actions which only concern a "private morality," which is the sphere of value judgments that relate to one's own acts and do not interfere with the set of values and moral rules shared by a group or community, . . . The recognition of an exclusive ambit in the behavior of men, reserved to each person and only subject to his occupation, that our Constitution consecrated since early times . . . is thus essential for guaranteeing the equilibrium between an increasingly omnipresent State and individuals who are increasingly dependent on the legal norms of their organized society. . . .[50]

Consequently, the law punishing the possession of drugs was declared unconstitutional.

On the same day the Court analogously decided the similar case *Capalbo*;[51] but in this decision Justice Fayt and Caballero expanded their dissent, based on Congress' power to define crimes of "abstract risks," which are in turn based on the legislator's presumption that there is harm to third parties, even when there is no concrete evidence of such harms. I think that this sort of legislation is unconstitutional because it invades the judiciary's nondelegable function to determine the true facts in the actual case.[52]

The majority of the Supreme Court applied the same doctrine to other kinds of cases during Alfonsín's presidency. An extremely important issue was that of divorce: the prohibition against divorce was included in the law of civil marriage enacted at the beginning of the century, but divorce and re-marriage remained a fact in society. During his campaign, Alfonsín's opponents pressed him to take a stand on the issue in order to put him in conflict with the Catholic Church. In response, he declared that he would neither propose nor veto a law of divorce. With the installation of the new Congress, deputies of the Radical Party presented a divorce project which the House approved. But the Senate, dominated by the Peronists, struck down the project during the ordinary period so as to oblige Alfonsín to include the project in the extraordinary sessions in which only projects presented by the Administration may be discussed. This created a stalemate.

The Supreme Court intervened with the extraordinary decision in *Sejean*,[53] where it declared the old law prohibiting divorce unconstitutional. This allowed the Administration to include the project, because a situation of grave legal uncertainty had been created when many lower courts ignored the Supreme Court. In *Sejean*, Justice Bacque, speaking for the majority of the Court, said that the Court recognized "that the National Constitution ensures all of the country's inhabitants the right to choose their personal plan of life, insofar as it does not harm third parties or offend public morality."[54] The Court distinguished between private ethics, where transgressions are reserved by the Constitution to the judgment of God, and collective ethics, where the rights of third parties are protected by courts.

Starting in 1990, the Court once again turned to a perfectionist stand. In August of 1990, the Federal Court in Criminal issues of Buenos Aires decided *Quesada*,[55] where crimes of abstract risks were held to be constitutional. The Court based its rationale on the authoritarian law 20.771, and reasoned that the possession of drugs should be punishable because the consumer and the drug-trafficker form a peculiar and harmful symbiosis. The Supreme Court subsequently decided *Montalvo*.[56] In that case, the majority of the Court upheld the contested statute on the grounds that it regulated a crime of abstract risk. The Court consequently found no obligation to prove that the harm ensued from the deed, and stated that such conduct was contagious and endangered all of humanity.

However, the newly integrated Court's decision in *Comunidad Homosexual Argentina*,[57] was even worse. In that case, an office of the Executive branch refused to grant legal personality to an association of homosexuals.

This denial was upheld as constitutional by the Court of Civil Appeals of Buenos Aires in its decision of December 7, 1990, on the basis that the Administration properly judged that homosexuality does not benefit the common good since it is against Christian ethics. The majority of the Court joined by all the Justices appointed by President Menem, used different rationales in affirming the decision of the lower tribunals. Justice Boggiano openly expressed the perfectionist view of the state, maintaining that the Court would not advocate the association's goal of protecting homosexuals from discrimination, because such advocacy could be interpreted as a public defense of that condition. He added that if the purpose of the statute of the Comunidad Homosexual Argentina was to allow ethical indifference and even approval of the homosexual condition, then it would subvert certain moral conceptions and would even accord homosexuals the protection of certain religions. Finally, he stated that a tolerated minority always requires a tolerant majority. However, "a situation may arise where so many minorities demand to be tolerated that there can be no majority at all. Democracy must be sustained by common values. The disintegration of these values may lead to the erosion of society, which is indispensable for government."[58] This opinion contains a gross misinterpretation of liberal democracy and deals solely with impersonal and social values, rather than with self-referring ones. Justice Boggiano ignores that the majority opinion is only as valid as individual opinion in evaluating the impact of actions on the life and character of the agent. Justices Fayt and Petracchi dissented, and the opinion of the latter is an enlightened statement of the implications of a liberal conception of society.

Therefore, we must conclude that the Supreme Court of Argentina and the other tribunals have been inconsistent over time both in defending personal autonomy and in protecting and promoting the democratic process. In both cases, the doctrine of the courts underwent deep oscillations in short stretches of time. These oscillations reflect the political backgrounds of their members, and show the instability of the Court's integration.

## C. The Argentine Supreme Court as Custodian of the Rule of Law

The role of the courts in preserving the continuity of legal and constitutional practice is conceptually different from that of protecting and promoting the democratic process, but these roles are considerably intertwined when the legal and constitutional convention endorses democratic mechanisms of discussion and decision. For example, when the Argentine Supreme Court undermined the democratic process by recognizing the validity of the laws enacted by authoritarian regimes, it showed a lack of concern both for the continuity of the rule of law and for the legal practice that evolved around the Constitution enacted in 1853-60. And yet the Court managed to be the only successful foundation of a more or less continuous legal practice, or at least of a recurrent aspiration of society to have such a practice. Notwithstanding the attempts to establish a different constitutional practice at times such as 1930, 1949, 1956, and 1972, society once again pressed to return to the old text of the middle of the past century as the only basis upon which the cooperation of different sectors seemed to be possible. Despite the overlapping between the requirements for maintaining the conventions grounded in that document and those for protecting democracy, in this section I shall concentrate on aspects of the process which have more to do with the stability of the political system than with its epistemic value.[59] I proceed by discussing the Court's attempts to oppose the Constitution by transgressing explicit constitutional text. These attempts disrupt the equilibrium between political and social forces whose stability and continuity depend upon that text.

One dimension of this disruptive action has to do with the balance between the powers of the State. I have argued elsewhere[60] that the formation of Argentine hyper-presidentialism -- which implied the transference of power from the provinces, Congress, and the judiciary to the Federal Executive -- has contributed to undermining the stability of the constitutional system. This is so because hyper-presidentialism implies, first, a personalization of power, an aspect of which is the reflection of all the weaknesses which may affect an individual (physical or psychological illnesses, involvement in scandals, downfall in the favor and trust of the people) on the institutional framework. Second, hyper-presidentialism leads to a great rigidity for reflecting changes in social consensus in the main center of power, so that there is no possibility of adapting that center and its policies to the changes in public opinion, and there is no escape valve when a critical situation arises. Third, this system of government, as Juan Linz has remarked,[61] has the dynamic of a "zero-sum game," because the power is concentrated in a unipersonal entity which cannot be divided among the political contenders. Consequently, a savage pugnacity among the parties normally ensues, particularly when parties are strongly disciplined and there is proportional representation, which causes blockages between the powers of the state, the submission of the Legislature to the Executive, and the refusal to form big coalitions, even in situations of deep crisis.

Though the formation of the Argentine hyper-presidentialism is caused by different factors -- which includes the impact of the organization adopted during the military regimes once the democratic system was re-established -- the judiciary, headed by the Supreme Court, contributed much to it. From a very early time the Supreme Court has acquiesced in the expansion of the Executive's power. For instance, in *Seste y Seguich c/Gobierno*

*Nacional,*[62] the Court decided that the Executive Power could not be the object of a legal claim, because the Judicial Power had no authority to make it obey. In *Montana,*[63] the Court decided that the Judicial Power had no jurisdiction over someone who was detained by the Administration's agents and was accused of the assassination of former President Urquiza. The Court in *Merk*[64] endorsed a presidential decree to appropriate a German pharmaceutical laboratory on the bizarre ground that this appropriation was justified by the grave necessity created by war. In fact, this was done when the war had already ended, and when there were never any real hostilities between the country and the Axis.

As discussed above, the doctrine of political questions was enormously expanded to cover judicial discretion regarding the enactment and application of the state of siege, which had been a true cemetery of the freedom of the Argentine people. Moreover, the Executive Power used this doctrine to justify the broadest application of its Constitutional authority to enact the state of siege doctrine during the long period when Congress is in recess. The same thing happened with the power to replace governments of provinces, which risks both social peace and republican institutions. The Constitution has an obvious omission because, in Article 6, it ascribes this power to the federal government without establishing which branch should properly apply it.[65] Initially, federal interventions were done by Congress, except when it was in recess; then they were performed by the Executive Power, communicating the act to Congress in case it wanted to revise it; finally, even this last requirement was forgotten.

The Supreme Court also permitted the delegation of legislative powers to the Administration, and thereby created a new channel to absolve administrative action. Although the Court prohibited this delegation in *Delfino,*[66] it used certain criteria to distinguish delegation from enactment, and recognized the Executive Power's authority to apply the law. The Court interpreted these criteria in a manner favorable to the Administration. In *Gabino,*[67] for example, the Supreme Court upheld the constitutionality of laws against speculation, which delegated to the Administration the power to fix maximum prices; and in *De Angelis,*[68] the Court upheld the constitutionality of the law of fiscal proceedings, which delegated to the Direccion General Impositiva (General Taxing Agency) the power to enact general rules to determine responsibility for paying taxes. On the basis of this permissive doctrine, a broad practice was established regarding the delegation of legislative authority to the Administration.

The Executive power over Congress is also advanced by the veto process, which allows it to veto partially a Congressional bill and then promulgate the unobjectionable part, allowing the Executive Branch to shape new

laws out of pieces of Congressional bills. The Supreme Court declared this
procedure unconstitutional in *Colella c/Febre y Basset*,[69] but the courts
eventually allowed this practice because of the enthusiasm with which the
Administration continued resorting to it.

The Supreme Court has permitted the greatest expansion of Executive
power through the doctrine that allows the Administration to enact decrees
in situations of "necessity and urgency," which has been interpreted to allow
almost any Executive proposal. Over the years, beginning at the turn of the
century with President Roca, there has been an increasing deployment of
this supposed authorization. There was some use of this doctrine during
President Alfonsín's government, such as the enactments of the Austral plan
-- which even changed the currency -- and a "forced savings" plan, but this
power was never used more extensively than during the present administration. President Menem confiscated bank deposits by decree and converted
them into state bonds; he also extended the law of economic emergency,
regulated the constitutional right of strike that was, according to the
Constitution, only properly regulated by legislation, and deregulated the
economy by abrogating dozens of laws. A case in which the Supreme
Court, as expanded by President Menem, upheld the constitutionality of
these decrees was *Peralta*.[70] In that case, the Court upheld presidential
decrees that converted bank deposits into state bonds, thereby permitting the
infringement of the owner's property rights, and even implying that
Congress is an inefficient institution for dealing with serious issues.

*Peralta* leads us to the final topic regarding the Court's responsibility to
protect the continuity of a morally justifiable legal practice against factors
which may destabilize the political system upon which that practice depends.
In previous works[71] I noted the temporal coincidence between the enormous expansion of real political participation in the country -- with the introduction in 1912, and the first application in 1916, of the law of secret,
universal, and obligatory voting which tripled electoral participation -- and
the beginning (since 1930) of a long period of political instability. This
suggested the hypothesis that the incorporation of popular sectors into the
electorate resulted in clean and unrestricted elections which were won by
conservative parties that alternated peacefully in power; therefore the privileged sectors sought other ways to have access to power. Fred Riggs
completed this hypothesis[72] with the idea that under presidentialism, electoral apathy is functional for the stability of the democratic system, since a
broad participation makes it more difficult for presidential candidates to
form wide coalitions of different interests and ideologies (inducing them to
being as vague as possible in their proposals), and exhibits the zero-sum
dynamics of the political confrontation.

At this point, I want to add to my hypothesis the fact that the ensuing instability after the expansion of electoral participation was favored by the fact that, unlike what happened in the United States during the so-called *"Lochner* era," the Supreme Court was weak in Argentina in protecting the right of property while the political gates were being opened. Possibly, in many stable democracies, the expansion of political participation was neutralized by entrenching the vested interests of dominant groups, notably the existence of an independent, and quite conservative judiciary charged with applying a Constitution with a paramount right of property. In Argentina this failed: at the same time that the popular sector of the electorate began to participate intensely and to press for social reforms, the Court acquiesced to these reforms.

For example, under the government of the Radical President Hipolito Yrigoyen, the Supreme Court headed by the former conservative President Figueroa Alcorta upheld the constitutionality of some progressive measures. For instance, in the famous case *Ercolano c/Lanteri Renshaw*,[73] the constitutionality of a law freezing housing rents for two years was disputed. The majority of the Court upheld the law's constitutionality, maintaining:

> Neither the right of using and disposing property, nor any other right is absolute. The conception of an unlimited right would be antisocial. The need to regulate and limit individual rights derives from the requirements of social coexistence. . . . The law's intervention is based not only on reasons of humanity and social justice, but also on the community's direct interest, since it is obvious that an afflictive situation of most of the population must have an unfavorable impact on the general economy. . . .[74]

Justice Bermejo dissented on the basis of the untouchability of the right of property and that this sort of measure was an abuse of the police power that could lead to State communism. Later on, in *Cornu c/Ronco*,[75] the Court admitted that the terms of the rental contract could be changed by law.

It is true that this doctrine was later limited.[76] But, on the whole, the courts were acquiescent to the expansive social policies of the successive governments, and a sort of circular process ensued: the democratic system was assaulted by those who felt that their interests would be better protected outside of it, and, as a result, courts became unstable and overlooked constitutional rules, giving even less security to the established powers.

Adam Przeworski[77] may help explain this phenomenon when he says that

> [D]emocracy is consolidated when it becomes self-enforcing, that is, when all the relevant political forces find it best to continue to submit their

interests and values to the uncertain interplay of institutions. Complying with the current outcomes even if it is a defeat, and directing all actions within the institutional framework, is better for the relevant political forces than trying to subvert democracy. To put it somewhat more technically, democracy is consolidated when compliance acting within the institutional framework constitutes the equilibrium of the decentralized strategies of all the relevant political forces.[78]

He adds that compliance depends on the probability that winning the political competition will be greater than some minimum,[79] and putting it conversely, this implies that "if some important political forces have no chance to win distributional conflicts . . . they will turn against it;"[80] "democratic institutions . . . must give all the relevant political forces the chance to win from time to time in the competition of interests and values."[81]

It is possible that what has happened in Argentina is that, when popular participation in elections was achieved, there were no political or judicial mechanisms to ensure the dominant economic groups that their basic interests would be protected against the strong pressures for social reforms processed through the democratic process. These groups lost any expectation to have a chance of winning again a substantial part of the political power, and their strategies turned to the subversion of the democratic system, which offered them greater gains. The judiciary was an actor in this dynamic, since, for better or for worse, it followed the policies decided through the democratic process, without trying to resist it, unlike what happened in the United States during the "*Lochner* era."

The dynamics of power which evolved in Argentina between 1930 and 1983 may also be analyzed by resorting to the structures of interaction unearthed by the theory of games. For instance, E. Ullman Margalit[82] describes the situation that arises between two or more parties when one of them pretends to maintain a status quo of inequality for its own benefit. Among the variety of situations in which this may take place, there is one where, in a second alternative state of affairs, the inequality is reduced, but the party who benefitted from the greater inequality in the first situation may threaten to move to a third alternative, in which the other party is still worse than in the first if he attempts to move to the second one. This latter party may have no other way than to attempt to move to a fourth alternative state of affairs in which he is even worse off than in the first, and of course than in the second, but better than in the third.

This is represented in figure 1. Each square identified with the cardinal points stipulates the utilities that each party obtains (the number to the right corresponds to A, and the left to B). In it B, in order to preserve his best option, which is that of the NW square, and to avoid moving to the best option of A, which is that of the NE square, threatens A with moving to his second option which is the worst for A, that is the option of the SE square. That obliges A to move West. If B would have precommitted himself to move to the South, in case of which A attempted to move to the West, both of them would end up being worse than they were at the beginning or than they would be if B would have accepted moving to the situation of greater equality towards A.

Figure 1:

```
         NW        A        NE
       ┌──────────────────────┐
       │  10/3    │   6/4     │
    B  │          │           │
       ├──────────┼───────────┤
       │  8/1     │   5/2     │
       └──────────────────────┘
         SW                 SE
```

In the case of the situation described with regard to Argentina, we might say that the situation before the application of the law of universal, secret, and obligatory ballot in 1916 was that of a restricted democracy; that the application of that law provoked a change toward almost a full liberal democracy; that the displaced conservative groups reacted mainly since 1930 and during the so-called "infamous decade" -- from 1932 to 1943 -- producing a movement towards authoritarian regimes which involved a highly unequal representation of the diverse sectors. However, all the sectors, even the dominant economic and social groups, suffered a loss of representation in comparison to the situation of the restricted democracy. After 1945, the popular sectors reacted, achieving a populist democracy which insured them better representation than they had in either the authoritarian regimes or in the situation of restricted democracy, but that was worse than that of full liberal democracy. From 1955 to 1983, there was a permanent oscillation between authoritarian regimes, restricted democracies, and populist democracies, and the most serious attempt to re-establish a full liberal democracy has only been carried out since 1983.

This dynamic of the political forces in Argentina may be represented again with a matrix, that of figure 2: "CS" represents the conservative sectors, "PS" the popular sectors, "RD" restricted democracy, "LD" liberal democracy, "MR" the military regimes, and "PD" populist democracy, while the numbers represent the hypothetical intensity of the preferences, which coincide with the abstract case represented in the previous matrix. We could say that the status quo of political representation until 1916 was located in the NW square; that the application of the law of universal suffrage and some other subsequent measures, such as the federal interventions of Yrigoyen, provoked a radical change towards the NE square; that the displaced conservative groups reacted since 1930, provoking a movement to the SW square, which implied a highly unequal representation of the diverse sectors, but of inferior quality with regard to all of them; that in 1945 there was a reaction of the popular sector, with a movement to the SE square, improving their representation but worsening the representation of all in comparison to the situation of full democracy; that between 1955 and 1983, the results of the political struggle implied a continuous oscillation between the NE, SE, and SW squares, and that only after 1983 has there been a serious attempt to achieve an equilibrium in the NW square. Perhaps a smoother transition from a restricted democracy to a full democracy, by replacing fraud with judicial guarantees, would have been a more efficient result, taking into account the interests of all the parties concerned.

Figure 2:

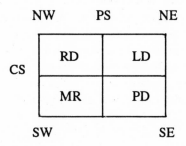

Perhaps the courts might have helped to achieve this most efficient solution from 1916 onwards, if they would have been independent enough of the political forces to give the losing but economically dominant groups the impression that their basic interests were protected. Perhaps this was impossible, given the unwillingness of these groups to relinquish some of their privileges so as to achieve social peace and a stable regime. In any event, with regard to this aspect of the court's function to preserve the existing legal practice, I am not formulating normative but explanatory hypotheses. Even when decisions like *Ercolano*[83] were risky for the preservation of the existing legal practice, perhaps they have been the right decisions from the moral point of view, and often justice cannot be materialized without undertaking some risks.

The only critical point that I dare to make with regard to this aspect of the exercise of judicial review is one that connects with the evaluative judgments made about the tasks that legitimize judicial power: the Argentine judiciary headed by the Supreme Court, even when reaching, from time to time, some good decisions in the exercise of judicial review, was more influenced by the ideological climate of the day and by the pressures of the dominant powers, than by the conscious assumption of its triple role as custodian of democracy, personal autonomy, and the existing legal practice.

## Notes

[1] I have already developed this theory in other papers and books. *See* CARLOS S. NINO, FUNDAMENTOS DE DERECHO CONSTITUCIONAL (1992); CARLOS S. NINO, THE COMPLEX CONSTITUTION (forthcoming 1993).

[2] The majoritarian view of democracy arises where the majority opinion is binding, after all the people concerned have had a full discussion and reached a collective decision. Counter-majoritarianism is moral epistemic elitism, where some people, who are not directly responsible to those whose interests are at stake, decide that they are better than the majority in determining impartial rules.

[3] I develop this view more fully in CARLOS S. NINO, THE ETHICS OF HUMAN RIGHTS (1991), chapter 7, and Carlos S. Nino, *The Epistemological Moral Relevance of Democracy*, 4 RATIO JURIS 36 (1991).

[4] Translation: Truth, not authority, makes law.

[5] *See* NINO, THE COMPLEX CONSTITUTION, *supra* note 1.

[6] *See* RONALD DWORKIN, TAKING RIGHTS SERIOUSLY (1977).

[7] *See* BRUCE A. ACKERMAN, WE THE PEOPLE (1991).

[8] *See* JOHN H. ELY, DEMOCRACY AND DISTRUST (1980).

[9] *See, generally*, LAURENCE TRIBE, AMERICAN CONSTITUTIONAL LAW 1062-1153 (2d ed. 1988).

[10] 347 U.S. 483 (1954).

[11] For further discussion on this point, see THE ETHICS OF HUMAN RIGHTS, *supra* note 3, chapter 5. Additionally, attempts to impose those ideals with the coercive or facilitating force of the law are usually self-defeating because these ideals, unlike intersubjective standards, cannot be satisfied if they are not spontaneously adopted.

[12] 381 U.S. 479 (1965).

[13] 478 U.S. 186 (1986).

[14] For a further overview on this point, see generally NINO, *supra* note 1.

[15] There is an early statute, number 48 of 1863, 49 (R.N. 1863-1869)(Arg.), which recognizes and regulates the power of judicial review on the part of the Supreme Court, but the constitutionality of this statute is itself contestable.

[16] 1 Fallos 36 (1863).

[17] 1 Fallos 345 (1864).

[18] 32 Fallos 125 (1887).

[19]5 U.S. (1 Cranch) 137 (1803).

[20]33 Fallos 162, 194 (1888).

[21]*Id.* at 194.

[22]*Id.* at 194.

[23]2 Fallos 127 (1865).

[24]*Id.*

[25]208 Fallos 185 (1947).

[26]209 Fallos 26 (1948).

[27]*Id.* at 27.

[28]Carlos S. Nino, *Una Nueva Estrategia para el Tratamiento de las Normas De Facto*, D LA LEY [L.L.] 935 (1983).

[29]306 Fallos 73 (1984).

[30]306 Fallos 175 (1984).

[31][1991-C] L.L. 390 (1991).

[32]97 L.L. 525 (1960).

[33][1986-B] L.L. 184 (1986).

[34]287 Fallos 31 (1973).

[35][1987-C] L.L. 245 (1987).

[36]33 Causa CCCL III, 54 Fallos 432, 433 (1893).

[37]167 Fallos 145 (1933).

[38]*Id.*

[39]142 Fallos 80 (1924).

[40]277 Fallos 63 (1970).

[41]Inter-Am. Ct. H.R. (ser. A) No. 7 (1986) (advisory opinion on Enforceability of the Right to Reply or Correction).

[42]196 Fallos 249 (1943).

[43]CONST. ARG. art. 19 (Arg.).

[44]*See* Nino, THE ETHICS OF HUMAN RIGHTS, *supra* note 3, chapter 5.

[45]153 Fallos 331 (1928).

[46]*See* GEORGE F. WILL, STATECRAFT AS SOULSCRAFT (1983).

[47]296 Fallos 15 (1976).

[48]300 Fallos 254 (1978).

[49]308 Fallos 1392 (1986).

[50]*Id.* at 1398, 1432.

[51]308 Fallos 1392 (1986).

[52]As I argued above, the epistemic value of the democratic process extends neither to ideals of personal excellence nor to factual issues.

[53]121 E.D. 522 (1987).

[54]*Id.* at 536.

[55]Quesada, Ignacio Juan s/estupefacientes, Cámara Nacional Federal Criminal y Correcional, Sala D (a/c Drs. Casanovas y Michel) Official Records, Aug. 1, 1990 (Arg.).

[56][1991-C] L.L. 80 (1991).

[57][1991-E] L.L. 679 (1991).

[58]*Id.* at 700.

[59]Of course, any departure from the conventional interpretation of the text adopted in 1853/60, which is the salient factor allowing the coordination of political action, undermines the continuity of the Argentine legal and constitutional practice. This applies to situations like the disregard for the prescription, repeated three times in the Constitution and never complied with, that criminal trials should be conducted with juries.

[60]*See* FUNDAMENTOS DE DERECHO CONSTITUCIONAL, *supra* note 1, chapter 14.

[61]*See* Fred Riggs, *Presidentialism v. Parliamentarism,* CONSEJO PARA LA CONSOLIDACIÓN DE LA DEMOCRACIA (1987).

[62]1 Fallos 387 (1864).

[63]9 Fallos 387 (1870).

[64]211 Fallos 193 (1945).

[65]There is, however, a reserve clause in article 67 inc. 28, by which Congress is given all the powers assigned to the federal government.

[66]148 Fallos 430 (1927).

[67]243 Fallos 276 (1958).

[68]304 Fallos 438 (1982).

[69]268 Fallos 352 (1967).

[70][1991-C] L.L. 158 (1991).

[71]*See, e.g.,* CARLOS S. NINO, FUNDAMENTOS DE DERECHO CONSTITUCIONAL (1992).

[72]Fred Riggs, Address at the International Conference of Political Science, (1991). [It took place in Buenos Aires.]

[73]136 Fallos 161 (1922).

[74]*Id.* at 171.

[75]142 Fallos 80 (1924).

[76]In *Horta c/Harguindeguy,* 136 Fallos 59 (1922), the Court refused to allow retroactive application of the freeze on rent prices, and in *Mango c/Traba,* 144 Fallos 220 (1925), the Court rejected its application to cases which had already been judicially decided.

[77]*See* ADAM PRZEWORSKI, DEMOCRACY AND THE MARKET: POLITICAL AND ECONOMIC REFORMS IN EASTERN EUROPE AND LATIN AMERICA 26 (1991).

[78]*Id.*

[79]*Id.*

[80]*Id.* at 32.

[81]*Id.* at 33.

[82]*See* E. ULLMAN MARGALIT, THE EMERGENCE OF NORMS (1977).

[83]136 Fallos 161 (1922).

# 22

# The Role of the Judiciary in the Review of Human Rights Violations in Argentina

## *Eduardo Rabossi*

On December 13, 1983 -- only three days after assuming the Presidency -- Raúl Alfonsín addressed the Argentine nation with an important message. He announced that there would be legal action taken against the officials of the military government who committed massive human rights violations between 1976 and 1983. Alfonsín's policy was atypical in comparison to international standards because the policy was not the outcome of a deal with the Armed Forces, the political parties, or influential corporations; it was a political decision made by Alfonsín himself and his political party.[1] The policy excluded the possibility of "exception" laws or courts: the policy was to be implemented by constitutional courts, using ordinary procedures, and abiding strictly to the due process of law. This policy's target was terrorism, both lay and state; that is, the policy was directed against all persons who had affected human dignity in their systematic use of indiscriminate violence. In the case of state terrorism, the policy placed the responsibility for human rights violations on commanding officers (allowing for the use of the due obedience exception for lower ranking officials). Thus the policy charged the Armed Forces itself with "institutional" responsibility. Its expected outcome was not to be assessed on mere retributionist grounds, but according to consequentialist criteria and was supposed to strengthen democratic institutions and, in particular, enhance the positive evaluation of the rule of law.

The judiciary was given a leading role in the enforcement of the policy. Indeed, the point did not pass unnoticed in Alfonsín's speech. Its opening and closing paragraphs were explicit in that respect: The democratic government has "a firm decision to re-establish the rule of law in Argentina." "The magistrates will allocate responsibilities. This will show that our only aim is an ethical one: to have Justice definitely realized in our republic."[2]

A policy of such vast design and important consequences necessarily involves a number of influential actors, is subjected to countless strains, and may be assessed on disparate grounds. It is, indeed, a large field for inquiry. In this chapter, I will select from such a large field a rather narrow problem. I will analyze: (1) the precise role that the policy assigned to the courts; (2) the judiciary's actual response; and (3) the factors that were influential in such a response. My aim is to describe and to evaluate this aspect of the Argentine experience on the judicial review of human rights violations.

However, I have a larger aim in mind. Democratic transitions are difficult processes in which the judiciary plays an essential role. The attitude and the decisions of the judges have a decisive influence in the shaping of democratic values and in the establishment of legal and ethical criteria for the community at large. But, how does one encourage a judiciary to meet the proper standards of review of human rights violations so that professional ethics and a balanced frame of mind coexist with strong democratic views? How does one break the influence of years of constitutional illegitimacy in the minds of those who are supposed to consider legitimacy as their *raison d'etre*? How does one set up an equitable process for the selection of nominees and what procedures should be followed for confirmation? These are vexing questions that confront democratic transitions. I do not, however, directly address them in this paper. Nevertheless, my remarks about the role of the judiciary in the review of human rights violations in Argentina may be taken as a case-study obviously relevant to all of these questions.

## I.
## Preparations for the Trial of the Generals

To assign the courts a neat, consistent, and effective role, on strictly legal grounds, was not an easy task. There were many hurdles to successful prosecution. First, in April 1982, the Military Junta passed a law (the "Amnesty Law") granting amnesty to the military personnel possibly involved in the commission of criminal offenses in the context of antisubversive actions.[3] Amnesty was also granted to lay terrorists. The legal consequence of such a law was clear: even if the Constitutional Congress abrogated the law in the future, the terrorists sentenced by the courts would have recourse to amnesty under the principle of "the more benign law."[4] Second, the secrecy and methods characteristic of terrorism in general, and state terrorism in particular, made the gathering of evidence by the courts a Herculean task that would take years to fulfill. A data bank was needed to assemble the information on the identity of the disappeared, the location of clandestine detention centers, the testimonies of persons illegally detained, and the design and systematic features of state terrorism. Third, according to the Argentine Military Code, the military courts had jurisdiction over the criminal offenses (military and non-military) committed by its personnel.[5] Such courts were the "natural judges" at the time of the commission of the offense. Civil courts were simply not recognized as competent on matters concerning military personnel. So, in principle at least, a would-be investigation of the deeds of the military would be exclusively in their own hands.

Alfonsín's government removed these hurdles to prosecution in the following ways. First, at the initiative of the President, the Congress passed a law nullifying Law 22.924;[6] that is, the Congress did not abrogate the Amnesty Law but declared it void and thus without legal consequences. The main argument was moral: the *de facto* authorities exempted *themselves* from legal responsibilities. Thus, they had produced a self-amnesty which affected an elementary ethical principle concerning the exercise of power.

Second, the President created a blue-ribbon commission -- the National Commission on the Disappeared (CONADEP) -- to inquire about the fate of the *desaparecidos* (the disappeared), to gather relevant data and to produce a report to the President. After nine months of exhausting work, CONADEP produced a list of almost nine thousand *desaparecidos*, located a number of clandestine detention centers, and somehow assembled the puzzle of state terrorism. CONADEP produced a long report to the President, edited afterwards as *Nunca Más*.[7] In September 1984, the President created the Undersecretariat for Human Rights to follow up on the work of CONADEP. For purposes of this essay, it is important to point out that by December 1985, and in the early months of 1986, the Undersecretariat for Human Rights had presented to the Supreme Council of the Armed Forces and the Federal Courts all of the testimonies it gathered concerning disappearances and the lists of military personnel possibly involved in those disappearances.

Third, again at the initiative of the President, the Congress passed a law modifying the Military Code.[8] This law asserted the right of the accused to be tried by his "natural judge," but stated that the particular Federal Court of Appeal with jurisdiction over the place where the offense was committed was entitled to review the decisions of the military court. Six months after beginning the inquiries, the Supreme Council of the Armed Forces -- to which the original jurisdiction for these crimes was recognized -- had to report its progress to the appropriate Federal Court of Appeal. The Federal Court of Appeal could grant extensions or assume jurisdiction over the case. The law also established, as a general principle, that the courts may presume the innocence of low ranking culprits under the due obedience principle.[9]

The year of 1984 was, indeed, a busy one. In spite of various difficulties faced by the new democratic government, the President and the Congress did a very good job in these matters. In less than one year the field was ready for the neat, consistent, and effective work of the courts. How did the courts fare?

## II.
## The Trial of the Generals

From the very beginning, the Supreme Council of the Armed Forces was a source of difficulty. Nominating its members was a complicated affair. High ranking officers were reluctant to investigate the deeds of their comrades. When nominated, they formally expressed their reluctance. The Supreme Council of the Armed Forces concluded that in the "war against subversion" the Armed Forces had abided strictly by internal ordinances and operative planning, and that they found nothing irregular in the contents of or in the way in which the Armed Forces had carried out its orders.

It is true, of course, that the President and the Congress anticipated such behavior. The reform of the Military Code granting the Federal Courts of Appeal the authority to monitor the Supreme Council of the Armed Forces and, eventually, to assume its jurisdictional powers, was motivated in part by the necessity of preventing such behavior. But it is also true that most civil authorities expected that at least the most aberrant behavior would be the object of some exemplary punishment. The stone-like attitude of the Supreme Council of the Armed Forces reflected the attitude of the Armed Forces, an attitude that persists even today -- an attitude unacceptable in a democratic society.

What about the Federal Courts of Appeal? In October 1984, the Federal Court of Appeal of Buenos Aires decided to take jurisdiction from the Supreme Council of the Armed Forces. Thus, the trial of the members of the Juntas fell into the appellate court's hands. The trial started on April 22, 1985, after some preliminary hearings and procedural decisions. On December 9, 1985, the Federal Court sentenced Lieutenant General Jorge Rafael Videla, President and Army Commander from March 1976 to March 1981, and Admiral Emilio Massera, Navy Commander from March 1976 to March 1981, to life in prison. Lieutenant General Roberto Viola, President and Army Commander from March 1981 to December 1981, Admiral Armando Lambruschini, Navy Commander from March 1981 to December 1981, and Brigadier Orlando Agosti, Air Force Commander from March 1976 to March 1981 were sentenced to seventeen, eight, and four years in prison, respectively. The appellate court absolved the remainder of the members of the Junta.[10]

Once it completed the trial of the members of the Junta, the Federal Court of Appeals of Buenos Aires tried the military and the police personnel of the First Army involved in state terrorism, and the navy personnel that manned a most daunting clandestine detention center: the so-called ESMA.[11]

The performance of the court was nearly perfect. Its judges acted with determination, consistency, effectiveness, and a permanent respect for the procedural forms of justice. Moreover, the substantive legal arguments displayed in sentencing the members of the Juntas met the very highest of international standards.

Unfortunately, the performance of the rest of the Federal Courts of Appeal for the provinces was very poor. They granted the Supreme Council of the Armed Forces successive extensions -- in spite of the fact that it did not carry out serious inquiries. Moreover, in the exercise of jurisdiction, these courts were reluctant to implement systematic inquiries leading to the trials of entire groups of military personnel, which was, of course, the only way of disentangling the plot behind state terrorism. The courts also refrained from taking advantage of the practical and legal consequences of the trial of the members of the Juntas in the Federal Court of Appeal of Buenos Aires insofar as it established the existence of state terrorism. Finally, some of the courts involved themselves in conflicts of interest that were additional sources of delay.

By 1986, it was obvious that the implementation of President Alfonsín's policy was unsatisfactory: the number of military personnel subjected to indictment was uncertain, the unrest in the Armed Forces increased, and the Federal Courts of Appeal remained in their low-profile patterns. The Minister of Defense instructed the General Prosecutor of the Supreme Council of the Armed Forces to reopen the cases and to apply the due obedience exception where applicable.[12] But the instruction was ineffective. Finally, at the initiative of the President, the Congress passed a law which gave the Federal Courts of Appeal sixty days to indict military personnel.[13] The law stated that criminal responsibilities were automatically extinguished in the case of non-indicted personnel.[14] The Federal Courts of Appeal engaged, then, in frantic activity. By the end of the sixty days, in April 1987, the courts indicted 139 officers, thirty of whom were still in active service.

But Law 23.492 did not settle the matter. The non-governmental organizations ("NGOs") and the political opposition saw the law as a setback, a sign of the government's weakness *vis-a-vis* the military. Within the Armed Forces the judgment was also negative, but for exactly the opposite reason:

the indictment of so many officers was taken as an attack against their institutional basis. This was, many argued, the real goal of Alfonsín's policy.

Over the Easter weekend in 1987, a small group of infantry officers asked for the removal of the Commander of the Army. They also asked to stop the judicial review of the "war against subversion." Although they were unable to engender much support, the President was also unable to control the mutiny in an effective and quick way. The situation deteriorated at an alarming pace.

In May 1987, at the initiative of the President, the Congress passed a law by which the due obedience exception was applied *jure et de jure* to the military personnel involved in the antisubversive actions, restricting criminal responsibility to high ranking officers in command.[15] As a consequence, only fifteen generals, two admirals, and a group of naval officers were liable to be tried and sentenced.

## III.

The policy inaugurated on December 13, 1983, no doubt deserves enthusiastic praise. It broke a long tradition of arbitrariness in Argentina, enhanced the value of the rule of law, and established -- at an international level -- a new model to deal with systematic human rights violations. But, on the other hand, it is a fact that the implementation of the policy was problematic. From 1986 on, it was subjected to strains culminating in the unwanted Due Obedience Law.[16]

What can be learned from this experience? One obvious point is this: a policy of such vast institutional and political consequences must be implemented within a certain span of time. To put it another way, the failure of timing was a major shortcoming of the Argentine policy on human rights violations. December 1986 was a proper deadline for the *final* allotment of responsibilities by the Federal Courts of Appeal. However, at that time, the Congress instead passed Law 23.492 to force the Federal Courts of Appeal to make a decision concerning the indictment of military personnel involved in state terrorism. All the actors involved in the implementation of the policy were responsible for such a failure. The Federal Courts of Appeal had a rather large share.

Why did the Federal Courts of Appeal fail to make full use of the legal instruments at hand? Alfonsín's government confirmed or promoted many of the judges to their positions. How can the asymmetry in the performance of the Federal Court of Appeal of Buenos Aires and that of the other Federal Courts of Appeal be explained? A possible answer is that almost without exception those judges confirmed or promoted by Alfonsín's government served under the military regimes. As such, the judges were related -- by action or by omission -- to the events they were supposed to investigate. It was naive, therefore, to expect a different performance. In the new democratic situation, the judges played the rule of law game, but the motivations and goals of the policy designed by the President were alien to them. Therefore, the wrong criteria were used to select and confirm the nominees to the Federal Courts of Appeal. This was a crucial mistake. Different nominees, selected on different criteria, would have performed in a very different way.

This answer deserves attention. First, it is true that almost without exception the judges of the Federal Courts of Appeal served under military regimes. Second, that fact does not seem to be sufficient to explain by itself the performance of the judges. "The Federal Court of Appeal of Buenos Aires was constituted by six judges none of whom became a judge as a consequence of the settling of the democratic government, although some of them were promoted by Alfonsín's Government."[17]

Third, the crucial issue then is not whether the judges served under the military regime, but whether they were prepared to make an ideological break with the past and to assume the advent of democracy as having the highest legal, political, and social value. The judicial review of human rights violations and, in particular, of state terrorism, was a good opportunity to determine whether such a break with the past was real or not. And most of the judges got low grades in passing the test.

If this brief argument is correct -- and I think it is -- the problem is transferred to the criteria for selecting nominees to the Federal Courts of Appeal, to the procedures used to confirm the nominees, and to the identification and availability of alternate candidates.

In the first place, as far as I know, no general criteria for selecting and confirming nominees to the Federal Courts of Appeal were actually applied. The nomination of Federal judges became a long and boring bargaining game between the Peronist Senators (the Senate majority) and the Radical Senators. Generally, Senators from the province in which the Federal Court of Appeal was located supported candidates for nominees to the Federal Courts of Appeal from their province. Thus, the potential nominee was usually born in the province or was related to the province through family or political ties. Potential nominees were supposed to be democratic souls, and I am sure that judicial review of human rights violations was not part of the criteria used in choosing nominees. This situation was also helped by the secrecy in which the Senate was allowed to deal with the nominations.

Second, the President did not draw a firm alternative strategy for the selection of nominees for judges for the Federal Courts of Appeal, nor did he have the possibility of imposing one: the Peronists practiced a strong and harsh opposition and their majority in the Senate gave them the power to condition a large number of necessary decisions in all fields. Bargaining was unavoidable.

In addition, the President made up and imposed his own criteria for the selection of candidates in Buenos Aires (the Federal District). The nominees to that Federal Court of Appeal were -- not by coincidence -- the judges of the only Federal Court of Appeal that applied Law 23.049 to the letter.

Finally, the method of identifying potential nominees was, with the exception of the Federal Court of Appeal of Buenos Aires, provincial and short-sighted. Obviously, it was not the only possible way to identify potential nominees. However, the question about alternative strategies was not easy to answer *at that very moment*. Low salaries prompted successful and well skilled lawyers to reject positions in the courts. Lawyers' associations were not exempted from having provincial views on the matter. And the lawyers who risked their lives assuming an active role before the courts during the military regime, were not, by necessity, prospective judges. So, alternative strategies to identify candidates for the judiciary were not addressed.

Marvin Frankel has said that judges cannot do much to make changes "unless those in command of the troops are prepared to move in a [certain] direction."[18] He is certainly correct, but with one proviso. The political decisions of those in "command" are always a necessary condition before judges can produce changes in exceptional situations. But they are not sufficient ones. The Argentine case is a clear example of such constraints: Those in constitutional command designed a policy concerning human rights violations, but the judiciary did not fare well -- to say the least -- in its implementation of that policy. To identify and enhance the operative elements of such a condition is, no doubt, a vexing question in any transition to democracy.

## Notes

[1] Alfonsín's political party is known as the Civic Radical Party (UCR).
[2] President Raúl Alfonsín, Address to the Argentine Republic (Dec. 13, 1983).
[3] Law 22.924.
[4] COD. PEN., art. 2 (Arg.).
[5] CODE OF MILITARY JUSTICE, art. 108.

[6]Law 23.049.

[7]*See* COMICIÓN NACIONAL SOBRE LA DESAPARICIÓN DE PERSONAS, NUNCA MÁS: INFORME DE LA COMISIÓN NACIONAL SOBRE LA DESAPARICIÓN DE PERSONAS (1985) [NEVER AGAIN: THE REPORT OF THE ARGENTINE NATIONAL COMMISSION ON THE DISAPPEARED].

[8]Law 23.049.

[9]COD. PEN., art. 34(5) (Arg.). *See also* CODE OF MILITARY JUSTICE, art. 514 (Arg.).

[10]This is not the place to comment on the technical aspects of the trial or to assess its extraordinary consequences, legal, political, and institutional. *See generally* Ronald Dworkin, Introduction, NUNCA MÁS, NEVER AGAIN: THE REPORT OF THE ARGENTINE NATIONAL COMMISSION ON THE DISAPPEARED (American edition 1986); AMNESTY INTERNATIONAL, ARGENTINA: THE MILITARY JUNTAS AND HUMAN RIGHTS: REPORT OF THE TRIAL OF THE FORMER JUNTA MEMBERS (1987).

[11]Escuela de Mecánica de la Armada (Mechanics School of the Navy).

[12]*See supra*, note 10.

[13]Law 23.492. Known as the *punto final* or "full stop" law.

[14]*Id.*

[15]Law 23.521. This became the new Due Obedience Law.

[16]*Id.*

[17]AMNESTY INTERNATIONAL, *supra* note 10, at 15.

[18]Marvin L. Frankel, *Concerning the Role the Judiciary May Serve in the Proper Functioning of a Democracy, in* TRANSITION TO DEMOCRACY IN LATIN AMERICA: THE ROLE OF THE JUDICIARY 23, 27 (Irwin P. Stotzky ed., 1993).

# 23

## The Tradition of
## Constitutional Adjudication

### *Irwin P. Stotzky*

### Introduction

The recognition and protection of human rights is perhaps the most significant aspect of social life in a democratic society. Indeed, human rights constitute an indispensable instrument that governments employ to avoid social catastrophes that often threaten the lives of large numbers of people. This is, of course, especially important in the transition from authoritarianism to democracy, precisely because the transition is such a long and arduous journey.

Yet several prominent problems in any such transition must be successfully resolved if the transition is to succeed without great harm to masses of people. Institutional structures must be developed and secured. Economic and political stability must be assured. Corporatist social and political structures must be transformed so that the powerless get their fair shares of the necessities of life. The rule of law must become paramount in the formal institutions and practices of government, and in the affairs of daily life. The transition process is, however, quite fragile, and the wrong choices by public officials on the many complicated issues that confront them can prove fatal to a democracy and thus lead to serious deprivations of human rights.

The problem is even more complicated than it first appears. One of the major factors that weakens the quest to promote human rights is the perception that once legally recognized, they are forever secured. Although such recognition is important because it makes it possible to block certain kinds of human rights violations carried out by the state, it is not enough. It is insufficient because those who have a monopoly on coercion may employ the state machinery to carry out the most brutal and devastating violations of rights. Legal recognition of rights simply does not ensure their practical enforcement when the state engages in these acts. International covenants, while helpful, also have their limits. The ideological divergence among governing powers in different nations leads to recognition of only a limited set of undisputed rights. In addition, notions of sovereignty restrict acceptance of international obligations, including outside intervention in aid of the investigation and punishment of human rights violations. The failure of legal recognition to protect fully human rights is connected to another barrier to their continued viability -- naked interests. These naked interests, however, are often concealed behind a mask of ideology. Moreover, attacks on human rights often come from true believers of ideologies contemptuous of these rights.

Because legal recognition does not ensure promotion or protection of rights, some have suggested additional approaches. Carlos Nino, for example, has argued that one must look beyond the legal recognition of human rights to "the creation of a moral consciousness of humanity which recognizes the value of those rights and abhors any action that disregards them."[1] Moreover, he claims that such a consciousness, if fully rooted, constitutes "the most permanent and efficacious barrier against the enemies of human dignity."[2] But how can moral consciousness be achieved? Nino's answer: through rational discussion or propaganda. To Nino, however, the latter is insufficient because "it conditions the mind to a kind of answer which may well adapt itself to the opposite stimulus" and because it "implies an elitist attitude" which "is pragmatically inconsistent with the defence of the rights promoted by the propaganda."[3]

Rational discourse, on the other hand, encompasses a broader range of interests than that of human rights. Almost every human being, even a tyrant, feels obligated to justify his acts. That attempt at justification, even if extremely hypocritical and unsophisticated, may lead to illuminating analysis. To Nino, the issue runs even deeper. The very proponents of human rights attempt to avoid moral discussion necessary to justify these rights. Moreover, Nino claims that "the commitment is a moral one and, if it is not justified on the basis of reasons, one remains defenseless before those who reject it."[4] Finally, he argues that it is necessary to determine both what rights must be recognized and their scope.

In the United States, the establishment of a constitutional adjudicative tradition and certain forms of remedies, such as structurally transforming injunctive remedies, have aided in the process of protecting human rights by establishing methods of rational discourse that have helped to develop a moral consciousness in the citizenry. This tradition, exemplified by *Brown v. Board of Education*[5] and its progeny, and the decisions interpreting the guarantees of the Bill of Rights,[6] has led to the protection of human rights and to structural reform of government institutions to make them conform to our constitutional values.

Many Latin American nations have failed to develop this type of constitutional adjudicative tradition.[7] Although fragile, such a process can be useful to developing democracies. My thesis is that the process of constitutional adjudication has been significant in the United States precisely because it establishes a tradition that ultimately protects individuals against the arbitrary actions of government. This tradition, by helping to create a moral consciousness in the citizenry through the process of rational discourse, has acted as a barrier against abuses by the government. This chapter is an attempt to illustrate such a tradition.

At the same time, however, a caveat is in order. The constitutional adjudicative tradition is not a magic elixir that will cure all the diseases of any society attempting to consolidate a democracy. It may be that such a tradition is not wholly sufficient to protect these rights even in a developed democracy. In the United States, for example, it is also true that the tradition has not always been faithful to the premise of developing and perpetuating moral consciousness. Indeed, since the early 1970s, the Rehnquist-led Court has interpreted Bill of Rights' guarantees in a manner calculated to restrict severely their scope.[8] I believe that it is not the necessary outcome of such a tradition, but the failure to adhere to its stringent demands, that has led to an erosion and derogation of the very human rights that are meant to be celebrated.

Furthermore, the methods of adjudication established in the United States are not necessarily transferable to developing democracies. Differences in cultures, history, and the role of law in each specific nation shapes and defines the methods of adjudication. Nevertheless, I believe that the establishment of a constitutional adjudicative tradition in the Latin American nations making the transition to democracy will be extraordinarily important in perpetuating respect for the rule of law and ultimately will act as a barrier against deprivations of human rights.

## I.
## Constitutional Adjudication in the United States

One of the major functions of law is to regulate the use of state power by describing the conditions under which its exercise is legitimate. In the United States, as in most other nations striving to become democracies, a system of constitutional law marks the boundary line between legitimate and illegitimate forms of power, thereby creating communities and claiming freedom and autonomy as a goal for the members of those communities. Some of the most significant public values protected and perpetuated by the

United States Constitution, such as the Fourth Amendment right to be free from unreasonable searches and seizures,[9] give individuals a zone of privacy free from governmental interference. To put it another way, the Constitution creates fences between the state and the individual, thus protecting "the living space of freedom."[10]

In constitutional democracies, where the state is pervasive, the values one finds in a constitution, such as liberty, equality, and freedom from unreasonable searches and seizures, to a large degree determine the quality of the people's social existence. But these values are also clearly ambiguous. They are capable of being given a great number of different meanings. Each part of the government -- the executive, legislative, and judicial branches -- has a role to play in giving these values meaning and content as well as in protecting them. Courts, however, have a particularly important role to play in this process. Indeed, adjudication on constitutional questions is, in my mind, the social process by which judges give meaning to our values.[11] This is not, however, the whole of the matter. This process is significant not only because it helps give meaning to our values but also because it gives rise to a dialogue -- rational discourse -- between the courts and society at large. The dialogue, in turn, defines and shapes the protective contours of these values.

The process runs even deeper. The development of constitutional law in the United States, in general, and of the jurisprudence of specific Bill of Rights' guarantees -- such as Fourth Amendment jurisprudence -- in particular, is a dynamic, not a static process; it is constantly in a state of development and reinterpretation. But this dynamic process always lives within the regime of a methodological tradition. It can never escape the confines of that tradition. Moreover, each of the amendments has a somewhat unique tradition, which itself fits within the broader constitutional interpretive tradition. The changes and interpretations of the amendments, if they are to retain the precious feel of legitimacy so vital to the constitutional adjudicative process, must always remain subject to that tradition.

In this chapter, I wish to explore the tradition of constitutional adjudication -- its methods and results -- in the context of the Fourth Amendment's barrier against unreasonable searches and seizures.[12] I intend to show that there is a deep significance in preserving a judicial constitutional process that has the possibility of promoting and protecting democracy, autonomy, and the rule of law. I choose the Fourth Amendment because, as Justice Jackson observed, the rights guaranteed in the Fourth Amendment "are not mere second-class rights but belong in the category of indispensable freedoms."[13] Indeed, legal barriers against unreasonable searches and seizures are among the first set of freedoms to be denied by authoritarian regimes.[14]

The approach I take in this chapter is to pay close attention to the particularities of specific Fourth Amendment problems. My approach follows from my view of the  nature of the Supreme Court's achievement.  The Court may not have harmonized its answers to various questions, but it has attempted to work with patience and skill to discern the criteria appropriate to particular problems.  To put it another way, the Supreme Court's achievement resides in the close analysis of particulars through a process of rational discourse.  I believe that this approach combines this narrow focus on the precise character of particular problems with a broad perspective on what we are doing as a society when we engage in certain types of social activity.[15]

I begin by establishing and developing the place of the Fourth Amendment as a tradition within the interpretive process itself.  Indeed, it is adherence to the tradition in all the senses described in this essay that best explains how a society may aspire to have a government of laws and not of men and women.

## II.
## The Fourth Amendment Tradition

### A. *Introduction*

In 1991, the people of the United States celebrated the bicentennial of the Bill of Rights. This is a particularly appropriate time, therefore, to reflect on the historical, political, social, and economic forces that held sway when a band of discontented people helped construct the document upon which the integrity of the political life of the people of the United States stands or falls.  It is often forgotten that the history that makes up a part of the tradition of the Fourth Amendment is complex and somewhat uncertain, and that the founding fathers were not themselves innocent of wrongdoing under the laws of their day.  Indeed, many of those most strongly opposed to the writs of assistance were guilty of systematic violations of the customs laws. The founders' objections to the writs were not necessarily that the writs violated the rights of innocent people, but that they permitted the enforcement of laws which, in their view, were substantively evil.[16]  I do not claim from this history that we should read into the Constitution a partiality for the criminal elements of our society.  Rather, I mean to say that we must recognize that the Fourth Amendment, like other Bill of Rights' guarantees, is at bottom a political right.  It is grounded in a fundamental distrust of government, and of those who govern, and it is intended to reserve to the people specific rights to freedom and security which they may well choose to exercise in ways disapproved of or even abhorred by the ruling majority.  Thus, talking about Fourth Amendment interpretations as solutions to "our" problems of crime control is dangerous and misleading because it assumes that the people and the government always have identical interests. The use of this mindset -- the notion that it is "we" (the law-abiding citizens) against "them" (the criminals) -- directly identifies the speaker and the people with the government. The relevant "we," however, includes not only the citizen sympathetic to government positions and the government, but also those most strongly and vociferously opposed to the government. It includes the executive as well as those subject to executive action. Neither police officers nor suspects must be objectified. Both must be seen as what they are: real, live, human beings. They must also be viewed within the context of the situation that has brought them to the point of conflict.

Once people become objectified and perceived as not quite human or part of the community and, therefore, not protected by its laws, it is a small step to the commission of atrocities by the state against whole classes and races of people done in the name of "justice" and "law." The objectification of human beings frees individuals from taking responsibility for their actions, thus making such atrocities more likely to occur. This is, of course, the hallmark of totalitarianism.[17] The struggle against a vision which portrays particular classes of human beings as being outside the protection of the Constitution, and thus subjects such people to tyranny in the guise of law and order and self-preservation, is an oft-forgotten but indispensably significant lesson of the Fourth Amendment Tradition. The Fourth Amendment, then, must be seen for what it is: a profoundly anti-government edict. But it is also more than that.

## B. The Tradition: A Basis for Legitimacy

Freedom from unreasonable searches and seizures by government officials is one of the most remarkable and most celebrated aspects of American constitutional law. It helps define the relationship between the government and the individual. It suggests a sphere of private activity that must be left free from government intrusion. In so doing, it also helps shape our relationships with other private individuals and groups by protecting our right to be let alone, and thus our right to develop to the fullest our capacities as individuals.[18] Through the Constitution's richly generative text, the value of personal autonomy is given permanence and secured against the changing demands of perceived social necessity. The Fourth Amendment is, therefore, more than a profoundly anti-government document. At its most significant level, it helps define what the United States stands for as a democratic nation.

This principle is rooted in the text of the Constitution. Nurturing the Fourth Amendment's textual principle, however, like nurturing other Bill of Rights guarantees, has been the task of the Supreme Court over the past two centuries. They have given the Fourth Amendment much of its present day shape. Their decisions also account for much of its force and sweep.

In speaking of a Fourth Amendment Tradition, I suggest that it encompasses an all embracing perspective.[19] Tradition in this sense includes a corpus of writings and practices passed down to the next generations. This corpus is respected, debated, limited, revered, and simultaneously exerts a force on the past, present, and future. It includes the unwritten sources as well as the written ones, and ideas and values which we unconsciously internalize as well as those accepted with full consciousness.

Moreover, there are at least four senses in which law responds to tradition. First, there is tradition in the sense of the unwritten complement of a legal order. To put it another way, courts may draw on the unwritten traditions of the people as a source for decision. For example, in support of an individual's claim against overreaching warrants, courts often discuss the history of the colonists' struggle against arbitrary government action in issuing writs of assistance, which allowed blanket authority to customs inspectors and their deputies to search for smuggled goods whenever and wherever they wished.[20]

Furthermore, there is an unmistakable uniformity in the style of professional legal education, and there are traditions of the profession itself -- a legal culture -- within which lawyers must live. These include aspirations to meet a high level of service, skill, courage, and independence in defense of the unconventional, and ethics in the practice itself. There is also the expectation that judges give public reasons for their decisions. These aspects of the unwritten complements to law are also clearly passed on from generation to generation. They appear in the style, tone, and substance of judicial opinions, and they help shape the tradition.

Second, there is also the notion of a tradition in the use of precedent of past decisions as a control on future decisions. Indeed, the predominant characteristic of legal argument is the requirement that it tie up with past precedents. In theory, but certainly not in practice, precedent controls and dictates present judgment. In practice, however, the role of precedent is meant to legitimate the process of decision. Past cases, invoked by analogy, help shape present debate, rather than simply determine results. This use of precedent, in the best sense of that notion, allows for growth, change, and self-correction.[21]

Third, when I speak of tradition, I also mean the rather complicated ways of arguing, writing, and thinking about legal problems that have been employed by the actors in our legal system throughout the past two centuries. These methods of arguing, writing, and thinking affect the behavior of individuals, groups, and, more generally, society and its institutions.

Further, the search for the ideal result, whether it be justice or commercial wisdom, is limited by the means and methods one can employ to reach that result -- tradition. This very limitation, however, liberates as well as binds the legal artist. By limiting his choice of materials, it frees up the artist to devote his creative energies to the content of his work. The tension between ideal result and limitation of means, therefore, is a necessary aspect of constitutional adjudication, which allows the process a measure of legitimacy.

Finally, there is the more difficult sense in which precedent, and even practice, embody values that transcend technical limits. An excellent example of this centers on the development in the last seventy-five years of the First Amendment -- the tradition of freedom of speech, press, religion, and political action. The development of the Fourth Amendment clearly fits within this aspect of tradition.

Thus, in speaking of a Fourth Amendment Tradition, everything related to the Fourth Amendment is included. Every encounter between the government, the individual, the Supreme Court, and the Fourth Amendment is part of the Tradition. Included within this Tradition is the discourse created by the Court to resolve constitutional issues. This discourse is significant because it helps elaborate and define the materials and methods the Court uses to reach its conclusions. It provides us with a new way to give meaning to events, and in so doing creates a central social and moral significance for the events with which it deals. Further, this discourse gives us a creative and imaginative as well as an analytical resource. Over the past 200 years, this method of rational discourse has helped create a moral consciousness in the citizenry and thus has acted as a barrier for the protection of human rights.

Indeed, as I mentioned above, one of the major factors that legitimates constitutional adjudication is the requirement that judges write opinions justifying their conclusions. Furthermore, judges must take on issues they may otherwise wish not to decide. They are not in control of their agenda, but must respond to the cases as they arise. This, of course, creates an opportunity for a dialogue between the society and the Court over the proper meaning of public values. It helps instill a moral consciousness in the citizenry. Thus, it becomes the essence of the democratic tradition to ensure that the Supreme Court Justices are satisfying this requirement. From this view, it follows that the judicial opinion has a function beyond stating the decision of a particular case. The judge has an obligation to explain his decision and to do so in a way that attempts not only to persuade the readers of its rightness, but to establish the terms in which other cases are to be dealt with by judges and lawyers in the future. More important, the judicial opinion establishes the discourse for a public debate over the meaning of those constitutional rights.[22]

In the Fourth Amendment field, for example, the Supreme Court has given us less a body of rules or principles than a language in which it compels us to think and talk about new issues as they emerge. This discourse includes thought and debate about the language of the preconstitutional history which gave birth to the Fourth Amendment; the wishes, motives, and desires of those who drafted, negotiated, voted for or rejected the amendment; factual assumptions or judgments about political and social issues related to the interpretation of the amendment; linguistic interpretations of the words and values emanating from the Fourth Amendment itself; the language of values that appear in other parts of the Constitution, but which shed light on the Fourth Amendment; those values found outside of the Constitution; and the values of past precedent and emerging views on controversial issues.

The judicial literature elaborating the Fourth Amendment also has certain special functions which suggest questions by which it can be evaluated. For example, one function of these cases is to provide directions to the police and prosecutors, telling them how they should behave, and to judges telling them how to decide cases, when to give warrants, and the like; they also speak to persons whose rights have been violated, and to ordinary citizens afraid of the criminal elements and proud of their constitutional rights. It might be said that one goal of this literature is to offer a way in which the policeman, the citizen, the judge, the defendant, and the victim can all look at the same events the same way and talk about them intelligibly -- not so that they can agree, but so that they can articulate their differences in mutually comprehensible ways, so that each can feel that his view is at least understood by the others. This is an attempt at rational discussion.

Furthermore, the discourse the Court has made is, among other things, a method for claiming a central social and moral significance for the events with which it deals, events that often could be represented as trivial, seamy, insignificant. The stop of a narcotics addict for questioning, the search of an alleged robber, the arrest of a small-time gangster, could all be described -- in a political speech, say, or in a novel -- in very different terms from those the Court uses in the cases discussed in this essay. The language in which these claims of meaning are made, and the institutions which express that language in the world of social reality, can be regarded as a cultural achievement of the first order. They provide us with a new way to give meaning to events, they constitute a narrative and imaginative as well as an analytical resource, and they create a climate for moral consciousness.

Constitutional law and thus Fourth Amendment adjudication is not, however, simply a separate culture. It is also part of the broader culture.

Indeed, Fourth Amendment interpretations bear a strong relationship to the ways people act, organize, and use their intellectual and material resources. Not least of all, constitutional adjudication forces us to think about justice.

When I speak of an all-encompassing perspective, therefore, I do not mean to suggest that the above catalog should be seen as a mere set of factors listed in encyclopedic form and required to be checked off when a final decision is made in a case. Rather, these factors are meant to be viewed in the nature of a shared understanding of the materials to be employed in resolving new fact situations. Indeed, it is crucial to understand that interpretations of Fourth Amendment problems, like interpretations of other Bill of Rights guarantees, must be perceived as part of a living, dynamic process, and not a static, predetermined ritual. Thus, when I speak of a Fourth Amendment Tradition, I suggest that it is meant to employ the broadest vision consistent with the protection of individuals against arbitrary government actions. The development of Fourth Amendment jurisprudence depends crucially upon seeing all the decisions, and abstracting from them an understanding of what freedom from unreasonable searches and seizures means: what lies at the center and what at the periphery; what is included and what is beyond the scope of the Fourth Amendment; and the reasons for these conclusions. The tradition also requires us to subject these conclusions and their rationale to analysis and criticism. The shape of the tradition is not, of course, fixed for eternity. Rather, each new decision is included in the tradition and therefore contributes to the meaning of the whole. It is also true, however, that the tradition acts as a constraining force on present and future decisions. The tradition is the background against which the issues are defined, and it provides the resources by which the lawyer, judge, and scholar confronts those issues. The tradition orients the actors in these dramas. It is the background against which every relevant actor must think, argue, and write.

One of the major sources of the tradition is history. One of the major questions is this: How is history used in the tradition? The history of the Fourth Amendment is said to be more certain than the history of most other parts of the Constitution. It is clear that the Fourth Amendment was the product of particular events that closely preceded the Constitution and the Bill of Rights, and that we can find specified in the pages of history the abuses against which it was particularly directed.[23] Should the specific history preceding the adoption of the amendment be the entire measure of its limits for constitutional interpretive purposes, or should the broad purpose of preventing tyranny by the government against the people be the basis for interpretation? Merely to ask the question, within the tradition, suggests an answer. The tradition has developed the notion that the Constitution is a document which is meant to expand its meaning in favor of the protection of the people. The broad view is therefore required. The appropriate metaphor for the Constitution is that of an evolving organism.

Further, the language of the Fourth Amendment itself supports a broad and liberal view of its interpretation. To understand the Fourth Amendment Tradition, therefore, it is necessary to look not only at the uses of history, but also to look at the words and structure of the Fourth Amendment itself, and to see the principles that have been judicially interpreted to make up a significant part of that tradition. The Fourth Amendment provides:

> The right of the people to be secure in their persons, houses, papers, and effects, against unreasonable searches and seizures, shall not be violated, and no Warrants shall issue, but upon probable cause, supported by Oath or affirmation, and particularly describing the place to be searched, and the persons or things to be seized.

The Fourth Amendment is a broad, general statement about the relationship between the individual and the government. Its function, according to the tradition, is to secure the permanence of personal autonomy against the constantly changing demands of perceived social necessity. But there is a fundamental problem with the language and structure of the amendment: it is general and does not answer specific questions. It has the virtue of brevity and the vice of ambiguity.[24]

The amendment divides neatly into two clauses. The first clause contains a general protection against "unreasonable" searches and seizures; the second clause specifies the conditions for issuance of a warrant. This latter clause makes it clear that a valid arrest or search warrant may issue only upon a showing of probable cause for the arrest or search. Nowhere in the amendment, however, is the relationship between the two clauses discussed or clarified. Nor does it contain a definition of what kind of governmental action may constitute an unreasonable search and seizure. Neither the structure nor the language of the Fourth Amendment answers the question of whether searches or seizures are reasonable and therefore constitutionally permissible without a warrant or probable cause.

To answer some of these questions, the Court has built upon the tradition of the amendment by measuring its language and structure against the values perceived to undergird the relationship between the citizen and the government. In this light, the tradition suggests several possible readings of the amendment. According to one reading, the second clause may be seen as a partial explanation of the first, so that any search or seizure conducted without a warrant is, by that fact alone, unreasonable. Alternatively, it is possible to argue that the first clause provides an additional requirement by implying that some searches and seizures may be unreasonable even when made under the authority of a warrant. Finally, one can plausibly claim that the first clause provides additional search and seizure power which is reasonable even when done without a warrant.

While the manifest purpose of the Fourth Amendment is to restrict searches and seizures by government officials that invade individual privacy, today it is clear that the tradition created by the Supreme Court's interpretation of the amendment classifies as reasonable some searches and seizures independently of the warrant clause. To put it another way, in limited circumstances, the first clause does provide some additional power to government officials. They may search and seize without a warrant in very carefully circumscribed situations. For example, the police are free to search movable vehicles without a search warrant when the exigencies are such that it is not feasible to obtain a warrant beforehand.[25] Moreover, the police may sometimes make an arrest without a warrant even when they had ample time to obtain one prior to the arrest.[26] But in neither of these described circumstances is the warrantless activity constitutional under the Fourth Amendment unless the police had probable cause for the search and seizure.

There are, however, even more narrowly circumscribed situations in which a warrant is not required and probable cause standards are lowered or not required at all. In certain "stop and frisk" circumstances, for example, a warrantless seizure of the individual may be made upon information which is less than that needed for a "full-fledged" arrest.[27] There are even situations in which neither probable cause, a reduced cause standard, nor a warrant are required for the validity of a search or seizure. For example, if someone crosses our international border, a search and seizure of that person and his property is said to be reasonable simply by virtue of the entry from outside our territory.[28] These narrowly circumscribed exceptions, however, are judicially recognized only because of serious and compelling governmental interests which are said, in the context of these exceptions, to outweigh the intrusion on individual privacy. But there is no "natural" limit to this reasoning. Expanding these exceptions can lead only to the Fourth Amendment Tradition becoming a "mere form of words."

In sum, the broad outline of the Fourth Amendment Tradition is not difficult to express. The Fourth Amendment prohibition of unreasonable searches and seizures means that government officials may neither search nor seize an individual or his private property unless there is probable cause. But probable cause alone is not necessarily sufficient. In most circumstances, there must also be a warrant or exigent circumstances to excuse the failure to obtain one. There are exceptions to these general principles, but they are carefully defined and narrowly limited ones.

The Supreme Court, particularly in the past two decades, has not always been faithful to the Fourth Amendment Tradition. As a perceptive constitutional observer has noted, "[f]or clarity and consistency, the law of the Fourth Amendment is not the Supreme Court's most successful product."[29] The cases are often confusing, complex, and seemingly irreconcilable with earlier precedents. I might add that I believe that many of the Court's Fourth Amendment problems can be traced directly to its failure to adhere strictly to the Fourth Amendment Tradition. Even with this said, however, the Court has been forced by the tradition to engage in rational discourse to explain its doctrinal changes. This requirement has in turn limited the speed and the scope of its retrenchment. Indeed, the tradition of constitutional adjudication clearly demands that the judiciary protect human rights.

## III.
## Tension Within the Tradition

The tradition of constitutional adjudication, particularly Fourth Amendment adjudication, like the art of law in general, is founded upon and practiced within a set of tensions between aims not simultaneously realizable in full. On the one hand, we are confronted with the aim of attaining Fourth Amendment justice. To put it another way, judges are obligated by the tradition to interpret the Fourth Amendment in a manner which accords due deference to the protection of individual privacy against the tyranny of government action. On the other hand, we are confronted with the desire of many politicians and others to rid our society of criminals, sometimes at the cost of our precious liberties. Both of these value systems confront another tension in constitutional adjudication -- the aim of using the authority of law in a legitimate manner, employing but not straining the techniques sanctioned as legitimate in our legal culture. Living and working within this tension is not made any easier by the fact that no reasoning about justice or even about practicability, and no reasoning about legal legitimacy, can ever be altogether demonstrative. Unlike a demonstration in mathematics or even in the physical sciences, constitutional decision-making is not based on objectively verifiable conclusions. What can be asked of the judge, lawyer, or scholar working within the legal system is not that he present or espouse utterly certain conclusions -- for if he tries to do this, he is following an illusion indeed -- but rather that he continually explore, with disciplined imagination, the means to justice within the legal system, and that at the same time he be continually responsive to the demand for reasoned justification within that system. The continual search for creative resolution of this tension is one of the main functions of the art of constitutional adjudication.

United States Supreme Court Justices have not, of course, always been faithful to their adjudicative obligations in Fourth Amendment cases. Most recently, they have failed to work within the confines of the Fourth Amendment Tradition. It is most appropriate, therefore, to interpose here a thought about the present trend in the Supreme Court and in some academic circles to discard altogether the traditional techniques of constitutional adjudication, and to drive toward what is conceived as the right result, usually on the basis of something labelled as a "philosophy." I regard this as a dangerous and potentially baneful tendency for several reasons. First, because it seems to me certain to erode public acceptance of the legitimacy of legal work without offering adequate critique or viable substitutes. Second, and even more important, this type of result-oriented adjudication demeans and thus deprives us all of our precious and fragile Fourth Amendment rights. Finally, this kind of adjudication passes over the almost infinitely rich resources of traditional law -- including the framework of ordered development and change -- in favor of comparatively thin and incomplete systems of thought. The conception of law as a tradition, and constitutional adjudication as the art of rights theory, demands that we adhere closely to the ways to the Fourth Amendment Tradition. Without a strict adherence to this tradition, we will soon be without the precious liberties we all assumed would be with us forever.

## Conclusion

In this chapter, I have employed what I refer to as the Fourth Amendment Tradition to illustrate the significant role that a constitutional adjudicative practice plays in the protection of human rights in the United States. I do not claim that the same tradition is fully applicable to the newly emerging democracies of Latin America. Each nation has its own social, political, and legal culture. These differences suggest that each nation will employ different methods of constitutional adjudication.

The problem is even more complicated than it first appears. It is, of course, correct to say that a constitutional adjudicative tradition, in and of itself, is not sufficient to fully protect human rights. Nevertheless, both in emerging and developed democracies such a process and practice certainly aids the perpetuation of rational discourse, which is a prerequisite to the creation of a moral consciousness of humanity in the society as a whole. This consciousness, in turn, creates a recognition of the values of human rights and may act as a powerful barrier against any action that disregards them.

It is, therefore, crucially important for the Latin American nations in the process of transition to democracy to consolidate the rule of law. This will not only help to secure respect for human rights and for observance of the democratic process, but will also help in the development of economic and social stability. Indeed, if judicial, executive, and legislative institutional structures are consolidated, and economic and political forces stabilized, a tradition of constitutional adjudication will most assuredly enhance and strengthen a democracy. Although this may seem like an almost impossible task, the results -- the protection and enhancement of human rights -- are most certainly worth the hardships of the journey.

A note of caution is, however, in order. While it is correct to say that such an adjudicative tradition is significant, it simply cannot develop in a vacuum. This means that the independence, reliability, and efficiency of the judicial process must be strengthened simultaneously with changes in the economic, social, and political spheres.

While the full breadth and depth of the promise of constitutional adjudication has not been fulfilled even in the United States, the promise itself remains as a vibrant symbol of the hopes and possibilities of ensuring the protection of human rights in developing democracies, and as a forceful challenge to those who have either become complacent or oppose the process itself in the name of political expedience. Constitutional protection exists precisely for what is too precious and fragile to be left to politics. The tradition of constitutional adjudication is indeed a worthy commitment for any nation.

## Notes

[1] CARLOS S. NINO, THE ETHICS OF HUMAN RIGHTS 3 (1991).

[2] *Id.*

[3] *Id.*

[4] *Id.* at 4.

[5] Brown v. Board of Education, 347 U.S. 483 (1954) (Brown I); Brown v. Board of Education, 349 U.S. 294 (1955) (Brown II).

[6] Although cases such as Brown v. Board of Education, 347 U.S. 483 (1954) (banned racial segregation in public schools), and Baker v. Carr, 369 U.S. 186 (1962) (recognized the principle of one person-one vote), are often viewed as the most significant modern decisions, and although they were certainly great steps forward for the nation and the Constitution, I believe that the decisions incorporating the guarantees of the Bill of Rights were even more significant. These decisions bind the states to almost all of the restraints of the Bill of Rights. The vehicle for this impressive development was the Fourteenth Amendment. Simply put, it has served as the legal instrument of an egalitarian revolution -- a revolution in judicial legal method as well as in substance. The Supreme Court employed this amendment, as well as the other Civil War amendments, to protect citizens from the

employment of government authority that violates our national conceptions of human dignity and liberty. The United States has been radically transformed by the standards, promises, and power of the Fourteenth Amendment. Citizens of all states are now no less citizens of the United States. Each person is entitled to due process and equal protection of the laws from all levels of government, state as well as federal. For an elaboration of this theme see Irwin P. Stotzky, Federalism, Judicial Review, and the Protection of Individual Rights (1992) (unpublished manuscript on file with the author).

[7]In many Latin American nations, the institutional structures and practices needed to establish and perpetuate a constitutional adjudicative tradition simply do not exist. In Argentina, for example, institutional judicial instability is caused by the large degree of dependence by the highest courts on the political process, by the rapid changes in doctrine, and by the regular wholesale replacement of judges. *See*, Irwin P. Stotzky & Carlos S. Nino, *The Difficulties of the Transition Process, in* TRANSITION TO DEMOCRACY IN LATIN AMERICA: THE ROLE OF THE JUDICIARY 3 (Irwin P. Stotzky ed. 1993) [hereinafter TRANSITION].

[8]For a discussion of this problem in the Fourth Amendment context *see, e.g.*, Irwin P. Stotzky, Some General Reflection on the Fourth Amendment and Its Literature (1988) (unpublished manuscript on file with the author).

[9]The Fourth Amendment reads:

> The right of the people to be secure in their persons, houses, papers, and effects, against unreasonable searches and seizures, shall not be violated, and no Warrants shall issue, but upon probable cause, supported by Oath or affirmation, and particularly describing the place to be searched, and the persons or things to be seized.

U.S. CONST. amend. IV.

Article 19 of the Argentine Constitution of 1853 also contains a provision relating to searches and seizures which reads in relevant parts: "No person may be . . . arrested except by virtue of an order signed by the competent authority . . . . The domicile is inviolate, as well as written correspondence and private papers; a law must prescribe in which cases and under which justifications the domicile may be searched and occupied." CONST. ARG. art. 19 (1853).

Judicial interpretations of the Fourth Amendment and Article 19 have, no doubt, not been parallel, given the striking differences in values, assumptions, and method between the Argentine and United States systems of government, and the role of the judiciary within each of those systems. On its face, for example, Article 19 could be interpreted to suggest that written correspondence and private papers may never be searched for and seized. Moreover, one could argue that even if such articles could be searched for and seized, they could not be used in evidence to convict an individual of a crime. In the United States, however, the "property theory" of the Fourth Amendment first enunciated in Boyd v. United States, 116 U.S. 616 (1886), has been rejected. *See, e.g.*, Andresen v. Maryland, 427 U.S. 463 (1976); Fisher v. United States, 425 U.S. 391 (1976).

[10]HANNAH ARENDT, THE ORIGINS OF TOTALITARIANISM 466 (1951).

[11]For an intriguing analysis of this point see Owen M. Fiss, *1978 Term Foreword: The Forms of Justice*, 93 HARV. L. REV. 1 (1979).

[12]Although this is not the place to explore the issue fully, it may be necessary, in order to provide support for my explanation of constitutional adjudication, that I locate the role of judicial interpretations, of the Fourth Amendment, for example, within the broader context of a democratic system of government. The democratic conception that I have in mind is explicitly a conception of a political order. It is a conception of a social system in which public debate over the direction of social life is not only expected, but actively encouraged. I view democracy, in part, as a public forum for moral discourse, where principles rather than special interests prevail. I believe that the best means for countering the overpowering influence of special interests is to create a polity governed by universal and impersonal principles where individual citizens, who preserve the ability to adopt new interests and are not necessarily identified with any special interest, make choices in a process of public justification and dialogue. For elaboration of this theme *see* CARLOS S. NINO, ETICA Y DERECHOS HUMANOS (1984); Carlos S. Nino, *Transition to Democracy, Corporatism and Constitutional Reform in Latin America*, 44 U. MIAMI L. REV. 129 (1989). *See also* Irwin P. Stotzky, *The Fragile Bloom of Democracy*, 44 U. MIAMI L. REV. 105 (1989).

Implicit in this conception of democracy is the realization that the removal of existing barriers to free deliberation would not necessarily eliminate all grounds for political disagreement. The task of a democratic conception, therefore, is not to describe a social order in which all disputes would be trivial, or indicative of a failure to realize the principles of the order. Rather, the burden is to outline a political order in which disagreements over the direction of that order can be socially addressed through free deliberation.

In view of these considerations, it follows that the democratic order must satisfy several major requirements. The principles of that order must be clarified by describing the justification or principle of democratic legitimacy. Some description and explanation must then be given of a set of institutional requirements rooted in those fundamental principles. Finally, an account must be offered of the motivations that might lead people to support and maintain such institutions over time.

The necessarily brief description of my conception of a democratic order sketched out in this footnote is strongly influenced by the writings of John Rawls. *See* JOHN RAWLS, A THEORY OF JUSTICE (1971); John Rawls, *Kantian Constructivism in Moral Theory*, 57 J. OF PHIL. 515-72 (1988). Moreover, the "triple theory of judicial review," which assigns judges the task of being guardians of democracy, personal autonomy, and the rule of law is, in my opinion, the best justification for the legitimacy of judicial review in a democratic system of government. See Carlos S. Nino, *On the Exercise of Judicial Review in Argentina*, in TRANSITION, *supra* note 7, at 309, for a description and elaboration of this thesis.

[13]Brinegar v. United States, 338 U.S. 160, 185 (1949) (J. Jackson dissenting).

[14]Argentina furnishes a particularly harsh example. Between 1976 and 1983, three separate military juntas ruled the nation. Under the guise of fighting terrorism, they eliminated between 7,000 and 30,000 persons. The extermination took

place under a veil of state secrecy. The disappearances followed a similar pattern. An armed unit simply burst into a victim's home in the early hours of the morning and kidnapped the victim. They warned family members that appeals to the authorities would be useless. (Civilian authorities, such as the police, were ordered not to interfere in certain targeted areas.) They carried off the victim in unmarked cars, usually Ford Falcons. These victims were questioned, tortured, and murdered. No judicial constitutional adjudicative tradition protected the victims from these illegal seizures and murders. *See* Stotzky, *supra* note 12, at 112; Paula K. Speck, *The Trial of the Argentine Junta: Responsibilities and Realities*, 18 INTER-AM. L. REV. 498-99 (1987). For a brilliant, haunting novel about the disappearances see LAWRENCE THORNTON, IMAGINING ARGENTINA (1987).

[15]For a more thorough elaboration of the process of judicial decision-making and a response to some criticisms of it, see Soia Mentschikoff & Irwin P. Stotzky, *Law - The Last of the Universal Disciplines*, 54 U. CIN. L. REV. 695 (1986); Irwin P. Stotzky & Alan C. Swan, *Due Process Methodology and Prisoner Exchange Treaties: Confronting an Uncertain Calculus*, 62 MINN. L. REV. 733, 756-765 (1978).

[16]Among the laws seen as evil by the Colonists were a number of navigation and trade acts passed by Parliament which were designed to prevent the colonies from trading with areas outside Europe. Their main weapon was the imposition of prohibitive import duties. The writs of assistance so hated by the Colonists had given custom officials virtually blanket authority to search where they pleased for goods imported in violation of British tax laws such as these. Smuggling thus became rampant in the colonies and was engaged in by even the most respectable persons in order to circumvent laws they regarded as oppressive and unjustifiable. Among the prominent men allegedly engaged in smuggling, for example, was John Hancock. He was accused of smuggling in 1769 and defended by John Adams. JACOB W. LANDYNSKI, SEARCH AND SEIZURE AND THE SUPREME COURT 30-31 (1966). Adams used the argument, *inter alia*, of no taxation without representation. The law, he said "was made without our Consent. My Client Mr. Hancock never consented to it. He never voted for it himself, and he never voted for any Man to make such a law for him." The case, along with Adams's arguments, is reported in Quincy's Reports of Cases Argued and Adjudicated in the Superior Court of Judicature of the Province of Massachusetts Bay, Between 1761 and 1772, at 457 (1865).

In one sense then it is no exaggeration to say that the Colonial smuggler can be viewed as the analogue to the liquor smuggler (bootlegger) of the twenties and the drug smuggler of today.

[17]Totalitarianism can rightly be called the political plague of the twentieth century. Hannah Arendt has written a masterful analysis of Totalitarianism. See ARENDT, *supra* note 10, at 466. Moreover, the disappearance of thousands of people during the military rule in Argentina from 1976 until 1983 is a particularly harsh example of this problem in the Latin American context. Under the guise of combating terrorism, the military regime murdered people in the name of preserving their society. *See supra* note 14.

[18]Hannah Arendt related this view of law by stating that "the space between men as it is hedged in by laws, is the living space of freedom." ARENDT, *supra* note 10 at 466.

[19]Perhaps the best example of this view of tradition in constitutional law is Harry Kalven's work on the First Amendment. *See* HARRY KALVEN, JR., A WORTHY TRADITION: FREEDOM OF SPEECH IN AMERICA (1988).

[20]A prime example of the use of unwritten tradition as the background for interpreting the Fourth Amendment is Justice Bradley's opinion in Boyd v. United States, 116 U.S. 616 (1886).

[21]*See* KARL N. LLEWELLYN, THE COMMON LAW TRADITION (1960); SOIA MENTSCHIKOFF & IRWIN P. STOTZKY, THE THEORY AND CRAFT OF AMERICAN LAW: ELEMENTS (1981). For an intriguing recent discussion of the use of precedent see Justices Souter, O'Connor, and Kennedy's discussion in Planned Parenthood of Southeastern Pennsylvania v. Casey, 112 S. Ct. 2791 (1992).

[22]For example, a decision such as Terry v. Ohio, 392 U.S. 1 (1968), allowed a public debate on the nature of stops and frisks, and helped create a new language to be employed in the debate. This language, in turn, helped create a climate of moral consciousness which acted as a barrier against government intrusions against the individual.

[23]For a general discussion of this history, see LANDYNSKI, *supra* note 15, at 19-48; NELSON B. LASSON, THE HISTORY AND DEVELOPMENT OF THE FOURTH AMENDMENT TO THE UNITED STATES CONSTITUTION 13-78 (1937); TELFORD TAYLOR, TWO STUDIES IN CONSTITUTIONAL INTERPRETATION 19-44 (1969).

[24]Even the second clause, which is a rather narrow prescription about the form and content of search warrants, leaves many questions unanswered. It does not, for example, address the questions of who may issue a warrant, how it must be executed, or in what circumstances seized property may be retained. The problem of interpretation of ambiguous text is, of course, endemic to many constitutional amendments, as well as to any text.

[25]Carroll v. United States, 267 U.S. 132 (1925).

[26]United States v. Watson, 423 U.S. 411 (1976).

[27]Terry v. Ohio, 392 U.S. 1 (1968).

[28]United States v. Ramsey, 431 U.S. 606 (1977).

[29]Anthony G. Amsterdam, *Perspectives on the Fourth Amendment*, 58 Minn. L. Rev. 349 (1974).

# 24

## The Negative Constitution: Transition in Latin America

### *Cass R. Sunstein*

### Introduction

In this chapter[1], I argue that in thinking about what constitutional courts should do, we should think not only about the best substantive theory of constitutional rights, but also about the limitations faced by constitutional courts. Or to put it another way, constitutional law, in the courts, is a mixture of substantive theory and institutional constraint. Sometimes courts do what they do in part because courts, as courts, face institutional limitations.

Several themes emerge from this claim. The first is that courts should protect, first and foremost, a firm negative constitution, protecting individuals from government impositions.[2] The second is that courts should be reluctant to protect positive rights, such as the right to welfare, to a clean environment, or to social security. The third and perhaps most surprising is that constitutions should be directed against the most dangerous or pathological aspects of their own, distinctive political culture.

The last point deserves emphasis, since it is somewhat unconventional. People often say that a constitution must be well adapted to the nation it governs, in the sense that it must be consistent with the nation's particular culture and customs. In some respects this is undoubtedly true. But it may be even more fruitful to think of constitutions as working best when they are self-consciously countermanding -- that is, when they are designed to counteract particular tendencies of the nation's political culture. From this it might follow, for example, that protection of freedom of contract would be unnecessary in the United States, but quite valuable in Russia. My use of the term "negative" can therefore be seen as double-edged. I mean to exclude positive rights, like the right to welfare, largely because they are difficult to enforce through courts. But I also mean to insist that a constitution should be "negative" in the sense that it should be directed against the deepest risks in the relevant nation's political culture. Much of the following discussion can be seen as an elaboration of these basic ideas.

This chapter comes in several parts. The first briefly discusses negative rights that should, I propose, play a principal role in Latin America. Part II discusses the function of negative economic liberties. Part III distinguishes two different kinds of constitutionalism, in order to identify the features of a positive constitution that I mean to criticize. Part IV argues against a positive constitution. Part V sets out a charter of economic liberties.

# I.
# The Negative Constitution

The first task for any country in the midst of a transition to democracy and constitutionalism is the creation of a firm negative constitution. Here it is indispensable to see constitutional rights through the lens of the capabilities of constitutional courts. It follows that the relevant rights should be ones that courts are fully able to enforce. Most of the negative rights are indeed capable of judicial enforcement. Moreover, most of them are central not only to individual liberty, but also to democracy, which is my principal concern here. I list them in what seems to me to be descending order of importance; but all of them are important. From this we can obtain a simple set of duties for constitutional courts. These duties, if satisfied, will accomplish an enormous amount in moving Latin American nations toward democracy, without unduly straining the powers and capacities of the judiciary.

The first and most important of these negative rights is the right to bodily integrity. This includes rights against torture, unjustified imprisonment, constraints on movement, and forced labor. The right to bodily integrity is often seen as part of individual autonomy, and the characterization is fully appropriate. People are not free if they cannot control their bodies. But it is equally useful to think of this most fundamental of rights as a precondition for citizenship. If your body is not your own -- if it is subject to the discretionary power of the state -- you will be deprived of the kind of security and independence that is a precondition for citizenship.

Second are the basic political rights: freedom of speech, the right to vote, and the right of association. These rights are the foundations of a democratic system. A government determined to prevent democracy will regularly infringe on these rights. One of the most valuable functions of a constitutional court is to prevent any such infringements. It is important, moreover, to see the rights of speech and association through the lens of democracy, and to be especially alert to any governmental incursions on these rights that threaten democratic processes.

Third are antidiscrimination principles. These include most prominently the right not to be discriminated against on the basis of race, religion, or gender. Antidiscrimination principles of this kind are part and parcel of political equality, a precondition for a democratic system. One of the most serious obstacles to democracy is second-class citizenship, in which one group is systematically below another, with corresponding violations of the principle of political equality. Indeed, in Latin America, such violations -- on the basis of religion and sex -- are a special threat. A firm antidiscrimination principle is crucial here because some such discrimination, when it occurs, might seem acceptable or even invisible. In Latin America, we have an especially important case for a negative constitution in the second of my two senses; that is, a negative, countermanding constitution, directed to counteract the most distinctive risks in the nation's own political culture.

Fourth, and finally, constitutional courts should protect the two major economic liberties, the right to private property and freedom of contract. These rights are familiarly thought to be central to economic growth and prosperity; and so they are. Less frequently, they are understood to be a component of democracy, a point to which I will be devoting some attention. In the United States, however, it is most controversial to say that courts should use the constitution aggressively to protect private property and freedom of contract. The controversy makes a good deal of sense. United States culture is highly protective of property and contract rights, and in these circumstances it is unnecessary and potentially dangerous to use the Constitution for the same purpose. (Recall the second sense of the negative constitution.) But in other cultures, it may well make sense to experiment with firmer protection of these rights. Because this proposition is also likely to be controversial, more detail is necessary.

## II.
## Why Protect Property and Contract?

### A. *Private Property and Economic Prosperity*

It is generally agreed that a system of private property helps to bring about economic prosperity. There are several reasons for this conclusion.[3] First, the institution of private property creates and takes advantage of the powerful human inclination to bring goods and services to oneself and to people one cares about.[4] A system without private property stifles incentives and thus induces both sloth and waste. These points do not depend on especially cynical accounts of human nature. It is necessary only to glance briefly at history, past and present, and to acknowledge that human beings will frequently attempt to accumulate resources. Social institutions appealing to this inclination will increase social productivity.

Second, a system of private property performs a crucial coordinating function. It ensures that the multiple desires of hundreds, thousands, or millions of consumers will be reflected in market outcomes. In this way, it protects against the perverse forms of scarcity produced by a command economy. Every citizen of Eastern Europe and Latin America has seen multiple illustrations.

Third, the institution of private property solves, all at once, a serious collective action problem faced by people in any system without that institution.[5] When property is unowned, no one has a sufficient incentive to use it to its full advantage or to protect it against exploitation. The creation of private property overcomes this problem. It ensures that externalities from use will be internalized by people who are producing either social harms or social benefits.

Finally, a system of private property creates the kind of stability and protection of expectations that are preconditions for investment and initiative, from both international and domestic sources. A company deciding whether to invest in a country will have a greater incentive to do so if it knows that its investment will be protected, and that government confiscation is prohibited by the government's basic law. A citizen who is seeking to begin a business will be far more likely to do so if he can operate against a secure and stable background, protected against the vicissitudes of government policy. In this way, too, economic development can be facilitated by property rights.

### B. Property and Democracy

The connection between property and prosperity may be reasonably well understood; but the right to private property has not always been considered a precondition for democracy. On the contrary, private property has frequently been thought an obstacle to democracy, and for this reason highly objectionable, or perhaps at best an institution necessary for economic growth and therefore to be reluctantly accepted, despite its corrosive effects on the democratic process.

There is indeed some tension between a system of property rights and a system of democracy. If property rights are secure, there is a firm limit on what the democratic process is entitled to do. In this sense, the tension is a real and enduring one. Notably, markets impose conspicuous short-term costs -- unemployment and inflation -- and in the emerging Eastern Europe and Latin American democracies, there will probably be a continuous temptation to slow down the transition to markets or perhaps to reject the transition altogether. In important respects, however, it is quite plausible to think that the right to a stable system of property rights -- one with which the state will interfere only occasionally or in a limited way, with a provision for compensation -- is actually necessary to democracy and not opposed to it at all.

The most fundamental point about the relationship between property and democracy is that a right to own property has an important and salutary effect on the citizens' relationship with the state and -- equally important -- on their understanding of that relationship. Because of this effect, it can be seen as a necessary precondition for the status of citizenship. Personal security and personal independence from the government are guaranteed in a system in which rights of ownership are protected through public institutions.

In this sense, the ownership of property is closely associated with the rule of law.[6] Both of these create a realm of private autonomy in which the citizenry can operate without fear of public intrusion. That realm is indispensable to the public sphere itself. Only people with a degree of security from the state are able to participate without fear, and with independence, in democratic deliberation. In this manner, a sharp, legally-produced distinction between the private and the public can usefully serve the public sphere. Contrary to a conventional understanding, it need not harm it at all.[7] A central point here is that in a state in which private property does not exist, citizens are dependent on the good will of government officials, almost on a daily basis.[8] Whatever they have is a privilege and not a right. They come to the state as supplicants or beggars, rather than as right holders. Any challenge to the state may be stifled or driven underground by virtue of the fact that serious challenges could result in the withdrawal of the goods that give people basic security. A right to private property, free from government interference, is therefore a necessary basis for a democracy.

Like the right to freedom of religious conscience,[9] moreover, the right to property helps create a flourishing civil society, an intermediate level between the government and the individual. The development of a civil society can in turn be understood as a mechanism both for creating economic prosperity and for promoting democratic self-governance. A constitutional system that respects private property should be regarded not as an effort to oppose liberal rights to collective self-government, but instead as a way to fortify democratic processes.

I have not dealt with the question of redistribution. In the West, enthusiasm for property rights is often thought to entail a reluctance to allow redistribution, or (worse) complete indifference to the poor. The proper response is twofold. First, property rights help create wealth, and greater wealth will often benefit the most vulnerable as well. Time and again it has been shown that economic growth does more than welfare and employment programs to benefit the disadvantaged.

Of course growth does not do everything, and it must be supplemented.[10] The second point, then, is that welfare and employment programs are a necessary part of any system of property rights. Such rights are best defended in self-consciously instrumental terms, because of the good things that they do. When they do not accomplish good, or enough good, they must be accompanied by other social strategies. Indeed, it is important to ensure not merely that everyone has a right to private property, but also (what is not the same thing) that everyone has private property. Property rights without property involve a degree of dependence that is debilitating to citizenship.

Properly understood, the defense of property rights is a defense of programs of redistribution as well. These programs are not designed to produce economic equality -- a truly disastrous goal -- but instead to bring about genuine equality of opportunity. In addition, these programs must bring about certain forms of freedom for all people in society: freedom from desperate conditions and from circumstances that impede human functioning.[11] There are extremely good arguments for seeing the right to minimally decent conditions as a basic human right. A defense of economic liberties should not be seen as inconsistent with that right. I will be arguing that positive rights should not be constitutional rights even if they are genuinely understood as rights; but this point results from the fact that the Constitution is a legal document for judicial enforcement. It is not an argument against government provision of decent opportunities and results to all citizens.

Moreover, no one should understand property and contract rights to be a constitutional obstacle to help for the disadvantaged, through, for example, aggressive education programs, employment and training programs, and welfare benefits. Ordinary interferences with property or contract rights -- taking someone's house, abolishing a contractual duty -- are hardly good ways of helping the disadvantaged. Instead, they typically serve to help some well-organized interest group.

I have dealt with property rights at this length because they may well be the most controversial on my list. I hope I have said enough to suggest that such rights do belong in a negative constitution. Now I want to argue against a very different understanding of constitutional rights; but first some background is in order.

## III.
## Two Conceptions of Constitutionalism

We should begin by distinguishing between two sorts of constitutions. From the experience in Eastern Europe -- with some overlap in Latin America -- we can roughly identify the features of constitutionalism in the West and the North, and the competing features in the East and the South. First, and crucially, the latter constitutions do not sharply distinguish between public and private spheres. They apply their prohibitions and permissions to everyone. They are not limited to government.

Second, such constitutions typically contain duties as well as rights. They do not merely grant privileges to citizens but also impose obligations on them. Third, and most important of all, the central provisions of these constitutions set out very general social aspirations or commitments. Their provisions are designed to state those aspirations, not to create concrete entitlements that citizens can attempt to vindicate, through an independent judiciary, against government officials. These aspirations include a wide range of "positive" rights.

Thus, for example, the former Soviet Constitution of 1977 included the right to work,[12] the right to rest and leisure,[13] the right to health protection,[14] and the right to maintenance in old age, sickness, and disability.[15] It imposed on citizens the duty to "preserve and protect socialist property" and to "enhance the power and prestige" of the Soviet State.[16] The Polish Constitution of 1991 includes the right to work,[17] the right to rest and leisure,[18] and the right to health protection.[19] The former Bulgarian Constitution of 1971 offered the right to a holiday,[20] the right to work,[21] the right to labor safety,[22] the right to social security,[23] and the right to free medical care.[24]

Along each of these dimensions, constitutions in the West and the North are quite different. The provisions of such constitutions generally apply only to the government, and not to private actors. They do not impose duties. Most important, they aim to create solid individual rights, ones that can be invoked by individual citizens, as of right, in an independent tribunal authorized to bar governmental action. Positive rights are the exception, and when they exist they are usually not subject to judicial enforcement.[25]

## IV.
## Against the Positive Constitution

With this background, I am now prepared to argue against the positive constitution. Such a constitution would protect aspirations or positive duties on government; impose such duties on private citizens; and erase the distinction between the public and private sphere. I want to suggest that all of these strategies would be mistakes.

*Aspirations.* A constitution might be used as a place for setting out very general social aspirations, or for imposing positive duties on government (such as the provision of a social welfare state, including such guarantees as equitable remuneration, leisure time, social security, and occupational safety and health). There are three reasons why this would be a dangerous strategy for Latin America, at least under current conditions.

First, to state aspirations and impose positive duties -- prominent of course in the Soviet Constitution -- runs the risk of turning a constitution into something other than a legal document with real-world consequences. It is important to remember that if it is to create rights realistically enforceable in the world, a constitution should not list all things to which a country aspires. It should limit itself, for the most part, to rights that it is genuinely able to enforce. A constitution that creates positive rights is not likely to be subject to judicial enforcement, because these rights are vaguely defined, simultaneously involve the interests of numerous people, and depend for their existence on active management of government institutions -- something for which judges are ill-suited. The existence of unenforceable rights will in turn tend to destroy the negative rights -- freedom of speech, freedom of religion, and so forth -- that might otherwise be genuine ones. If some rights are shown to be unenforceable, it is likely that other rights will be unenforceable as well.

The second problem with positive rights is that they will work against the general current efforts to diminish the sense of entitlement to state protection, and to encourage individual initiative and self-reliance. Both markets and democracy tend to develop these highly salutary characteristics. Sometimes liberal constitutionalism is praised because it responds accurately to "human nature," and does not try to tinker with it. There is undoubtedly something to this idea; efforts fundamentally to revise human character are usually doomed to failure. But liberal constitutionalism might be defended precisely on the ground that it has healthy effects on human character. Markets and democracy tend to create certain types, with many valuable characteristics.[26]

To say this is emphatically not to say that in the post-reform era, nations in Latin America should eliminate social welfare protections and leave their citizens to the vicissitudes of the market. Such a route would be a recipe for disaster, since it would allow for mass suffering of the kind that is unacceptable in any nation. But these protections should be created at the level of ordinary legislation, and subject to democratic discussion, rather than placed in the foundational document.

The third problem with positive rights is that they establish government interference with markets as a constitutional duty. The current effort is to limit such interference, and to establish the preconditions for private markets, free trade, and free contract. To impose a constitutional duty of interference is to move in precisely the wrong direction.

A possible response to these points would be that constitutions should be understood not merely as a place for setting forth legal rights but also as a forum for the identification of national ideals.[27] The identification might serve educative and other functions; it might inform statutory interpretation. The point suggests that aspirations and positive rights may well belong at least in some western constitutions, to encourage political attention to fundamental matters (such as shelter, subsistence, medical care, and environmental quality) and to ensure that statutes are interpreted in the light of a full range of social commitments. Ambiguities might therefore be resolved favorably to, for example, environmental protection.

In Latin America as well, these ideals may be less appealing. But perhaps a section outlining explicitly unenforceable positive rights could enhance the chances of ratification, play a beneficial role in public debate, and accomplish this without compromising the effort to produce genuinely enforceable "negative" rights. At most, any positive rights and aspirations, in proposed or existing constitutions, should generally be understood to be unenforceable.

*Duties.* Another strategy, posing similar risks, is to use the constitution as a place for creating "duties" as well as rights. Such duties are not likely to be enforceable through courts. Their statement in a constitution tends to weaken the understanding that the document creates protected rights, with real meaning, against the state.

*No Distinction Between Public and Private Spheres.* Yet another dangerous strategy is to make constitutional provisions binding against private people and private organizations as well as against the state. In almost all legal systems in the North and the West, the constitution applies only to the government, not to the people in general. This is extremely important, because it recognizes and helps create a private sphere -- a civil society that operates independently of the state. It also frees up private organizations -- employers, religious organizations, unions, and so forth -- to act as they choose. If the people want to apply particular constitutional provisions to particular private organizations, of course they can do so, through ordinary legislation. But it is a mistake to apply such provisions through the constitution itself. Above all, this strategy works to erase the distinction between the private and public spheres, a distinction that should be enthusiastically embraced on substantive political grounds.

It may be that, in Latin America, some private organizations effectively function as public ones, because of their size, their importance, and their enjoyment of a *de facto* or *de jure* legal monopoly. The first response to this situation is to try to break up the monopoly. If this is impossible, selective constitutional safeguards may well make sense. But this is an exception to what should be the general rule.

## V.
## A Bill of Economic Liberties?

In the next few years, it may be useful to develop a set of potential provisions for inclusion as an "economic freedoms" section of the proposed constitution, or for judicial interpretation of the existing document. There is no such section in western constitutions. Its design should be understood not as an effort to export western ideas to Eastern Europe and Latin America, but instead as an exercise in constitutional drafting intended specifically for problems in these parts of the world.

I provide in this section a preliminary outline of constitutional provisions that might be adopted in the interest of creating a well functioning system of property rights and economic markets. The outline amounts to little more than a list; it is intended only to provide a starting point for discussion.

*The Rule of Law.* In order to comply with the rule of law, a government must ensure that action may not be taken against citizens unless it has laid down, in advance, a pertinent law. The rule of law requires that any such restriction must be clear rather than vague and publicly available rather than secret; and it must operate in the world as it does on the books.[28]

A guarantee of the rule of law is both an economic and a democratic right. It creates a wall of protection around citizens, giving a guarantee of immunity and ensuring them that they may engage in productive activity without fear of the state. Moreover, by creating this wall of protection, the guarantee creates the kind of security and independence that are prerequisites for the role of a citizen in a democracy.

*Protection of Property Against Takings Without Compensation.* Many constitutions contain protection of this kind. The American Constitution embodies this idea in the Fifth Amendment, which says, "nor shall private property be taken for public use, without just compensation."[29] A provision of this general sort is indispensable on both economic and democratic grounds. Without such a provision, there is not, in fact or in law, a system of property rights.

*Protection of Property Against Takings Without Due Process.* This is a procedural rather than a substantive protection of property. It means that citizens will be provided with a hearing before government may interfere with their holdings. A provision of this sort accomplishes two functions.

First, it promotes accurate fact-finding. A hearing before an independent tribunal ensures that property will not be taken capriciously, or on the basis of whim, or for discriminatory or irrelevant reasons. In the hearing, it is necessary to show the facts that would justify a deprivation of property as a matter of law. Second, the hearing right carries out an important dignitary and participatory function. To say that people cannot be deprived of property without a hearing is to say that before it acts against them, the government must listen to what they have to say. This constraint improves governmental legitimacy as well. There is considerable evidence that people feel more secure and trustful if government affords them an opportunity to be heard before it undertakes action harmful to their interests.

*Protection of Contracts.* Many constitutions protect contractual liberty from governmental invasion -- as in, for example, a provision to the effect that government shall not pass any "Law impairing the Obligations of Contracts."[30] Constitutional protection of contracts ensures citizens that when they engage in economic arrangements, they can do so free from the specter of governmental interventions. Without this right, there will be a serious deterrent to productive activity.

For those countries that choose this route, there are two central questions. The first is whether the protection applies prospectively, or only retroactively. One might think that the state should be free to create the background against which people enter into agreements, and that therefore there should be no limit on the state's power to set out, in advance, limits on the terms on which people may contract. This is the approach taken in United States law, which allows the government to affect contractual ordering however it wishes, so long as it does so in advance.

The second and related question is the extent of the "police power," pursuant to which limits on contractual freedom will be permitted. It is obvious that the state can forbid contracts for murder or assault. It will probably be agreed that the state may forbid contracts to work for less than a certain monthly wage, or for more than a certain number of hours per week. But does this mean that a state can impair a contract retroactively, simply because it believes that the outcome is unfair to one side?[31] If so, freedom of contract becomes a dead letter.

*Occupational Liberty.* There are several possible provisions for protecting occupational liberty.

1.  <u>Protection of free entry into occupations, trades, and business</u>. A provision of this sort can be found in the German Constitution.[32] This is a salutary protection against governmental restrictions on an important form of liberty, one that is part and parcel of free labor markets.

It does, however, contain an ambiguity, similar to that arising under the protection of freedom of contract. It seems clear that government can impose certain limits requiring that jobs be performed by people who are trained to do them. It can, for example, ensure that doctors actually know something about medicine, or that lawyers are trained in the law. If this is so, it will be necessary to distinguish between legitimate and illegitimate interferences with free entry into occupations, rather than simply to say that the government has no role to play in this regard. This issue is probably best resolved through judicial interpretation, not in the text itself.

2.  <u>The right to choose one's occupation</u>. A provision of this general sort can be found in the German Constitution.[33] It overlaps a good deal with protection of free entry into trades, and has similar virtues. It also raises a similar interpretive difficulty, involving the legitimacy of provisions designed to ensure that people are genuinely qualified for jobs.

3.  <u>A prohibition on forced labor</u>. This provision seems indispensable to the emerging Latin American democracies. It nicely complements the right to choose one's occupation, by saying that government cannot require people to engage in work that it prefers them to undertake. It also tends to guarantee free labor markets. Such a provision also carries forward, in a particularly crisp way, the traditional liberal prohibition on slavery, embodied in the general idea that "we were not made for one another's uses."[34]

*Prohibition on Government Monopolies (de jure)*. If the goal is to create a market economy, the Constitution should say that government may not give itself a legal monopoly over any sector of the economy. A right of exclusive management of agriculture or telecommunications is a sure way of stifling competition and of impairing economic productivity. Indeed, such a right will reintroduce all of the problems discussed in Part I of this chapter. The government should be banned from embarking on this course.

Under certain narrow conditions, an exception might be permitted -- as, for example, where government cannot efficiently perform a certain function unless it creates a monopoly, and where competition is impossible. This is an extremely rare circumstance, however, and a strong burden should be imposed on government to show that it is present in any particular case.

It would probably be a mistake to create a constitutional prohibition on government monopolies that exist in fact but that are not created through law. In any system, some *de facto* monopolies are likely, and it is hard to see how a constitutional court can prevent them. Here we encounter again one of the limits of constitutionalism: the narrow remedial power of the judiciary.

*Nondiscrimination Against Private Enterprises.* It probably follows from what has been said thus far that government should be constrained from imposing special disabilities on private enterprises, that is, from taxing, regulating, or otherwise discouraging private entities from operating on equal terms with official organs. Government might well seek to create such disabilities as a way of insulating itself from competition or of protecting its own instrumentalities. If it does so, it will create severe harms to civil society and to economic markets. A prohibition could accomplish considerable good.

Of course there will be some hard interpretive questions here. To see whether there is discrimination, one will have to explore whether private and public enterprises are similarly situated. This will not always be an easy question to answer.

*The Right to Travel Within the Nation and To and From the Nation.* Protection of the right to travel serves both economic and democratic functions. Especially in a system with some degree of jurisdictional decentralization, the right to travel is a safeguard against oppressive regulation. If citizens can leave, there is a powerful deterrent to such regulation; people are able to "vote with their feet." It is fully plausible to think that in the United States, the right to travel has been one of the greatest safeguards against legislation harmful to economic development. The right to travel internally creates a built-in check on tyranny, at least in a federal system. The right to leave one's nation serves the same function. In this sense the right is simultaneously an economic and a political one.

## Conclusion

I have argued here for a constitution that is negative in two senses. First, it should limit itself to rights that courts are genuinely able to enforce, rather than including all rights that people ought, in principle, to have. It follows that the Constitution should protect the conventional negative rights: bodily integrity, including freedom from torture and unjustified imprisonment; vote, speech, and association; antidiscrimination principles, most notably race, religion, and sex; and the basic economic liberties of private property and freedom of contract. Generally, the Constitution should not protect positive rights, or rights against the private sphere. And if it does protect these rights, courts should not enforce them. These are best suited to the democratic process. Courts do not have the necessary tools.

I have also argued for a negative constitution in a second sense; that is, a constitution that is self-consciously directed against the most dangerous tendencies of a nation's particular political culture. In the United States, the point suggests a strong argument in favor of a right prohibiting racial subordination. In Eastern Europe, it argues for powerful economic liberties. In Latin America, it argues for a right to bodily integrity and (as in Eastern Europe) against discrimination on the basis of religion and sex. These rights are fully capable of judicial enforcement.

I am aware that some of my arguments -- especially those opposed to positive rights -- are likely to be controversial. But even if these arguments are wrong, it may be proper to insist that constitutions are (among other things) legal documents, and that they should be written and interpreted with their legal enforcement in mind. In Latin America, a good step in the transition to democracy is to insist that courts will protect those rights most indispensable to that form of government, and most capable of vindication through the judiciary. For the future, Latin American courts could do far worse than to proclaim that they will be especially unsympathetic to any governmental efforts to infringe on rights to bodily integrity, political participation, nondiscrimination on the basis of race, religion, and sex, and the basic liberties of private property and contractual liberty.

## Notes

[1]Parts of this essay appeared, in somewhat different form, in Cass R. Sunstein, *Constitutionalism, Democracy, Prosperity: Transition in Eastern Europe*, 2 CONSTITUTIONAL POLITICAL ECONOMY 161 (1991).

[2]In a way the term is misleading, but I trust that its meaning will emerge from the discussion. Rights of private property, for example, are not truly negative; they depend for their existence on a government willing and able to protect such rights. Even bodily integrity depends importantly on a legal machinery willing to protect people against public and private incursions. By using the term "negative," I seek not to make controversial claims about when the government is "present," but instead to build on some usual (if misleading) terminology in order to refer to the conventional catalogue of liberal rights.

[3]*See* JEREMY WALDRON, THE RIGHT TO PRIVATE PROPERTY (1988).

[4]Aristotle made the basic point: "Men pay most attention to what is their own: they care less for what is common; or, at any rate, they care for it only to the extent to which each is individually concerned." *See* ARISTOTLE, THE POLITICS OF ARISTOTLE 1261, at 44 (E. Barker trans., 1958).

[5]*See* Harold Demsetz, *Toward a Theory of Property Rights*, 57 AM. ECON. REV. 347 (1967).

[6]FRIEDRICH A. VON HAYEK, THE ROAD TO SERFDOM (1945).

[7]*Cf.* Stephen Holmes, *Gag Rules or the Politics of Omission, in* CONSTITU-TIONALISM AND DEMOCRACY 19 (J. Elster & A. Hylland eds., 1988). The division between private and public spheres is hard to defend or even to understand if it is treated as a metaphysical one, or as a claim that public power is not behind the private sphere. But if we understand the division as a political one, to be justified in public terms, it becomes both intelligible and indispensable. The (legal) creation of a private sphere, undertaken by the state, is a key part of the process of creating civil society and market ordering. If these can be justified, the private sphere itself becomes unproblematic, at least in the abstract. Of course its particular content can always be criticized, and is frequently subject to democratic redefinition.

[8]The demoralizing effects of such regimes are well known to citizens of Com-munist nations, and indeed to visitors as well. Continuous dependence on govern-ment officials has a range of predictable corrosive effects on both character and spirit -- a worthy subject for inquiry by a modern de Tocqueville.

[9]*Cf.* Holmes, *supra* note 7.

[10]*See* JEAN DREZE & AMARTYA K. SEN, HUNGER AND PUBLIC ACTION 20-34 (1989).

[11]*See* Martha C. Nussbaum, *Aristotelian Social Democracy, in* LIBERALISM AND THE GOOD (R. Bruce Douglass et al. eds., 1990); AMARTYA K. SEN, COMMODITIES AND CAPABILITIES (1985).

[12]KONST. [CONSTITUTION] SSSR art. 40 (1977) (Union of Soviet Socialists Republic [hereinafter, SOVIET CONSTITUTION]). Unless otherwise noted, the translation of SOVIET CONSTITUTION can be found in I COLLECTED LEGISLATION OF THE USSR AND CONSTITUENT UNION REPUBLICS; CONSTITUTIONS: CONSTITUTION OF THE UNION OF SOVIET SOCIALIST REPUBLICS (William E. Butler ed., 1985).

[13]SOVIET CONSTITUTION, *supra* note 12, art. 41.

[14]*Id.* art. 41.

[15]*Id.* art. 43.

[16]*Id.* art. 62.

[17]KONSTYTUCJA [CONSTITUTION] art. 68 (Poland) [hereinafter, POLISH CONSTITU-TION]. Unless otherwise noted, the translation of POLISH CONSTITUTION can be found in XIV CONSTITUTIONS OF THE WORLD, REPUBLIC OF POLAND (Albert P. Blaustein & Gisbert H. Flanz eds., 1991).

[18]POLISH CONSTITUTION, *supra* note 17, art. 69.

[19]*Id.* art. 70.

[20]BULG. CONST. of 1971 art. 42 [hereinafter, BULGARIAN CONSTITUTION]. Unless otherwise noted, the translation of the Bulgarian Constitution of 1971 can be found in II CONSTITUTIONS OF THE WORLD, BULGARIA (Albert P. Blaustein & Gisbert H. Flanz eds., 1991).

[21]BULGARIAN CONSTITUTION, *supra* note 20, art. 40.

[22]*Id.* art. 41.

[23]*Id.* art. 43.

[24]*Id.* art. 47.

[25]The German Constitution is, in its basic text, not an exception. The Constitutional Court has, however, used the text to create some positive rights.

[26]*See* JOHN S. MILL, CONSIDERATIONS ON REPRESENTATIVE GOVERNMENT (C.V. Shields ed., 1958) (1865).  To say this is not of course to say that all of those characteristics are always good ones.

[27]I defend this idea in CASS R. SUNSTEIN, THE PARTIAL CONSTITUTION (forthcoming 1993).

[28]*See* LON L. FULLER, THE MORALITY OF LAW (1964).

[29]U.S. CONST. amend. V.

[30]*Id.* art. 1, § 10.

[31]Sometimes people think that the appropriate remedy for a harsh bargain is to disallow the bargain. But it is not at all clear that this remedy helps the weaker side. Usually someone in bad circumstances will be presented with a range of unfavorable alternatives, and will choose the least unfavorable of them.  To disallow this option does nothing to improve the bad circumstances, and simply forces the person to choose the second-least unfavorable option.  It is crucially important for the emerging democracies to understand this point.  Efforts to close off market options are tempting when those options seem few and produce harsh results; but the closing off is an utterly ineffectual remedy.

[32]GG [CONSTITUTION] art. 12 (Federal Republic of Germany), *translated in* VI CONSTITUTIONS OF THE COUNTRIES OF THE WORLD, FEDERAL REPUBLIC OF GERMANY 85 (Albert P. Blaustein & Gisbert H. Flanz eds., 1991).

[33]*Id.*

[34]JOHN LOCKE, TWO TREATISES ON GOVERNMENT 311 (Laslett ed., 1960).

# 25

# Constitutions, Constitutionalism and Constitution-Mongering

## *William Twining*[1]

In 1833, John Stuart Mill wrote: "Our utilitarian radicals . . . will no longer rely on the infallibility of constitution-mongering."[2] This was only one year after the Great Reform Act and the death of Jeremy Bentham. It could be said to mark the start of modern caution about rationalism and universalism in constitution-making, even among liberals.

In 1992, we are witnessing a global debate. Constitutional reform, constitution-making, and constitution-mongering are high on the agenda not only in Latin America, but also in the former Soviet Union, Eastern Europe, South, East and West Africa, the Islamic world, Hong Kong, and even the United Kingdom.

Two truisms have been the subtexts of the papers in this volume. On the one hand, we belong to an interdependent world, even if it is not quite yet a global village. On the other hand, it is generally agreed that local history and conditions are crucial to the development of legitimate, stable, and workable constitutional orders.

The tension between these ideas is apparent in a puzzle about the current global debate. The terms of the debate seem to be widely shared:[3] almost everywhere one goes one hears talk of democracy, constitutionalism, human rights, limited government, the rule of law, free elections, an independent judiciary, and even judicial review. Do these terms suggest that there is a widely shared agenda of problems with a limited range of solutions, as some constitution-mongers suggest? Or does an ambiguous discourse conceal a much greater range of issues that are more context-dependent and more sensitive to local knowledge than the common vocabulary reveals?

The academic and political discourse on these questions is, at times, highly sophisticated. Indeed, there has been explicit recognition by the authors of this volume that a variety of conceptions underlie the key terms -- even such seemingly innocuous words as "judge" and "judiciary" -- and that both local conditions and international trends influence the meanings and conceptions adopted in particular debates.

Moreover, the chapters in this part of the book reflect a tendency to adopt a thick and sophisticated notion of a constitution, strong versions of democracy, and an Americanized conception of judicial review. If this is correct, it has important implications for interpreting the ideas expressed by these authors. It is accordingly worth pausing briefly to consider how these three terms may have been used.

The term "constitution" is often used merely to refer to a formal written text or set of texts or to such documents overlaid with a set of principles of interpretation, which are typically contested, and with a particularized set of interpretations embodied in judicial decisions, constitutional conventions, and official practice (what might be called constitutional doctrine). Sometimes the term is used more broadly to include one or other version of the ideology of "constitutionalism;" for example, the idea that a good constitution necessarily involves limited government and an entrenched bill of rights.

Such normative conceptions can be contrasted with two "realist" ones. A constitution can be conceived as a map of *de facto* political power, a description of how such power is in fact distributed and the processes by which important political decisions are made in practice.[4] Such descriptions can be constructed in terms of crude real politik or by more sophisticated methods of interpretive sociology or political science. In an increasingly interdependent world such maps, to be "realistic," have to be set in the context of a picture of the world's political and economic order.

A more complex "realist" conception combines the normative and the empirical. Viewing a constitution as a "going institution," as in the phrase "the living constitution," can include all of the above ingredients and a good deal more. In short, a thick account of a constitution as an institution could include ideology, canonical texts, constitutional doctrine, maps of power, and an account of local legal culture and tradition, and of personnel and their ways of doing things.[5]

Different conceptions of "constitution" should lead to correspondingly different conceptions of constitutional design and of constitution-mongering. There is an enormous difference between the tasks of drafting a formal text, developing a body of constitutional doctrine over time, constructing a coherent constitutional theory or ideology, drawing a map of power, or creating a viable "living constitution." The modern constitution-monger, epitomized by the foreign expert, may have progressed from being a mere purveyor of designer models (the Westminster model, the Presidential model, a bespoke bill of rights) to a skilled negotiator and draftsperson of political settlements. Nevertheless, such experts have a very limited role to play in the evolutionary growth of constitutional doctrine or a living institution.[6] In discussions of constitutional reform it is rather easy to slip from a thick "realist" conception of constitution to a thinner, more rationalistic conception of constitution-making.

Strong conceptions of democracy have also tended to dominate the literature. While different versions have been on offer, very few scholars have accepted a simple statistical or majoritarian view of democracy, and some have explicitly rejected it.[7] Nearly everyone has taken formal protection of human rights for granted. Similarly, many assume a strong, American-style version of "judicial review," which includes judicial power to determine the constitutionality of legislation as well as to rule on the legality of administrative action.

Applying these relatively strong conceptions to my own country, one might conclude that the United Kingdom does have a constitution (which many doubt)[8] but may not be a democracy and does not have judicial review.[9] This is not English flippancy. As we shall see, each of these points is central to contemporary debates about constitutional change in the United Kingdom.

The main question is this: Is judicial review consistent with and supportive of democracy? There appears to be a consensus among the authors that the answer to the first half of the question should be an unequivocal "Yes."[10] To put it another way, the majority of scholars believe that the judiciary should be given a role in limiting both executive and legislative power and in protecting rights and that this is justified by and possibly required by democratic theory. This is hardly surprising if one accepts a non-statistical theory of democracy, even in relation to a relatively strong version of judicial review -- provided that it is not too strong. There is, however, less of a consensus about the rationale for judicial review, its scope, and its likely effectiveness in the specific conditions of different Latin American countries.

I lack sufficient local knowledge to comment on the details of the arguments as they apply to Latin America. It may, however, be relevant to make two general points about this kind of debate in relation to the international context. The first is cautionary, the second is more optimistic.

As an academic and some kind of liberal, I am naturally attracted by sophisticated conceptions of constitutions and related concepts and by strong versions of democratic theory. I am less skeptical than some of my British colleagues[11] about the wisdom of entrusting significant constitutional powers to our judiciary. However, in the context of contemporary world politics there is a real danger that a strong version of constitutionalism and particular versions of democracy may be crystallized into a new dogmatism which could become a dangerous form of ideological imperialism. The export of "democracy, human rights, and good governance" is high on the current agenda of Western powers and even if one likes the message, one needs to be wary of the messenger.

I visit parts of Africa quite frequently. I have no sympathy for the repression and brutality of some modern African regimes. I applaud the influence of organizations like Amnesty International and Africa Watch in restraining human rights abuses and in giving indirect support to opposition at the grass roots level. I have even criticized the British government for being slow and selective in bringing pressure to bear on some governments in respect of domestic violations of international standards. But Western pressure through aid with strings, the World Bank, the International Monetary Fund, and even well-intentioned non-governmental agencies need to be viewed with extreme caution. The campaign to foster good governance, democracy, and human rights could well degenerate into a doctrinaire, simplistic, universalist, yet highly selective, form of neo-colonialism -- if it has not done so already. I find it ironic that a Tory government that has eroded civil liberties and weakened democracy at home and which for nearly all of the post-imperial period treated law as being "not developmentally relevant,"[12] had a deathbed conversion to human rights and good governance abroad, while opposing constitutional reform and a bill of rights at home.[13] The judgment of history may be that in the Thatcher era the United Kingdom exported civil liberties.

As Jonathan Miller has argued, however, there is a positive side to international pressure: the importance of the international rights movement in fostering local democratic orders.[14] I would add three glosses to his account. First, the international human rights movement is not only governmental and its influence does not operate solely or even mainly through courts. For example, this is clearly illustrated by the recent publication *Put Our World to Rights*.[15] This is a report by the Commonwealth Human Rights Initiative which was sponsored by five Commonwealth non-governmental organizations ("NGO"s). The report is addressed to local, regional, and international NGOs, and individuals as well as to governments. One of the central themes of that report is the importance of networking non-governmental human rights activities, especially in strengthening "bottom-up" democracy at the grass roots level. Most of its recommendations are proactive. Even in respect of human rights violations the court of public opinion is treated as being more important than official courts, whether domestic or international. Such themes are repeated in numerous other reports and writings and could be said to represent part of the consensus that underlies the international human rights movement.

Second, appeals to international human rights standards are consistent with most democratic theory in that they are, at least nominally, based on consent. These standards, despite all the dilemmas of universalism and disagreements about detail, do represent a remarkably broad international consensus about values, at least at the level of rhetoric. Insofar as many governments which regularly violate international norms are signatories to at least some of the various declarations, covenants and conventions, they have formally and publicly accepted these standards. At the very least this acceptance exemplifies De La Rochefoucauld's dictum: "L'hypocrisie est un hommage que la vice rend a la vertue."[16] Both in current practice and potentially, public subscription to such standards, however reluctant or hypocritical, often involves more than lip-service.

Third, international rhetoric can itself transform domestic reality. Let me turn again to my own country. Before the General Election of April 1992, there seemed to be at least more than an even chance that within ten years the United Kingdom would have an entrenched domestic bill of rights backed by powers of judicial review of legislation as well as of administrative action. The first great constitutional debate since World War II began about 1988 and culminated in the general election campaign, with the Conservative party being the most skeptical of the need for substantial formal change of the electoral system, protection of civil liberties, and devolution. The debate continues, but in a considerably muted form since the Conservative victory. What is particularly significant in the present context is the extent to which our local debate has been structured and influenced by the fact the United Kingdom is a signatory to the European Convention on Human Rights and Fundamental Freedoms.

The story of our local debates about a domestic bill of rights might be summarized as follows.[17] In the first phase we became signatories to a number of international declarations and conventions absent-mindedly, rather as in an earlier age we acquired some colonies. In 1951, we reluctantly ratified the European Convention. In 1966, with virtually no debate, we accepted the jurisdiction of the European Court of Human Rights at Strasbourg and the right of individual petition. Neither of these events might have happened if the Convention had been perceived as involving serious obligations. British civil servants and judges went about their business as if the Convention was of no consequence, even if they knew of it. Then gradually in the 1970s, starting with refugees from Amin's Uganda, and spreading to Northern Ireland, then to the Isle of Man, and to prisons and other fringe elements of society, individual petitions to the European Court began to attract significant publicity and to cause official embarrassment. By the early 1980s, it was a much-publicized fact that the United Kingdom headed the league table of defendants before the Commissions and the Court.[18] The full story has yet to be told. So far as one can judge, however, the Convention began to have a significant impact on official practice, behavior, and expectations, more through quiet pressure applied on other Ministries by the Foreign and Commonwealth Office than by the direct influence of particular decisions of the Court. The first occasion on which a domestic court treated the European Convention as being admissible in argument as at best a persuasive authority was 1976,[19] twenty-five years after the ratification of the Convention. Today it is still not binding on domestic courts. However, it is increasingly cited as an aid to interpretation and its influence on the drafting of new legislation, on subordinate legislation and regulations, and on official practice is very significant indeed. The influence is largely proactive. The European Court is important not so much because of its particular decisions and its jurisprudence, which have been quite cautious, but because it is there. Civil servants and other officials are increasingly conscious of "The Judge over your Shoulder."[20]

The current debate on a domestic bill of rights represents a second, much more recent phase in the story. Although there have been advocates of such a change for many years, the issue has only been taken seriously by the main political parties in the very recent past. One might say that the founding of Charter 88 four years ago marks the start of a broader movement for constitutional reform which has gradually won significant political support, largely as a reaction to the Thatcher years and our membership in the European Community. The Conservative Party victory in the 1992 General Election was a set-back, but the debate continues.

What is significant in the present context is the form that the debate has taken. The main proposal, and the one most likely to win support, is that the European Convention should be embodied in domestic legislation with only minor modifications. The main support for such a change comes from the center and the center-left. It is opposed by most conservatives and many socialists, but in broad terms they seem to be losing the debate. The main neo-Burkean conservative argument is that we do not need a bill of rights and that civil liberties are best protected by tradition. The simple answer to that is that we already have a bill of rights -- the European Convention -- and that civil liberties have been significantly eroded in recent years by those who claim to be the guardians of tradition. The main argument from the left is twofold: first, that a bill of rights is undemocratic, to which the reply, developed by, for example, Ronald Dworkin in the United Kingdom[21] and Carlos Nino in Argentina,[22] is that this assumes a crude, statistical version of democracy. They maintain that an entrenched bill of rights is both justified and required by liberal democratic theory.

The second argument is that the British senior judiciary as at present constituted is too conservative, elitist, and formalistic to be entrusted with American-style powers of judicial review.[23] The response to this is that the judiciary is changing (for example, its recent activism in administrative law) and would inevitably change further over time as a result of being given such powers.[24] In any case, the main significance of a bill of rights is to provide a focus or setting for perpetual public debate in which the judiciary and the legal profession are by no means the only participants.

A third line of argument is that a bill of rights is inconsistent with some standard interpretations of socialism. This is still advanced by some,[25] but no longer has the support of all socialist commentators.[26]

My account of the British debate is, of course, a great simplification. But insofar as it is broadly true, the main lesson is that a most unlikely candidate for adopting a domestic bill of rights and judicial review, the United Kingdom, may well do so within the next decade. In that case the United Kingdom's return to democracy will in large part be a result of our membership in the European and the World Community.

## Notes

[1] I am grateful to Professors Terence Anderson, Yash Ghai and Csaba Varga for comments on an earlier draft.

[2] I THE LETTERS OF JOHN STUART MILL 37 (Hugh S.R. Elliot ed., 1910) (letter from J.S. Mill to Thomas Carlyle, March 9, 1833).

[3] They are not universal. For example, the discourse and rhetoric of debates within the Islamic world and in China are probably significantly different.

[4] I. Harden, *The Constitution and Its Discontents*, BRIT. J. OF POL. STUD. 489, 491-2 (1991).

[5] Karl Llewellyn expressed this "thick" idea of legal institutions in typical fashion as follows: "[A] sound sociology plays not alone, as Timasheff suggests, between the two poles of power and ethics, but between six poles which I prefer to call Might, Right, Skills, Rules, Results, and Law's People." Karl N. Llewellyn, *in* MY PHILOSOPHY OF LAW: CREDOS OF SIXTEEN AMERICAN SCHOLARS 181, 197 (Julius Rosenthal Foundation, 1941). These ideas were applied to constitutions in Karl N. Llewellyn, *The Constitution as an Institution*, 34 COLUM. L. REV. 1 (1934). Indeed, such a thick conception of a constitution seems to have been accepted either explicitly or implicitly in the papers of the authors in this section of this book.

[6] One of the most experienced of modern Constitutional advisers, Professor Yash Ghai, has emphasized the importance of maintaining a protracted relationship, as he had with Papua New Guinea, over several years rather than seeing constitution-making as a once-for-all episode of negotiation and drafting (personal communication to the author). Some of the themes of this comment owe much to his writings:

*see especially*, Yash P. Ghai, *Constitutional Issues in the Transition to Independence, in* FOREIGN FORCES IN PACIFIC POLITICS (A. Ahmed and R. Crocombe eds., 1983); *The Rule of Law in Africa: Reflections on the Limits of Constitutionalism*, THE NAIROBI LAW MONTHLY, Sept. 1990, No. 24, at 23; The Past and Future of Hong Kong's Constitution, Inaugural Lecture, Supplement to UNIVERSITY OF HONG KONG GAZETTE, May 6, 1991.

[7]*E.g.*, Raúl R. Alfonsín, *The Function of Judicial Power During the Transition, in* TRANSITION TO DEMOCRACY IN LATIN AMERICA: THE ROLE OF THE JUDICIARY 41 (Irwin P. Stotzky ed., 1993) [hereinafter, TRANSITION].  Carlos S. Nino, *On the Exercise of Judicial Review in Argentina, in* TRANSITION *supra*, at 309 (three important exceptions to the majoritarian denial of judicial review).

[8]*E.g.*, F. F. Ridley, *There is No British Constitution: A Dangerous Case of the Emperor's Clothes*, 41 PARLIAMENTARY AFFAIRS, 340-61 (1988); *cf.* F. F. RIDLEY, THE STUDY OF GOVERNMENT 20 (1975).

[9]Traditionally English and United Kingdom Courts have not had the power to review the constitutional validity of Acts of Parliament.  However, under legislation enacted as a result of the United Kingdom's membership in the European Community the courts have been required to interpret existing and future Acts of Parliament, and subordinate legislation, in accordance with directly effective Community law. *See generally*, L. COLLINS, EUROPEAN COMMUNITY LAW IN THE UNITED KINGDOM (3d ed. 1984) (discussing the European Communities Act of the United Kingdom 1972, Ch. 68); P.J.G. KAPTEYN & P.V. VAN THEMAT, INTRODUCTION TO THE LAW OF EUROPEAN COMMUNITIES AFTER THE COMING INTO FORCE OF THE SINGLE EUROPEAN ACT (2d ed. 1989).  These are themselves Acts of Parliament giving effect to treaties and, in theory, are not entrenched.

[10]*See, e.g.*, Nino, *supra* note 7, at 309; Irwin P. Stotzky, *The Tradition of Constitutional Adjudication, in* TRANSITION *supra* note 7, at 347.

[11]Leading examples are J. A. G. GRIFFITH, THE POLITICS OF THE JUDICIARY (4th ed. 1991 passim, especially chapter 9); KEITH D. EWING & CONOR A. GEARTY, FREEDOM UNDER THATCHER 262-74 (1990); Stephen Sedley, *Free Speech for Rupert Murdoch, Stephen Sedley writes about the Limitations of a Bill of Rights*, LONDON REV. OF BOOKS, Dec. 19, 1991, at 3-5.  For contrary views see, for example, RONALD DWORKIN, A BILL OF RIGHTS FOR BRITAIN (1990); INSTITUTE FOR PUBLIC POLICY RESEARCH, A BRITISH BILL OF RIGHTS, Constitution Paper No. 1 (1990).

[12]Keith Patchett, *The Role of Law in the Development Process*, 48 COMMONWEALTH LEGAL EDUC. ASSOC. NEWS. 33 (1987).

[13]EWING & GEARTY, *supra* note 11.

[14]*See, e.g.*, Jonathan Miller, *The Latin American Reformer's Stake in United States Human Rights Policy, in* TRANSITION *supra* note 7, at 155.

[15]ADVISORY COMMITTEE, COMMONWEALTH HUMAN RIGHTS INITIATIVE, PUT OUR WORLD TO RIGHTS (1991).

[16]FRANCOIS DUC DE LA ROCHEFOUCAULD, MAXIMES 218 (Dominique Secretan ed. 1967).

[17]A. Lester, *Fundamental Rights: The United Kingdom Isolated?*  The F. A. Mann Lecture, 1982 PUBLIC LAW 46 (1984).

[18]*Id.*

[19]R v. Secretary of State for the Home Department ex parte Bhafan Singh [1976] QB 198, 207 per Lord Denning M.R.; cp. R v. Chief Immigration Officer, Heathrow Airport ex p. Salamat Bibi [1976] I.W.L.R. 979, 984 CA (where Lord Denning recanted). The first citation in the House of Lords was in Waddington v. Miah [1974] 1 W.L.R. 692. Donaldson M.R. in British Airways v. Laker Airways [1983] 3 All E.R. 375 (c.A.) at 402h.

[20]THE TREASURY SOLICITOR'S DEPARTMENT, THE JUDGE OVER YOUR SHOULDER (1987). This guide to administrative law for civil servants is an indication of the growth in importance of the subject in the United Kingdom in recent years.

[21]DWORKIN, *supra* note 11.

[22]Nino, *supra* note 7.

[23]*See, e.g.,* Sedley, *supra* note 11; EWING & GEARTY, *supra* note 11.

[24]*E.g.,* DWORKIN, *supra*, note 11.

[25]*E.g.,* Sedley, *supra*, note 11.

[26]*See generally* TOM CAMPBELL, THE LEFT AND RIGHTS (1983).

# PART SEVEN

# Conclusion

# 26

## A Democratic Vision

### *Irwin P. Stotzky*

A democratic society can be conceived as an ongoing order characterized by a certain principle of justification -- a principle of democratic legitimacy. This principle requires a continuous order of mutually assured and encouraged autonomy in which political decisions are manifestly based on the judgments of members who are free and equal persons. It requires that the expression of self-governing capacities operate both within the formal institutions of politics and in the affairs of daily life. The democratic order must also satisfy the conditions of equal freedom and autonomy that give it definition.

Because the absence of material deprivation is a prerequisite for free and unconstrained deliberation and individual development and fulfillment, a democratic society must provide a basic level of material satisfaction for all members of the political order. Further, to satisfy democratic values, the level of material satisfaction should be determined through a free process of deliberation among the people. Without such a system, and thus without the development of moral consciousness in the citizenry, those nations striving to become constitutional democracies will inevitably be plunged back into the abyss of authoritarianism.

As the essays in this book amply demonstrate, there is no such thing as an easy fix in the transition to democracy. Economic, political, and social stability has not yet been achieved. The corporatist political and social structure has to be transformed to allow the less privileged to enjoy the basic necessities that ensure a life of dignity. Institutional structures, such as an independent judiciary, a representative congressional branch, and limitations on the executive power must be developed and stabilized. The rule of law -- and thus the guarantees of due process -- have to be consolidated and become an accepted, basic requirement of social interaction. This is necessary not only to protect human rights and the democratic process, but also to reach a satisfactory level of economic and social development.

All of these factors are interconnected. Indeed, the problems inherent in the transition to democracy in Latin America are extremely complicated, and they are interrelated to one another in incredibly subtle ways. What this means, of course, is that the people of the region must internalize the importance and legitimacy of a constitutional system based on the rule of law. They must also internalize universal standards of achievement and competition necessary to the proper functioning of a democracy. The belief in the overpowering significance of status and connections, which severely cripples the transition to democracy, must be defeated.

The essays in this book reflect an attempt to understand the complexities of the issues and to propose solutions to these problems. While these problems may appear insoluble, there is also cause for hope and optimism. That hope ultimately rests with the people of Latin America. Many brave and dedicated people in that region are struggling daily to create and perpetuate a constitutional democratic system of government. In the vanguard of this effort is a core group of intellectuals, lawyers, and government officials who are writing about these issues and attempting to implement the necessary changes in their societies. These individuals clearly understand the almost intractable problems they face and the proposed solutions to these issues. They have not been remiss about taking action to effectuate these changes, even in the face of possible physical harm to themselves and their families. Their work and actions are nothing short of heroic.

# About the Contributors

**Raúl Ricardo Alfonsín** is the former President of Argentina (1983-1989) and former leader of the Radical Party, one of the major political parties in Argentina.

**President Jean-Bertrand Aristide** was elected in 1990 and is the first democratically elected President of Haiti.

**Robert A. Burt** is Southmayd Professor of Law at Yale University Law School. Prior to joining the Yale law faculty, he held a joint appointment at the University of Michigan Law School and the Psychiatry Department of the Medical School. Professor Burt's recent books include *Two Jewish Justices: Outcasts in the Promised Land* (1988) and *The Constitution in Conflict* (1992).

**Andrés José D'Alessio** is Professor of Criminal Law at the University of Buenos Aires, Argentina, where he teaches Criminal Law and Constitutional Law. Professor D'Alessio has been active in the Argentine government, previously serving as a Supreme Court clerk and as a Federal Appellate Judge, where he presided over the trials of the military juntas for violations of human rights. From 1987-1989 he served as Attorney General of Argentina. He has also published several articles in Argentina on criminal and constitutional law issues.

**Owen M. Fiss** is Sterling Professor of Law at Yale University Law School. His many books include *The Civil Rights Injunction* (1978), *Procedure* (with Robert Cover and Judith Resnik) (1978), and *Troubled Beginnings of the Modern State* (1993), part of the History of the Supreme Court sponsored by the Devise of Oliver Wendell Holmes, Jr.

**George P. Fletcher** is Beekman Professor of Law at Columbia University School of Law. During the 1970s and early 1980s he was active in supporting the rights of Jewish and dissident prisoners in the former Soviet Union. Professor Fletcher's numerous scholarly articles have been published in leading academic journals. His books include *Rethinking the Criminal Law* (1978) and *Loyalty, An Essay on the Morality of Relationships* (1993).

**Marvin E. Frankel** currently serves as the Chairman of the Lawyers Committee for Human Rights. He is a partner in the firm of Kramer, Levin, Naftalis, Nessen, Kamin & Frankel. Mr. Frankel served as a United States District Judge for the Southern District of New York for thirteen years and has been active in the practice of law since 1948. He has written and published many scholarly articles and several books, which include *Criminal Sentences: Law Without Order* (1973), *Partisan Justice* (1980), and with Ellen Saidman, *Out of the Shadows of Night: The Struggle for International Human Rights* (1989).

**Roberto Gargarella** is Professor of Law at the University of Buenos Aires, Argentina, and is currently a member of the Center for Institutional Studies of Argentina.

**Joseph Goldstein** is Sterling Professor of Law at Yale University Law School and Professor at Yale's Child Study Center. A political scientist, lawyer, and psychoanalyst, he is the author of several books, of which *Psychoanalysis, Psychiatry and the Law* (with J. Katz and A.M. Dershowitz) (1967), *In the Best Interests of the Child* (with A. Freud, A.J. Solnit, and J. Goldstein) (1986), and *The Intelligible Constitution* (1992) are leading examples.

**Philip B. Heymann** is James Barr Ames Professor at Harvard Law School, Director of that school's Center for Criminal Justice, and Professor at Harvard's Kennedy School of Government, where he directs the Program for Senior Managers in Government. Professor Heymann was Assistant Attorney General in charge of the Criminal Division of the Department of Justice from 1978-1981, and Associate Watergate Prosecutor from 1973-1975. He previously held several government posts in the State Department. His books include *The Politics of Public Management* (1988) and *The Social Responsibility of Lawyers* (1988).

**Elizabeth M. Iglesias** is Professor of Law at the University of Miami Law School, where she teaches Constitutional Criminal Procedure, Labor and Employment Law, and International Economic Law and Development. After graduating from law school, she worked with the Lawyers Committee for Civil Rights Under Law of the Boston Bar Association. Following a period of private practice, she became an associate researcher with the Harvard/Guatemala criminal justice reform project.

**Paul W. Kahn** is Professor of Law at Yale University Law School. He teaches in the areas of constitutional law and theory, international law, and philosophy. He has published numerous articles and recently published *Legitimacy and History: Self-Government in American Constitutional Theory* (1992).

**Jaime Malamud-Goti** was a senior advisor to President Alfonsín of Argentina from 1983-1987 and the Solicitor to the Supreme Court of Argentina from 1987-1988. He is currently Professor of Law at the University of Buenos Aires, Argentina, and a member of the Institute of Advanced Studies at that University. Professor Goti has written numerous articles and several books on law and social theory, such as *Derecho Penal de la Competencia* (1984), *Legitima Defensa y Estado de Necesidad* (1977), and *Smoke and Mirrors: The Paradox of the Drug Wars* (1992).

**Jonathan Miller** is Professor of Law at Southwestern University School of Law, teaching courses in Latin American Laws and Institutions, International Human Rights, and Civil Procedure. Between 1985-1987 he was a Jervey Fellow from Columbia University, spending several months in Argentina as a visiting professor at the University of Buenos Aires, teaching Argentine Constitutional Law and Human Rights Law. Professor Miller has published extensively on Argentine legal issues including casebooks currently used in Argentina, *Constitución y Poder Político* (with M.A. Gelli & S. Cayuso) (1987), and *Constitución y Derechos Humanos* (with M.A. Gelli & S. Cayuso) (1991).

**Carlos S. Nino** is Professor of Philosophy and Law at the University of Buenos Aires, Argentina. He has also been a Visiting Professor at the Yale Law School. He is Director of the Center for Institutional Studies of Buenos Aires and Secretary of the Argentine Analytic Philosophy Society. He has written numerous articles and books including *The Ethics of Human Rights* (1992), *Un País al Margen de la Ley* (1992), and *Fundamentos de Derecho Constitucional* (1992).

**Diane F. Orentlicher** is Professor of Law at The American University in Washington, D.C., teaching in the areas of evidence and international law. Professor Orentlicher has served in many capacities on various human rights committees, from general counsel to overseas human rights reporter. She is currently on the Board of Directors of the International League for Human Rights and the Advisory Council for the International Human Rights Law Group. She has authored many articles on the human rights practices of several countries, including the United States, Nicaragua, Honduras, and El Salvador.

**Eduardo Rabossi** is Professor of Philosophy and Law at the University of Buenos Aires, Argentina. He also served as Under Secretary of Human Rights under former President Alfonsín of Argentina.

**Marcela Rodriguez** is currently Professor of Law at the University of Buenos Aires in Argentina. She is also a member of the Center for Institutional Studies of Argentina.

**Stephen J. Schnably** is Professor of Law at the University of Miami School of Law, where he teaches International Law and Human Rights Law. He has represented petitioners in several cases before the Inter-American Commission on Human Rights, and has written articles on American constitutional law and the Organization of American States' role in promoting democracy.

**Cass R. Sunstein** is Karl N. Llewellyn Professor of Jurisprudence in the Law School and Department of Political Science at the University of Chicago. He is Co-Director of the Center on Constitutionalism in Eastern Europe. His books include *After the Rights Revolution* (1990), *Democracy and the Limits of Free Speech* (1993), and *The Partial Constitution* (1993).

**Jorge Correa Sutil** is Dean of the School of Law of the University Diego Portales of Chile, and teaches General Theory of Law. He has authored several articles, including *La Cultura Juridica Chilena en Relacion a la Funcion Judicial* and *Formacion de Jueces para la Democracia*. Professor Sutil was the General Secretary of the Chilean Group of Constitutional Studies, which was opposed to the military regime. During the first year of Chile's transition to democracy, he was appointed to be Chief of Staff of the National Commission for Truth and Reconciliation, responsible for reporting past human rights violations. Today he assists President Aylwin in legal matters.

**Ruti Teitel** teaches Comparative Constitutional Law, U.S. Constitutional Law, and Religion and the First Amendment at New York Law School. Professor Teitel was Assistant Director, Legal Affairs Department, of the Anti-Defamation League in New York for several years. She has published many articles on comparative constitutional law, human rights abuses, prosecution of war crimes, and religious freedom and democracy.

**William Twining** has been Quain Professor of Jurisprudence at University College, London, since 1983, where he is chairman of the Bentham Committee. Professor Twining has taught in Eastern Africa, Northern Ireland, and the United States, and is a regular visitor to the University of Miami. His books include *Analysis of Evidence* (with Terence Anderson) (1991), *How To Do Things With Rules* (with David Miers) (1991), and *Issues of Self-Determination*, (1991). He is also co-editor of the *Law in Context* series and the *Jurists* series.

# About the Book and Editor

The transition to democracy in Latin America encompasses adjustments in norms and institutions regarding the strictures of the rule of law. This book addresses the critical role of the judiciary in the transition. The contributors examine the significance of the independence of the judiciary, which ensures institutional integrity and freedom from political pressures, and discuss various theoretical and practical aspects of the judicial process, most notably trials. They examine specifically how a system could be devised that would combine procedural formalities with the need for expedience in the pursuit of substantive justice.

The book also focuses on the role of the prosecution -- and particularly the independent prosecutor -- in the investigation of human rights abuses committed by government officials. The establishment of a judicial adjudicative tradition and justifications for judicial review are discussed as well.

The volume offers valuable insights into how peaceful transfers of power help strengthen and reinforce the defense of human rights. It also provides significant evaluations of the role the judiciary might play in this important process.

**Irwin P. Stotzky** is currently Professor of Law at the University of Miami School of Law. In 1986-1987, he was a Visiting Scholar at the Yale University Law School. In 1991-1992, he was a Fulbright Scholar in Argentina. For the past sixteen years, he has represented Haitian refugees on constitutional and human rights issues in many cases, including several cases in the U.S. Supreme Court. He teaches in the areas of constitutional law and theory, criminal procedure, and philosophy. He has published numerous articles and is the author of *The Theory and Craft of American Law: Elements* (with Soia Mentschikoff) (1981).